Workflow Management

Cooperative Information Systems
Michael Papazoglou, Joachim W. Schmidt, and
John Mylopoulos, editors

Advances in Object-Oriented Data Modeling, Michael P. Papazoglou,
Stefano Spaccapietra, and Zahir Tari, editors, 2000

Workflow Management: Models, Methods, and Systems, Wil van der
Aalst and Kees Max van Hee, 2002

Workflow Management

Models, Methods, and Systems

Wil van der Aalst and Kees van Hee

The MIT Press
Cambridge, Massachusetts
London, England

First MIT Press paperback edition, 2004
This translation © 2002 Massachusetts Institute of Technology

Originally published under the title *Workflow Management: Modellen, Methoden en Systemen*, 1997, by Academic Service.

This book was set in Sabon on 3B2 by Asco Typesetters, Hong Kong, and was printed and bound in the United States of America.

Library of Congress Cataloging-in-Publication Data

Aalst, Wil van der.
  Workflow management / Wil van der Aalst, Kees van Hee.
    p.   cm. — (Cooperative information systems)
  Includes bibliographical references and index.
  ISBN 978-0-262-01189-1 (hardcover : alk. paper), 978-0-262-72046-5 (paperback)
  1. Management information systems. 2. Production management.
3. Workflow. I. Hee, Kees Max van, 1946– II. Title. III. Series.
T58.6 .A17   2002
658.5′1—dc21   2001042602

10 9 8 7

Contents

Series Foreword

The traditional view of information systems as tailor-made, cost-intensive database applications is changing rapidly. The change is fueled partly by a maturing software industry, which is making greater use of off-the-shelf generic components and standard software solutions, and partly by the onslaught of the information revolution. In turn, this change has resulted in a new set of demands for information services that are homogeneous in their presentation and interaction patterns, open in their software architecture, and global in their scope. The demands have come mostly from application domains such as e-commerce and banking, manufacturing (including the software industry itself), training, education, and environmental management, to mention just a few.

Future information systems will have to support smooth interaction with a large variety of independent, multi-vendor data sources and legacy applications running on heterogeneous platforms and distributed information networks. Metadata will play a crucial role in describing the contents of such data sources and in facilitating their integration.

As well, a greater variety of community-oriented interaction patterns will have to be supported by next-generation information systems. Such interactions may involve navigation, querying, and retrieval, and will have to be combined with personalized notification, annotation, and profiling mechanisms. Such interactions will also have to be intelligently interfaced with application software, and will need to be dynamically integrated into customized and highly connected cooperative environments. Morever the massive investments in information resources, by governments and businesses alike, call for specific measures that ensure security, privacy, and accuracy of their contents.

All these are challenges for the next generation of information systems. We call such systems *Cooperative Information Systems*, and they are the focus of this series.

In layman terms, cooperative information systems are servicing a diverse mix of demands characterized by *content—community—commerce*. These demands are originating in current trends for off-the-shelf software solutions such as enterprise resource planning and e-commerce systems.

A major challenge in building cooperative information systems is to develop technologies that permit continuous enhancement and evolution of current massive investments in information resources and systems. Such technologies must offer an appropriate infrastructure that supports not only development, but also evolution of software.

Early research results on cooperative information systems are becoming the core technology for community-oriented information portals or gateways. An information gateway provides a "one-stop shopping" place for a wide range of information resources and services, thereby creating a loyal user community.

The research advances that will lead to cooperative information system will not come from any single research area within the field of information technology. Database and knowledge-based systems, distributed systems, groupware, and graphical user interfaces have all matured as technologies. While further enhancements for individual technologies are desirable, the greatest leverage for technological advancement is expected to come from their evolution into a seamless technology for building and managing cooperative information systems.

The MIT Press *Cooperative Information Systems* series will cover this area through textbooks and research editions intended for the researcher and the professional who wishes to remain up-to-date on current developments and future trends.

The series will present three types of books:

• Textbooks or resource books intended for upper level undergraduate or graduate level courses;
• Research monographs, which collect and summarize research results and development experiences over a number of years; and
• Edited volumes, including collections of papers on a particular topic.

Authors are invited to submit to the series editors book proposals that include a table of contents and sample book chapters. All submissions will be reviewed formally and authors will receive feedback on their proposal.

John Mylopoulos
jm@cs.toronto.edu
Dept. of Computer Science
University of Toronto
Toronto, Ontario
Canada

Joachim W. Schmidt
j.w.schmidt@tu-harburg.de
Software Systems Institute
Technische Universität TUHH
Hamburg, Germany

Michael Papazoglou
M.P.Papazoglou@kub.nl
Tilburg University
INFOLAB
P.O. Box 90153
5000 LE Tilburg
The Netherlands

Acknowledgments

This book was prepared in close cooperation with the workflow groups at Deloitte & Touche Bakkenist, the Faculty of Mathematics and Computing Science, and the Faculty of Technology Management at Eindhoven University of Technology. The authors would like to thank all (former) members and students of these groups, in particular Twan Basten, Silvia de Gast, Ernst Kleiberg, Selma Limam, Michel van Osch, Jaap Rigter, Eric Verbeek, Marc Voorhoeve, Laurens Vrijnsen, Gerd Wagner, and Jaap van der Woude. We would also like to thank Michiel Bos and Niels van Riel for helping us preparing the English version of our book and Monique Jansen for proofreading the final version.

Special thanks are also due to our co-authors, André Blommers and Peter van der Toorn, each of whom contributed a chapter. Last but not least, we would like to thank the Dutch Tax Authority for permission to use the Sagitta 2000 project as a case study for this book.

December 2000
Wil van der Aalst
Kees van Hee

Introduction

This book is about the management of business processes. This is certainly not a new topic. Since the beginning of the Industrial Revolution, it has been written about from every possible point of view—economic, sociological, psychological, accountancy, mechanical engineering and business administration. In this book, we examine the management of business processes from the perspective of computing, or—to put it more broadly—of information technology. The reason is that information technology has made huge leaps forward in recent years, resulting in the creation of completely new ways of organizing business processes. The development of generic software packages for managing business processes—so-called workflow management systems (WFMS)—is particularly important in this respect.

Until recently, the golden rule was: "First organize, then computerize." This implied that processes were developed with the implicit assumption that the business process would primarily be managed by people. Then an organizational structure would be developed under which groups of people, or departments, were allocated particular tasks. Only then did people consider whether computers—or rather, information systems— could partially support, or even take over, the work. This approach does not sufficiently examine the opportunities offered by information systems. We have now reached a turning point: we first design business processes in a more abstract way, without considering implementation, and then we design the information systems and the organization hand in hand. In fact, we decide whether each task in a process should be performed by an information system or a person.

There are still some problems with this depiction. First, the notion that we can organize business processes differently using information systems is not new. People have long done this with business processes whose primary task is the processing of information. During the 1970s, serious efforts were made to completely computerize the management of business processes using information systems. This proved impossible with the technology then available. Even today, and for the foreseeable future, there are and will remain many tasks in the business process which can only be performed by people. In reaction to the reckless attempts of the 1970s, the role played by information technology has been somewhat restricted.

Information systems are used to reduce people's workload, particularly in offices. By analyzing thoroughly what people in offices do—by asking why they do it—the following information processing functions have been identified: text writing, drawing, calculating, filing, and communicating information. These analyses have led to the development of the following products: word processors, drawing systems, spreadsheet systems, database systems and electronic-mail systems. All these systems are generic in nature: they are not limited to a specific business application— as, say, accounting systems are—and so are widely used. Thanks to widespread distribution, this software is of high quality and relatively cheap. (In fact, accounting systems are widely usable, but not as extensively as word processors.)

Partly because of this development, the impact made by information technology has increased enormously, which in turn has led to many more people studying the possibilities presented by it. And this has resulted in the "BPR wave." BPR stands for business process redesign (or business process re-engineering) and is a method for improving the effectiveness and efficiency of business processes. BPR is based upon the notion that, if full use is made of information technology, business processes could be entirely different than at present. It therefore is wise to redesign the current processes completely, in the way described above. How business processes are organized is thus no longer the sole prerogative of the organizational or business expert: the information technologist now also has a major role to play. This is a good thing, because the information technologist is a developer of processes par excellence. After all, every algorithm defines a process. Until recently, however, the role of the information technologist was limited to the processing of information in computer systems—whereas, in fact, the main task of many other business processes is information processing.

In the past, it was the functional structure of an organization that played the most important role in how it was organized. Now the business processes are crucial. For this, a good frame of reference is required so that processes can be defined and analyzed clearly. Definition is important when preparing a (re)design, and before deciding whether to actually implement a new process it is very important to first establish whether it will work properly. To do this, one must be able to analyze the process defined. This can be done in a number of ways. For example, formal methods can be used to identify processes' properties, or lack of them. Another analysis method uses simulation techniques, sometimes supported by computer animation. Supporting software tools are essential to this.

This book presents a reference framework for defining processes and discusses analytical methods. In doing so, extensive use is made of Petri nets, a formal concept that has been developing since the 1960s and that made particularly significant leaps forward during the 1980s. Petri nets are ideally suited for defining and analyzing complex processes. Another useful property is that they make the definitions easy to understand for non-experts. This eases communication between designers and users. There also exist software tools which support the definition and analysis of processes.

Once new business processes have been developed, they then have to be implemented. The management and, in part, the execution of processes are handled by people, with the help of information systems. As already mentioned, during recent years a new class of generic software has been evolving: workflow management systems. This software supports business processes by taking on their information logistics. In other words, workflow management systems ensure that the right information reaches the right person at the right time, or is submitted to the right computer application at the right moment. A workflow management system does not, therefore, actually perform any of the tasks in a process. Herein lies both its strength—it is generic software and so can be used in many situations—and its weakness: usually actual application software is also needed.

The term "workflow" is used here as a synonym for "business process." We shall, as far as possible, use the terminology developed by the WorkFlow Management Coalition (WFMC). This is an organization dedicated to developing standard terminology and standard interfaces for workflow management systems components.

This book begins by describing the organization of workflows. This is important in order to be able to understand the role which workflow management systems can play and how they should be applied. The terms that are required in order to be able to deal with processes are introduced in an informal way, thus providing a basis for the rest of the book. Then there follows a chapter about modeling workflows. This includes a simple introduction to Petri-net theory. The next chapter covers the management of resources that contribute to business processes. These resources may be people, but can also be machines or computer systems. Techniques for analyzing processes are also considered. Then workflow management systems are introduced, with both their functions and architecture being covered. Then there follows a methodology for developing workflow applications. The final chapter is devoted to a case study of an actual application.

As an appendix, we have included an alphabetical glossary containing all the relevant terms used with their synonyms and short definitions. The first time that an important term is used, it is printed in italics.

This book is intended for students in information technology, industrial engineers, and for those who are professionally involved in implementing BPR using WFMS.

1

Organizing Workflows

1.1 Ontology for Workflow Management

The objective of this chapter is to develop a reference framework. This framework has three functions in this book. First, it is used to define the business-management context within which workflow management systems operate. Second, it is used to model and analyze processes. And third, it is used to describe the functionality and architecture of workflow management systems. A reference framework is a system of straightforwardly defined terms that describe a particular field of knowledge. It is also known as an *ontology*.

The ontology in which we are interested is that of processes. The terms used are generic in nature and can be applied in virtually all working situations. In practice, however, many have various synonyms which are widely used; for the sake of clarity, we will try to use a single "preferred term" as often as possible. This will be in line with the terminology used by the Workflow Management Coalition. In this chapter, we first discuss the role of work in society. Then we examine processes, followed by the distribution of work. The relationship between the principal and the contractor plays an important role in this. Specifically in electronic business these relationships are extremely important. We then study organizational structures and the management of processes. Finally, we look at the role played by (computerized) information systems in the establishment and management of business processes.

1.2 Work

People work to live—even though some become so involved that they give the impression of living for their work. In fact, we work because we need products to maintain our lives (for example: food, clothing, a home, a means of transport, not to mention entertainment). We do not produce all the things that we need ourselves, because that is inefficient. It actually would be impossible to manufacture all the products that we use during our lives in a modern society, ourselves. We would have to learn so many different and complex skills that they alone would take up our entire lives. We would need many lifetimes just to make the tools needed to produce the necessities of life. This is why we are instead organized into specialized "business units," in which people produce a limited range of products in a highly efficient way, with the help of machines. These products are supplied to other people through a market mechanism and a distribution structure in exchange for money, which enables the producers to buy those products that they do not make themselves. With production distributed in such a way, there is also created work that would not exist if everybody was entirely self-sufficient in producing all the products they need. For example, managing money—what the banks do—and preparing advertising materials would not be necessary.

There have thus developed all kinds of services and products that do not make a direct contribution to keeping us alive, but are necessary to keep the organization operating. Despite this "burden," we are able to produce so efficiently that we have a large amount of free time—thus further stimulating the demand for entertainment. The leisure industry therefore is also a flourishing one.

Modern society has become so complex that nobody can entirely survey it any longer, and many people do not know what role their work plays in the overall scheme of things. This "alienation" is a major social problem that falls outside the scope of this book. But even within large companies there exists a high degree of work specialization, which results in the "big picture" being lost and employees not always realizing why they have to do the things they are told to do. Such alienation from work has a negative effect upon productivity. This is why many companies are organizing their work in such a way that their employees clearly understand that they are working for a particular customer. Among the objectives of such customer-oriented work is an increase in employees' motivation, and hence their productivity. The fact that we have moved from living in a supply-driven economy, in which the means of produc-

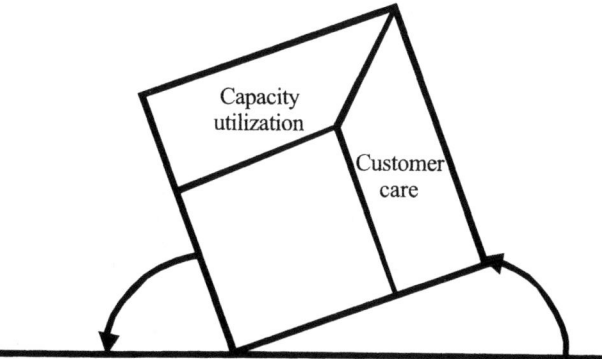

Figure 1.1
Organizational paradigm shift

tion were scarce, to a demand-driven one in which it is the customers who are scarce, has only served to reinforce this tendency. This shift of focus from the means of production to the customer is also known as "organizational paradigm shift" (see figure 1.1).

In order to make work "controllable" and to encourage communication between employees, *workflow management systems* have evolved. These are a new class of information system. They make it possible to build, in a straightforward way, a "bridge" between people's work and computer applications.

1.3   Business Processes

There are many different types of work, such as baking bread, making a bed, designing a house or collecting survey results to compile a statistic. In all of these examples, we can see the one tangible "thing" that is produced or modified: the bread, the bed, the house, or the statistic. In this book, we shall call such a "thing" a *case*. Other terms used are work, job, product, service, or item. A case does not need be a specific object; it can also be more abstract—like, say, a lawsuit or an insurance claim. A building project or the assembly of a car in a factory are also examples of cases.

Working on a case is discrete in nature. That is, every case has a beginning and an end, and each can be distinguished from every other case.

Each case involves a *process* being performed. A process consists of a number of *tasks* that need to be carried out and a set of *conditions* that determine the order of the tasks. A process can also be called a *procedure*. A task is a logical unit of work that is carried out as a single whole by one *resource*. A resource is the generic name for a person, machine or group of persons or machines that can perform specific tasks. This does not always mean to say that the resource necessarily carries out the task independently, but that it is responsible for it. We will examine this subject more closely in the next section.

As an example of a process, we shall examine how a (fictional) insurance company deals with a claim. We can identify the following tasks:

1. *recording* the receipt of the claim;
2. establishing the *type* of claim (for example, fire, motor vehicle, travel, professional);
3. checking the client's *policy*, to confirm that it does in principle cover what has been claimed for;
4. checking the *premium*, to confirm that payments are up to date;
5. *rejection*, if task 3 or 4 has a negative result;
6. producing a *rejection letter*;
7. estimating the *amount to be paid*, based upon the claim details;
8. appointment of an *assessor* to research the circumstances of the damage and to establish its value;
9. consideration of *emergency measures* to limit further damage or relieve distress;
10. provision of *emergency measures* if approved as part of task 8;
11. establishment or revision of *amount to be paid* and offer to client;
12. recording of client's *reaction*: acceptance or objection;
13. assessment of *objection* and decision to revise (task 11) or to take legal proceedings (task 14);
14. legal *proceedings*;
15. *payment* of claim; and
16. *closure* of claim: filing.

Here we can see sixteen tasks that do not necessarily need to be performed in the order shown. Two or more tasks that must be performed in a strict order are called a *sequence*. For some cases, certain tasks do not need to be carried out. One example is the appointment of an expert, if the claim report is clear and the amount of the claim is below a particular value, the involvement of an expert is not necessary. Other tasks that do not always need to be performed are taking emergency measures, assessing an objection, or taking legal proceedings. Sometimes, therefore, a choice between two or more tasks can be made. This we call a *selection*.

There are also tasks that can be performed *in parallel*, for example checking the policy and checking the premiums. These tasks must both be completed before the "rejection" task can begin. This is called *synchronization*.

This example of a process also includes *iteration*, or repetition—namely, the repeated assessment of an objection or the revision of the amount to be paid. In theory, this could go on forever. Figure 1.2 shows the order of the tasks as a *process diagram*: an arrow from task A to task B means that A must be done before B. We can also see that the diagram contains more information than the list of tasks. For example, it shows that a claim can only be closed once any emergency measures required have been taken. Each task is indicated by a rectangle. If a task has more than one successor task—that is, if it has more than one arrow leading from it—then precisely *one* of these subsequent tasks must be chosen during the task in question. If a task has more than one predecessor—more than one arrow leading to it—then *all* of these must be completed before that task can begin (synchronization). The circles indicate where particular workflows meet or split. The gray circles have *several* precursor tasks and only *one* subsequent task. They indicate that only one of the preceding tasks needs to be performed in order to continue. The black circles have *one* predecessor and *several* subsequent tasks. They show that all the subsequent tasks must be performed. (The circles can be regarded as "dummy" tasks.) Chapter 2 introduces a process notation which makes it easier to express such properties.

To summarize, we can identify four different basic mechanisms in process structures: sequence, selection, parallelization, and iteration. All are very commonplace in practice, and in principle all processes can be modeled using these four constructions. We shall consider them in greater detail in chapter 2.

Some tasks can be performed by a computer without human interference. Other tasks require human intelligence: a judgment or a decision. For instance, a bank employee decides if a client's loan request will be granted or not. Human workers need *knowledge* to execute tasks. This

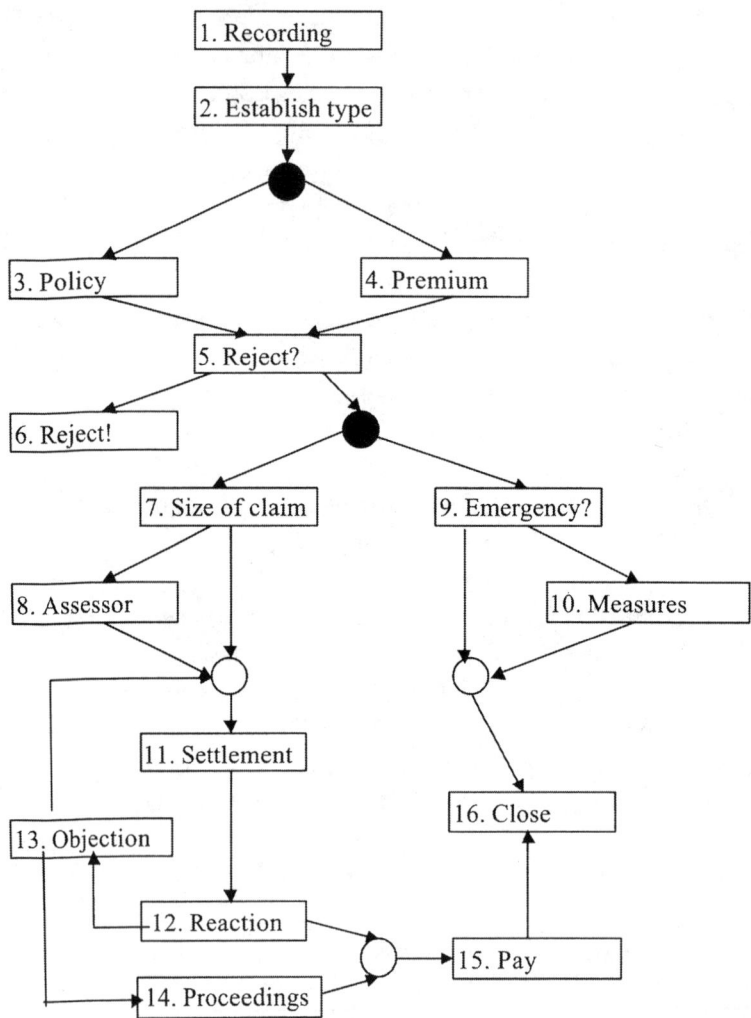

Figure 1.2
Insurance claim process

knowledge is stored in their minds by experience, the so-called *tacit knowledge*. Other forms of knowledge can be obtained by learning and information retrieval, the so-called *explicit knowledge*. *Knowledge management* is concerned with the acquisition, enrichment, and distribution of knowledge so that the right knowledge is at the right time with the person who has to fulfill a task.

A task can also be defined as a process that cannot be subdivided any further: an *atomic* process. There is a subjective element in this—what one person regards as a single task may be a nonatomic one to another. For an insurance company, for example, the compilation of an assessor's report of damage to a car is a single task, whereas for the expert himself it is a process comprising various tasks, such as checking the chassis, engine, and bodywork. A task is therefore an atomic process for the person defining or ordering it, but for the person carrying it out it is often a nonatomic one.

A single process is carried out on each case. We call the performance of a task by a resource an *activity*. Various cases may have the same process, but each case may follow a different route through that process. In the insurance company, for example, one claim may involve an objection and another not. The route taken depends upon the specific characteristics of the case—the *case attributes*. The number of processes in a company is (generally) finite and far smaller than the number of cases to be handled. As a result, a company can develop a routine for performing processes and thus operate efficiently.

This is clearly seen in the clothing industry: it is much faster to make one hundred skirts with the same pattern than one hundred skirts using different patterns. Off-the-rack is cheaper than made-to-measure. What's more, producing one thousand skirts of the same pattern is less expensive than ten times making one hundred in that pattern. This is called the economy of scale: the costs per case fall as the number of cases increases. Companies therefore endeavor to keep the number of processes small and to make the number of cases that each can perform as high as possible—at least, as long as they can earn something from each case. Profit, after all, is the ultimate objective.

An insurance company wants to keep the number of claims as low as possible—but this is generally a factor that it cannot control. It will also try to keep the number of processes low. There is, however, a catch:

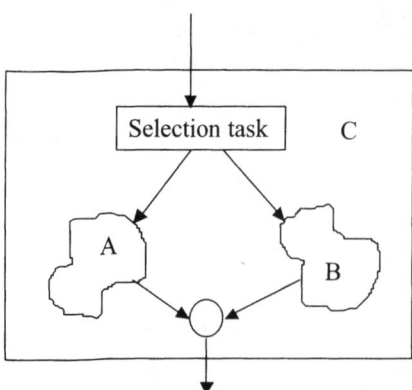

Figure 1.3
Combination of two processes into one

the processes must not become too complicated. It is better to have a few more, but simpler, processes than a few which are overly complex. Remember that, in theory, it is possible to combine two or more processes into one, as shown in figure 1.3. Processes A and B are joined to form a single process, C.

Here one additional task has been added: deciding what type of case we are dealing with and so choosing which of the processes to follow. This is therefore a false economy. In order to reach an efficient process structure, calculations need to be made which cannot generally be performed without the aid of computer simulations.

The situation that we have just described is the most common: a small number of processes with a lot of cases. There are, however, exceptions to this rule. A tailor, for example, produces every suit made-to-measure; one could therefore say that he must design and start up a new process for each case. This also applies to an architect who has to design every new house or office block from scratch. But we can also view this in a different way: both the tailor and the architect will certainly use a standard approach, and thus a process which they always follow. The tailor will start by taking the customer's measurements, then show him a number of patterns and try to establish with him which best matches his wishes, and then make changes to the pattern. Then the fabric is chosen and the tailor starts drawing the pattern. There are also many other tasks that can be identified as a part of each case. The same applies to the architect. What we can see here is that there is indeed a process, but the tasks performed are highly dependent upon the case. This is, therefore, a yardstick for the complexity of a process: the degree to which the tasks depend on the cases.

Although we shall deal primarily with situations in which many cases pertain to a single process, there are many situations in which a new process needs to be designed for each case. We call these "one of a kind" processes. In these, the first stage in tackling the case is the design of its specific process. Even here, there are frequently standard tasks from which the process is compiled. In such cases, we say that every case has its own *project*. The words "project" and "process" are here synonymous.

We have already seen that the work carried out on cases is of a discrete nature: each has a single beginning and a single end. However, there is also work of a continuous nature which does not clearly belong to a single case. Take, for example, a doorman whose work consists of assisting people to enter a building, or a policeman who has to guarantee security in a district by patrolling it. In both examples a case can still—with a little goodwill—be defined by identifying periods and regarding door keeping or patrolling for a particular period as one case. The employee thus automatically receives a continual sequence of cases, one for each period. Another way of regarding work of a continuous nature in case terms is to regard the work as a whole as one case comprising a continual repetition of tasks. In this book, we concentrate upon discrete work—but in doing so we do not exclude continuous work. It can serve as an extreme example with which the principles presented in the book can be put to the test.

To conclude this section, we shall subdivide processes into three categories: *primary*, *secondary*, and *tertiary*:

• Primary processes are those that produce the company's products or services. They therefore are known also as *production processes*. They deal with cases for the customer. As a rule, they are the processes that generate income for the company, and are clearly customer-oriented. Sometimes the customer is not yet known, as when firms produce to stock. Examples of primary processes are the purchase of raw materials and components, the sale of products and services, design and engineering, and production and distribution.

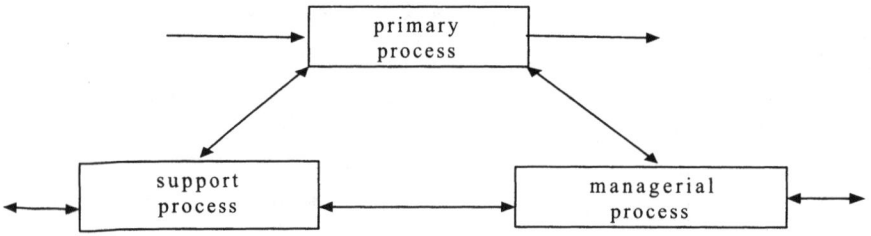

Figure 1.4
Links between the three types of processes

• Secondary processes are those that support the primary ones. They therefore are also known as *support processes*. One important group of secondary processes concentrates upon maintaining the means of production: the purchase and maintenance of machinery, vehicles, and premises. A comparable group of processes is that involving personnel management: recruitment and selection, training, work appraisal, pay-rolls, and dismissal. Financial administration is also a secondary process, as is marketing.

• Tertiary processes are the *managerial processes* that direct and coordinate the primary and secondary processes. During these, the objectives and preconditions within which the managers of the other processes must operate are formulated, and the resources required to carry out the other processes are allocated. The managerial processes also encompass the maintenance of contacts with financiers and other stakeholders.

Figure 1.4 shows the relationships between the three types of processes.

The managerial processes have objectives and capital as their input, and must deliver performance—often in the form of profit. Support processes receive, from the managerial processes, the means to buy in resources, and they dispose of resources which are no longer functioning. The resources managed by the secondary processes are placed at the disposal of the primary processes, which return them after use. As input, the primary processes receive orders on the one hand and raw materials and components on the other. As output, they deliver products and services. They receive assignments and purchasing budgets from the managerial processes. Support and primary processes report back to the managerial processes and submit their income.

The secondary and tertiary processes are often continuous in nature, although they may contain discrete subprocesses, whereas the primary processes are usually case driven and thus have a discrete character.

1.4 Allocating and Accepting Work

Animals and machines work on *orders*, or *assignments*, given by people. But most people's work is also assigned or outsourced to them by other people: their principals. Exceptions are artists, scientists, and politicians, who can—to some extent—decide for themselves what work they are going to do.

There are two forms of principals: the *boss* and the *customer*. Ultimately, assignments ordered by bosses are directly or indirectly related to work for customers. The relationship is "direct" if the work carried out results in a product or service for a customer, which may be unknown. This mainly applies to the primary processes. The relationship is "indirect" if the work involves maintaining or improving the production process: the secondary and tertiary processes.

In most organizations there exists a hierarchy under which assignments that people receive can (in part) be passed on to people further down the hierarchy. A person who is assigned a task is a *contractor*, also known as a *resource*. We mainly use the latter term because assignments can be carried out by machines—in particular, computer applications—as well as by people. Thus far we have discussed principals and contractors as if they are individual people, but they can in fact also be company departments or separate firms. We will therefore use the term *actor* to describe principals and contractors in general. An actor may play both roles—as a principal and a subcontractor (or resource)—at the same time.

A contractor does not necessarily carry out the work itself, but may redirect or subcontract it to third parties. But the contractor always *directs* the work which it accepts.

In larger organizations, employees carrying out an assignment often do not know for which customer the task is being performed. This is particularly the case when products are being produced to stock, because during production the identity of the customer is still unknown. (And sometimes there is eventually no customer at all for the product.)

As indicated before, a principal is either a customer or a boss. There is also a wide variety among customers. For the Prison Service, criminals (prisoners) are its customers; the Inland Revenue's customers are the taxpayers, a hospital's customers are its patients. The role of a customer is dependent upon the situation: the baker is the gardener's customer when the gardener looks after the baker's garden, but the gardener is the baker's customer when he buys bread.

In large organizations, there is a marked tendency to accentuate the role of the customer more clearly. The principle that "the customer is always right" is winning ground over "working for the boss." Customer awareness ensures that people are more conscious of who they are working for, which leads to a more careful approach to their work: after all, if they deliver poor quality work, they will be unsure whether the customer will order more. (For a prison "customer," this principle works the other way around.)

For all work a principal and a contractor exist who have a—sometimes unwritten—*contract* with one another about the case to be performed, the deadline for its completion, and the price to be paid. If the contractor is a separate company, then a communications process will be created between principal and contractor before the contract is entered into, and communications between the two actors may continue to be necessary during the performance of the task. When the relationship between the contractor and the principal is formalized, a *communications protocol* can be observed. This can be very complex. Figure 1.5 shows an example of a communications protocol.

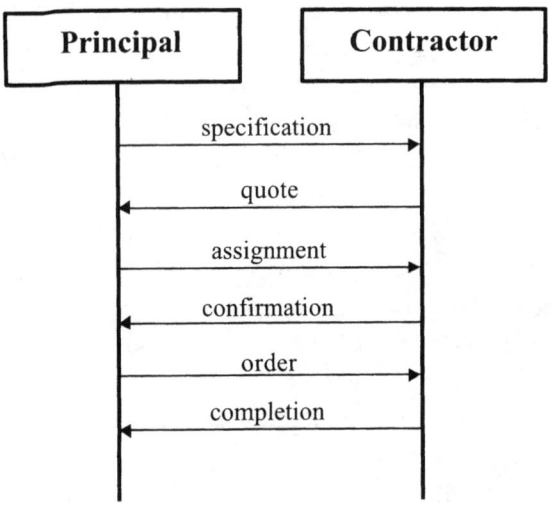

Figure 1.5
Communications protocol

In this example, we can see the successive steps in the relationship. The principal first provides a specification of the work to be carried out. Then the contractor produces a plan for performing the work and fixes a price. This is the "quote" that it submits to the principal. The latter studies the quote and orders the work in accordance with it. In practice, there can be a lot of discussion between the parties in the meantime, with the principal making supplementary demands—about the price, for example—and the contractor explaining how it intends to carry out the work. In many cases, the moment when the order is confirmed is not the same as when it actually begins. If the work forms part of a larger project that the principal is directing, then the work can only begin once other elements in the project have been completed; the principal thus determines at what point the work can start. The number of steps in a communications protocol between a principal and a contractor therefore can vary from case to case according to the specific characteristics and handling of each, and so does not need to be fixed in advance.

An actor responsible for a process may assign or outsource a task as a whole to a contractor or he may decompose it into a process, that is, a network of tasks, each of which he assigns to a contractor. At their turn these contractors may repeat this decomposition process. This decomposition leads to a *contract tree*. Execution of a task for a particular case requires the enactment of a communications protocol between principals and contractors. Instead of decomposing a task into a process and outsourcing the subtasks of this process for all cases that pass the task, it is also possible to do this for each case in a different way. Then the execution of a task for a particular case starts with a "design phase," in which the network of tasks is created and in which the (sub)contractors are selected. Figure 1.6 shows an example of this. In this example, the task is the transportation of a cargo from point A to point K. The principal P subdivides this work into two tasks: transportation from point A to point D, and transportation from point D to point K. Each of these tasks is subcontracted to a different contractor, that is, contractors Q and R. Each of the tasks is then subdivided again by these two: by principal/contractor Q into transportation from A to C and then C to D, and by principal/contractor R from D to J and then from J to K. This is illustrated in figure 1.6. Note that both Q and R act as principal *and* contractor.

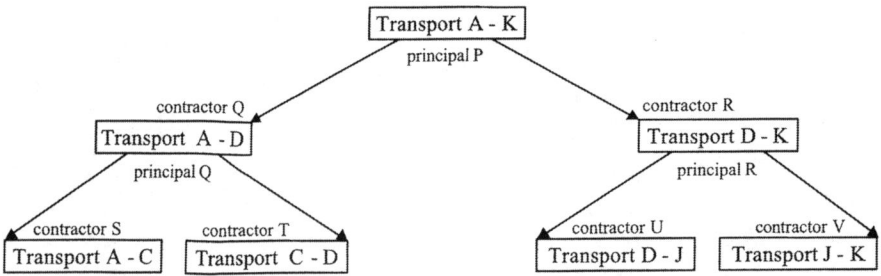

Figure 1.6
Contract tree

This tree contains "nodes," which are shown in the example as rectangles. "Branches" link two "nodes." The "nodes" show those actors who are responsible for a part of the work. In this example, the actors are identified by the tasks that they must perform. The "root" of the tree (which we actually show at the top of the diagram) receives the assignments directly from the principal. The "leaves" of the tree (that is, the lowest of the "nodes") are the actors who actually carry out the tasks. The other actors are both principals and contractors. An actor X is a subcontractor of another actor Y if there is an arc from Y to X. An actor is a principal if there is an arc leading from this actor to another actor. Consider for example figure 1.6. Actor Q is a subcontractor of P and a principal of S and T. Such decomposition and outsourcing processes occur frequently inside organizations but also between different organizations. In electronic business we try to automate/computerize these processes as much as possible. If we want to support business processes by information systems, we need very detailed and precise descriptions of these business processes. If we want to couple business processes of different organizations in an automatic/computerized way, this becomes even more important.

1.5   Organizational Structures

A great deal of literature has been published about organizational structures, and any attempt to summarize it in a few paragraphs is doomed to fail. Therefore we shall not try to do so. We shall, however, discuss those properties of the three most important forms of organizational structure that are relevant to workflow organization.

An organizational structure establishes how the work carried out by the organization in question is divided up amongst its staff. In most cases this does not mean the people themselves, but rather the *roles* or *functions* that they fulfill. A single person can fulfill several roles during her or his lifetime. Somebody can, for example, begin as an administrative assistant and end up as head of accounts. People may also fulfill different roles in time. It may be that the same person is both a driver and a messenger, delivering messages when there is nobody to be driven. One important aspect of an organizational structure is the division of authorities and responsibilities. If an executive has specific responsibilities, then he also has to have particular authorities. These often involve the authority to assign work to other members of staff—in other words, to outsource work to others. Conversely, an executive is responsible for ensuring that the work assigned to him by authorized colleagues actually is carried out.

The three most important forms of organizational structure—or rather, coordination mechanisms—are:

1. the hierarchical organization;
2. the matrix organization; and
3. the network organization.

The *hierarchical organization* is the best known of these, and is characterized by a "tree" structure. Such a structure is called an *organizational chart*. We already have encountered tree structures in the previous section in the form of contract trees. In an organizational chart, each node which is not a "leaf" indicates an individual role or function. The "leaves" of the tree usually represent groups of staff or departments. The "branches" show authority relationships: the person at the start (top) of the branch is authorized to order work from the person or department at the end (bottom) of it.

There is also another definition of the organizational chart that closely resembles ours but is, in fact, different. Under this definition, each "leaf" shows a person and each node at a higher level represents a department. The "root" node indicates the entire company, and every other node a part of that above it. The people indicated in each leaf thus belong to the department shown in the node immediately above them. Whereas the

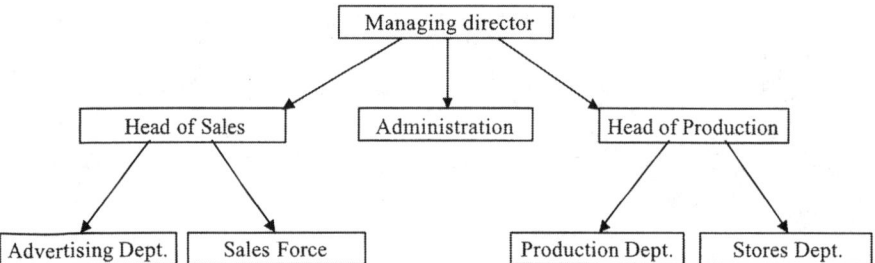

Figure 1.7
Organizational chart

first definition shows the person who is responsible for all the people below him in the tree for whom he represents the root, the second regards each of these collections of staff as one department. The similarity between organizational charts and contract trees is that both express principal-contractor relationships as "branches." The difference is that in an organizational chart this relationship is not linked to any specific case, whereas this relationship is very relevant for a transaction tree. In a strictly hierarchical organization, communication between two nodes always passes through their closest common predecessor. Figure 1.7 shows an example of an organizational chart.

In this example, formal communication between the sales force and the stores department must go through the head of sales, the managing director and the head of production. The "management" or "board" is often at the "root" of an organizational chart. Its "leaves" are the company's departments. One typical example of a hierarchical organization is the army. In practice, there exists a lot of informal communication between the various individual members of staff and departments, allowing communication to be quicker than if it were to follow hierarchical lines. Purely hierarchical organizations are virtually extinct now, since this structure is too inflexible. In many firms it is too unwieldy to allow the delegation of work only through fixed, hierarchical channels.

In designing a hierarchical organization, we are free to choose what departments are created and what management layers exist above them. In allocating staff into departments, we can select from three principles:

• *The capacity group.* Put people with the same skills together in the same department. In principle, such people are interchangeable. The task of the head of department is to keep its members "up-to-date"—through training, for example—and to do his best to "sell" them to other business units for whom they perform their work. Typical examples are typing pools and pools of maintenance engineers.

• *The functional department.* This performs an interdependent group of tasks, each often requiring the same skills. Responsibility for the work of the department rests with its head. Typical examples are departments like accounting, marketing, and maintenance.

• *Process or production departments.* In this case, the department is responsible for a complete business process or for the manufacturing of a product.

The first or second type of organization is often chosen for the secondary processes. In the primary ones, the third form begins to gain importance. Superseding the departments are the hierarchical management layers. In choosing these, the following question plays an important role: is the amount of coordination required between the departments large or small? There should be as few layers as possible between departments which need to coordinate to a great extent, so they should preferably have a single manager.

A manager has a maximum *span of control*. In other words, he cannot direct an unlimited number of subordinates. How large a particular manager's span of control is depends to a great extent upon the nature of the work and her own experience.

This is how the *matrix organization* came about. This form of organization is structured in accordance with two dimensions: the *functional* and the *hierarchical*. The hierarchical part is the same as described above and is usually based upon functional or capacity groups: people with the same skills belong to the same group. The functional part is based upon the tasks which have to be performed. (The terminology can be rather confusing.) Each person thus has a hierarchical boss—the head of the department to which he belongs—and a functional boss, who is responsible for the task to be carried out. The tasks—which in the context of matrix organizations are usually called "projects"—are unique; in other words, no fixed structure can be created based upon the tasks, so the hierarchical (fixed) structure is based upon the skills of the people concerned. The functional bosses are known as "project leaders."

Matrix organizations are found mostly in companies that operate on a project basis, such as building contractors, installation firms, and soft-

	Project-1	Project-2	Project-3
Supervisors	Louise	Anita	John
Carpenters	Pete	Karl	Geraldine
Masons	Henry	Tom	Jerry
Painters	Bert	Simone	Simone
Plasterers	Charles	Peter	Paul

Figure 1.8
Staff allocation in a matrix organization

ware houses: in other words, in businesses that do not carry out serial production but rather unique projects. The functional structure thus is constantly subject to change. It is quite possible that person A is for a while the leader of a project in which person B participates, and then a little later B becomes the leader of a project involving A. Figure 1.8 shows an example of staff allocation in a matrix organization. The columns show the functional allocation and the rows the hierarchical.

We can see how one person can take part in more than one project. Naturally, one person may be involved only in one project at a time, but it is equally possible for someone to work alternately on several projects during the same period. Often several people within one department work on the same project. In the matrix, this would mean more than one person being included in the same cell. For the sake of simplicity, this is not shown in figure 1.8. A form of organization which strongly resembles the matrix type occurs when processes are managed by a process manager and cases by a *case manager*. The former is responsible for the quality and efficiency of "her" process, whereas the latter ensures the rapid and correct completion of "her" cases. This can lead to a conflict of interests.

The last form of organization which we can identify is the network organization. In this, autonomous actors collaborate to supply products or services. To the customer, though, they appear to be one organization—which is why the network organization is sometimes called a *virtual organization*. The actors perform as principals and contractors. The autonomy means that there exists no formal permanent (employment) relationship, which means that an actor can choose whether or not she wishes to carry out a particular task. The actors required to perform each task therefore must be recruited individually on each occasion. This may be done through a protocol and a contract tree, as discussed in the previous section. This can be a time-consuming business, so "framework" contracts are often drawn up for regular assignments. Such a contract determines that a party is available upon request to perform a particular type of work. Just as in a matrix organization, party A can be party B's principal for one type of work but its subcontractor for another.

More and more network organizations are being created. There are two main reasons for this. First, firms are trying to keep their permanent workforce as small as possible instead making more extensive use of temporary staff and subcontractors. This, together with the fact that many people are now working part time, is known as the flexibilization of labor. In this way firms can control their fixed costs. The use of *comakers* and *outsourcers*, which are examples of contractors, is very common in the building and motor industries. The second reason is that specialist companies, each with only a limited product range, can supply together an entire product. Examples are found in the construction industry—in which a range of actors join forces to build a bridge—and amongst consultancy firms, which package their individual knowledge to offer an integrated product incorporating, say, financial, legal, fiscal, and IT advice. A network organization is, to a certain degree, comparable with a matrix organization. After all, the resources for each project are assembled individually. The difference, however, is that in this case those resources do not have the same employer.

1.6   Managing Processes

One established way of studying the management of processes is to distinguish between a *management system* and a *managed system*. The word "system" here means all those people, machines, and computerized information systems that carry out particular processes. A managed system can even be further subdivided into a lower-level management system and a managed system (see figure 1.9). The managed system at the lowest level of this subdivision is an *enactment system*. At the highest level, a system is always part of a managed system. A management system can manage several systems, and in doing so, it ensures the ability of

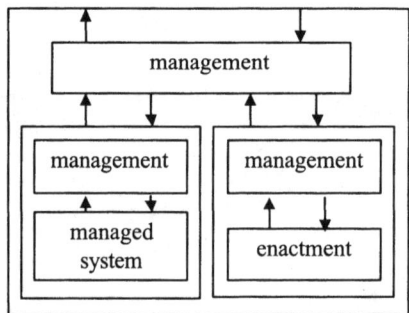

Figure 1.9
Recursive management paradigm: The whole entity is a managed system

the managed systems to communicate with one another and with the outside world—that is, the managed system at a higher level.

Between the management system and the managed system there occurs an exchange of information. This enables the management system to communicate objectives, preconditions, and decisions to the managed system, and the managed system—conversely—reports back to the management system. Based upon these reports, the management system may revise the objectives, preconditions, and decisions. This so-called *planning and control cycle* can be identified in every organization.

Process management has long been divided into four levels. The distinction between these is based upon the frequency and scope of the decisions to be made. By scope, we mean two things: the period of time over which the decision has an influence, and its (potential) financial impact. The four levels are as follows (see figure 1.10):

1. *Real-time management.* Decisions can be made very frequently (intervals range from microseconds to hours). The period of time during which the decision has an effect is very short, and the financial consequences of a wrong decision are small.

2. *Operational management.* Decisions are made very regularly (from hours to days) and their scope is limited. In other words, the influence of the decision is no longer noticeable after a short period.

3. *Tactical management.* Decisions are made periodically (from days to months), and their scope is limited.

4. *Strategic management.* Decisions are made only once, or no more than every couple of years, and their scope is wide. The influence of a strategic decision can remain noticeable for many years.

Management level	Time horizon	Financial impact	Type of decisions	Supporting methods
Real-time	Seconds–hours	Low	Equipment control	Control theory
Operational	Hours–days	Limited	Resource assignment	Combinatorial optimization (e.g., scheduling)
Tactical	Days–months	High	Resource capacity planning and budgeting	Stochastic models (e.g., queueing models)
Strategic	Months–years	Very high	Process design and resource types	Financial models, multi-criteria analysis

Figure 1.10
Four levels of process management

Another distinction between these levels of management is the types of decisions which are made. Real-time and operational management involve only dynamic aspects, not the structure of the business processes. Real-time management involves the control of machines and vehicles. Operational management mostly concerns the allocation of resources to cases and the routing of those cases. Typical examples of operational management are *production scheduling* and the *routing* of trains.

Tactical management concerns: *capacity planning* and *budgeting* for operational management. Capacity planning involves determining the quantities of resources required per type of case. This means not only human resources, but also the machines and raw materials used in performing the case. Stocks management is a typical example, involving not only the management of the raw-materials stocks themselves but also that of reserve resources. Budgeting concerns the allocation of financial means and the formulation of targets in financial terms.

Strategic management is concerned with the *structural* aspects of processes and types of resources. One strategic question is whether the company should carry out a particular process itself, or source it out. Another question is how the processes should be structured and what procedures should be followed.

Each management level, except for real-time management, also has the task to take care of exceptions to rules that are made for the lower levels. Tactical management may be involved if the resource allocation at the operational level does not succeed.

Decision making is an important feature of (process) management. The discipline of operations research (OR) searches for the best possible solutions to decision problems using mathematical techniques. Artificial intelligence (AI) tries to develop computer systems that can imitate human techniques for solving decision problems (heuristics). Organizational sociology tackles such things as methods by which people can cooperate to find a solution. Here, we shall confine ourselves to summarizing the four phases that are always passed through when solving decision problems:

1. *Definition* involves establishing exactly what the problem is and, in particular, within what scope a solution to it must be found. Drawing up optimization criteria often forms part of this phase.

2. *Creation* involves formulating one or more solutions that fall within the scope defined or satisfy an optimization criterion.

3. *Evaluation* involves assessing different solutions, for instance by multi-criteria analysis.

4. *Selection* involves selecting one solution that works in order to implement it.

In principle, computer support is available for all these tasks, particularly the second and third. This is sometimes possible using a simple spreadsheet but usually requires mathematical techniques or simulation models.

1.7 Information Systems for Business Processes

The organization of work, both within and between companies, is becoming more and more complicated. This is why (computerized) information systems have been developed that support the management of processes and their coordination. We shall first offer a method of classifying information systems. Then we shall outline how they have been developed in the past and how they will probably be developed in the near future.

Information systems can be categorized in many ways. The one we have chosen to use here is based upon the role played by the system in the processes. The list below is in ascending order of functionality: the first type of system listed contains very little knowledge of the processes and should only be used to support the people who actually do the work, whereas the final one can manage processes without any human intervention:

• *Office information systems.* These systems assist the staff responsible for carrying out and managing processes with basic information processing: writing, drawing, calculating, filing, and communication. They include word processors, drawing packages, spreadsheets, simple database management systems, and electronic mail. These systems do not themselves contain any knowledge of the processes. Although the information that they process may contain business knowledge, they themselves cannot do anything with this.

• *Transaction-processing systems.* These systems, also called registrational systems, register and communicate the relevant aspects of changes in the circumstances of a process and record these changes. Transaction-processing systems that specialize in communication between different organizations are called *interorganizational information systems.* These often use electronic data interchange (EDI) using standards for data exchange like XML. The heart of such a system generally is a database management system, but today a workflow management system also becomes an essential component. The latter type of system does have some knowledge of the processes, as proven—for example—by the fact that it can independently interpret incoming transactions and thus determine where and how the input data should be stored.

• *Knowledge-management systems.* These systems take care of acquisition and distribution of knowledge to be used by knowledge workers, either case workers or managers. The knowledge they handle is explicit knowledge that can be represented in digital form. One of the simplest forms of a knowledge-management system is a search engine coupled to a document-management system. With such a system, a knowledge worker is able to find relevant text fragments produced by himself or others by means of keywords or free-text search. A more advanced facility is a case-based reasoning system that searches through a database of best-practice cases and finds cases with a high level of similarity to the actual case. The solution presented by the cases found might be applicable for the actual case as well. Managers are interested mostly in aggregated data about the processing of cases or about the cases themselves. Here we often use *data warehouses* that are connected to tools for statistical analysis. A data warehouse is a database that stores aggregated data in multidimensional cells, for instance the number of customers that bought a typical kind of product in a specific time period and a geographical region.

• *Decision-support systems.* These compute decisions through interaction with people. There are two types of decision-support systems. The first type is based upon mathematical models. Examples include budgeting and investment systems and production-planning systems. The second type is based upon logical reasoning systems. They are also known as *expert systems.* One example is a system for establishing the cause of a defect in a machine. These systems are used at all levels of management (operational, tactical, and strategic).

• *Control systems.* Also known as programmed decision-making systems, these systems calculate and implement decisions entirely automatically, based upon the recorded state of a process. Examples are automatic ordering, climate control, and invoicing systems.

An information system is often a combination of the four types described above. From the viewpoint of efficiency, the control system appears to be the ideal because it requires no staff. In practice, the number of applications in which such systems can be used turns out to be very limited, and only well defined decision situations can be approached in this way. Nevertheless, they do work for some operational management

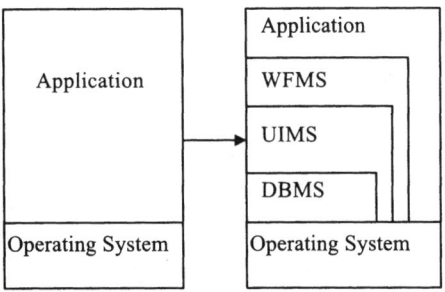

Figure 1.11
Decomposition of generic functionality

problems. The decision-support systems, which solve management problems through interaction with people, offer the most potential because they combine human insight with the computer's calculating power. We still have absolutely no idea how an information system should make a decision about many problems at the strategic level. In practice, most information systems are office-information and transaction-processing systems.

We shall now examine the way in which we develop information systems. This will be done by means of a historical summary. The boundaries of the time periods given should not be regarded as clear-cut, but that is not the most important point. The summary below highlights the influence of workflow management systems. What the history shows is that more and more generic tasks have been taken out of programs and put into decomposed management systems. Figure 1.11 illustrates this evolution.

1. *1965–1975: decompose applications.* During this period, information systems comprised decomposed applications, each with its own databases and definitions. The applications ran directly on the operating system and either had no user interface or one entirely of their own. Data were stored between two runs of the application program, originally on punch cards and paper tapes, and later on magnetic tape and in disk memory. There was no exchange of data between different applications. It thus was possible for a member of staff to have different names in the payroll program and the personnel program. It was impossible to achieve added value by combining different sources of data.

2. *1975–1985: database management—"take data management out of the applications."* This period is characterized by the rise of the *database*

management system (DMBS). Originally these were hierarchical and network databases, later relational ones. A database is a permanently available, integrated collection of data files which can be used by many applications. The use of databases has the advantages that data managed by different applications can be combined, that data structures only need to be defined once, that the organization of data can be handed over to a database management system, and that the same data item only needs to be stored once. A DBMS is a piece of generic software that can be used to define and use databases: to add, view, revise, and delete data. The use of database management systems has also radically changed the system-development process: once the database has been defined, different developers can work on designing applications on it at the same time. To do this, methods were developed for establishing data structures before the applications were defined. This is the data-oriented approach to system development. This period thus can be characterized as that during which the data organization was beginning to be extracted from application programs.

3. *1985–1995: user-interface management—"take the user interface out of the applications."* It was during this period that the next bottleneck in system development appeared. Because we were developing more and more interactive software, a great deal of time was being spent developing user interfaces. Originally these were designed by the developers screen by screen, field by field. Not only did this take up a lot of time, but also each designer had her own style, which meant that every system had to operate in a different way. There are now *user-interface management systems* (UIMS) that solve both these problems: a user interface can be defined rapidly and the designer is "invited" to do this in a standard way. In recent years, a transition has taken place from character-based user interfaces to graphics-based ones, and as a result the utilization of user-interface management systems has increased. Today the functions of user-interface management systems are integrated in other tools, like database management systems, program environments, and web browsers. During this period the user interfaces were extracted from the application programs.

4. *1995–2005: workflow management—"take the business processes out of the applications."* Now that data management and user interfacing have largely disappeared from applications themselves, it seems that much of the software is devoted to business processes (procedures) and the handling of cases. Therefore, it has become attractive to isolate this component now and find a separate solution for it. Not only can this accelerate the development of information systems, but it also offers the added advantage that the business processes become easier to maintain.

Today, it occurs frequently that management wants to change an administrative procedure, but this would have far-reaching consequences for the software. As a result, the change is not carried through. *Workflow systems* should solve such problems. A workflow system manages the workflows and organizes the routing of case data amongst the human resources and through application programs. Just as databases are developed and used with the assistance of a database management system, so *workflow management systems* (WFMS) can be used to define and use workflow systems. This period can be characterized as that during which the processes were extracted from the applications.

To put workflow management in historical perspective, we should mention some of the early work on workflow management. The idea to have generic tools, or at least generic methods, for supporting business processes emerged in the 1970s with pioneers such as Skip Ellis and Michael Zisman. Zisman completed his Ph.D. thesis "Representation, Specification, and Automation of Office Procedures" in 1997 (University of Pennsylvania). In the 1970s, Ellis and others worked at Xerox PARC on "Office Automation Systems." Ellis already used Petri-net-based workflow models (the so-called information control nets) in the late 1970s. One could wonder why it took such a long time before workflow management systems became established as a standard component for enterprise information systems. There are several reasons for this. First of all, workflow management requires users linked to a computer network. Only in the 1990s did workers become connected to the network. Second, many information systems evolved from systems that are unaware of business processes and the organization to systems that are aware; therefore, workflow was never considered as a really new piece of functionality. Finally, the rigid and inflexible character of the early (and some of the contemporary) products scared away many potential users.

A workflow management system can be compared with an operating system: it controls the workflows between the various resources—people or applications. It is confined to the *logistics* of case handling. In other words, a change to the content of case data is implemented only by people or application programs. A workflow management system has a number of functions that can be used to define and graphically track workflows, thus making both the progress of a case through a workflow and the structure of the flow itself easy to revise. It therefore is not remarkable that workflow management systems have become the ideal tool for achieving BPR.

In the above evolution, we can see that *disentangling* functions from applications is the way to improve efficiency. By separating certain functions, generic solutions (management systems) can be developed for them. In this way information systems can be made *component-based*, by first *configuring* the components and then *integrating* them (a process also known as *assembling*). Configuration is the setting of parameters, which may take all sorts of forms. The input of a database scheme into a database management system and the definition of a process scheme in a workflow management system are examples of component configuration.

For integration of components we have the so-called middleware. Some form of middleware just is a set of standards and language features that create a communication structure at compile time. Another form is a component that takes care of the communication needs of other components.

Alongside these developments, we also increasingly observe companies buying—for specific processes—standard software packages that combine a large number of the functions defined above. For a specific process, such *generic* software has to be configured; that is, parameters must be set. The advantage of a standard software package is that there are no development costs, but one drawback is that the system may not meet all the wishes of its users. This disadvantage could, though, be seen as a benefit, because it forces the organization to work in the tried and trusted way embedded in the package. In fact, such a software package contains a generic *company model* that can be adapted to a specific business situation.

EXERCISES

Exercise 1.1
A workflow is defined as a network of tasks with rules that determine the (partial) order in which the tasks should be performed.

(a) Which are these essential ordering principles?
(b) Show that iteration can be made by the other ordering principles.

Exercise 1.2

In this chapter we have seen (figure 1.2) some notation to describe a network of tasks. (This is not the notation we will use in the remainder of the book.) A task is represented by a rectangle and it has one or more direct predecessors and one or more direct successors. The rules are: all predecessors should be ready before the task may be executed and exactly one successor will be executed. Further there are two kinds of connectors: open and closed circles with rules for passing signals. Change these rules as follows: tasks have exactly one incoming and one outgoing arc. Connectors may have one or more incoming and outgoing arcs. Open circles pass the signal from only one incoming to one outgoing arc exactly. Closed circles require from all incoming arcs a signal and pass it to all outgoing arcs. Model the claim handling example of figure 1.2 with these new rules. (It is allowed to connect circles to each other.)

Exercise 1.3

The concept "task" has two meanings, depending on the point of view. Give these two meanings and explain them.

Exercise 1.4

Give the three principles to assign employees to departments in a hierarchical organization and give pros and cons for each choice.

2

Modeling Workflows

2.1 Workflow Concepts

The success of a workflow system stands or falls on the quality of the workflows put into it. This book therefore devotes considerable attention to the modeling and analysis of workflows. In this chapter, we shall limit ourselves initially to the process itself. As a tool, we use Petri nets. With their help, we can represent a process in a straightforward way. We can also use them to analyze these processes. We shall go into this aspect more extensively in chapter 4. Before any of this, we should first examine some of the concepts introduced in chapter 1 in more detail.

2.1.1 The case

The primary objective of a workflow system is to deal with *cases*. Examples of cases include an insurance claim, a mortgage application, a tax return, an order, or a patient in a hospital. Similar cases belong to the same *case type*. In principle, such cases are dealt with in the same way.

Each case has a unique *identity*. This makes it possible to refer to the case in question. A case has a limited lifetime. Consider, for example, an insurance claim. This case begins at the moment when the claim is submitted and disappears from the workflow system at the point when the processing of the claim has been completed. Between the appearance and disappearance of a case, it always has a particular *state*. This state consists of three elements: (1) the values of the relevant *case attributes*; (2) the *conditions* that have been fulfilled; and (3) the *content* of the case.

A range of variables can be associated with each case. These case attributes are used to manage it. Thanks to them it is, for example, possible to indicate that a task may—under certain conditions—be omitted.

When handling an insurance claim, we may use the case attribute "estimated claim value." Based upon the value of this variable, the workflow system can decide whether or not to activate the "send assessor" task. Note that the value of a case attribute may change as the case progresses.

We cannot use a case attribute to see how far a case has progressed. To do this, we use conditions. These are used to determine which tasks have been carried out, and which still remain to be performed. Examples of conditions include "order accepted," "application refused," and "under consideration." We can also regard a condition as a requirement that must be met before a particular task may be carried out. Only once all the conditions for a task within a particular case have been met can that task be performed. For any given case, it is at all times clear which conditions have been met and which not. We can also use the word *phase* instead of condition. This, however, is confusing when several conditions have been met: the case would be in more than one phase simultaneously.

In general, the workflow system does not contain details about the content of the case, only those of its attributes and conditions. The content is contained in documents, files, archives, and/or databases that are not managed by the workflow management system.

2.1.2 The task

The term *task* already has been mentioned extensively. It refers to one of the most important concepts in this book. By identifying tasks, it is possible to structure workflows. A task is a logical unit of work. It is indivisible and thus is always carried out in full. If anything goes wrong during the performance of a task, then we must return to the beginning of the entire task. In this respect, we refer to a *rollback*. However, the indivisible nature of a task depends upon the context within which it is defined. A task which is contracted out by a client to a supplier is regarded as "atomic" (indivisible) by the former. This does not have to be the case for the supplier, though: he may well split the task set into smaller ones.

Typing a letter, assessing a valuation report, filing a complaint, stamping a document, and checking personal data are all examples of tasks. We can differentiate between *manual, automatic* and *semi-automatic tasks*. A manual task is entirely performed by one or more people, with-

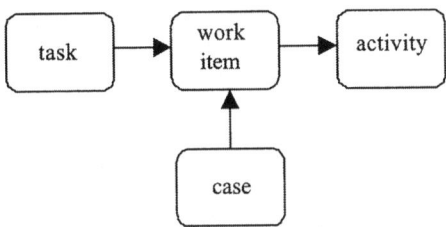

Figure 2.1
The relationship between the terms task, case, work item, and activity

out any use of an application: for example, carrying out a physical check. By contrast, an automatic task is performed without any intervention by people. This usually means that an application—a computer program—can carry out the task entirely based upon previously recorded data. Both a person and an application are involved in a semi-automatic task. For example, the completion of a valuation report by an insurance assessor supported by a specially developed program.

A task refers to a generic piece of work, and not to the performance of an activity for one specific case. In order to avoid confusion between the task itself and the performance of that task as part of a particular case, we use the terms *work item* and *activity*. A work item is the combination of a case and a task which is just about to be carried out. A work item is created as soon as the state of a case allows it. We thus can regard a work item as an actual piece of work which may be carried out. The term *activity* refers to the actual performance of a work item. As soon as work begins upon the work item, it becomes an activity. Note that, unlike a task, both a work item and an activity are linked with a specific case. Figure 2.1 shows this diagrammatically.

2.1.3   The process

The way in which a particular category of cases should be carried out is described by the relevant *process*. This indicates which tasks need to be carried out. It also shows the order in which this should be done. We can also regard a process as a *procedure* for a particular *case type*. In general, many different cases are handled using a single process. It therefore is possible to enable a specific treatment based upon the attributes of a certain case. For example, it may be that one task in the process is only performed on some of the cases. The order in which the tasks are performed may also vary depending upon the properties of the case. Conditions are used to decide which order is followed. In essence, a process is therefore constructed from tasks and conditions.

It is possible to make use of previously defined processes as part of another process. So, in addition to tasks and conditions, a process may also consists of (zero or more) subprocesses. Each of the subprocesses again consists of tasks, conditions, and possibly even further subprocesses. By explicitly identifying and separately describing subprocesses, frequently occurring ones can be used repeatedly. In this way, complex processes can also be structured hierarchically. At the highest level of process description, we see a limited number of subprocesses. By examining one or more of these we can, as it were, "zoom in" on particular sections of the process.

The lifecycle of a case is defined by a process. Because each case has a finite lifetime, with a clear beginning and end, it is important that the process also conforms with this. So each process also has a beginning and an end, which respectively mark the appearance and completion of a case.

2.1.4   Routing

The lifecycle of a case is laid down in the process. In this respect, we refer to the *routing* of the case. Routing along particular branches determines which tasks need to be performed (and in which order). In routing cases, we make use of four basic constructions:

• The simplest form of routing is the *sequential* execution of tasks. In other words, they are carried out one after the other. There is usually also a clear dependency between them. For example, the result of one task is input to the next.

• If two tasks can be performed simultaneously, or in any order, then we refer to *parallel* routing. In this case, there are two tasks which both need to be performed without the result of one affecting the other. The two tasks are initiated using an *AND-split* and later resynchronized using an *AND-join*.

• We refer to *selective routing* when there is a choice between two or more tasks. This choice may depend upon the specific properties of the case, as recorded in the relevant case attributes. Such a choice between alternatives is also known as an *OR-split*. The alternative paths are reunited using an *OR-join*. As well as selective routing, we also use the terms alternative or conditional routing.

• In the ideal situation, a task is carried out no more than once per case. Sometimes, however, it is necessary to perform a particular task several times. Consider, for example, a task which needs to be repeated until the result of the subsequent "check" task is satisfactory. We call this form of routing *iteration*.

We shall return to these four forms of routing in more detail later.

2.1.5 Enactment

A work item assignment can only be carried out once the state of the case in question allows it. But actual performance of such an assignment often requires more than this alone. If it has to be carried out by a person, he must first take the assignment from his "in tray" before an activity can begin. In other words, the work item is worked on only once the employee has taken the initiative. In such a case we refer to *triggering*: the work item is triggered by a resource (in the example, an employee). However, other forms of triggering are possible: an external event (for example, the arrival of an EDI message) or reaching a particular time (for example, the generation of a list of orders at six o'clock). We thus distinguish between three types of triggers: (1) a resource initiative, (2) an external event, and (3) a time signal. Work items which must always be carried out immediately—without the intervention of external stimuli—do not require a trigger.

The concepts summarized above are the central themes of this chapter. We thus shall focus mainly upon the modeling of the processes which underlie the workflows. In the next chapter, we shall turn our attention to the allocation of work items, the arrangement of the organizational structure, and specific staff skills. In chapter 4, we shall see how we can analyze the workflows modeled.

2.2 Petri Nets

Unlike many other publications on workflow management, this book takes a formal approach based upon an established formalism for the modeling and analysis of processes—Petri nets. The use of such a formal concept has a number of major advantages. In the first place, it forces precise definition. Ambiguities, uncertainties, and contradictions are thus prevented, in contrast to many informal diagramming techniques. Secondly, the formalism can be used to argue about processes. It thus becomes possible, for example, to establish certain patterns. This is closely linked with the fact that a formalism often enables the use of a number of analytical techniques (those for analyzing performance, for instance, as well as those for verifying logical properties). As we shall see later, it becomes possible to check whether a case is successfully completed after a period of time. There thus are various good reasons to opt for a formal method. Before we depict the concepts listed earlier in this chapter within Petri nets, it is important to know something about this technique. For the sake of completeness, we shall go deeper into them than is strictly necessary for the purposes of workflow management.

Petri nets were devised in 1962 by Carl Adam Petri as a tool for modeling and analyzing processes. One of the strengths of this tool is the fact that it enables processes to be described *graphically*. Later, we shall see that we can use it to present workflow processes in an accessible way. Despite the fact that Petri nets are graphical, they have a strong mathematical basis. Unlike many other schematic techniques, they are entirely formalized. Thanks to this formal basis, it is often possible to make strong statements about the properties of the process being modeled. There are also several analysis techniques and tools available which can be applied to analyze a given Petri net.

Over the years, the model proposed by Carl Adam Petri has been extended in many different ways. Thanks to these, it is possible to model complex processes in an accessible way. Initially, however, we shall confine ourselves to the classic Petri net as devised by Petri himself.

2.2.1   Classical Petri nets

A *Petri net* consists of *places* and *transitions*. We indicate a place using a circle. A transition is shown as a rectangle. Figure 2.2 shows a simple Petri net, consisting of three places (*claim, under_consideration*, and *ready*) and three transitions (*record, pay*, and *send_letter*). This network models the process for dealing with an insurance claim. Arriving at the place *claim*, it is first recorded, after which either a payment is made or a letter sent explaining the reasons for rejection.

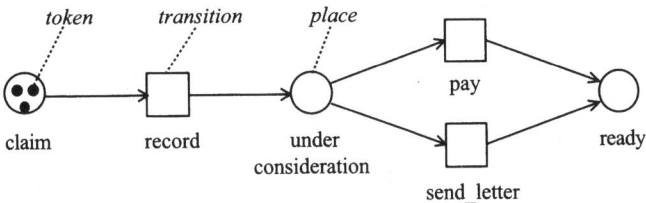

Figure 2.2
A classic Petri net

Places and transitions in a Petri net can be linked by means of a *directed arc*. In figure 2.2, for example, the place *claim* and the transition *record* are linked by an arrow pointing from the former to the latter. There are two types of arcs: those that run from a place to a transition and those that run from a transition to a place. Arcs from a place to a place or a transition to a transition are not possible.

Based upon the arcs, we can determine the *input places* of a transition. A place *p* is an input place for a transition *t* if—and only if—there is a directed arc running from *p* to *t*. Similarly, we can determine the *output places* of a transition. A place *p* is an output place for a transition *t* if—and only if—there is a directed arc running from *t* to *p*. As it happens, in figure 2.2 each transition precisely has one input and one output place.

Places may contain tokens. These are indicated using black dots. In figure 2.2 the place *claim* contains three tokens. The structure of a Petri net is fixed; however, the distribution of its tokens among the places can change. The transition *record* can thus take tokens from the *claim* input place and put them in *under_consideration*. We call this the *firing* of the transition *record*. Because the firing of transitions is subject to strict rules, we shall first introduce a number of terms.

The *state* of a Petri net is indicated by the distribution of tokens amongst its places. We can describe the state illustrated in figure 2.2 using the vector (3,0,0). In other words, there are three tokens in *claim*, none in *under_consideration*, and none in *ready*.

A transition may only fire if it is *enabled*. This occurs when there is at least one token at *each* of its input places. The transitions are then, as it were, "loaded": ready to fire. In figure 2.2, the transition *record* is enabled. The other two are not.

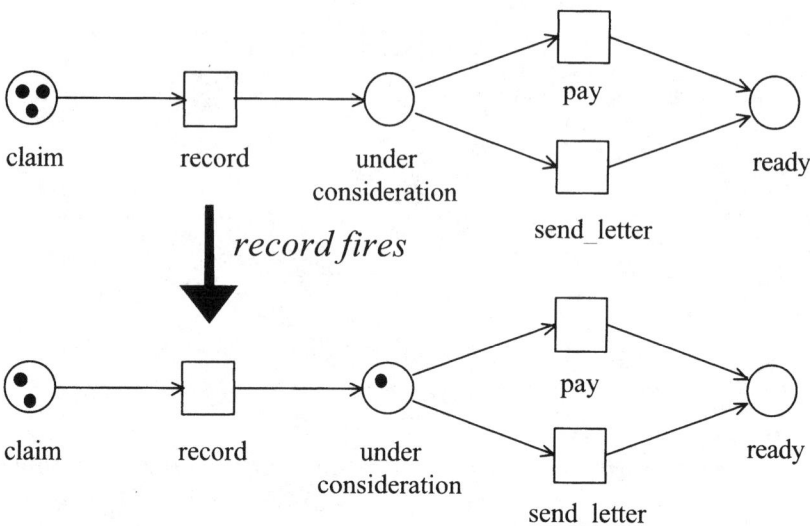

Figure 2.3
State before and after the transition "record" fires

A transition may fire from the moment it is enabled. As it fires, one token is removed from each input place and one token added to each output place. In other words, the moment it fires, a transition *consumes* tokens from the input place and *produces* tokens for the output place. Figure 2.3 shows the effect of firing the transition *record*. Its result is that one token is transferred from the place *claim* to the place *under consideration*. We can also describe the new situation using the vector (2,1,0).

Once *record* has fired, a situation arises in which three transitions are enabled. The transition *record* can fire again because there is at least one token in *claim*, and the transitions *pay* and *send letter* can fire because there is a token in *under_consideration*. In this situation, it is not possible to tell which transition will fire first. If we assume—for the sake of convenience—that it is the transition *pay* which fires, then the state illustrated in figure 2.4 will be reached.

Note that the transition *send_letter*, which was enabled before firing, is no longer enabled. The transition *record* is still enabled and will therefore fire. Eventually, after a total of six firings, the Petri net will reach the state (0,0,3). That is, a state with three tokens in the place *ready*. In this state, no further firing is possible.

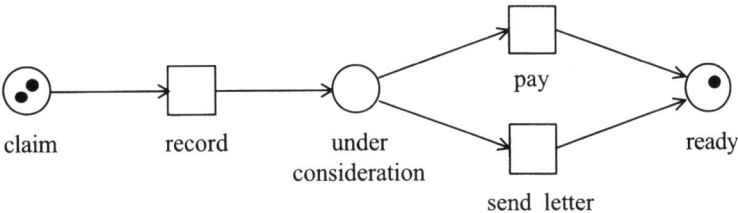

Figure 2.4
State after "pay" fires

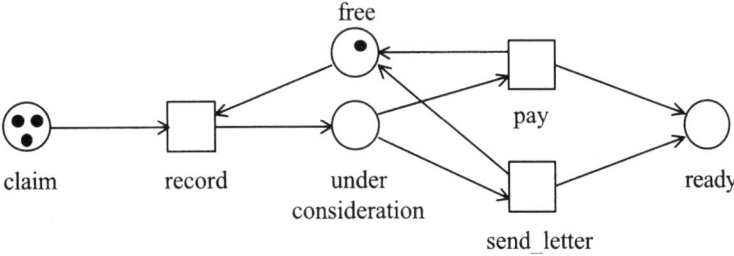

Figure 2.5
The modified Petri net

Transitions are the *active* components in a Petri net. By firing a transition, the process being modeled shifts from one state to another. A transition therefore often represents an event, an operation, a transformation, or a transportation. The places in a Petri net are *passive*, in the sense that they cannot change the network's state. A place usually represents a medium, buffer, geographical location, (sub)state, phase, or condition. Tokens often indicate objects. These can be physical ones, but also objects representing information. In the network considered above, each token represents an insurance claim.

In the Petri net shown in figure 2.2, it is possible for several cases to be in progress simultaneously. If the transition *record* fires twice in succession, then there will be at least two tokens in the place *under_ consideration*. If, for some reason, we wish to limit the number of cases which can be under consideration at the same time to a maximum of one, then we can modify the Petri net as shown in figure 2.5. The additional place *free* ensures that the transition *record* is blocked as soon as a claim goes under consideration.

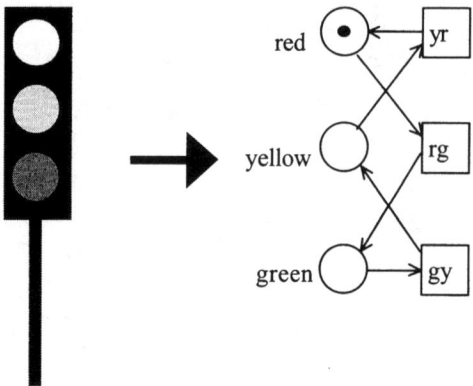

Figure 2.6
A set of traffic lights illustrated on a Petri net

In the initial state depicted, *record* is enabled because there is at least one token at each of the input places. Once transition *record* has fired, the state is such that *record* is no longer enabled, but the other two transitions are. Once one of these has fired, there is again a token in the place *free*. Only at this point is *record* again enabled. By adding the place *free*, the maximum number of cases that can be under consideration at any time has indeed been limited to one. If we wish to limit the number of cases in progress at any time to a maximum of n, then we can model this simply by placing n tokens in the place *free* at the start.

Using Petri nets, we can also describe processes that are repetitive in nature. Figure 2.6 shows how we can model the cyclical activity of a set of traffic lights.

The traffic lights' three possible settings are illustrated by three places: *red, yellow,* and *green.* The three possible light changes are shown by the transitions *rg, gy,* and *yr.* Imagine now that we want to model the traffic lights at the crossing of two one-way streets. In this case, we require two sets of traffic lights that interact in such a way that one of the two is always red. Obviously, the Petri net shown in figure 2.6 needs to be duplicated. Each set of lights is modeled using three places and three transitions. This, however, is not sufficient, because it does not exclude unsafe situations. We therefore add an extra place x, which ensures that one of the two sets of lights is always at red (see figure 2.7).

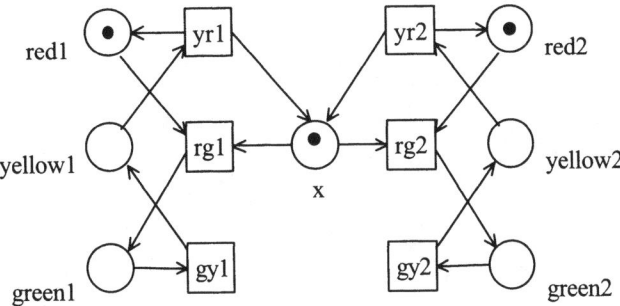

Figure 2.7
Two sets of traffic lights

When both traffic lights are red, there is a token in the place x. As one set of lights changes to green, the token is removed from x and so the other set is blocked. Only when both sets of lights are again red is the other able to change to green once. In chapter 4, we use an analytical technique to show that the traffic lights do indeed operate safely.

2.2.2 High-level Petri nets

Because Petri nets are graphical, they are easily accessible and easy to use. They also have a strong mathematical basis and there are many analytical techniques available for them. In chapter 4, we shall see that we can use these techniques to analyze workflows. Despite this strength, the classic Petri net has shortcomings in many practical situations. It becomes too large and inaccessible, or it is not possible to model a particular activity. This is why the classic Petri net has been extended in many ways. Thanks to these extensions, it is possible to model complex situations in a structured and accessible way. In this section we shall focus upon the three most important extensions: (a) color extension, (b) time extension, and (c) hierarchical extension. We call Petri nets extended with color, time, and hierarchy *high-level Petri nets*. Because a complete description of high-level Petri nets would go too far, we shall confine ourselves to those aspects that are important in the context of workflow management.

(a) **The color extension** Tokens are used to model a whole range of things. In one model they can represent insurance claims, in another the state of traffic lights. However, in the classic Petri net it is impossible to distinguish between two tokens: two in the same place are by definition indistinguishable. In general, this is an undesirable situation. In the case of two insurance claims, for example, we want to incorporate the separate characteristics of the two claims in the model. We want to include such things as the nature of the claim, the policy number, the name of the policyholder, and the assessed value of the claim. In order to enable the coupling of an object's characteristics with the corresponding token, the classic Petri net is extended using "color." This extension ensures that each token is provided with a *value* or *color*. A token representing a particular car will, for instance, have a value which makes it possible to identify its make, registration number, year of manufacture, color, and owner. We can notate a possible value for such a token as follows: *[brand: 'BMW'; registration: 'J 144 NFX'; year: '1995'; color: 'red'; owner: 'Johnson']*.

Because each token has a value, we can distinguish different tokens from one another. By "valuing" tokens, they are—as it were—given different colors.

A firing transition produces tokens that are based upon the values of those consumed during firing. The value of a produced token therefore may depend upon those of consumed ones. Unlike in the classic Petri net, the *number* of tokens produced is also variable: the number of tokens produced is determined by the values of those consumed.

To illustrate this, we shall use a process for dealing with technical faults in a product department. Every time a fault occurs—for example, a jammed machine—it is categorized by the department's mechanic. The fault can often be put right as it is being categorized. If this is not the case, then a repair takes place. After this has been done, a test is carried out, with three possible results: (1) the fault has been solved; (2) a further repair is required; or (3) the faulty component must be replaced. This process is modeled in figure 2.8 using a Petri net.

A token in the place *fault* means that a fault has occurred which needs to be dealt with. For each token in *fault*, the transition *categorize* will fire precisely once. During each firing precisely one token will be produced, in either the place *solved* or the place *nr* (needs repair). In contrast with the classic Petri net, it is now possible for an output place not to receive a token. During the execution of transition *categorize*, a choice is now made based upon the information available. As a result of this choice, the

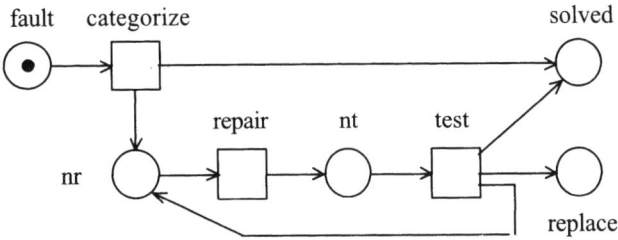

Figure 2.8
The process for dealing with faults

fault is either regarded as solved or a repair is carried out. The token in the place *fault* has a value in which the relevant properties of the fault are recorded (for example: the nature of the fault, the identity of the non-functioning component, its location code, and fault history). If a repair is required, then the transition *repair* will fire, bringing the token to place *nt*, followed by the firing of transition *test*. The transition *test* produces precisely one token, which appears in one of the three output places. The relevant information about the fault is always retained in the value of the token in question.

In a color-extended Petri net, we *can* set conditions for the values of the tokens to be consumed. If this is the case, then a transition is only enabled once there is a token at each of the input places and the *preconditions* have been met. A transition's precondition is a logical requirement connected with the values of the tokens to be consumed. In the Petri net illustrated in figure 2.8, we could for example add the following precondition to the transition *categorize*: "The value of the token to be consumed from the place *fault* must contain a valid location code." The consequence of this precondition is that faults without a valid location code are not categorized; they remain in the place *fault* and are never consumed by the transition *categorize*.

We can also use a precondition to "synchronize" tokens. By this we mean that a transition only fires if a particular combination of tokens can be consumed. We use the transition *assemble*, illustrated in figure 2.9, to illustrate this.

Based upon a production order, the transition *assemble* takes a chassis, an engine, and four wheels and produces a car. (This is the first example

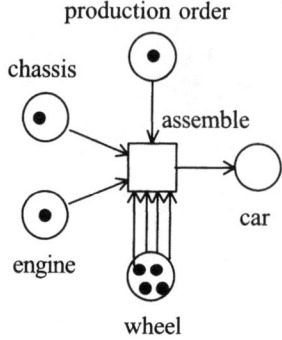

Figure 2.9
The transition "assemble"

we have seen in which more than one arrow leads from an input point to a transition. In this case, there must be at least four tokens in *wheel* before *assemble* can be enabled. The number of incoming arrows thus shows how many tokens there must be at the input point from which they come. When a transition fires, the number of tokens consumed is equal to the number of incoming arrows.) When the transition *assemble* fires, tokens are not taken at random from the input places. For example, the four wheels must be of the same type, the engine must fit the chassis, the wheel diameter must suit the chassis and the engine power, and so on. Tokens thus are only taken from the input places in certain combinations. This is determined by means of a precondition.

The result of the color extension is that, in contrast to the classic Petri net, the graphic representation no longer contains all the information. For each transition, the following factors must be specified:

· Whether there is a precondition. If there is a precondition, then this must be defined precisely.
· The number of tokens produced per output place during each firing. This number may depend upon the values of the tokens consumed.
· The values of the tokens produced. This, too, may depend upon the values of the tokens consumed.

Depending upon the objective for which the Petri net has been produced, the transitions are specified by a piece of text, a few lines of pseudo-code, a formal specification, or a subroutine in a programming language.

(b) The time extension Given a process modeled as a Petri net, we often want to be able to make statements about its expected performance. If we produce a model of the traffic lights at a road junction, then we are probably also interested in the number of vehicles that this junction can handle per hour. If we model the production process in a car factory, then we also want to know the expected completion time and the capacity required. To be able to answer these questions, it is necessary to include pertinent information about the timing of a process in the model. However, the classic Petri net does not allow the modeling of "time." Even with the color extension, it is still difficult to model the timing of a process. Therefore, this classic Petri net is also extended with *time*.

Using this time extension, tokens receive a *timestamp* as well as a value. This indicates the time from which the token is available. A token with timestamp 14 thus is available for consumption by a transition only from moment 14. A transition is enabled only at the moment when each of the tokens to be consumed has a timestamp equal or prior to the current time. In other words, the *enabling time* of a transition is the earliest moment at which its input places contain sufficient *available* tokens. Tokens are consumed on a FIFO (first-in, first-out) basis. The token with the earliest timestamp thus is the first to be consumed. Furthermore, it is the transition with the earliest *enabling time* that fires first. If there is more than one transition with the same enabling time, a nondeterministic choice in made. Moreover, the firing of one transition may affect the enabling time of another.

If a transition fires and tokens are produced, then each of these is given a timestamp equal to or later than the time of firing. The tokens produced thus are given a *delay* that is determined by the firing transition. The timestamp of a produced token is equal to the time of firing plus this delay. The length of the delay may depend upon the value of the tokens consumed. However, it is also possible that the delay has a fixed value (for example, 0) or that the delay is decided at random. Firing itself is instantaneous and takes no time.

To illustrate the time extension, we can use the example of the two sets of traffic lights, which must not simultaneously be at green or yellow. At moment 0 both sets are at red. As we can see in figure 2.10, the timestamps of the tokens in the places *red1*, *x*, and *red2* are 0.

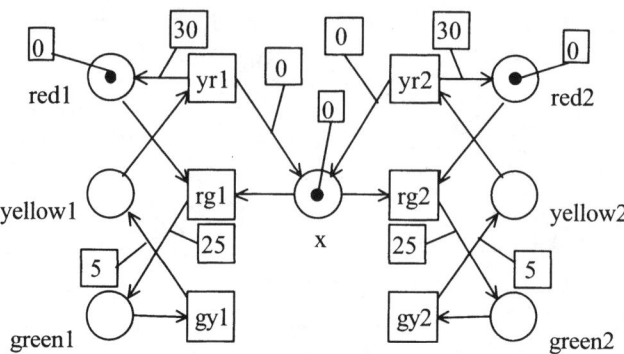

Figure 2.10
The two sets of traffic lights with time

The enabling time of the transition *rg1* is also 0, the maximum of the timestamps of the tokens in *red1* and *x*. The enabling time of *rg2* is also 0. There hence exists a nondeterministic choice between *rg1* and *rg2*. Let us assume that *rg1* fires. The transition *rg1* consumes the two tokens from the input places and produces one token for the place *green1* with a delay of 25 time units. In figure 2.10, each delay is shown as a label linked to an arrow emerging from a transition. (If the delays were dependent upon the values of the tokens consumed, this would no longer be possible.) After the firing of *rg1*, there is a token in *green1* with a time stamp of 25, and *gy1* is the only enabled transition. The transition *gy1* thus will fire at moment 25 and produce a token at *yellow1* with a timestamp equal to $25 + 5 = 30$. At moment 30, the transition *yr1* will fire. During this firing, *yr1* produces a token for *red1* with a delay of 30 and a token for *x* without delay. As a result of the firing, *rg1* has an enabling time of 60 and *rg2* an enabling time of 30. Therefore transition *rg2* now fires. By adding time to the model, we thus have not only specified the timing of the various phases, but also forced the traffic lights to change to green alternately.

(c)   **The hierarchical extension**   Although we can already describe very complex processes using the color and time extensions, usually the resulting Petri net still will not provide a proper reflection of the process being modeled. Because the modeling of such a process results in a single, extensive network, any structure is lost. We do not observe the *hierar-*

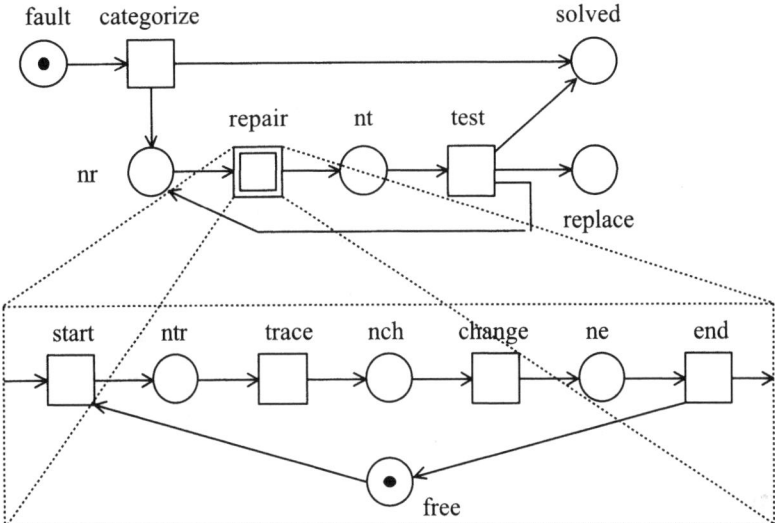

Figure 2.11
The process "solve fault" contains one subprocess: "repair"

chical structure in the process being modeled by the Petri net. The hierarchical extension therefore ensures that it becomes possible to add structure to the Petri net model.

In order to structure a Petri net hierarchically, we introduce a new "building block": a double-bordered square. We call this element a *process*. It represents a subnetwork comprising places, transitions, arcs, and subprocesses. Because a process can be constructed from subprocesses that in turn also can be constructed from (further) subprocesses, it is possible to structure a complex process hierarchically. In order to illustrate this, we shall refine the process modeled in figure 2.8. This refinement concerns the activity *repair*. We no longer wish to regard repair as a single, indivisible action, but as a subprocess consisting of the following steps: (1) start, (2) trace, (3) change, and (4) end. Moreover, there is never more than one fault under repair at a given point in time. To model this refinement, we replace the transition *repair* with a subprocess consisting of four transitions and four places—see figure 2.11.

In figure 2.11, we can see clearly that a process can take two forms: (1) as a subprocess within a hierarchically superior process (the double-bordered square), and (2) as the definition of the process (a summary of the elements from which the process is constructed). We find the meaning of a process constructed from subprocesses by replacing each of those subprocesses with the appropriate definition. The process *solve fault* illustrated in figure 2.11 is thus in fact a Petri net consisting of six transitions and nine places.

By using (sub)processes, we can structure a Petri net hierarchically, using either a top-down or a bottom-up approach. The *top-down approach* begins at the highest level, with processes increasingly being broken down into subprocesses until, at the lowest level, these consist only of transitions and places. Repeated decomposition results in a hierarchical description. The *bottom-up approach* works in the opposite direction. It begins at the lowest level. First, the most elementary components are described in detail. These elements (subprocesses) are then combined into larger processes. Repeated composition eventually results in a description of the entire process.

When modeling complex processes, a hierarchical method of description is often an absolute necessity. Only by dividing the main process into ever-smaller subprocesses can we overcome its complexity. In this respect, we refer to the *divide-and-conquer strategy*. However, the identification of subprocesses has yet another important advantage. It enables us to *reuse* previously defined processes. If a particular subprocess recurs several times, one definition used repeatedly will suffice. The reuse of (sub)processes often makes it possible to model a complex process more quickly.

In this section, we have studied the three most important types of extensions: (a) the color extension, (b) the time extension, and (c) the hierarchical extension. We call Petri nets which incorporate these extensions *high-level Petri nets*. In the remainder of this book, we shall use the high-level net to model and analyze processes in the context of workflow management.

2.3   Mapping Workflow Concepts onto Petri Nets

The time has now come to illustrate the concepts described earlier—the case, task, condition, process, trigger, and so on—using the Petri net technique.

2.3.1   The process

Using a process in a workflow management system, we can indicate in which way a particular category of cases should be handled. The process defines which tasks need to be carried out. As well as information about the tasks to be performed, a process also contains information about conditions. In this way, it defines the order in which the tasks need to be carried out. It is also possible to use previously defined processes within a larger process. Thus process may also consist of more than one sub-process, as well as tasks and conditions. It therefore is obvious to *specify a process using a Petri net*. This network should have one "entrance" (a place without incoming arcs) and one "exit" (a place without outcoming arcs). We show conditions as places and tasks as transitions. This also is obvious, because transitions are the active components in a Petri net, and places its passive components.

In order to specify a process using a Petri net, we shall examine a process for handling complaints. An incoming complaint first is recorded. Then the client who has complained and the department affected by the complaint are contacted. The client is approached for more information. The department is informed of the complaint and may be asked for its initial reaction. These two tasks may be performed in parallel—that is, simultaneously or in any order. After this, the data are gathered and a decision is taken. Depending upon the decision, either a compensation payment is made or a letter is sent. Finally, the complaint is filed. Figure 2.12 shows how we can illustrate the process just described using a Petri net.

Each of the tasks *record, contact_client, contact_department, pay*, and *file* is modeled using a transition. The assessment of a complaint is modeled using two transitions: *positive* and *negative*. The transition *positive* corresponds with a positive decision; the transition *negative* corresponds with a negative decision. (Later we shall see how this task can also be modeled using just one transition.) The places *start* and *end* correspond with the beginning and end of the process being modeled. The other places correspond with conditions that are or are not met by every case in progress. The conditions play two important roles: on the one hand they ensure that the tasks proceed in the correct order, and on the other hand that the state of the case can be established. The place $c8$, for example, ensures that a complaint is filed only once it has been fully

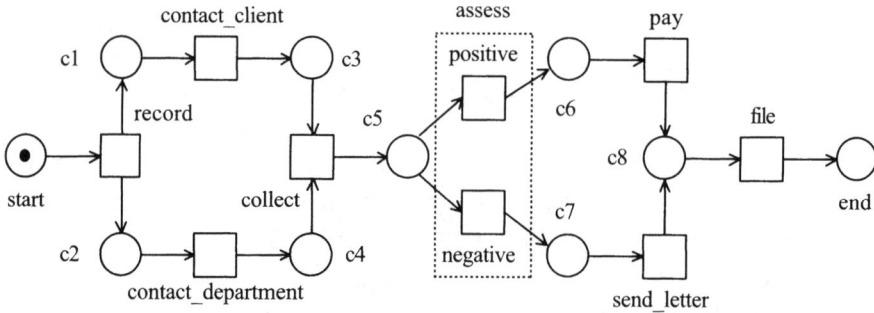

Figure 2.12
The process "handle complaint" modeled as a Petri net

dealt with. It also corresponds with the state that exists between a complaint being fully handled and its filing.

From the above, it should be more or less clear that a case is represented by one or more tokens. Cases thus are illustrated using tokens. In figure 2.12, the token in the place *start* shows the presence of a case. Once *record* has fired, there are two tokens—one at *c1*, one at *c2*—that represent the same case. As a case is being handled, the number of its tokens thus may fluctuate. The number of tokens that represent a particular case is equal to the number of its conditions that have been met. Once there is a token in *end*, the case has been completed. In principle, each process should fulfil two requirements: (1) it should at any time be possible to reach—by performing a number of tasks—a state in which there is a token in *end*; and (2) when there is a token in *end*, all the others should have disappeared. These two requirements ensure that every case that begins at the place *start* will eventually be completed properly. Note that it is not possible to have a token in *end* while there remain tasks still to be performed. The minimum requirements just mentioned, which every process must meet, can be checked effectively using standard Petri net tools.

The state of a case is not determined solely by the conditions that have been met; to steer it, the case may have one or more attributes. For these, it seems obvious to use the color extension. The value of a token contains information about the attributes of the case in question. We shall go into this in more detail later.

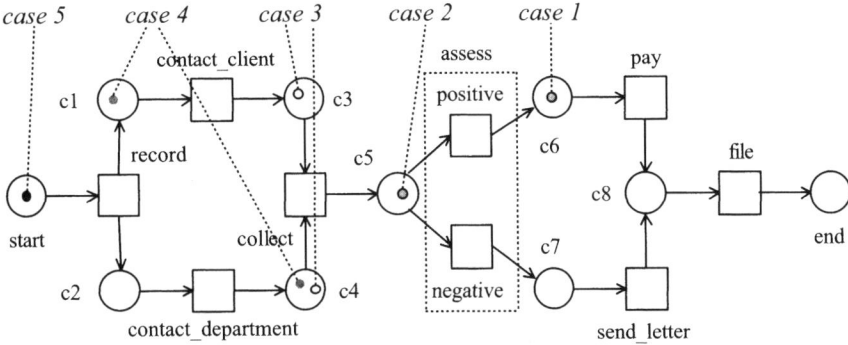

Figure 2.13
Each case is illustrated using one or more tokens

Tokens that correspond with particular cases are kept strictly separate (by the workflow management system). We can translate this into Petri net modeling in two ways. Because tokens belonging to different cases cannot influence one another, we can produce a separate copy of the Petri net for each case. Each thus has its own process, as illustrated in figure 2.12. However we can also use just one Petri net by making use of the color extension. Thanks to this, we can provide each token with a value from which it is possible to identify the case to which the token refers. This is shown diagrammatically in figure 2.13.

The state of the Petri net illustrated here indicates that there are currently five cases in progress. Case 1 has almost been completed, whereas case 5 is still at the start state. In order to ensure that the token belonging to different cases do not get "mixed up," each transition is provided with a precondition that states that only tokens from the same case may be consumed at any one firing. If the transition *collect* in the situation shown in figure 2.13 now fires, this precondition will ensure that the two tokens for case 3 are consumed.

Figure 2.12 shows a nonhierarchical process. However it goes without saying that a process may be constructed from subprocesses. To illustrate this, we can for example combine the first four tasks (*record, contact_client, contact_department,* and *collect*) into a single subprocess called *phase1*. Figure 2.14 shows how the corresponding Petri net would look, with two levels.

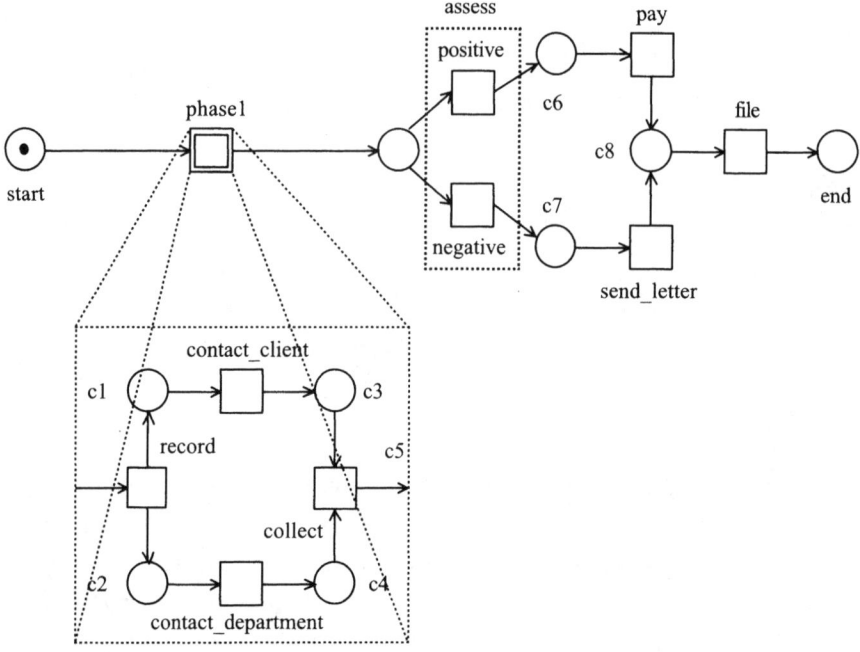

Figure 2.14
The process "handle complaint" now contains the subprocess "phase 1"

2.3.2 Routing

Tasks may be optional. That is, there may be tasks that only need to be carried out for a number of cases. The order in which tasks are performed may also vary from case to case. By routing a case along a number of tasks, we can determine which tasks need to be carried out (and in what order). As indicated earlier, four basic constructions for routing are recognized. For each of these, we shall show the corresponding Petri net modeling.

(a) Sequential routing We refer to the sequential performance of tasks when these have to be carried out one after another. If two tasks need to be carried out sequentially, there usually is a clear interdependence between them. For example, the result of the first is required in order to perform the second. In a Petri net, this form of routing is modeled by linking the two tasks using a place. Figure 2.15 shows an example of sequential routing.

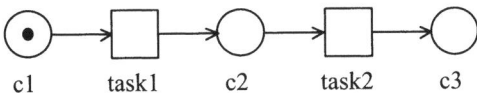

Figure 2.15
Sequential routing

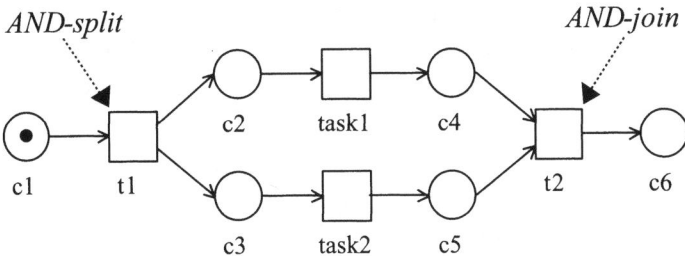

Figure 2.16
Parallel routing

The task that corresponds with the transition *task2* is only performed once the task corresponding with transition *task1* has been completed. This is enforced by place *c2*, which corresponds with the condition that must apply before *task2* can be carried out.

(b) Parallel routing If more than one task can be carried out at the same time or in any order, then we refer to parallel routing. If we confine ourselves to the situation with two tasks, *task1* and *task2*, then there are three possibilities: both tasks can be performed simultaneously; *task1* can be carried out first, then *task2*; or *task2* can be first, followed by *task1*. Figure 2.16 illustrates how we can model this situation using a Petri net.

In order to enable the parallel execution of *task1* and *task2* in the case corresponding with the token in *c1*, we begin with a so-called *AND-split*. This is a task added so as to allow more than one task to be managed at the same time. In figure 2.16, the transition *t1* is the equivalent of an AND-split. It fires when there is a token in *c1*, and produces one token in each *c2* and *c3*. Once condition *c2* has been met for a particular case, *task1* can be carried out. Once condition *c3* has been met, *task2* can be carried out. Firing *t1* thus enables the performance of two tasks. We also say that *task1* and *task2* can be carried out in parallel. Only when both have been performed can transition *t2* fire. It is the equivalent of an *AND-join*: a task added to synchronize two or more parallel flows. Only when a particular case has fulfilled both condition *c4* and condition *c5* this task can be performed.

In figure 2.16, we have had to insert two tasks, *t1* and *t2*, to model the AND-split and the AND-join. We call such "artificial" additions *management tasks*, because they do not correspond with a recognizable piece of work. Thanks to them, we can carry out *task1* and *task2* in parallel. However, it is also possible for tasks such as *t1* and *t2* to correspond with an actual piece of work. In figure 2.12, for example, the task *record* corresponds with an AND-split. The task *collect* corresponds with an AND-join.

In a business process in which cases are carried out entirely manually (without the aid of a workflow system), sequential routing is often the rule due to, for example, physical limitations. For instance, the tasks in a particular case must be carried out one after the other because the accompanying document can only be in one place at a time. By introducing a workflow system, such limitations are largely eliminated. Tasks that previously had to be carried out sequentially can now be done in parallel. This can often achieve enormous time savings. Allowing parallel routing thus is clearly of major significance in the success of a workflow system.

(c) **Selective routing** A process lays down the routing for a specific type of case. But there may be differences in routing between individual cases. Consider, for example, a process for dealing with insurance claims. Depending upon the specific circumstances of a claim, a particular route will be selected. The task *send_assessor*, for example, is not carried out for small claims. We refer to such cases as selective routing. This involves a choice between two or more tasks. Figure 2.17 shows an example modeled in terms of a Petri net.

Once a case fulfils condition *c1*, either *t11* or *t12* fires. If it is the former, then *task1* is enabled. If it is the latter, then it is *task2* that is enabled. Thus there is a choice between the two tasks. We call the network consisting of transitions *t11* and *t12* and places *c2* and *c3* an *OR-split*. Once one of the tasks has been performed, the *OR-join* ensures that a token appears in *c6*. In this case, the OR-join is modeled using a network

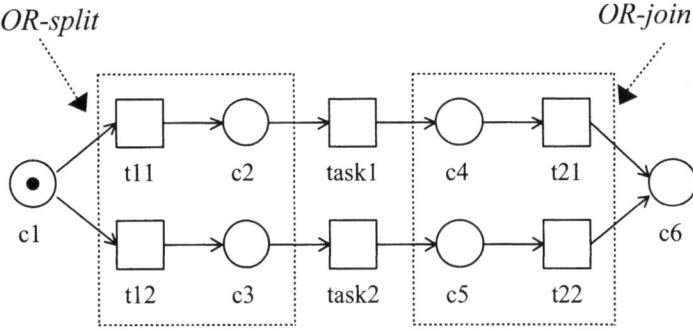

Figure 2.17
Selective routing (1)

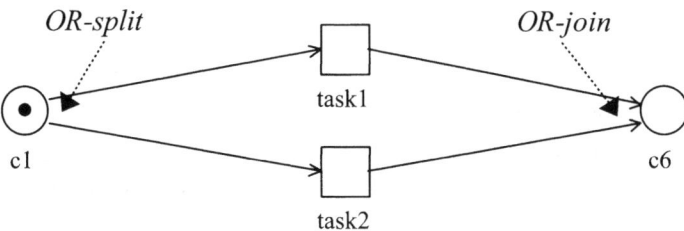

Figure 2.18
Selective routing (2)

consisting of two places (*c4* and *c5*) and two transitions (*t21* and *t22*). So the OR-split selects one of the two alternative streams and the OR-join brings them back together. In figure 2.17, we have explicitly modeled the OR-split and the OR-join by adding two small networks. This is neces-sary when we want to show the OR-split and OR-join as explicit man-agement tasks. However, it is also possible to model them implicitly, as shown in figure 2.18.

When a case fulfils condition *c1*, either *task1* or *task2* will be carried out. So this is another example of selective routing. If we look at the way in which the OR-join is modeled in the two previous figures, we notice little difference. Obviously, therefore, an OR-join can be modeled using several arrows leading into the same place. In the case of the OR-split, though, there is a difference. In figure 2.17, a choice is made at the mo-ment when there is a token in *c1* (that is, when a case fulfils condition *c1*). In figure 2.18, the choice comes later. Which of the two branches is actually selected is decided only at the moment when either *task1* or *task2* has to be carried out. This may appear to be only a subtle difference, but in fact the distinction between the OR-splits in figures 2.17 and 2.18 can be of crucial importance.

Let us assume, for example, that *task1* corresponds with the processing of a valuation report, and that *task2* has to be carried out if that report is not delivered within a given time. In this context, the model provided using the construction in figure 2.18 is excellent. When the token is in $c1$, two subsequent events are possible: either the report arrives and *task1* is carried out, or it is late and *task2* is carried out. The decision about which task to perform is delayed until either the report arrives or a fixed period of time has elapsed. In figure 2.17, however, the decision must be taken immediately. If $t11$, for example, fires, then it is no longer possible to carry out *task2*. Later on, we shall show some larger examples in which the *moment* the choice is made is of great significance.

Thus far, we have (automatically) assumed that the choice between two alternatives is nondeterministic. In other words, we have not explained how the choice between *task1* and *task2* is made, because—as far the process is concerned—it does not matter which task is performed: the selection is left to the environment of the workflow system. In most cases, however, the decision is made best according to the specific properties of the case. Depending upon the values of the case attributes (that is, the case's management parameters), we want to be able to choose between the alternatives. Figure 2.19 shows how we can model this situation.

Based upon the case attributes, transition $t1$ in figure 2.19 produces a token for either $c2$ or $c3$ (but not for both). In this case, therefore, we make use of color extension to enable a choice to be made in transition $t1$. Using the attributes of the case in question, the decision rule in $t1$ determines which task should be performed. In doing so, we assume that all the relevant attributes of this case are contained in the value of the token in $c1$. In the case of parallel routing, however, there may be more than one token assigned to the same case. Because the attributes concern the entire case, these tokens must have identical values. In other words, there must never be two tokens assigned to the same case but with different values. In order to enforce this, we must ensure that a change to a case attribute caused by the performance of a task updates the value of *every* token pertaining to that case.

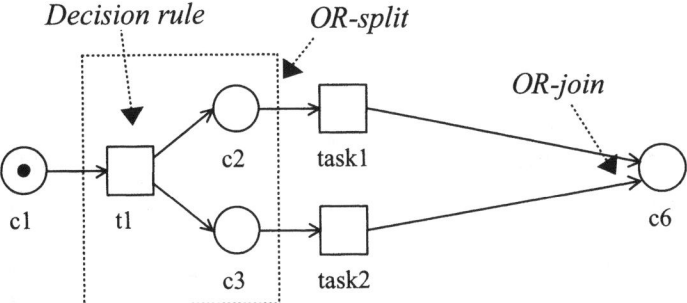

Figure 2.19
Selective routing (3)

We thus can regard a case attribute as information that can be inspected and revised by every task relevant to that case. In theory, the broad nature of a case attribute can be modeled explicitly by linking each transition with a common place. This place always contains one token whose value corresponds with those of the case attributes. Because illustrating this common place makes the process diagrams confusing, for the sake of convenience we shall omit it.

In figure 2.19, the number of tokens produced in each of the output places of *t1* is variable (0 or 1). A choice is made based upon the value (case attributes) of the token in *c1* and the decision rule in *t1*. However, we can also produce this choice by using two transitions containing the appropriate preconditions. Recall that a precondition is based on the colors of the tokens to be consumed and acts like a transition guard. Figure 2.20 shows how this is possible.

The precondition in transition *t11* corresponds with the requirements that need to be met to justify the choice for *task1*. The precondition in *t12* determines when *task2* should be selected. If the precondition in *t11* is the negation of the precondition in *t12*, then each token in *c1* will result in a deterministic choice for either *task1* and *task2*. In this case, therefore, the OR-splits in figures 2.19 and 2.20 are equivalent.

Because constructions such as the AND-split, AND-join, OR-split and OR-join occur frequently, we use a special notation to illustrate them. This is shown in figure 2.21.

We represent an AND-split by using the symbol ◁ on the output side. This indicates that a token must be produced for each of the output places under all circumstances.

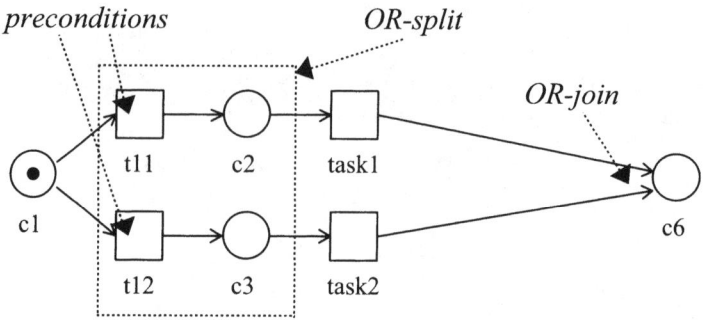

Figure 2.20
Selective routing (4)

We represent an AND-join by using the symbol ⊵ on the input side. This indicates that the task being modeled can only take place once there is a token at each of the input places. From figure 2.21, we can see that both the AND-split and the AND-join correspond with a "normal transition" like those encountered in the classic Petri net.

We represent an OR-split by using the symbol ⊵ on the output side. This indicates that a token must be produced for precisely one of the output places. As we saw earlier, we can model this in two ways. In the rest of this chapter, we shall use only the first of these.

We represent an OR-join by using the symbol ⊴ on the input side.

We can use the following technique to remember the difference between the AND and OR symbol. When, in principle, the arrows enter or leave the same large triangle, it is an AND. Otherwise, it is an OR.

The symbol ⊟ on the output side indicates a mixture of an AND-split and an OR-split. In this case one or more tokens will be produced, depending upon the value of the case attributes. Figure 2.21 shows two ways of using this mixed form in a Petri net.

(d) Iterative routing   The last form of routing is the repeated execution of a particular task. Ideally, a task will be performed only once per case. In certain situations, however, it is necessary to apply *iterative routing*. For example, when a certain task needs to be repeated until the results of a subsequent test prove positive. Figure 2.22 shows how we can model iterative routing.

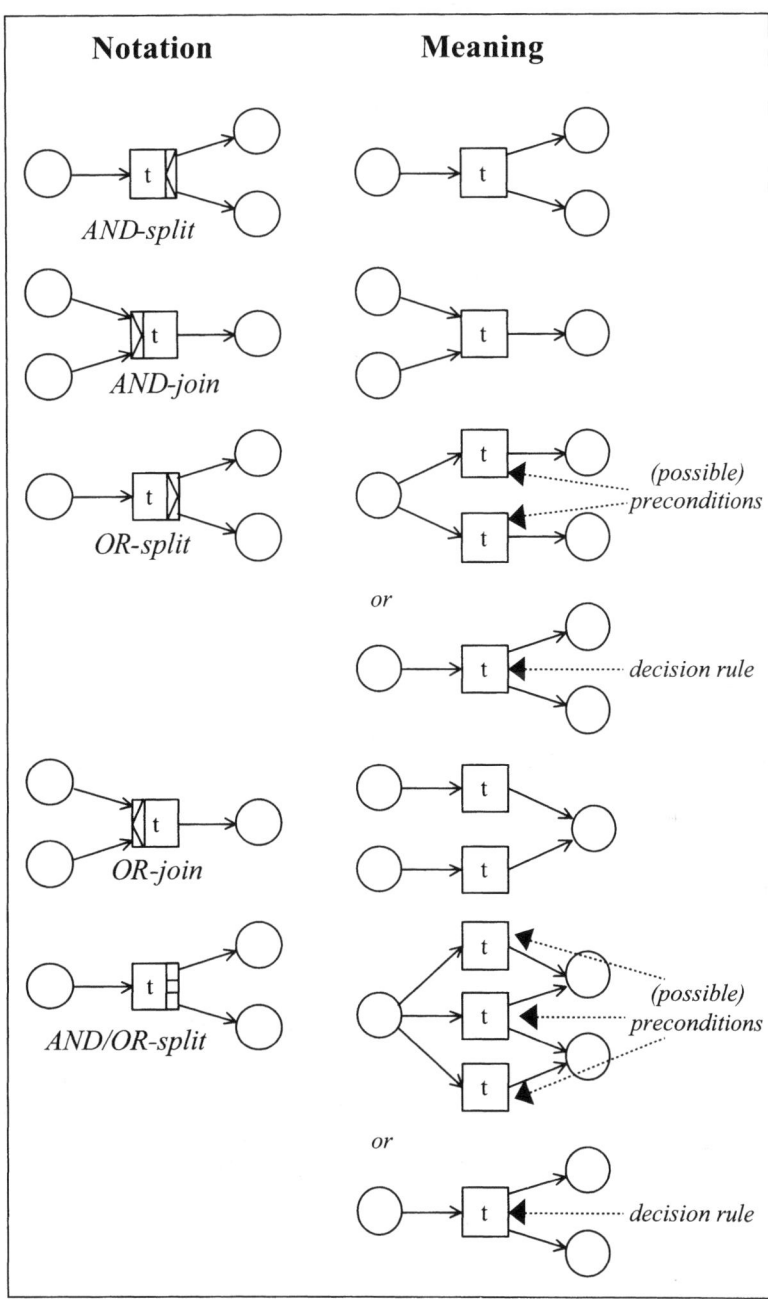

Figure 2.21
Notation method for common constructions

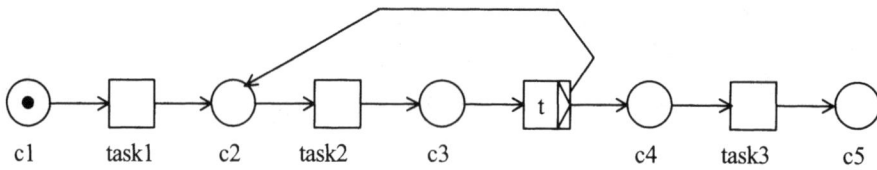

Figure 2.22
Iterative routing (1)

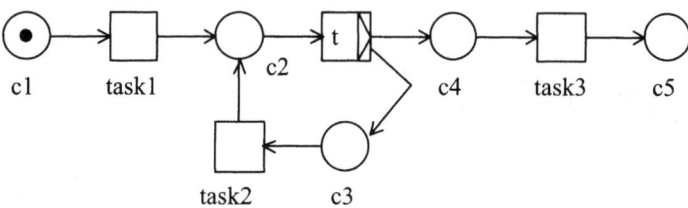

Figure 2.23
Iterative routing (2)

Taking the case corresponding with the token in *c1*, we see that *task1* and *task2* are performed successively. Once *task2* has been completed, OR-split *t* determines whether or not it needs to be performed once again. Once *task2* has been carried out one or more times, the case moves on to *task3*. *Task2* must be carried out at least once between *task1* and *task3*.

Figure 2.22 assumes that *task2* must be performed at least once ("repeat ... until ..."). If this is not the case, the construction illustrated in figure 2.23 applies ("while ... do ...").

Immediately upon completion of *task1*, OR-split *t* determines whether or not *task2* needs to be carried out. It now becomes possible for *task1* to be followed directly by *task3*.

In both examples, there exists an OR-split that makes its decision based upon the current values of the case attributes. Note that the two constructions illustrated correspond with the familiar "repeat ... until ..." and "while ... do ..." constructions that appear in many programming languages.

Example   Using the example described in the previous chapter, we can now illustrate the concepts defined thus far. The example concerns an insurance company's process for dealing with claims. Chapter 1 identifies sixteen tasks in this process. In chapter 1 we did not yet introduce the Petri net tool to model workflow processes. Therefore, we used an "ad hoc" notation technique to illustrate the routing. Now, however, we can show the process "properly," as shown in figure 2.24. But before looking at that diagram, try to model the process yourself.

For the sake of convenience, the conditions which are used to route the cases correctly are given "symbolic" names. In practice, however, symbolic names are of no use. For example, we could more appropriately call condition *c7 accepted*. Conditions *c1* and *c20* have a special role: *c1* represents the start of the process and *c20* its end. Note that the "informal" diagram in chapter 1 and figure 2.24 do closely resemble one another. The major difference between the two is that the conditions are explicitly named in figure 2.24. As a result, we can describe the state of a case.

2.3.3   Enactment

A *process* is a collection of tasks, conditions, subprocesses, and their relationships with one another. As we have seen, we can describe a process using a Petri net. Conditions are depicted using places and tasks using transitions. To simplify the representation of a process in terms of a Petri net, we have defined a method of notating a number of typical constructions. (See figure 2.21.)

A process is designed to deal with a particular *category* of cases, and so may handle many individual cases. A task is not specific to a particular case. However, when a case is being carried out by a process, tasks are performed for that specific case. In order to avoid confusion between a task as such and its performance on a specific case, we have introduced the terms *work item* and *activity*. A work item is the combination of a case and a task which is ready to be carried out. The term activity refers to the actual performance of a work item. At the point when a work item is actually being worked on, it is transformed into an activity. Note that, unlike a task, both a work item and an activity are linked to a specific case. The distinction between (1) a task, (2) a work item, and (3) an activity becomes clear as soon as we translate them into Petri net terms. A task corresponds with one or more transitions, a work item with a transition being enabled, and an activity with the firing of a transition.

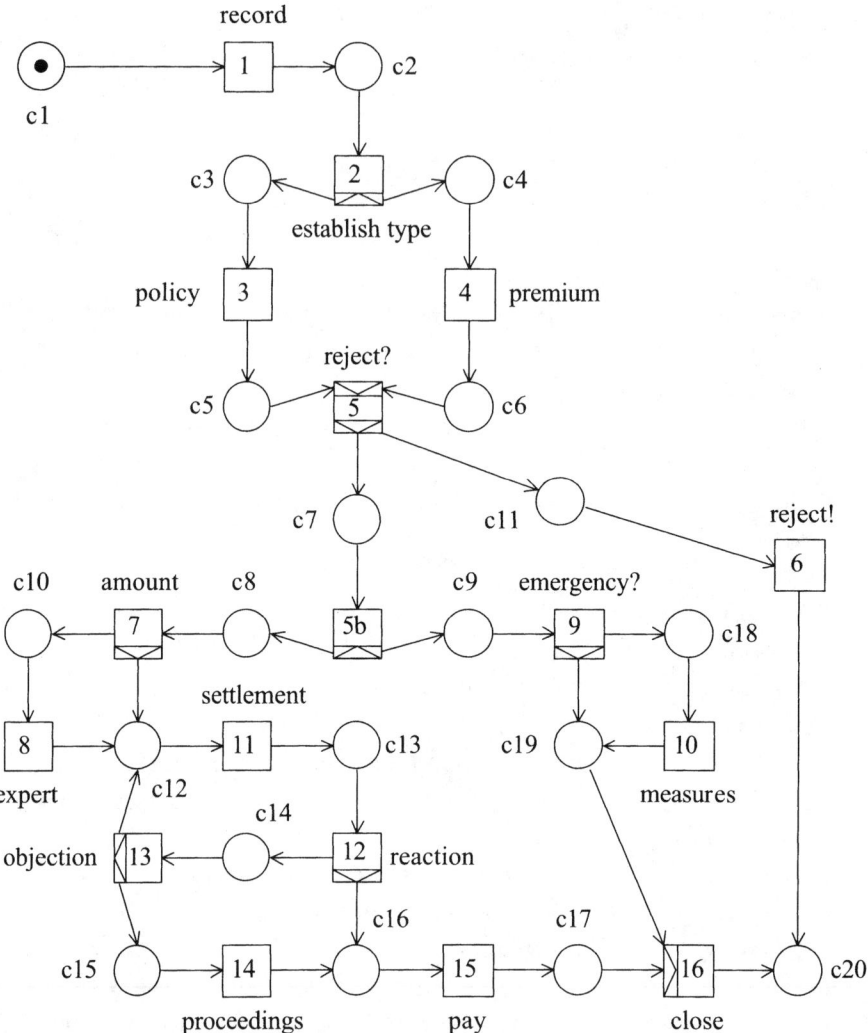

Figure 2.24
The process for dealing with insurance claims

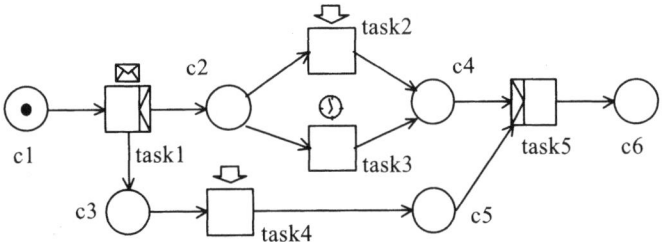

Figure 2.25
An example with various forms of triggering

Transitions in a Petri net are "eager." In other words, they fire as soon as they are enabled. As we have just established, the enabling of a transition corresponds with a work item. For an assignment to be carried out, however, more is often required than simply the relevant case having the right state. If it is to be carried out by a person, she must first take it from her "in tray" before an activity begins. In other words, the work item is only carried out once the employee has taken the initiative. This is why we recognized the existence of *triggering*. Certain work items can only be transformed into an activity once they have been triggered.

We differentiate between three types of triggers: (1) a resource initiative (such as an employee taking a work item from her in tray); (2) an external event (such as the arrival of an EDI message); and (3) a time signal (such as the generation of a list of orders at six o'clock). Work items that must always be carried out immediately, without the intervention of a resource, do not need a trigger. We can illustrate in a Petri net which form of triggering applies. Tasks triggered by a resource are shown using a wide, downward-facing arrow. Those triggered by an external event have an envelope symbol. And those that are time dependent have a clock symbol. Figure 2.25 shows an example of a process containing "triggering information."

Task2 and *task4* are handled by a resource. *Task3* is time-dependent, and *task1* requires an external trigger (for example, an EDI message). The only automatic task is *task5*.

The notion of triggering is of major importance. It is not the workflow system that is in charge, but the environment. The system cannot force a client to return a form; it cannot even force an employee to perform a work item at a particular time. It is easy to model the triggering mechanism in Petri net terms. To each transition belonging to a task requiring a trigger an extra input place is added. A token in such an extra input place represents the trigger. So a token appears in that extra input place when the trigger is recorded by the workflow system.

The triggering mechanism also shows that the *timing of an OR-split choice* is crucial. In figure 2.25, the timing of the nondeterministic choice between *task2* and *task3* is as late as possible. Once condition *c2* has been met there are two possibilities. The first is that an employee begins the work item corresponding with *task2* before the moment specified for the performance of *task3* is reached. Alternatively, no employee takes the initiative to carry out *task2* before that moment. In the first case *task2* fires, in the second *task3* fires. A choice between the two alternatives thus is delayed until the moment when the first trigger is received. Because it is not known in advance which one will be activated, the implicit OR-split in the form of place *c2* cannot be replaced by an explicit OR-split in the form of one or two additional transitions. So the OR-split comes in two forms: *implicit* and *explicit*. Figure 2.26 shows these diagrammatically.

Like the firing of a transition, an activity—that is, the actual performance of a task for a specific case—is an atomic unit. It thus is always carried out in full. However, a fault may occur during the performance of the task related to the activity. For example, it may make use of a resource (such as an employee) which interrupts it for some reason or another. An employee may notice, say, that certain data required to carry out the task are missing. Or the activity may use an application (such as a program for calculating interest charges) that crashes while performing

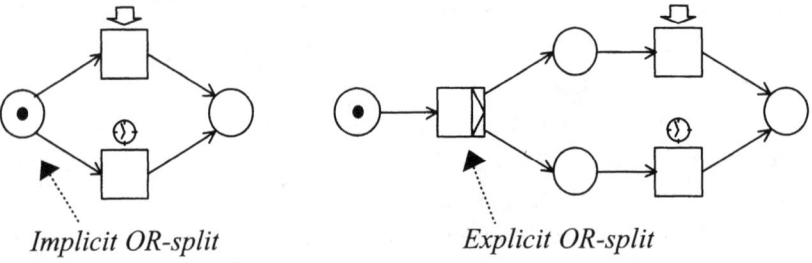

Implicit OR-split   *Explicit OR-split*

Figure 2.26
There is an essential difference between the implicit and explicit OR-split

the task. Moreover a failure in the workflow system itself—perhaps due to a system error—during an activity cannot be ruled out.

In all such cases, a so-called *rollback* is required. This involves returning the workflow system to its state prior to the start of the activity. Following the rollback, the activity can be restarted. Only when the activity has been successfully completed does a so-called *commit* occur and all changes made become definitive. As far as the process is concerned, a rollback is very simple: the case attributes and all valid conditions are returned to their original values. For the application (which has been cut off in the middle of performing a task), a rollback can be more complicated.

2.3.4   Example: Travel agency

Let us consider an example where triggers play an important role. To organize a trip, a travel agency executes several tasks. First the customer is registered. Then an employee searches for opportunities which are communicated to the customer. Then the customer will be contacted to find out whether she or he is still interested in the trip of this agency and whether more alternatives are desired. There are three possibilities: (1) the customer is not interested at all, (2) the customer would like to see more alternatives, and (3) the customer selects an opportunity. If the customer selects a trip, the trip is booked. In parallel, one or two types of insurance are prepared if they are desired. A customer can take insurance for trip cancellation or/and for baggage loss. Note that a customer can decide not to take any insurance, just trip cancellation insurance, just baggage loss insurance, or both types of insurance. Two weeks before the start date of the trip the documents are sent to the customer. A trip can be cancelled at any time after completing the booking process (including the insurance) and before the start date. Note that customers who are not insured for trip cancellation can cancel the trip (but will get no refund).

Based on this informal description, we create the corresponding process using the constructs introduced in this chapter. Figure 2.27 shows the result.

The process, like any workflow process in this book, has a source place which serves as the start condition (i.e., case creation) and a sink place which serves as the end condition (i.e., case completion). First, the tasks

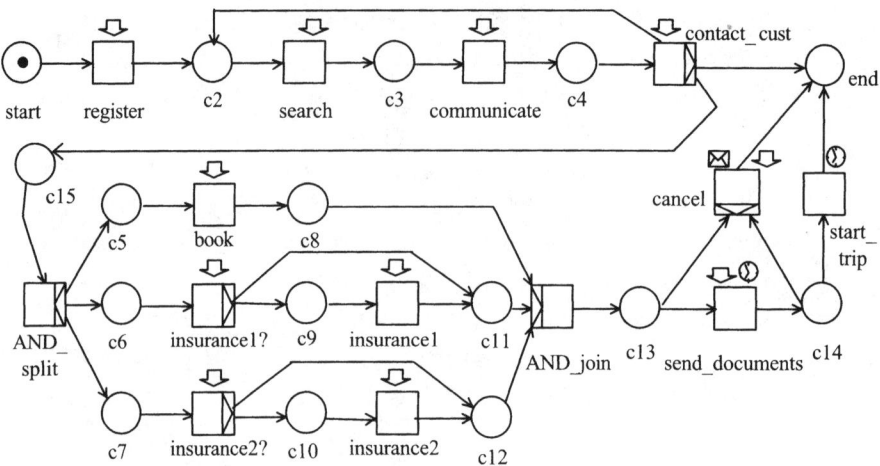

Figure 2.27
The travel agency

register, *search*, *communicate*, and *contact_cust* are executed sequentially. Task *contact_cust* is an OR-split with three possible outcomes: (1) the customer is not interested at all, that is, a token is put into *end*, (2) the customer would like to see more alternatives, that is, a token is put into *c2*, and (3) the customer selects an opportunity, that is, a token is put into *c15* to initiate the booking. Tasks *AND_split* and *AND_join* have just been added for routing purposes. These routing tasks enable the parallel execution of the booking and insurance tasks. The task *book* corresponds to the actual booking of the trip. Tasks *insurance1* and *insurance2* correspond to handling both types of insurance. Since both types of insurance are optional, there is a bypass for each of these tasks. The OR-split *insurance1?* allows for a bypass of task *insurance1* by putting a token in *c11*. After handling the booking and optional insurances the AND-join puts a token in *c13*. The remainder of the process is, from the viewpoint of triggers, very interesting. Note that all tasks executed before this point are either tasks that require a resource trigger or automatic tasks added for routing purposes only. The downward-facing arrows denote the resource triggers. If the case is in *c13*, then the normal flow of execution is to first execute task *send_documents* and then execute *start_trip*. Note that task *send_documents* requires both a resource trigger and a time trigger. These two triggers indicate that two weeks before the beginning of the trip a worker sends the documents to the customer. Task *start_trip* has been added for routing purposes and requires a time trigger. Without task *start_trip*, that is, putting the token in *end* after sending the documents, it would have been impossible to cancel the trip after sending the documents. Task *cancel* is an explicit OR-join and requires both a resource trigger and an external trigger. This task is only executed if it is triggered by the customer. Task *cancel* can only be executed when the case is in *c13* or *c14*, that is, after handling the booking and insurance related tasks and before the trip starts.

Using the travel agency example, we point out *two guidelines for modeling*. The first guideline concerns the use of OR-joins. *OR-join tasks should be avoided as much as possible.* In most situations it is possible to use places/conditions instead of explicitly modeling OR-join tasks. If an OR-join task has two or more input conditions and these conditions are not input for any other task, then these conditions can be fused together because, from a semantical point of view, they are identical. As a result the number of elements in the diagram is reduced and there is no need to use an OR-join. For example, place *c2* in figure 2.27 can be split into two conditions; one condition for new cases and one condition for cases that require more work. Such a split would introduce the need for an OR-join task *search*. The resulting diagram only becomes more complex without changing the actual behavior. Therefore we prefer the solution with one condition *c2* with two incoming arcs. Only in rare situations are OR-join tasks needed to obtain the desired behavior. Consider for example figure 2.27. Task *cancel* is an OR-join. It is not possible to remove this OR-join by fusing the input conditions *c13* and *c14*. Conditions *c13* and *c14* correspond to different states, that is, in *c13* *send_documents* is enabled and in *c14* *start_trip* is enabled. The second guideline for modeling concerns the *use of triggers for the first task* in the process. In figure 2.27 we could have added an external trigger to task *register*. This trigger would correspond to the request of the customer. Another interpretation is that the request of the customer corresponds to the creation of the initial token in condition *start*. This interpretation is used in figure 2.27. Therefore the external trigger was not added to task *register*. In this book we prefer to use this interpretation. However the interpretation that the first task requires an external trigger to initiate the process is also allowed.

And finally ...   In this chapter, we have introduced a process-modeling technique for the specification of workflows. It is based upon the theory of Petri nets and has a number of advantages. First, the technique is graphical and easy to apply. As we have seen using several examples, workflow concepts can be illustrated elegantly using Petri nets. Second, it is a technique with a good formal foundation: the meaning of each process is precisely defined. As a result, we have for example discovered that two types of OR-split exist. Another important advantage over many other process-modeling techniques is the fact that (interim) states are explicitly indicated. This enables us to differentiate between an implicit and an explicit OR-split. Explicit states also make it conceptually easier to cancel cases. Cancellation can be achieved simply by removing all the tokens belonging to that case. An explicit notion of states is also essential when transferring a case from one workflow system to another. Finally—because Petri nets have a formal basis—various analytical methods are possible.

EXERCISES

Exercises Classical Petri Nets

Exercise 2.1   German traffic light
There are some differences between traffic lights in different countries. The traffic lights described in this chapter are Dutch traffic lights. The traffic lights in Germany have an extra phase in their cycle. German traffic lights do not turn suddenly from red to green, but rather give an additional yellow light just before turning to green.

(a) Identify the possible states and model the transition system. A transition system lists all possible states and state transitions.

(b) Provide a Petri net that is *able* to behave like a German traffic light. There should be three places indicating the state of each light and all state transitions of the transition system should be supported.

(c) Give a Petri net that *exactly* behaves like a German traffic light. Make sure that the Petri net does not allow state transitions that are not possible.

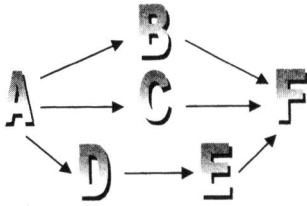

Figure 2.28
Project X

Exercise 2.2   Project X
A secret project by the government (let's call it Project X) will be executed by one person and consists of 6 tasks: A, B, C, D, E, and F. Figure
2.28 specifies the order in which the tasks need to be executed (precedence graph, cf. PERT/CPM). A possible execution trace is for example
ABDCEF.

(a) Model the project in terms of a classical Petri net.
(b) How does one model so that E is optional?
(c) How does one model so that D and E should be executed consecu-
tively, that is, B and C are not allowed between D and E?

Exercise 2.3   Railnet
A circular rail network consists of four tracks. Each track is in one of the
following three states:

• Busy, that is, there is a train on the track.
• Claimed, that is, a train has successfully requested access to the
track.
• Free, that is, neither busy nor claimed.

There are two trains driving on the circular track. The track where a
train resides is busy. To move to the next track a train first claims the
next track. Only free tracks can be claimed. Busy tracks are released
the moment the train moves to another track. One can abstract from
the identity of trains only the state of the rail network is considered.

(a) Model the dynamic behavior of the rail network in terms of a Petri
net.
(b) Is it easy to model the situation with 10 tracks (160 states)?

Exercise 2.4   Binary counter

The following (binary) counter is to be modeled as a Petri net. The marking of a place represents a binary value (1 or 0). The combination of the markings of these places represents the natural number that is displayed by the counter. For example, the binary number 101, that is, 5, marks two places corresponding to a "1" (i.e., the places 2^2 and 2^0) and one place corresponding to a "0" (i.e., the place 2^1).

Make a model of a counter able to count from 0 to 7.

Exercises High-Level Petri Nets

Exercise 2.5   Driving school

A driving school is trying to set up an information system to track the progress of the students' training and the deployment of instructors. As a starting point for a formal process model the following description can be used.

New students register with the driving school. A registered student takes one or more driving lessons followed by an examination. Each driving lesson has a beginning and an end. Instructors give driving lessons. The driving school has five instructors. Each driving lesson is followed by either another lesson or an examination. The examination has a beginning and an end and is supervised by a driving examiner. In total there are ten driving examiners. For the outcome of an examination there are three possibilities:

1. The student passes and leaves the driving school.
2. The student fails and takes additional lessons in order to try again.
3. The student fails and gives up.

(a) Model the driving school in terms of a classical Petri net.
(b) Use a colored Petri net to model that one takes ten lessons before taking the exam and people will drop out if they fail three times.
(c) Add time to model that a lesson takes one hour and an exam thirty minutes.

Exercise 2.6   Bicycle factory

A factory produces bicycles (just one type). The Bill Of Materials (BOM) is given in figure 2.29.

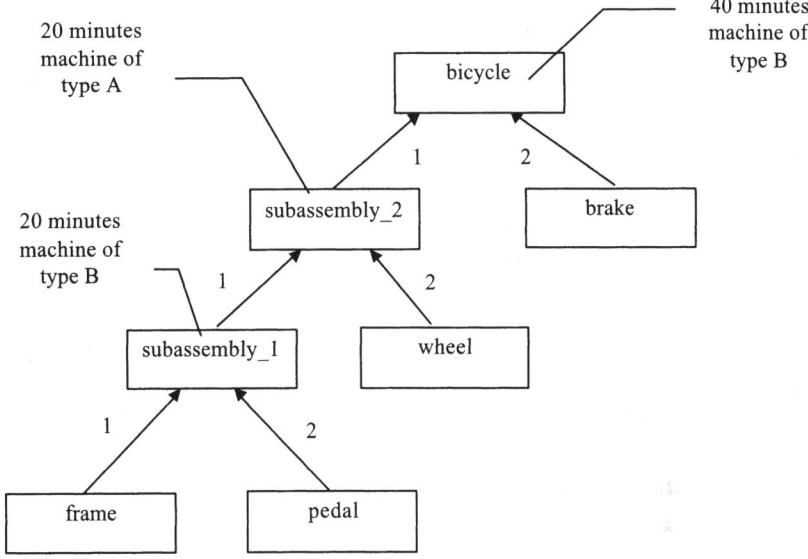

Figure 2.29
Bicycle factory

Suppliers deliver the raw materials. First the frame and two pedals are assembled. This takes twenty minutes and is done by a machine of type B. The other two assembly steps are defined in a similar fashion (see figure 2.29). Finally, the end product is delivered after three assembly steps. The factory has three machines of type A, and seven machines of type B. Each of the machines has a capacity 1, that is, a machine is either free or busy.

(a) Model the factory in terms of a Petri net. Make sure to model the states of the machines (busy/free) explicitly and abstract from time.

(b) Add time to model the temporal behavior. What is the maximal throughput per hour?

Workflow Process Definitions

Exercise 2.7   Insurance company
Insurance company X processes claims that result from traffic accidents with cars where customers of X are involved in. Therefore, it uses the following procedure for the processing of the insurance claims.

Every claim, reported by a customer, is registered by an employee of department CD (where CD is Car Damages). After the registration of the claim, the insurance claim is classified by a claim handler of rank A or B within CD. There are two categories: simple and complex claims. For simple claims two tasks need to be executed: check insurance and phone garage. These tasks are independent of each other. The complex claims require three tasks to be executed: check insurance, check damage history, and phone garage. These tasks need to be executed sequentially in the order specified. Both for the simple and complex claims, the tasks are done by employees of department CD. After executing the two respectively three tasks a decision is made. This decision is made by a claim handler of rank A and has two possible outcomes: OK (positive) or NOK (negative). If the decision is positive, then insurance company X will pay. An employee of the finance department handles the payment. In any event, the insurance company sends a letter to the customer who sent the claim. An employee of the department CD writes this letter.

Model the workflow by making a process definition in terms of a Petri net using the techniques introduced in this chapter.

Exercise 2.8   Complaints handling

Each year travel agency Y has to process a lot of complaints (about 10,000). There is a special department for the processing of complaints (department C). There is also an internal department called logistics (department L) which takes care of the registration of incoming complaints and the archiving of processed complaints. The following procedure is used to handle these complaints.

An employee of department L first registers every incoming complaint. After registration a form is sent to the customer with questions about the nature of the complaint. This is done by an employee of department C. There are two possibilities: the customer returns the form within two weeks or he does not. If the form is returned, it is processed automatically resulting in a report that can be used for the actual processing of the complaint. If the form is not returned on time, a time-out occurs resulting in an empty report. Note that this does not necessarily mean that the complaint is discarded. After registration, that is, in parallel with the form handling, the preparation for the actual processing is started.

First, the complaint is evaluated by a complaint manager of department C. Evaluation shows that either further processing is needed or it is not. Note that this decision does not depend on the form handling. If no further processing is required and the form is handled, the complaint is archived. If further processing is required, an employee of the complaints department executes the task "process complaint" (this is the actual processing where certain actions are proposed if needed). For the actual processing of the complaint, the report resulting from the form handling is used. Note that the report can be empty. The result of task "process complaint" is checked by a complaint manager. If the result is not OK, task "process complaint" is executed again. This is repeated until the result is acceptable. If the result is accepted, an employee of the department C executes the proposed actions. After this the processed complaint is archived by an employee of department L.

Give the process, that is, model the workflow by making a process definition in terms of a Petri net.

Exercise 2.9   Let's have a party

A group of students wants to set up an agency to organize parties. The customer should indicate the amount of money to be spent, the number of persons the party is meant for, and the area in which the party is to be given. With that information, the agency looks for a suitable location and takes care of the rest.

Locations are indoors or outdoors. If the location is indoors, a room is to be hired. In case of an outdoor location, however, a party tent and a terrain have to be arranged, possibly along with a permit for making noise (music). There are two sorts of music: live or CDs. The choice between these alternatives is not made by the customer, but by the agency itself: live music is preferred, but expensive, so most parties will have to do with CDs. CDs are also chosen if there is not enough time left to ask a band. If CDs are chosen, a sound system has to be arranged. In case of live music, however, things are more complicated. First, a band is selected. Then this band is sent a letter inviting it to play on this party. If the band does not react within a week, a new band is selected and the procedure is repeated. If they do react, there are again two possibilities: they are interested or not interested. In the latter case, a new band is selected and the procedure is repeated. In the first case, however, the band is not hired immediately. First the agency should see and hear the band to see if they are good enough. Because the students only take the best, about thirty percent of the bands is considered good enough. For the other seventy percent, a new band is selected, and so on. If the students cannot find a band quickly enough, they switch to CDs. Of course, the bands that have been hired before do not have to be evaluated first. They're hired immediately. After taking care of the location and the music, they also take care of food and drinks. In case of a band, they order extra food and drinks for the musicians. To make sure everything is fine, the students take a look at the party when it is being held. After that, a bill is sent to the customer.

(a) Model the workflow by making a process definition in terms of a Petri net using the techniques introduced in this chapter. Assign triggers to tasks whenever appropriate.

(b) Analyze the process and investigate possible improvements.

3

Management of Workflows

3.1 Resource Management Concepts

Using the definition of a process, we can indicate *which* tasks need to be performed for a particular category of case. We can also show the *order* in which they must be carried out. However, the process definition does not indicate *who* should do it. But the way in which the work items are allocated to resources (people and/or machines) is very important to the efficiency and effectiveness of the workflow. In this chapter, we shall concentrate upon the management of resources and the link between a process definition and the resources available. We shall also pay attention to improving workflows.

3.1.1 The resource

A workflow system focuses upon supporting a business process. In this process, work is carried out by means of production, also called *resources*. In an administrative environment, the term resource primarily refers to office staff. However, a doctor, a printer, a doorman, and an assembly robot are all examples of resources. The basic characteristic of a resource is that it is able to carry out particular tasks. We also assume that each resource is uniquely identifiable and has a certain capacity. In this chapter, we shall confine ourselves to resources with a capacity of one. In other words, each resource may be working on no more than one activity at any given time. This does not, however, have to be the case in practice.

3.1.2 Resource classification

In general, a resource is permitted to carry out a limited number of tasks. In a bank, for example, a teller is not allowed to grant a mortgage. A task usually can be performed only by a limited number of resources. Because it is impracticable to indicate which resources are able to carry out each task, we classify them using *resource classes*. A resource class is a group of resources. For example, the resource class *Counter_Staff* may consist of the people Annie, Hank, Mandy, Jack, and Tom. A resource may belong to more than one class. So Annie, say, could be a member of both the *Counter_Staff* and the *Travel_Agent* categories. In general, we differentiate between two forms of resource classification: (1) that based upon functional properties and (2) that based upon position within the organization.

A functionally based resource class is known as a *role*. It is also referred to as a function or qualification. A role is a group of resources, each of which has a number of specific skills. Such resource classes as *Counter_Staff, Travel_Agent, Assessor, C_Executive, Administrator, Printer, Hospital_Bed*, and *Junior_Doctor* are examples of roles. By linking a task to the correct role, one can ensure that the resource carrying out the task is sufficiently qualified (and authorized).

Resources can also be classified according to their place in the organization. Under this definition fall such resource classes as *Sales_Department, Purchasing_Department, Team_2*, and *Atlanta_Branch*. A resource class based upon organizational rather than functional characteristics also is called an *organizational unit*. This form of classification can be used to ensure that a task is carried out at the right place in the organization.

Figure 3.1 shows a resource classification diagrammatically. In total, there are eight resource classes. Of these, the resource classes *Atlanta, Denver, Purchasing_Department*, and *Sales_Department* are examples of organizational units. So the resource Jack works at the *Atlanta* branch in the *Sales_Department*. The remaining resource classes are based upon functional characteristics. The resource class *Secretary*, for example, contains all those resources which are qualified to act as a secretary. As we can see in figure 3.1, resource classes may overlap. It is even possible for one resource class to be a subset of another, larger one. The resource class *Salesperson*, for example, is contained entirely within the resource class *Office_Staff*. We can use a classification similar to the one shown in figure 3.1 to link a particular task to the appropriate resource(s). Say we need a salesperson based in Denver. In this case, only one resource

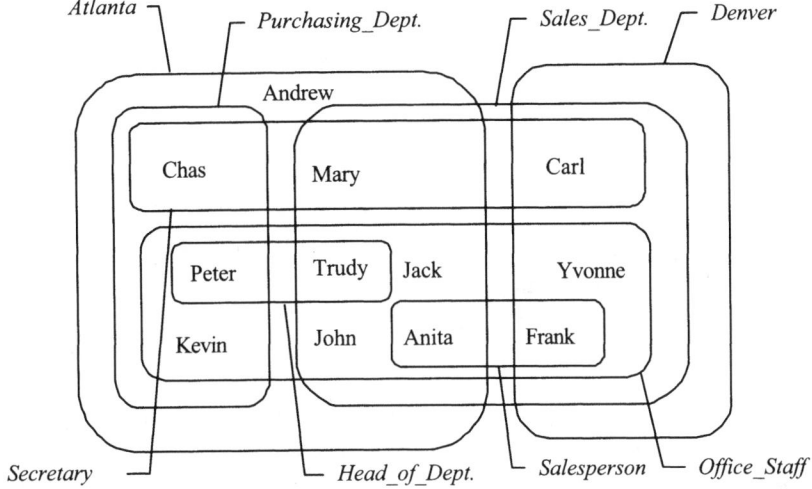

Figure 3.1
Resource classification

qualifies: Frank. If we need a secretary in the *Sales_Department*, two
resources are possible: Mary and Carl.

As already indicated, in most cases a resource classification consists of
two parts. We call that part containing the functional structure the *role
model* and that containing the organizational units the *organization
chart*. Note that the term organization chart usually has a broader
meaning, referring to the hierarchical structure of the organization.

3.1.3   Allocating activities to resources

In order to ensure that each activity is performed by a suitable resource,
we provide each task in the process definition with an *allocation principle* (see figure 3.2). This specifies which preconditions the resource must
meet. In most cases, the allocation specifies both a role and an organizational unit. The resource then must belong to the intersection of these
two resource classes. However it is also possible to define a much more
complex allocation. From figure 3.1, for example, we could specify the
resource classes *Office_Staff* and *Atlanta*, but exclude *Salesperson*. The
task with this allocation rule therefore may be carried out only by an
office worker in Atlanta who is not a salesperson. The allocation may
also depend upon the attributes of the case for which the task must be

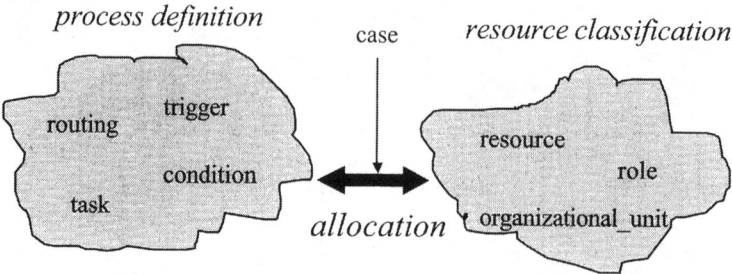

Figure 3.2
Allocation principles link the process definition with the resource classification

carried out. Depending upon these attributes we can, for example, select the organizational unit. To assess an insurance claim, for instance, we would select the nearest branch of the company. In such a case, we should use the customer's address as a case attribute. When the Internal Revenue Service deals with a tax return, the allocation may depend upon the name of the person making the return. A particular assessment team is selected based upon the name. In this case, it is of course the person's name that acts as a case attribute.

By making careful use of the case attributes, we can also ensure that an activity is performed by a specific resource. But the opposite is also possible. In a bank, for example, it may be that one member of staff is not allowed to perform two successive tasks on the same case. We call this *separation of function*. This term is taken from accountancy. Here, it is important that certain tasks not be carried out by the same person in order to prevent fraud. The financial settlement of a travel-expenses claim, for example, should not be done by the person who authorized the journey. The objective of separation of function is to combat abuse. Because each case is dealt with by several people, it becomes more difficult to commit fraud. If a number of successive tasks do need to be carried out by, or under the authority of, a single employee, then that person is referred to as a *case manager*. Because she is largely responsible for a case, she is naturally more involved in it. The appointment of a manager for each case can result in a better service to the customer and more rapid completion because of greater familiarity with the work.

By providing a task with an allocation principle, we specify the pre-conditions that the resource must meet. In most cases, there is more than one resource that may carry out the activity associated with a particular work item.

At the heart of a workflow system is the *workflow engine*. This ensures the actual enactment of a specified workflow. One of its core tasks is to allocate work items to resources. In doing so, it must take into account the resource classes specified, as well as such things as separation of function and case management. In many cases, the workflow engine nevertheless is able to choose between a number of resources when allocating work. It then has to decide which resource will carry out the activity. We shall return to this later.

3.2   Resource Management in More Detail

The allocation of resources to activities is not a simple issue. As we have seen, such concepts as the task, the case, the work item, the activity, the case attributes, the resource, the resource class, the role, the organizational unit, and allocation are all closely connected with one another. For the sake of clarity, we therefore make use of a simple data model which summarizes the concepts and their mutual relationships. Figure 3.3 shows an entity relationship (ER) diagram. Broadly speaking, this diagram consists of two types of elements: entity types and relationship types. The former is indicated using a rectangle and represents a group of entities. For example, the entity type *task* contains all the tasks that form part of a process. Relationship types are illustrated using a diamond. This represents a group of relationships. So the relationship type *belongs_to*, for example, contains a collection of relationships between resources and resource classes. If there exists a relationship between resource *r* and a resource class *c*, then this means that *r* belongs to *c*.

The relationship type *of* between *task* and *work item* indicates to which task a work item relates. Each work item has a relationship with precisely one task and each task may have an arbitrary number of work items (say N) associated to it. This is shown using the symbols 1 and N. These therefore refer to the cardinality of the relationship *of*. We can also say that there exists a 1-on-N relationship. In other words, each work item relates to precisely one case. It may be possible for more than one work item to have a relationship with the same case. This may, for example, result from parallel routing.

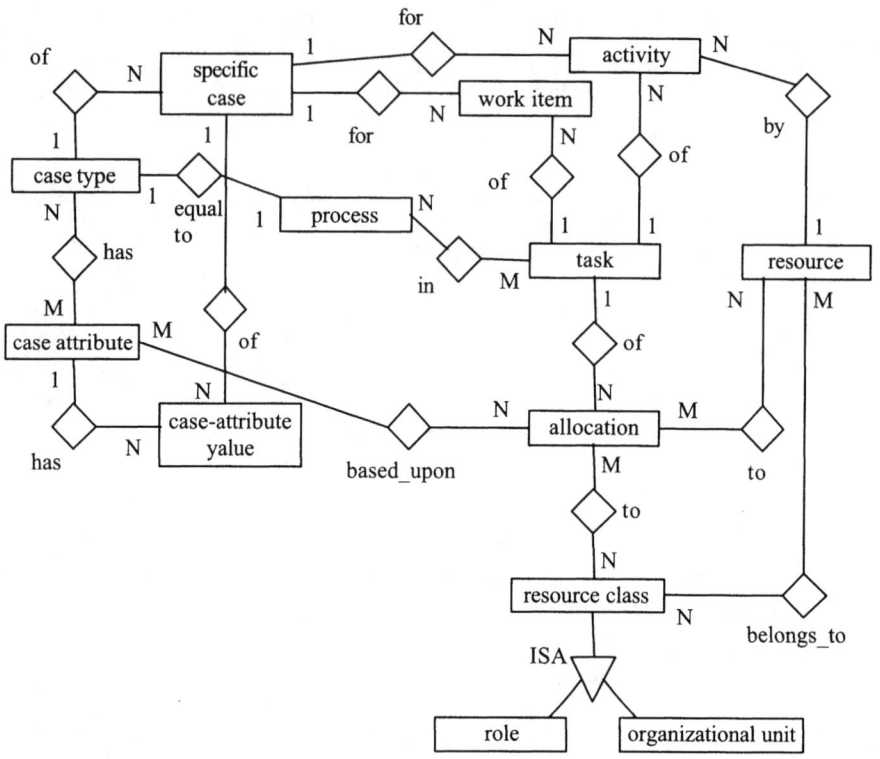

Figure 3.3
Using an ER diagram, we can illustrate the links between various entities

An entity of the entity type *activity* relates to the actual performance of a work item. So, like a work item, an activity relates to a single case and a single task. Moreover, zero or one resources are also attached to each activity. The relationship type *belongs_to* is an example of an M-to-N relationship, which specifies that a resource may belong to several resource classes and a resource class may contain several resources. A role and an organizational unit are examples of resource classes. Hence the entity types *role* and *organizational unit* are associated with the entity type *resource class* through a so-called ISA relationship type. This indicates that roles and organizational units are special cases of resource classes.

In the ER diagram, we differentiate between a specific case and a case type. The latter corresponds with a process: it is the category of cases that can be dealt with by that process. The ER diagram also indicates that there exists a one-on-one relationship between the case type and the process. We also differentiate between case attributes and specific case attributes associated with a specific case. The former refers to a logical name that expresses a particular property, the latter to the value of an attribute in a specific case that is in progress. The entity type *allocation* determines which conditions the relationship type *by* between the entity types *activity* and *resource* must fulfill.

As noted earlier, the preconditions formulated in the allocation policy can become highly complex. After all, an allocation relates tasks, resource classes, case attributes, and resources to each other. Each task has one or more allocations. And an allocation may depend upon one or more case attributes. In most cases, an allocation will point to the intersection of a role and an organizational unit. In special cases, though, a specific resource may be excluded (separation of function) or selected (case manager).

The ER diagram can only provide an impression of the *static* aspects of resource management. We can regard such a diagram as a "snapshot" of resource management at a particular moment, that is, the diagram only describes the structure of all possible states. Its *dynamic* aspects are not shown in figure 3.3. To illustrate these, we must look at the process shown in figure 3.4.

The process *handle complaint* consists of eight tasks, of which three are automatically handled (they do not involve intervention by a resource). Moreover there are four resource classes. Two of these are based upon functional characteristics: *Employee* and *Assessor*. Alongside these two roles there are two further resource classes based upon organizational characteristics: *Complaints* and *Finance*. These correspond with two of the company departments. Figure 3.4 also shows diagrammatically the allocation for each task. The task *contact_client* is linked with the role *Employee* and the organizational unit *Complaints*. This means that an employee in the complaints department is needed to approach the client. A resource from the intersection of the resource classes *Employee* and *Complaints* also is required for the tasks *contact_department* and *send_letter*. For the task *pay*, an employee from the financial department is needed. The task *assess* is carried out by a resource from the intersection of the resource classes *Assessor* and *Complaints*. In figure 3.5, these

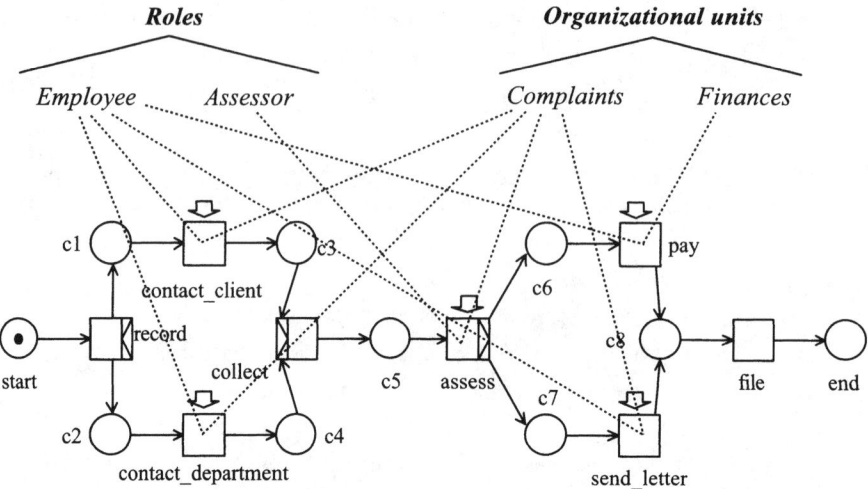

Figure 3.4
The process "handle complaint" and the resource classes involved in it

Resource class	Resources
Employee	John
	Jim
	Liz
	Jack
	Mandy
	Carl
Assessor	Mandy
	Carl
Complaints	John
	Jim
	Mandy
	Carl
Finances	Liz
	Jack

Task	Role	Organizational unit
record	-	-
contact_client	Employee	Complaints
contact_dept.	Employee	Complaints
collect	-	-
assess	Assessor	Complaints
pay	Employee	Finances
send_letter	Employee	Complaints
file	-	-

Figure 3.5
A summary of the composition of each resource class and those required for each case

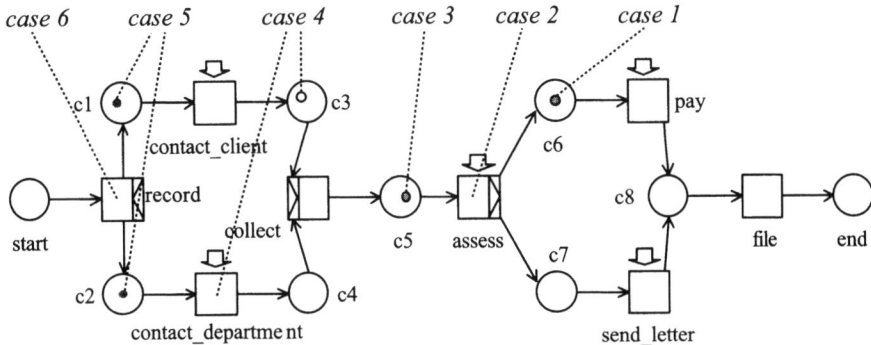

Figure 3.6
In the state illustrated, there are six complaints in progress

allocations are shown again, but in table form. The composition of each resource class is also given.

In figure 3.5 we see, for example, that Mandy belongs to the resource classes *Employee, Assessor,* and *Complaints.* She thus can carry out any task except *pay.* Liz and Jack, on the other hand, can only carry out the task *pay.*

Figure 3.6 shows the states of six cases. Case 1 has been assessed positively, resulting in a work item (*pay*). (In other words, the task *pay* is enabled for case 1.) For case 2, the activity *assess* is being performed. Based upon the states shown in figure 3.6, we can establish the relevant work items and activities. These are shown in the table in figure 3.7. However the opposite is not possible. Based upon the table in figure 3.7, we cannot directly work out the state of each case. For example, it is impossible to tell directly from the table that there is a token in the place corresponding to condition $c3$.

There is a total of four work items. Each corresponds with the potential performance of a task for a particular case. Note that in the situation depicted in figure 3.6 there are two work items for case 5. This is because of parallel routing, which enables the tasks *contact_client* and *contact_ department* simultaneously. There are three activities. Each of these corresponds with the actual performance of a task for a particular case. The first corresponds with the performance of the task *assess* for case 2 by resource Mandy. The second is carried out by Jim: the task *contact_*

Work items	
Case	Task
Case 1	pay
Case 3	assess
Case 5	contact_client
Case 5	contact_dept.

Activities		
Case	Task	Resource
Case 2	assess	Mandy
Case 4	contact_dept.	Jim
Case 6	record	-

Figure 3.7
The work items and activities for the state illustrated in figure 3.6

department for case 4. The last is the task *record* for case 6. As shown in figure 3.5, no resource is required for this.

Each of the work items shown in figure 3.7 can, in principle, be transformed into an activity. The first (task *pay* for case 1) requires a resource from the intersection of the resource classes *Employee* and *Finances*. Both Liz and Jack thus qualify. The second (task *assess* for case 3) can only be carried out by a resource from the intersection of *Assessor* and *Complaints*. Since Mandy is already busy assessing case 2, Carl is the only resource able to perform this work item immediately. The other two work items require a resource from the intersection of *Employee* and *Complaints*.

3.2.1   Allocation principles
The objective of a workflow system is to complete work items as quickly as possible. After all, a hold up affecting work items can result in the case as a whole taking longer. In order to transform work items into activities, two decisions always need to be made:

• *In what order are the work items transformed into activities?* If there exists an excess of work items at particular times, we cannot transform each into an activity immediately. There may, after all, be more work items than there are resources available. If this is the case, then a choice must be made as to the order in which the work items are selected.

• *By which resource are the activities carried out?* Because not all resources are the same, it may matter to which resource a particular work item is allocated. A specialist resource, for example, can carry out certain tasks more quickly. It may also be sensible to keep a flexible resource—one that is a member of a large number of resource classes—free for as long as possible.

It goes without saying that these two decisions are closely interrelated. The order can be important when selecting a resource. Conversely the choice of a resource can affect the order in which work items are transformed into activities.

Many different heuristics can be applied to select a particular order. In particular, we can borrow the various queueing disciplines for production management that are used in factories. The routing of a case through several resources exhibits many similarities with the routing of a product through machines in a production department. Some common queueing disciplines are as follows:

- *First-In, First-Out (FIFO)*. If work items are dealt with in the order in which they are created, we refer to a FIFO discipline. Rather than the time when the work item was generated, we can also use the moment when the case as a whole was created. FIFO queueing is a simple and robust allocation rule and is the most widely used in practice.

- *Last-In, First-Out (LIFO)*. LIFO is the opposite of FIFO. In this arrangement, the work items created most recently are dealt with first. In certain cases, this (unfair) allocation rule can lead to a higher average level of service.

- *Shortest Processing Time (SPT)*. We can sometimes estimate in advance, using the attributes of a case, how much time is required to perform an activity. A distinction can often be made between easy and difficult cases, and between simple and time-consuming tasks. By selecting first those work items that take the least time, it is often possible to reduce the average flow time of cases. It is also possible, however, to imagine situations in which it is actually better to give time-consuming tasks priority over simplest ones. We then refer to a Longest Processing Time (LPT) queueing discipline.

- *Shortest Rest-Processing Time (SRPT)*. If we have some insight into the time required to carry out particular activities for a given case, and into the routing of that case, then we can estimate its remaining total net processing time. By always prioritizing the case with the shortest remaining processing time, the quantity of work in progress (WIP) is generally minimized. If, conversely, we select the case with the longest remaining processing time, then we refer to a Longest Rest-Processing Time (LRPT) queueing discipline.

- *Earliest Due Date (EDD)*. An activity is always carried out in the context of a case. This was initiated at a certain time, and should preferably also be completed by a set time (the "due date"). The EDD queueing discipline determines the order based upon the case's deadline.

So a case that must be finished today takes priority over one that needs to be ready in a week. The tasks still to be carried out may also be taken into account when deciding the order.

Note that the information required by each queueing discipline can vary widely. FIFO needs virtually no information. SRPT, though, requires information about the expected processing times and the routing. There also exist very advanced queueing disciplines that take into account the work in progress, the expected supply of work, and the availability of resources. These disciplines are characterized by their use of the current state of the workflow or of forecasts of its future state.

When considering queueing disciplines, we thus far have assumed that the order is determined by the individual characteristics of a case. However it is also possible for it to be decided for a batch of cases. For a given batch, it is sometimes possible to improve the order using certain criteria.

In what order work items are transformed into activities is closely associated with the selection of the resource. If a work item could be carried out by more than one resource, then the following considerations come into play:

• *Let a resource practice its specialty.* A resource can often perform a large number of tasks. Usually, though, there are some in which it specializes. A tax inspector, for example, may be qualified to assess a whole range of tax returns but at the same time be specialized in those submitted by building contractors. It therefore is preferable to let this resource practice his specialty.

• *As far as possible, let a resource do similar tasks in succession.* Both people and machines require so-called set-up times. By this we mean the (additional) time required to begin performing a new task. The set-up time may, for example, be spent opening an application or getting used to a new task. By carrying out similar tasks one after the other, the set-up times can be cut down. Furthermore in the case of work of a repetitive nature, people can reduce their average processing time by using routine.

• *Strive for the greatest possible flexibility for the near future.* If we have a choice between two resources of equal value to perform a work item, it is wise to select the one that can carry fewer work items of other types. In other words, save the "generalists" until last. In the situation shown in figure 3.7, for example, it would not be sensible to allocate Carl to one of the work items for case 5. If we were to do so, all the resources from the resource class *Assessor* would be busy and case 3 could not proceed any further. By keeping the "generalists" free, flexibility for the near future is guaranteed.

So when allocating work items to resources, choices must continually be made. There are two ways in which this can be done:

• *The workflow engine matches work items and resources.* Within preset conditions, the workflow engine can choose which resource performs each work item. The resource itself thus is unable to choose. As soon as it has finished performing one activity, it is given a new work item. We refer to this as *push-driven*: the engine "pushes" work items onto resources.

• *The resources themselves match work items and resources.* In this scenario, it is the resources that take the initiative. Each has studied the work items that it is able to carry out. It then chooses one. We call this *pull-driven*: the resources "pull out" work items and all "eat" from the same basket of work items.

Usually an approach somewhere between push and pull-driven is taken. One common method is the pull principle supplemented by an ordering of the work items by the workflow engine. A resource thus sees an ordered list of the work items that it can carry out. This is supplied by the workflow engine, which sorts the work items according to such principles as FIFO, LIFO, SPT, or EDD. The resources preferably take the first work item on the list. They may, however—and for whatever reason—choose another. The advantage of this mixed approach is that the workflow engine is given an advisory role while the (human) resources still retain the freedom to decide what work they do.

3.3   Improving Workflows

A workflow system enables an organization to use and manage structured business processes. One important property of workflow systems is that, by comparison with classic information systems, it becomes easier to change business processes. Exchanging or combining tasks, or rearranging resource classes, are easy modifications. It therefore is interesting to examine how we can improve the workflows that are being managed by the system. Improvements influence performance criteria such as completion times, utilization of capacity, level of service, and flexibility.

3.3.1   Bottlenecks in the workflow
When should the process, resource classification, or resource management be changed? If a workflow is not working properly, we can often

observe all types of symptoms. These can be compared with the functions of our body. Symptoms like headaches, diarrhea, nausea, or coughing indicate problems. In a workflow, there also are typical symptoms that betray the presence of a bottleneck that is obstructing its proper operation. Some typical symptoms are listed below:

• *Number of cases in progress (too) large.* If there are many cases in progress, this can indicate a problem. This large number can be caused by major fluctuations in the supply of cases or by a lack of flexibility in the resources. However, it may also be that the process contains too many steps that need to be passed through sequentially.

• *Completion time (too) long compared with actual processing time.* The actual processing time of a case sometimes forms only a small part of the total time it is in progress. If this is the case, there may be a whole range of possibilities for reducing the completion time.

• *Level of service (too) low.* A workflow's level of service is the degree to which the organization is able to complete cases within a certain deadline. If the completion time fluctuates widely, then there is low level of service. It is not possible to guarantee a particular completion time. A low level of service also exists when there are many "no sales" occurring. (By this, we mean the inability to take on potential cases due to the long waiting times.) When the client knows that it will take a long time to complete a case (say, a loan application), it will approach another company. A low level of service can indicate a lack of flexibility, a poorly designed process or a structural lack of capacity.

These three symptoms point to possible bottlenecks. To identify them we need benchmark values for these measures, for instance from comparable processes. Usually, it is not sensible to combat the symptoms using only emergency measures. It is important to tackle their *causes*.

To alert us to problems and to measure the performance of a particular workflow, we use *performance indicators*. These express the performance of a particular aspect of the workflow. In general, we distinguish between two groups of performance indicators:

• *External performance indicators (case-oriented).* The external performance indicators focus upon those aspects that are important to the environment of the workflow. For example, indicators of the average completion time and reliability of the completion time. Note that these indicators can be subdivided according to the specific properties of the case.

• *Internal performance indicators (resource-oriented).* The internal performance indicators show what efforts are required to achieve the external performance (for example, the level of resource utilization, the number of cases per resource, the number of cases in progress, the number of rollbacks, and the rate of turnover). The latter is a measure of the speed at which cases proceed through the workflow system. It is calculated by dividing the length of a period (for example, a month) by the average completion time, or by dividing the average number of cases which come in during a period by the average number of cases in progress.

A poor external performance costs a lot of money. Consider, say, a bank: a long completion time for mortgage applications causes a loss of many clients. However, a good external performance can require a high degree of internal effort. Achieving a rapid completion time can, for example, require extra overtime or the allocation of additional resources. The objective of every organization is to minimize its total costs. As shown in figure 3.8, careful weighing of the costs of a poor external performance (no-sale costs) versus those of internal effort is required.

Nevertheless it is in many cases possible to improve the external performance of a workflow without allocating additional resources. Such an improvement can be achieved by restructuring the workflow or using a better allocation strategy.

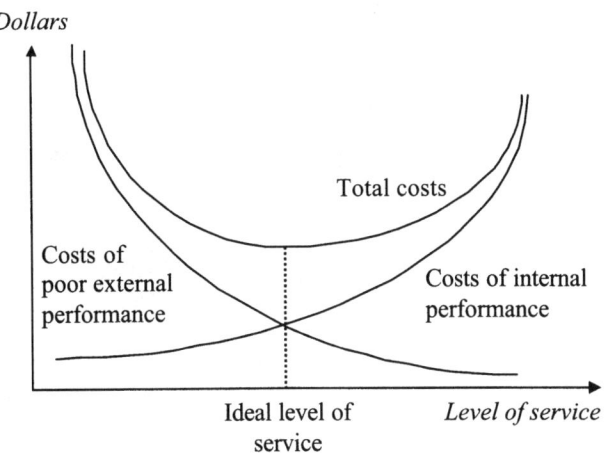

Figure 3.8
Weighing external performance versus internal effort

3.3.2 Business Process Re-engineering

Before focusing upon improving workflows, we shall consider the relationship between *business process re-engineering* (BPR) and workflow management. We can define BPR as the fundamental reconsideration of business processes. Its objective is to bring about entirely new business processes which enable drastic improvements to costs, quality, and service. In order to achieve this objective, radical changes are often necessary. For many administrative processes, the rise of workflow management systems is an "essential enabler" for BPR efforts. After all, the use of a workflow management system makes it easy to adapt processes.

The introduction of a workflow system makes it possible to work in a completely different way. Conversely, some BPR efforts result in the purchase of a workflow management system. Workflow management and BPR are natural partners. It is therefore important for work-process designers to be aware of the latest developments in BPR.

In their book *Re-engineering the Corporation*, Michael Hammer and James Champy write that BPR is characterized by four key words: fundamental, radical, dramatic, and process. The keyword *fundamental* indicates that, when revitalizing a business process, it is of great importance always to ask the elementary questions: why are we doing this, and why are we doing it like this? *Radical* means that the re-engineering must represent a complete break from the current way of working. BPR is not an improvement of the existing processes, but their replacement by completely new ones. The third keyword also refers to the fact that BPR must not effect merely marginal or superficial changes, but that these must be *dramatic* in terms of costs, service, and quality. But of all the keywords, *process* is perhaps the most important. In order to achieve a dramatic improvement, it is necessary to focus upon the business process. This means that the organization must be subordinated to the primary business process. To operate in a genuinely process-oriented way, one must abstract oneself from other aspects, such as people, functions, jobs, teams, and departments.

Process-oriented thinking is crucial in the use of workflow management systems. One of the great dangers threatening the successful introduction of a workflow system lies in simply computerizing existing (manual) practices. Supporting old processes with a workflow system will only deliver a limited amount of improvement. Dramatic improvements are only possible if the old processes are separated from and replaced by new ones. One common error when introducing a workflow system is the unnecessary sequencing of tasks. The fact that a physical document can only be in one place at a time led to sequential routing in many old style processes. However, computerization of the document and the use of a workflow system enable parallel routing in many cases. It is important to structure the new process in such a way that parallel routing also becomes possible (see chapter 6).

3.3.3 Guidelines for (re)designing workflows

Inspired by many experiences in BPR, we are able to propose a number of rules of thumb (i.e., best practices) for the design or redesign of workflows. These relate to process design, resource classification, and the allocation of activities to tasks:

1. *First establish the objective of the process.* When designing a new workflow or changing an existing one, it is crucial to consider the role played by the process in the greater scheme of things. Why do we need the workflow at all? By reflecting upon this fundamental question, it is possible to define the new workflow without misleading presuppositions.

2. *Ignore the existence of resources when defining a process.* The process definition is independent of the potential offered by people and machines. If the allocation of work to resources is already being considered when drawing up the process definition, one runs the risk that the resulting process will not be the best one possible. First list which tasks are required and in what order they should be carried out. Only then link the tasks to resources. In other words, do not allow yourself to be distracted by the traditional structure of the organization when designing a process. In all, we recognize four phases in the (re)design of a workflow: (1) *What?*, (2) *Why?*, (3) *How?*, and (4) *Whom?*. Figure 3.9 shows these phases diagrammatically.

During the first phase we select the process that needs to be redesigned. During the second we consider the objective of the process: what is its output, in terms of product delivered, and do we need this? During the third we determine the structure of the process. Only during the last phase do we focus upon allocating work to resources.

3. *As far as possible, make one person responsible for the processing of a case (case manager).* Processes supported by a workflow system can be quite complicated. For the client, it therefore is often very difficult to gauge the progress of a particular case. This is why it is sensible to appoint a manager for each case. He or she acts as a sort of buffer between

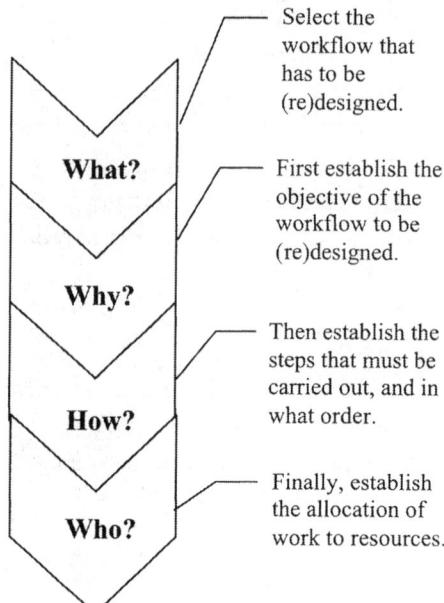

What? — Select the workflow that has to be (re)designed.

Why? — First establish the objective of the workflow to be (re)designed.

How? — Then establish the steps that must be carried out, and in what order.

Who? — Finally, establish the allocation of work to resources.

Figure 3.9
The four phases through which the (re)design of a workflow passes

the complicated process and the client. In doing so, it is important that the case manager behaves towards the client as if he or she is responsible for the entire process. This provides the client with a single point of contact, and the case manager feels more involved in the work. Note that the case manager is only responsible for the case itself. Other resources can be used to actually carry out the activities associated with the case.

4. *Check the need for each task.* Tasks are sometimes added for the sake of security: for example, monitoring tasks. Such tasks often are used as a stopgap to conceal a problem in one of the previous tasks. For the same reason, iterations should always be examined critically. In short, eliminate those tasks that add no value.

5. *Consider the scope of tasks.* A task is a logical unit of work. By combining separate tasks into one composite task, set-up times can be reduced. The involvement of the people performing them is also increased. However tasks should not be too large. Because a task always has to be performable in one go, without interruptions, "bite-size chunks" are desirable. Large tasks can also inhibit flexibility and make an advanced allocation of work impossible.

6. *Strive for the simplest possible process.* Complex process definitions lead to unmanageable processes. This is why it is important that a process not be unnecessarily complex. Processes can often be simplified by adding more "intelligence" to the tasks. If it is impossible to avoid a complex process, then it is essential to establish a clear hierarchical structure. When breaking down a process, it is important to ensure that tasks with a close relationship form part of the same subprocess. In addition, it is sensible to allow as few causal links as possible between different subprocesses. Ideally, each subprocess will have one entrance and one exit. However, the most critical consideration is that the process be understood by the people carrying out the work. If this is not the case, the result can be a difficult-to-manage process.

7. *Carefully weigh a generic process versus several versions of the same process.* Do not define a separate process for each type of case. Try to create a generic process that distinguishes between the various types of cases by using selective routing. Do not, though, attempt to handle two completely different types of cases in a single process. If a process begins with an OR-split which sends the case into a number of alternative subprocesses, then it is probably a good idea to use a number of separate subprocesses. Each of these will then correspond with a version of the same process.

8. *Carefully weigh specialization versus generalization.* The division of a generic task into two or more alternative tasks may have either a positive or a negative effect. One advantage can be that the tasks become better suited to the specific qualities of a resource. There can be drawbacks to specialization, though. It often detracts from the flexibility and accessibility of the process. It also can lead to monotonous work, which reduces motivation. Rather than specialization, the term *triage* is often used. This is the classification of cases in order to enable selective processing.

9. *As far possible, try to achieve parallel processing of tasks.* Always consider whether tasks can be performed in parallel. If two tasks can be carried out independently of one another, then it is very important that the process allows for their parallel execution. The unnecessary introduction of sequential order relationships results in longer completion times and the inefficient use of resources.

10. *Investigate the new opportunities opened up by recent developments in networking and (distributed) databases.* The elimination of physical barriers resulting from such developments as the computerization of documents often makes possible entirely new process structures. Tasks that previously had to be performed in sequence can be carried out in parallel following the introduction of, say, a workflow package.

11. *Treat geographically scattered resources as if they are centralized.*
The introduction of a workflow system lowers the physical barriers between the various sections of an organization. It makes it easier for two
organizational units to exchange work. If team A is struggling with a
flood of work, but team B is operating below capacity, it is logical to
transfer work from A to B. It is even better to treat geographically scattered resources as if they are centralized. This enables resources to be
allocated to those places where most of the work is waiting.

12. *Allow a resource to practice its specialty.* As mentioned earlier, it is
important to make use of a resource's specific qualities.

13. *As far as possible, allow a resource to perform similar tasks in succession.* By performing similar tasks one after the other, set-up times can
be reduced and the benefits of routine working can be exploited.

14. *Try to achieve as much flexibility as possible for the near future.*
When allocating work to resources, it is sensible to retain as much flexibility for the near future as possible.

15. *Allow a resource to work as much as possible on the same case.* If
an employee performs a number of successive tasks for a specific case, the
total processing time is usually shorter than if different employees carry
out those tasks. Less time is taken because the member of staff does not
have to "get used" to each new case.

Based upon the guidelines listed above, workflows can be designed that
result in the efficient and effective processing of cases. A number of these
guidelines highlight the fact that a balance needs to be struck between
two or more alternatives. In many cases, which should be chosen can
only be decided following a thorough analysis. Such an analysis is usually of quantitative aspects, with the emphasis being placed upon such
performance indicators as average completion time, level of service, and
utilization of capacity. There are various analytical techniques available
for establishing these performance indicators using a modeled workflow.
A number of these are addressed in the next chapter.

EXERCISES

Exercise 3.1   Insurance company
Consider the insurance company described in exercise 2.7.

(a) Make a resource classification with relations between roles (qualifications) and groups (organizational units).

(b) Assign a role and a group to each task in the process model.

Exercise 3.2   Complaints handling
Consider the complaints handling process described in exercise 2.8.

(a) Make a resource classification with relations between roles (qualifications) and groups (organizational units).
(b) Assign a role and a group to each task in the process model.

Exercise 3.3   Employment Office
Agency "*Job Shop*" accepts requests for new employees by companies all over the country. Requests can be sent by e-mail, by mail, or by phone to one of the agencies in Eindhoven and Leeuwarden. Handling these requests is a job for someone in the department of business relations (BR). For the Eindhoven agency this job is done by Johan in Leeuwarden Sietse, who is responsible for BR. The first thing being done is sending an acknowledgement back to indicate that the request has been received. Then "*Job Shop*" has several options: they always look in their database to find suitable people, but they can also place an advertisement in some of the greater papers in the country to ask for people, as well. Placing an ad is a job for those in public relations (PR): Jaap and Anke in Eindhoven, Rinske in Leeuwarden. The manager decides whether or not this option should be used. Being a manager is a job fulfilled by Ahmed (Eindhoven) and Dion (Leeuwarden).

The actual searching in the database is done by someone in recruitment. All candidates for the job get a marking that will be used later.

People who react to the ad can do this by phone, by completing a form (found at Internet), or by dropping off a letter with their data at the office. Someone from recruitment processes the data in the form/letter by adding it to the database and by marking candidates for the job. If someone uses the phone, a member from recruitment will interview this person to get his/her data for the database. Again, a marking is placed if the person fits the requirements for the job.

The Eindhoven recruitment team is formed by Annelies, Manja, and the people of both PR and BR. In Leeuwarden, Anja, Hakan, Rinske (also PR), and Sietse (also BR) take care of new people.

After some time, the deadline for a job expires and a candidate has to be chosen from the ones marked in the database. Reactions to the ad, if placed, will not be processed anymore from then on. One by one, the candidates will be called by someone in the recruitment team until someone has been found. In this call, she gets an invitation to come to the office to discuss the possible new job. Of course people may refuse to come. However, if someone agrees to come to the office, an appointment is made and she gets an interview with one of the employees (recruitment) of "*Job Shop*." Immediately after this interview an evaluation is made and the candidate is told whether or not she will be chosen. If no candidate can be found, or when no one is suitable for the job, a letter is sent to the company.

Once someone has been chosen, she gets a letter with all the data needed to prepare for the new job. This letter is composed by someone from recruitment. Also a letter is sent by BR to the company for which the new employee has been found. In this, all relevant data concerning the new employee is listed. Of course, the database will have to be updated in order to reflect the new status of this person. This is done after sending the letters, by the same person from recruitment who sent the letter.

Maintenance of the database in both agencies is done by Mahroud, the IT specialist.

(a) Make a resource classification with relations between roles (qualifications) and groups (organizational units).

(b) Construct a process model of the process sketched above.

Exercise 3.4   Have a nice flight with CRASH

We will look at the preparation of a flight plan for the aircraft of the company "CRASH" (*Cheap and Reliable Aerial Shipments*). This company transports freight for customers from place Y to place Z.

Each customer sends a form describing the freight and the wishes she has about it. Upon receipt of such a form, a secretary makes a copy of it. The original is taken to a loadmaster, who, with his knowledge of the capacity of all the company's aircraft, will decide which aircraft will be used. The copy is sent to the navigator. The navigator, responsible for setting out the flight plan, takes a flight plan paper and fills in the date, her data (name and employee number) and the client number. Then the navigator has to check the following things in sequence before planning the flight:

· What freight will be taken and, more important, where does it have to be delivered? Together with the loadmaster this will be discussed. The type of aircraft and its payload will influence the flight path: perhaps some extra stops are needed to refuel.

• What are the weather conditions? For this the navigator goes to the north side of the company's building to meet with someone in meteorology. Together they will discuss the weather for that day and that person will put the information on a map.

• There might be some exceptions: some areas have to be avoided because of military exercises, etc. At the south side of the building, the directors have their room. They know all about those exceptions and will tell the navigator what she needs to know. The same map is used to draw the areas for which exceptions hold.

Once the navigator has gathered these three pieces of information, she can start planning the flight in her room at the west side. For this she uses a special form, not the form she already has filled out in part. The reason for this is that she wants to be able to make corrections without spoiling the official flight plan. After that, she takes the flight plan to the directors. One of them will check this flight plan with other, already approved flight plans. This will ensure that collisions with other aircraft because of incorrect flight plans will be prevented. Also some mistakes the navigator might have made, however small the chances of that are, will be spotted then.

If the flight plan turns out to be unsafe, the navigator returns to her room to do the planning again and come up with an improved flight plan. This will be followed by another check with the directors, just as often as it takes to make the flight plan safe. Then both the navigator and the director will sign the flight plan, after it has been put on the official form by a secretary specially trained to do so.

Since the fuel has to be paid for by the company itself, a courier then has to take the flight plan to one of the company's logistics people (in another building two miles from where the navigator has her room). This person has to sign the flight plan to approve the use of fuel. Of course, he can refuse to sign. In that case, the refusal will be made clear to the navigator and a letter will be sent to the customer. In this letter, the company will send its excuses and explain why no acceptable flight plan could be produced. Of course, "CRASH" hopes to be of better service in the future.

However, if the person in logistics approves, a courier takes the flight plan back. Then the captain of the aircraft has to sign it. This is because she will be responsible for the aircraft every second of the flight. Again, the flight plan can be refused, with the same consequences as before. If the flight plan is accepted (by signature), the flight plan will be stored in the computer by one of the directors.

After a successful delivery (despite the company's name, most deliveries are!), the customer will also be sent a letter, accompanied by a bill. However, sometimes a crash does occur. Then an apologizing letter is sent to the customer. All letters to customers are composed and sent by a secretary.

Once a flight plan has been "released" for signing by logistics and the plane's captain, the navigator is available for planning another flight.

About the organization: most navigators are captains as well. Therefore all captains and navigators are united in the AIR division. (They say that AIR stands for "Aces with Incredible Reputations"; being humble is not their strength). Extra captains hired from KLM (Kaptains Looking for Money, an agency that "has" freelance pilots/captains) are also part of AIR, albeit temporarily. Ground support by the loadmasters, directors and meteorology people is covered by the SUPPORT division: SUPPort Of Reliable Transport. The logistics and secretary departments are part of CRASH, but since they couldn't come up with a good name, they don't have a group of their own. The couriers are hired from an agency close to the company.

(a) Construct a resource classification of CRASH, distinguishing roles and groups, using the techniques of the book.

(b) Construct a process model of the process sketched above. Define roles, and assign triggers and roles to tasks whenever appropriate.

(c) Analyze the process and investigate possible improvements.

4

Analyzing Workflows

4.1 Analysis Techniques

The introduction or modification of a business process can have far-reaching consequences. Because a process definition is the blueprint of such a process, it is vitally important that it contains no serious errors. The process should also be designed in such a way that the completion times of and capacity required for cases are kept as small as possible. For example, if two tasks can be carried out in parallel, it in general is sensible to ensure that the process allows this. After all, by "parallelizing" tasks, completion times usually can be reduced. Because the process definition is so important, it is useful to *analyze* it thoroughly prior to its enactment. In doing so, we differentiate between the analysis of (1) the *qualitative aspects* and (2) the *quantitative aspects* of workflows. The former mainly concern the *logical correctness* of the defined process, that is, the absence of anomalies such as "deadlocks" (when a case is "blocked" and no longer proceeds through the process) and "livelocks" (when a case becomes "stuck" in a never-ending loop). The quantitative aspects mainly concern the *performance* of the defined process. An analysis of the quantitative aspects focuses upon establishing the performance indicators, such as average completion time, level of service, and utilization of capacity.

In this chapter, we shall highlight a number of analysis techniques which can be extremely useful in the context of workflow management (see figure 4.1). We first introduce a simple technique designed to illustrate all the states attainable in a case. We then turn our attention to the errors that can be made when drawing up the definition of a process. We will show that, based upon the structure of the underlying Petri net, we

Figure 4.1
Analysis techniques can be applied to examine workflows both qualitatively and quantitatively

can decide whether a process definition is correct. In the second part of this chapter, we concentrate upon the analysis of quantitative aspects. Using a number of examples, we show how to improve the performance of existing processes. Finally, we study the subject of capacity planning.

4.2 Reachability Analysis

As we learned in chapter 2, we can define a process in terms of a Petri net. Figure 4.2 shows such a network.

A Petri net and its initial state determines which states are reachable and in what order they can be reached. (As we saw in chapter 2, the state of a Petri net corresponds with the distribution of tokens over places.) We therefore use a Petri net to specify the possible *behavior* of a modeled process. One way to illustrate the behavior is to draw up a so-called *reachability graph*.

This is a directed graph consisting of nodes and directed arrows. Each node represents an reachable state and each arrow a possible change of state. To illustrate this, we can examine the Petri net shown in figure 4.2. The possible states of this network are indicated using "triplets" (a, b, c), with a representing the number of tokens in the place *claim*, b the number in *under_consideration*, and c the number in *ready*. We therefore show

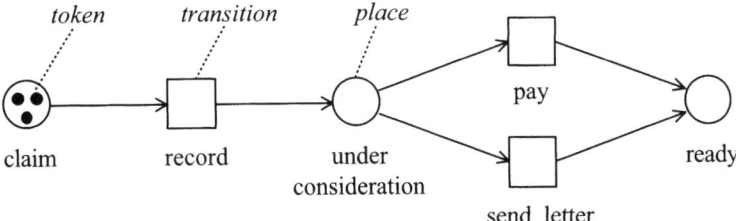

Figure 4.2
A classic Petri net

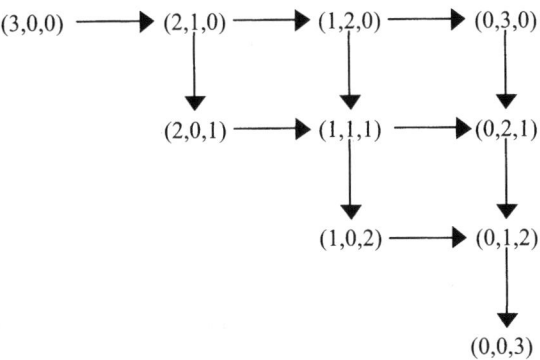

Figure 4.3
The reachability graph for the Petri net shown in figure 4.2

the initial state illustrated as (3,0,0). The reachability graph derived from this initial state is shown in figure 4.3.

Using this graph, we can deduce that there is a total of ten attainable states. Each node represents one of these. But not each reachable state actually has to occur. The state (1,2,0), for example, is reached only if the transition *record* fires for a second time when the state is (2,1,0). The number of arrows leading from a node indicates how many subsequent possible states there are. If there is more than one outgoing arrow, then the next state is not predetermined. We refer to this situation as a *nondeterministic choice*. If a node has no arrows leading from it, then it corresponds with an *end state*. This is a state in which no transition is enabled. The reachability graph in figure 4.3 shows that the Petri net beginning with the state (3,0,0) always results in the end state (0,0,3) after six firings.

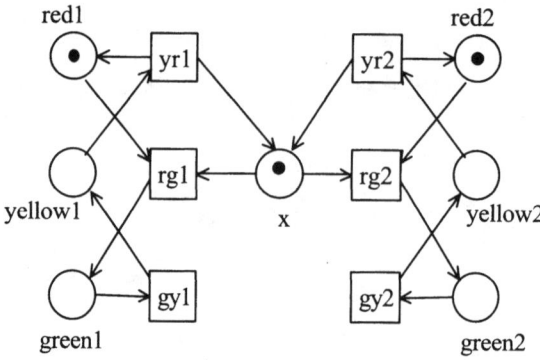

Figure 4.4
Two sets of traffic lights

We are paying considerable attention to the reachability graph because it embodies the behavior of the process being modeled. By drawing up the reachability graph for a number of cases, we can gain an insight into the operation of the Petri net tool. The fact that, given a diagram like figure 4.2 (that is, a Petri net and its initial state), we can compile a reachability graph, shows that Petri nets are an unambiguous and precise means of description. Because the operation of a Petri net is completely formalized, it therefore is also possible for a computer to construct the reachability graph.

As we saw in chapter 2, we can use Petri nets to describe processes with a repetitive nature. We used the network shown in figure 4.4 to model the traffic lights at the junction of two one-way streets. The two sets of lights operate in such a way that one is always at red.

When both sets of lights are red, there is a token in the place x. As soon as one of the lights changes to green, the token disappears from x and the other set of lights is blocked. Only when both sets have returned to red is the other light able to change to green. Using the reachability graph shown in figure 4.5, we can study whether the traffic lights do indeed operate in a safe way.

Each possible state in this case is represented by a septet. The figures show the number of tokens in *red1*, *green1*, *yellow1*, *red2*, *green2*, *yellow2*, and *x*, respectively. An inspection of the reachability graph shows that the traffic lights do indeed operate safely: in every possible state at least one of the sets of lights is red. However we can see that it

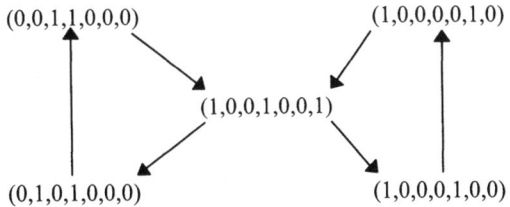

Figure 4.5
The reachability graph for the Petri net shown in figure 4.4

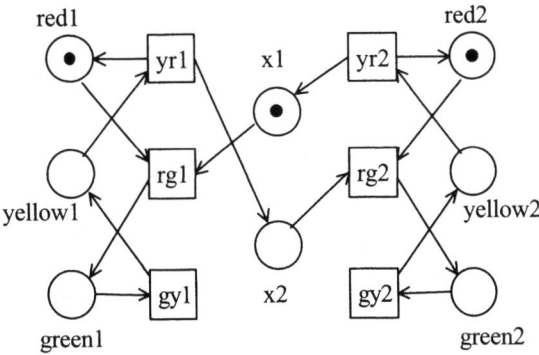

Figure 4.6
The two traffic lights now change to green alternately

is also possible that the first set always changes to green, while the second set remains constantly at red. We can avoid this by ensuring that each set of lights changes to green in turn. Figure 4.6 shows how this can be modeled.

It is easy to work out that the reachability graph associated with figure 4.6 has a total of six states. Just as we can verify the correct operation of traffic lights using the reachability graph, we can use it to determine the correctness of a workflow. Before we go further into checking correctness, we shall look at a number of typical errors that can occur when defining a process.

4.3 Structural Analysis

Before the introduction of advanced information systems—such as workflow systems—business processes generally had a simple structure.

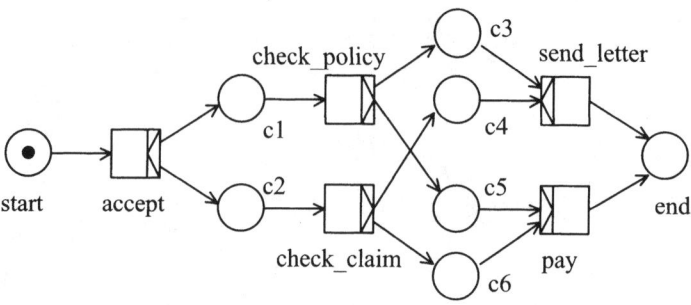

Figure 4.7
An example of an incorrect process

This was mainly due to the fact that a paper document was linked with each case and could physically only be in one place at any one time. The document acted as a sort of token which ensured that tasks were carried out sequentially. As a result of the many developments in information technology, however, it is now possible to arrange processes completely differently. By using databases and networks, information can be shared. Because different people can work on the same case at the same time, it is no longer necessary for tasks to be performed sequentially. Thanks to the "parallelization" of the business process, enormous reductions in completion times can be achieved. In the environment in which a workflow system operates, it therefore is often attractive to carry out tasks in parallel, as far as possible. But the use of sequential, parallel, selective, and iterative routing in the same process can make it very difficult to assess the correctness of the defined process. We can illustrate this using the simple example in figure 4.7.

At first sight, this appears to be a sensible process definition, with two checks being carried out in parallel following the acceptance of a claim. Based upon these checks, either a rejection letter is sent or a payment is made. However, owing to an incorrect combination of parallel and selective routing, errors have crept into this process definition. If *check_ policy* places a token in *c5* and *check_claim* a token in *c6*, *pay* will fire. This is the only scenario in which the case is completed correctly. If *check_policy* places a token in *c3* and *check_claim* a token in *c4*, then *send_letter* will fire twice. The consequence is that two tokens appear in *end*. If *check_policy* places a token in *c3* and *check_claim* a token in *c6*,

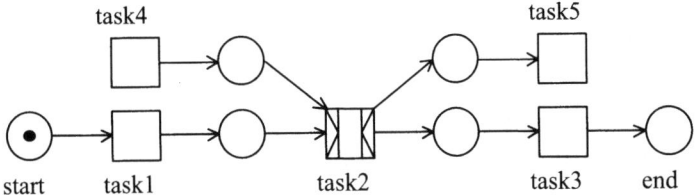

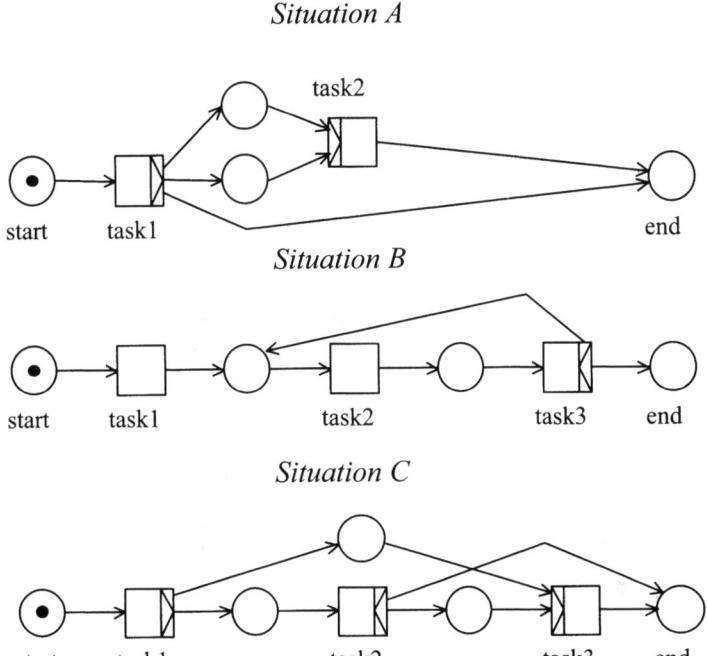

Figure 4.8
Four flawed situations

then *send_letter* will only fire once, but one token will remain in *c6*. The same happens if *check_policy* places a token in *c5* and *check_claim* a token in *c4*.

Figure 4.8 illustrates four situations that, as in the previous example, can result in incorrect processes. Using this figure, we can highlight a number of common *errors* that occur during the definition of a process:

1. *Tasks without input and/or output conditions.* When a task has no input conditions, it is unclear when it may be performed. When a task has no output conditions, it does not contribute to the successful completion of a case and so it can be dropped. Situation A in figure 4.8 contains one task without input conditions (*task4*) and one without output conditions (*task5*).

2. *Dead tasks: tasks that can never be carried out.* It is obvious that a process definition containing "dead" tasks is undesirable. In situation B, *task2* can never be performed; the same applies to *task3* in situation D.

3. *Deadlock: jamming a case before the condition "end" is reached.* If *task1* in situation B places a token in one of the two uppermost places, then the case will wait "ad infinitum" for *task2*. Only if *task1* delivers a token directly to the place *end* will this deadlock be avoided. In situation D a token can be "jammed" waiting for *task3*.

4. *Livelock: trapping a case in an endless cycle.* In situation C, every case will remain "ad infinitum" in the cycle consisting of *task2* and *task3*. There thus exists iterative routing without an opportunity to escape.

5. *Activities still take place after the condition "end" is reached.* A good process definition has a clear beginning (the condition *start*) and end (the condition *end*). Once the condition *end* is reached, no more tasks should be carried out. In situation C, *task2* and *task3* will be fired after the condition *end* is reached. In this way, an infinite number of tokens will reach the place *end*. This is clearly an undesirable situation.

6. *Tokens remain in the process definition after the case has been completed.* Once a token appears in the place *end*, all other references to the case must have disappeared. In situation D, if the case is completed as a result of the firing of *task2*, there will remain a token in one of the places before *task3*.

The above shows that, without any knowledge of the actual content of the process being defined, we can identify a number of typical errors in a given process definition. These are connected with the routing of cases. In order to computerize the check for these errors, we need a precise notion of correctness.

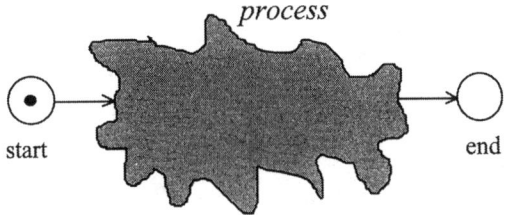

Figure 4.9
A process has one entrance and one exit

4.3.1   Soundness

In the remainder of this book, we use the following minimum requirement that every process must meet:

A process contains no unnecessary tasks and every case submitted to the process must be completed in full and with no references to it (that is, case tokens) remaining in the process.

We call a process that fulfills this minimum requirement *sound*. We shall formulate the *soundness* property of a process precisely using figure 4.9.

A workflow process defined in terms of a Petri net has a single input place *start* and a single output place *end*. Such a Petri net only makes sense if each transition (task) or place (condition) lies on a directed path from *start* to *end*. In other words, there should be no "loose" tasks and conditions. Thanks to this requirement, each task (or condition) can be reached from the place *start* by following a number of arrows, and the place *end* is always reachable from each task (or condition) by following a number of arrows. A transition that is not on a path from *start* to *end* does not contribute to the successful completion of the process or can be activated at any time. In this section, we only consider Petri nets satisfying this requirement. These Petri nets are called *workflow nets* (WF-nets).

A workflow net satisfies some syntactical requirements. However, it is still possible to have workflow nets that have anomalies such as potential deadlocks and the inability to terminate. Therefore we define a workflow net to be sound if, and only if, it fulfills the following three requirements:

1. For each token put in the place *start*, one (and only one) token eventually appears in the place *end*;

2. When the token appears in the place *end*, all the other places are empty; and

3. For each transition (task), it is possible to move from the initial state to a state in which that transition is enabled.

The first requirement means that every case will be completed successfully over a period of time. The second requirement means that once the case is completed, no references to it will remain in the process. If we combine the first two requirements, we come to the conclusion that—based upon the state illustrated in figure 4.9—there exists only one final state: that is, one with precisely one token in the place *end*. The last requirement excludes "dead tasks"; that is, each task can—in principle—be carried out.

The definition of soundness assumes a notion of *fairness*; that is, if a task can potentially be executed, then it is not possible to postpone its execution indefinitely. Consider for example iterative routing. Although, in principle, it is possible to repeat a part of the process infinitely often, we assume that iteration does not necessarily violate the soundness requirement. Similarly, we assume that two tasks cannot "starve" a third task indefinitely. If we would not make this assumption, any process with selective or iterative routing would not be sound.

How can we establish whether a given process corresponds to a sound workflow net? To do this, we must first check whether the Petri net representing the process is a workflow net. This can be checked by examining the structure of the process. Checking whether the process is sound is more involved. We can check the three soundness requirements using a reachability graph starting with the initial state in which there is only one token in the place *start*. To check the last requirement, we examine whether there is for each task a state transition in the reachability graph which corresponds to the firing of that task. The first two requirements are checked by confirming that the reachability graph has only one final state, and that this is one in which there is precisely one token in *end*. The requirements for correctness just formulated therefore can be checked entirely automatically by inspecting the reachability graph.

There are, however, two drawbacks attached to this approach. First, the construction of the reachability graph for large-scale processes can take up a lot of computer time. It therefore is almost impossible to perform this analysis without a computer. Second, the reachability graph provides little support in repairing a nonsound process definition. Note that the reachability graph is infinite if tokens can accumulate in a place. It is possible to use variants of the reachability graph, such as the so-called coverability graph, which allows for the detection of such unbounded behavior (see appendix). Nevertheless, these "brute force" approaches can be quite time consuming and do not provide good diagnostics.

Fortunately, there are techniques available for Petri nets that do not suffer from these drawbacks. We do not have the space here to discuss these techniques in depth. However, we shall outline two alternative methods of determining whether or not a process is sound. The first method is based on advanced computer support; the second one can be used manually.

4.3.2   Method with computer support

The first method to determine soundness translates the soundness property to two well-known properties which have been investigated for decades. In order to analyze a process defined in terms of a Petri net, we add an additional transition to the network: t^*. This has *end* as its input point and *start* as its output point. The net without transition t^* is called the workflow net; the net with this transition is called the short-circuited net. With this addition, the soundness of the workflow net corresponds with two well-known properties: *liveness* and *boundedness* of the short-circuited net. A Petri net is *live* when it is possible to reach—for each transition t and from every state reachable from the initial one—a state in which transition t is enabled. In a live Petri net, therefore, it remains possible to fire every transition an arbitrary number of times. A Petri net is *bounded* when there is an upper limit to the number of tokens in each place. In other words, it is not possible for the number of tokens in a place to rise without limit if the process is started in the initial state. The traffic lights modeled in figures 4.4 and 4.6 are live and bounded.

Liveness and boundedness are properties which have been researched extensively during the past thirty years. As a result, efficient algorithms and tools are available to analyze them. A process is sound if its Petri net, with the additional transition t^*, is live and bounded. The correctness of a defined process thus can be verified by using standard tools. For a number of important subcategories—including the so-called *free-choice Petri nets*—liveness and boundedness of a network can be established in polynomial time. Thanks to the many results achieved in the field of Petri-net theory, the soundness of a process can hence be determined efficiently. When a process is not sound, diagnostics can be generated that indicate *why* this is the case.

The above is merely an illustration of the many analysis possibilities offered by the Petri net representation of a given process. For more information, we refer to the appendix of this book and the very extensive literature about Petri nets.

4.3.3   Method without computer support

The translation of soundness to liveness and boundedness allows for the application of efficient analysis techniques. Unfortunately, the translation is not very intuitive and requires computer support to be relevant. Therefore we propose an alternative method which is easy to apply without computer support or deep theoretical knowledge. We add one requirement to "good" workflow nets in addition to soundness: we will require that the workflow nets are also *safe*, which means that the number of tokens in each place will never be larger than one. (This means that they are bounded by value one.) It is often easy to check if a net is safe by inspection of the net structure. The method is based on an important property that is very easy to understand in an intuitive way:

If we have two sound and safe workflow nets V and W and we have a task t in V which has precisely one input and one output place, then we may replace task t in V by W and then the resulting workflow net is sound and safe again.

In figure 4.10 this replacement is illustrated.

This property is intuitively clear because a sound workflow net behaves like a transition: it consumes one token from its input place and, after a while, it produces one token in its output place. The environment therefore will not discover the replacement of t by W. The safety of the nets is required in order to avoid the situation that in W two or more tokens will be active at the same time, which may violate the soundness of W.

This replacement property is proved in the appendix. Here we focus on the application of this property. The main idea is as follows:

Suppose we have some set of sound and safe workflow nets, called "building blocks," to start with. If it is possible to derive the workflow

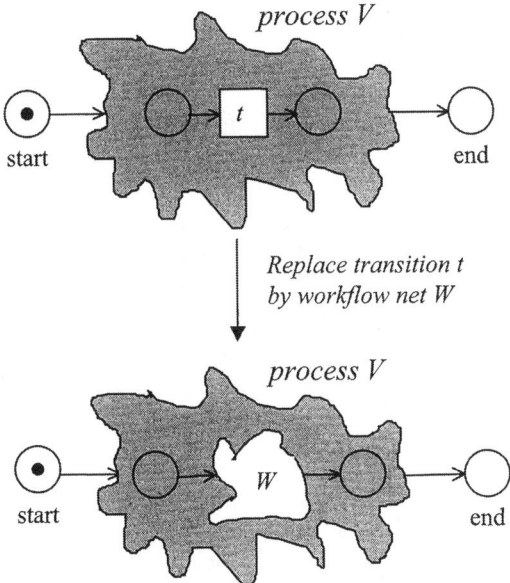

Figure 4.10
If a transition is replaced by a sound workflow net, then the resulting workflow net is also sound (assuming safeness)

net under consideration by a sequence of substitutions of nets from this set of building blocks, then we have proved that our net is sound and save as well.

To illustrate this method we start with a small set of nets for which the soundness and safety is obvious. See figure 4.11. The workflow nets correspond to the typical constructs introduced in chapter 2. There are of course other sets of building blocks possible but this set is already quite powerful.

First we show how we can apply the method. Consider the workflow net shown in figure 4.12.

For this net we can find the derivation presented in the subsequent figures. The method starts with the basic building block shown in figure 4.13.

In the first step, the AND construct is applied to put task b in parallel with task a. The resulting workflow net is shown in figure 4.14. Note that we simply applied the AND construct shown in figure 4.11 with $x = a$ and $y = b$.

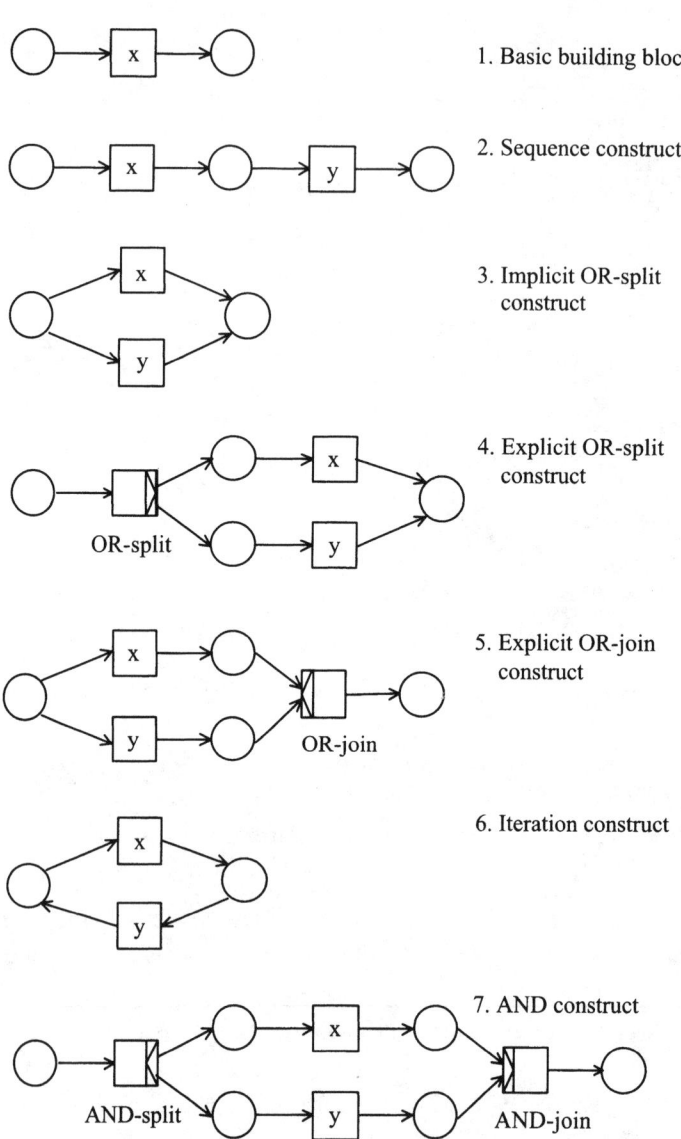

1. Basic building block

2. Sequence construct

3. Implicit OR-split construct

4. Explicit OR-split construct

OR-split

5. Explicit OR-join construct

OR-join

6. Iteration construct

7. AND construct

AND-split

AND-join

Figure 4.11
Sound and safe nets

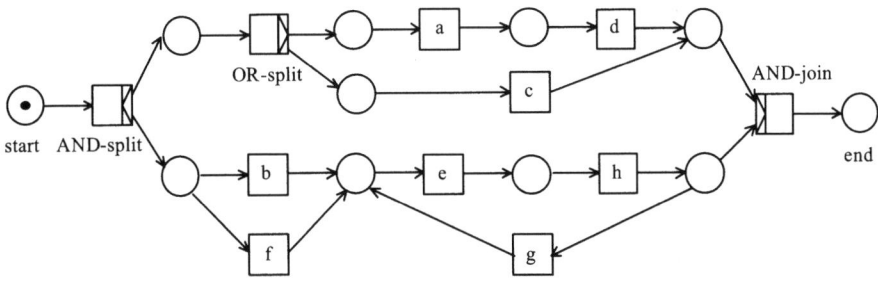

Figure 4.12
A safe and sound process

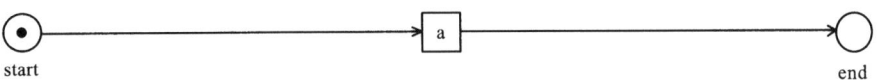

Figure 4.13
Apply the AND construct to a (Step 1)

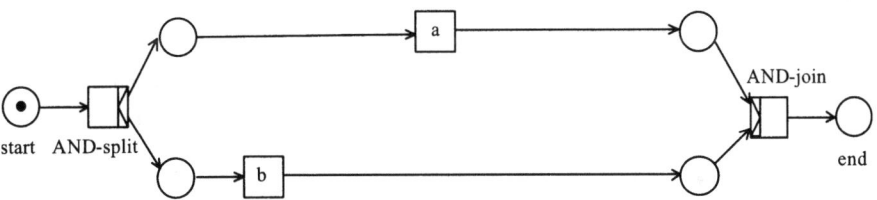

Figure 4.14
Apply the explicit OR-split construct to a (Step 2)

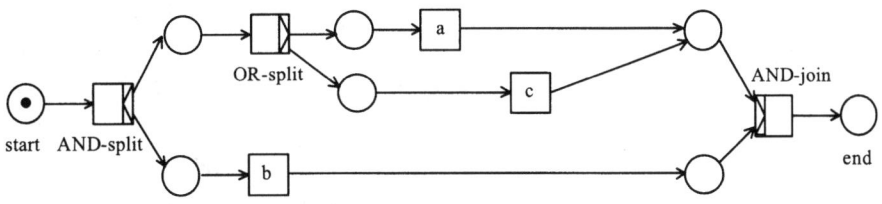

Figure 4.15
Apply the sequence construct to a (Step 3)

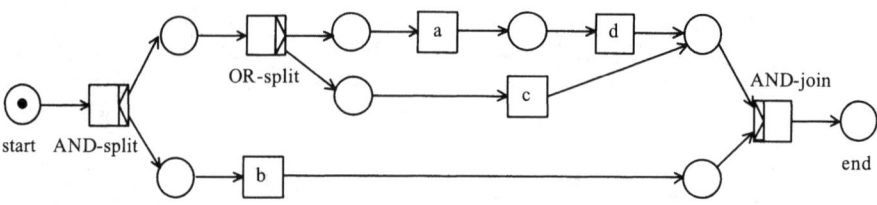

Figure 4.16
Apply the sequence construct to b (Step 4)

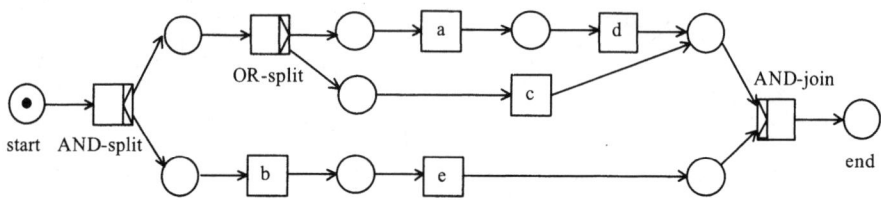

Figure 4.17
Apply the implicit OR-split construct to b (Step 5)

In the second step, the explicit OR-split construct is applied to a, that is, the explicit OR-split "pattern" shown in figure 4.11 is applied with $x = a$ and $y = c$. The resulting workflow net is shown in figure 4.15.

In the third step, we apply the sequence construct: task a is followed by task d.

Then the sequence construct is applied to b.

In the fifth step an implicit OR-split construct is applied to b with the addition of task f as result.

Then the iteration construct is applied to task e. As a result, task g is added to the workflow net.

Finally the sequence construct is applied to task e. The resulting workflow net shown in figure 4.20 is exactly the process we wanted to construct. Since we just applied the design patterns shown in figure 4.11, this workflow net is guaranteed to be safe and sound.

As we can see there can be more than one derivation for a particular net. In the example we could have interchanged steps 3 and 4. Not all sound and safe nets have a derivation as is shown in the example presented in figure 4.21.

The reason that we cannot find a derivation here is that two paths that originated at one AND-split should come together in the same AND-join

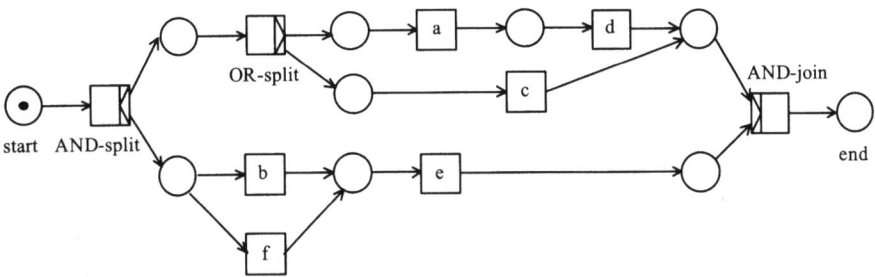

Figure 4.18
Apply the iteration construct to e (Step 6)

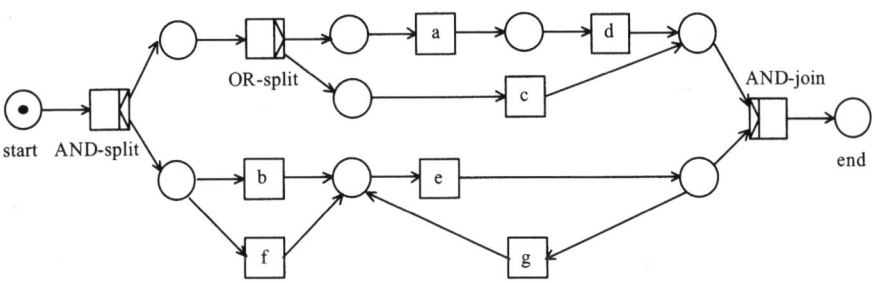

Figure 4.19
Apply the sequence constrcut to e (Step 7)

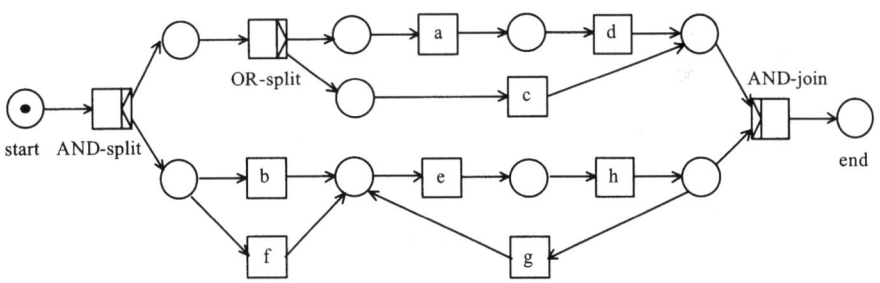

Figure 4.20
The complete process

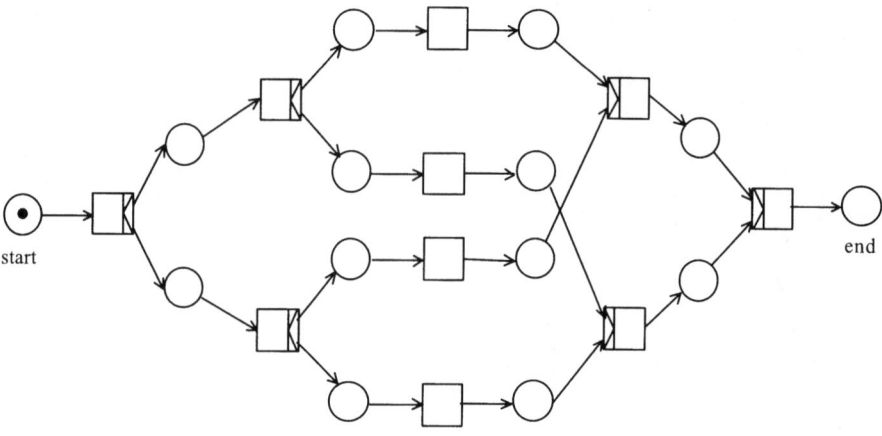

Figure 4.21
A process that cannot be constructed using the standard constructs shown in figure 4.11

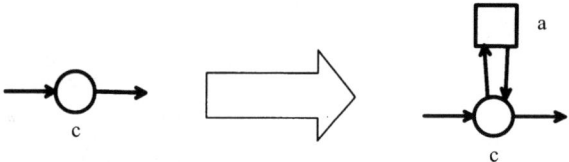

Figure 4.22
The loop construct

due to the replacement rules presented in figure 4.11. This is not the case in figure 4.21. This example shows that in case we cannot find a derivation for a particular workflow net, it is not allowed to conclude that the net is not sound and safe: the workflow net shown in figure 4.21 is both safe and sound but it is not possible to construct this net using the standard design patterns shown in figure 4.11.

Note that it is always permissible to add a sound and safe net to our collection of building blocks, so also the net shown in figure 4.21. A particular extension of our replacement rules is a rather trivial one: every place (excluding source and sink places) may be replaced by a place and a task for which this place is the input as well as the output place. In figure 4.22 this transformation is represented.

Suppose that we have found a derivation for a net and that we have to modify the net during a design process. If the modifications are only

Table 4.1
Each Step in a Derivation

step	set of tasks	selected task	used block	new task
1	a	a	AND	b
2	a,b	a	explicit OR-split	c
3	a,b,c	a	sequence	d
4	a,b,c,d	b	sequence	e
5	a,b,c,d,e	b	implicit OR-split	f
6	a,b,c,d,e,f	e	iteration	g
7	a,b,c,d,e,f,g	e	sequence	h

replacements of tasks by sound and safe building blocks, everything is fine. But suppose that we have to do another modification: is it necessary to find a new derivation from scratch? The answer is no. We may always go back in the derivation and take another sequence of steps from there after which we continue with the rest of the former sequence. To clarify this we note that in each replacement rule treated so far, we replaced one transition by two other ones with exactly one input and one output place (constructs shown in figure 4.11). In each case the number of transitions with one input and one output increased exactly with one. If we identify the replaced transition with one of the new transitions (with one input and one output) then we have to give the other one a new, unique name. So we can characterize each step in a derivation by a triplet: the selected task, the used building block, and the name of the new task. In the derivation shown in figures 4.13 through 4.20, all tasks have a name. In the table 4.1 we represent this derivation in tabular form.

It is easy to verify that the result of this derivation is the net with tasks $\{a, b, c, d, e, f, g, h\}$ shown in figure 4.20. Note that we do not mention tasks just added for routing purposes, that is, *AND-split*, *AND-join*, and *OR-split* are omitted.

Suppose that we want to extend the workflow nets shown in figure 4.20 with one additional task x to obtain the workflow net shown in figure 4.23.

Note that task x is added by introducing an implicit OR-split. As was argued before we can use the former derivation and simply add a

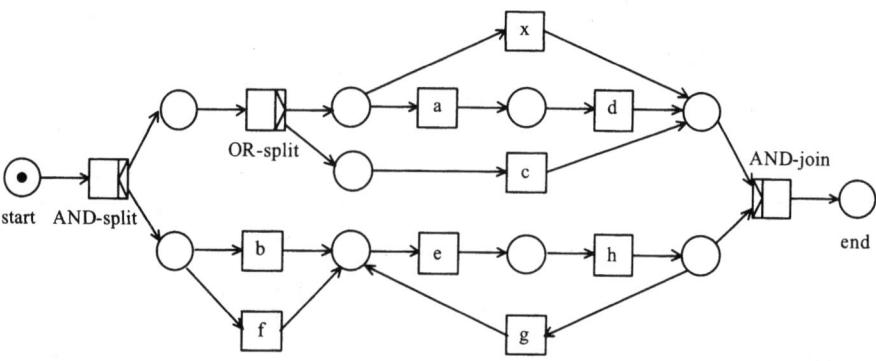

Figure 4.23
An alternative process with one additional task *x*

step between 2 and 3 (step 2.5). After this modification we can continue the derivation as before which results in the net with tasks $\{a, b, c, d, e, f, g, h, x\}$ shown in figure 4.23. Table 4.2 shows this derivation. Using this simple technique we can construct a large set of sound and safe workflow nets.

4.4   Performance Analysis

As well as the correctness of a defined workflow, we are also interested in its *performance*. By this, we mean such quantitative aspects as completion times of cases, the number of cases which can be processed per time unit, the utilization of staff, and the percentage of cases that can be completed within a preset, standard time. To gain insight into the performance of a defined workflow, various analysis techniques can be used. The three techniques most commonly used in this respect are as follows:

1. *Markovian analysis*. Based upon a given workflow, it is possible to generate a Markov chain automatically. This can be used to analyze particular aspects of a workflow. Such a chain contains the possible states of a case and the probability of transitions between them. In fact, the Markov chain is a reachability graph with the probability of transitions added to it. These probabilities are determined based upon measured or expected properties of a case type. Various properties can be established using a Markov chain, for example, what are the chances of a case taking a particular route through a process. By expanding Markov chains with cost and time aspects, a range of performance indicators can be generated. The disadvantage of this approach is that not every aspect

Table 4.2
Each Step in a Derivation (with 2.5)

step	set of tasks	selected task	used block	new task
1	a	a	AND	b
2	a,b	a	explicit OR-split	c
2.5	a,b,c	a	implicit OR-split	x
3	a,b,c,x	a	sequence	d
4	a,b,c,d,x	b	sequence	e
5	a,b,c,d,e,x	b	implicit OR-split	f
6	a,b,c,d,e,f,x	e	iteration	g
7	a,b,c,d,e,f,g,x	e	sequence	h

can be incorporated into the analysis. Markov-chain analysis can also be very time-consuming (if not intractable).

2. *Queueing theory.* Queueing theory is intended for the analysis of systems in which the emphasis is placed upon such performance indicators as waiting times, completion times, and utilization of capacity. It therefore is quite a logical way to analyze workflows. In a workflow, there may be queues of cases waiting for resources that cannot process a particular inflow of cases immediately. If we are interested in the formation of a single queue for a number of resources of equal value, then we can confine ourselves to a system consisting of one queue. There are many results available for the analysis of a single queue, which are in general simply to apply. If we wish to evaluate the entire workflow, then we need to consider a network of queues. For queueing networks, some questions can be answered by mathematical methods. Unfortunately, many of the assumptions used in queueing theory are not valid for workflow processes. For example, in the presence of parallel routing, it is often impossible to apply the results obtained from queueing theory.

3. *Simulation.* Simulation is a very flexible analysis technique. It almost always is possible to analyze a workflow using it. In fact, simulation boils down to the following of a path in the reachability graph. In doing so, particular choices are made based upon various probability distributions. Because simulation is nothing more than the repeated execution of a process with the aid of a computer, it is a technique that is accessible to people without a mathematical background. Simulation therefore results in a better insight into the operation of the process being modeled. Because most simulation tools offer an animation option, the workflow can

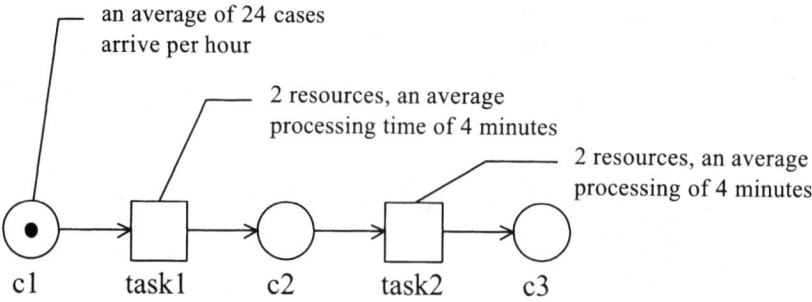

Figure 4.24
Situation 1

be tracked graphically. Moreover simulation can be used to answer a wide range of questions. It is also easy to extend a simulation model with a new aspect (for example, faults). However, the establishment and analysis of a model for a detailed simulation can be a time-consuming affair. Moreover, the careful processing of simulation results requires thorough statistical knowledge.

In this book, simulation is the main analysis technique. The reason for confining ourselves just to one analysis technique is that simulation usually is the only tool supported by the workflow management system. And when we examine the analysis techniques used in BPR, we again see that simulation usually is the only tool available for carrying out quantitative analyses. To illustrate the use of an analysis technique like simulation, we use the process definition shown in figure 4.24.

As figure 4.24 shows, the process consists of two tasks to be performed sequentially. The average number of new cases that arrive at the process per hour is 24. The average time between two successive arrivals therefore is 2.5 minutes. The average time required to carry out both *task1* and *task2* is 4 minutes each. For each task, 2 resources are devoted exclusively to completing the work item associated with it. These therefore are highly inflexible resources, which can work on only one task. Based upon the figures just given, we can calculate that the average level of resource utilization, that is, the number of arrivals per time unit divided by the number that can be served per time unit, is 80 percent: on average, a resource spends 80 percent of its time working on a task for a particular case. The resource is idle for the remaining 20 percent of the time.

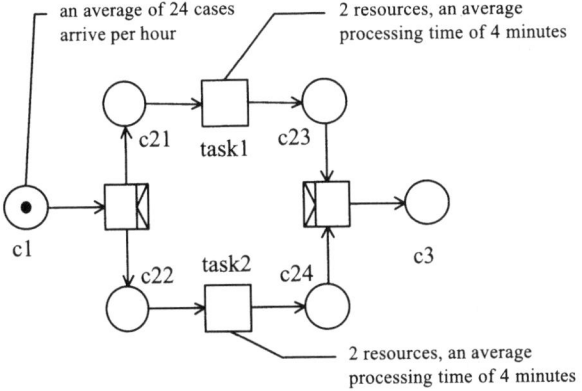

Figure 4.25
Situation 2

We can now ask ourselves what the average completion time for a case is. In order to determine this, we need to know more about the arrival pattern of new cases and the processing time. For the sake of convenience, we shall assume that the interarrival times are distributed in a negative exponential way. On this hypothesis, it can be determined using either simulation or queueing theory that the average completion time is approximately 22.2 minutes. In other words, it takes an average of 22.2 minutes for a case to move from place $c1$ to place $c3$. But of these 22.2 minutes, an average of only 8 minutes is spent on actually working on the case. The remaining 14.2 minutes are waiting time. In this case, therefore, the average waiting time is actually longer than the processing time. In fact, this is actually the case in many real-life situations. Consider, for example, the time spent on waiting to see a doctor. In many administrative processes, things can be even worse: actual processing times are only a small fraction of the total completion time.

As indicated in one of the guidelines for developing workflows, it is sensible—where possible—to perform tasks in parallel. Figure 4.25 shows the process that could be used if it were possible to carry out the two tasks for each case simultaneously. In this situation, the average level of resource utilization remains 80 percent—after all, the supply of cases and the average processing time have not changed. However, the average completion time can be significantly reduced in this way. Using simulation, we can show that the average completion time is now approxi-

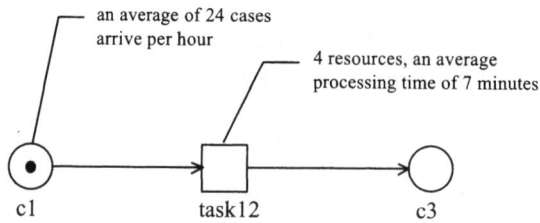

an average of 24 cases
arrive per hour

4 resources, an average
processing time of 7 minutes

c1   task12   c3

Figure 4.26
Situation 3

mately 15 minutes. By performing tasks in parallel, we can in this instance achieve a considerable reduction in completion time with the same resources.

It can sometimes be useful to combine two tasks into one larger task. Figure 4.26 shows a process in which *task1* and *task2* have been fused into a single *task12*. The average processing time for this new task is 7 minutes. We therefore have assumed that it takes 1 minute less to perform the combined task than to carry out the two original tasks. This reduction is explained by the elimination of set-up time. As a result of the shorter processing time, the average level of resource-capacity utilization has fallen to 70 percent. Moreover, the completion time has dropped dramatically, to an average of 9.5 minutes. So for each case there is now an average waiting time of 2.5 minutes. Compared with the original average waiting time of 14.2 minutes, we thus observe a considerable improvement, which is primarily attributable to increased resource flexibility. The new *task12* can be performed by each of the 4 resources. In contrast to the previous situation, each of the resources is busy as long as there is a case to be carried out.

To illustrate the positive influence of resource flexibilization, consider the original process shown in figure 4.27. In this process the two tasks again have to be carried out sequentially. However in this case the resources are not linked to a specific task: each can perform both *task1* and *task2*. As a result, the average completion time is only 14.0 minutes. Compared with the original situation, the average waiting time has fallen from 14.2 to 6 minutes.

Thus far we have assumed that the cases are indistinguishable from one another. In other words, we do not know whether the processing of a particular case will take little or much time. Figure 4.28, though, shows

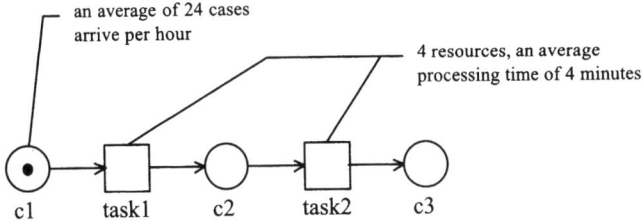

Figure 4.27
Situation 4

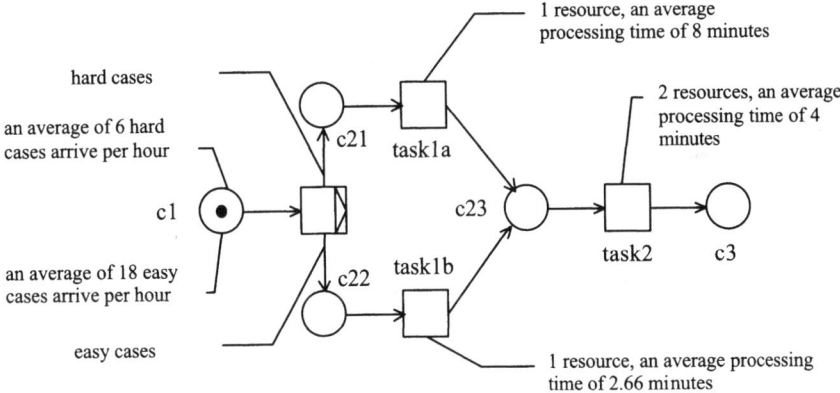

Figure 4.28
Situation 5

a situation in which we can differentiate between "easy" and "hard" cases. Performing *task1* for an easy case takes an average of 2.66 minutes, whereas for a hard case it takes an average of 8 minutes. On average, 25 percent of the cases are classified as hard, 75 percent as easy. In figure 4.28, we have tried to make use of this information. A special resource has been assigned to perform *task1* for hard cases. Besides, there is also a special resource to perform *task1* for easy cases. The idea is that the total average completion time can be reduced by separating the two flows. This is the principle also known as *triage*. In this case, however, it has disastrous results: the average completion time rises to no less than 31.1 minutes. So there is considerable worsening of the situation.

There are instances when triage can have a beneficial effect, though. Consider, for example, the "baskets only" checkout in a supermarket. (Triage is a term which existed long before the rise of BPR and WFM. It is also used to describe the selection and prioritization of war or disaster casualties according to the nature and seriousness of their injuries.) There are two circumstances in which triage can be useful: (1) when the allocation of specialized resources reduces the average processing time, and (2) when small clients no longer have to wait for large ones to be processed, which reduces the overall average waiting time. The reason that triage has a negative effect in figure 4.28 is that the flexibility of the resources is reduced. For example, only one resource can perform *task1* for an easy case. This example shows that thorough quantitative analysis is often required to reach a well-considered workflow design.

The introduction of triage in a supermarket (the "baskets only" checkout) usually shortens the overall completion time because those clients with only a few items do not have to wait behind those with a lot of items. In fact, triage operates in this case as a *prioritization rule*. In general, we find that triage leads to short completion times when easy cases are actually handled earlier than hard ones. If this is not the case, longer completion times will result. However, we can also apply a prioritization rule without using triage (in other words, without introducing a special queue). Figure 4.29 shows a situation in which for each task the easy cases (those with an average processing time of 2.66 minutes) are given priority over the hard ones (those with an average processing time of 8 minutes). With the aid of simulation, we can show that this results in an average completion time of approximately 14 minutes. So prioritization rules can also deliver considerable savings in completion time. Figure 4.30 lists all the situations again in summary.

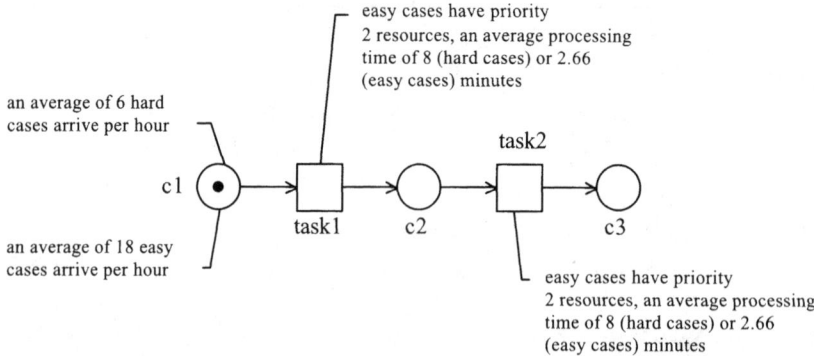

Figure 4.29
Siutation 6

The above shows that we can use an analysis technique like simulation to support the design of a workflow. Depending upon the workflow's design, we have seen the average waiting time for a case vary from 2.5 minutes (situation 3) to more than 23 minutes (situation 5). Which design is preferable depends upon the circumstances. There are, however, three guidelines that apply in most situations.

1. *When possible, perform tasks in parallel.* The implementation of parallel processing generally results in short completion times.

2. *Strive for high resource flexibility.* Ensure that resources can perform as many tasks as possible. The use of flexible resources results in higher levels of resource utilization and shorter completion times.

3. *When possible, handle cases in order of processing time.* In general, it is sensible to give cases that have a short processing time priority over those with a longer one. This can be done using triage or prioritization rules.

These guidelines illustrate the fact that there are considerable similarities between the structure and management of logistical and production systems. In fact, a workflow system is a logistical management system. It therefore is important that, when designing workflows, one bears in mind the principles, methods, and techniques which have been developed for structuring and managing logistical and production systems.

4.5   Capacity Planning

Thus far we always have assumed that the number of resources in each resource class is fixed. In practice, of course, this is not the case. Employees may fall ill, go on vacation, or leave the company. The

Situation	Description	Average completion time	Average processing time	Average waiting time
Situation 1	Sequential	22.2	8.0	14.2
Situation 2	Parallel	15	4	11
Situation 3	Composition	9.5	7.0	2.5
Situation 4	Flexibilization	14.0	8.0	6.0
Situation 5	Triage	31.1	8.0	23.1
Situation 6	Prioritization	14.0	8.0	6.0

Figure 4.30
A summary of the performances in the six situations described

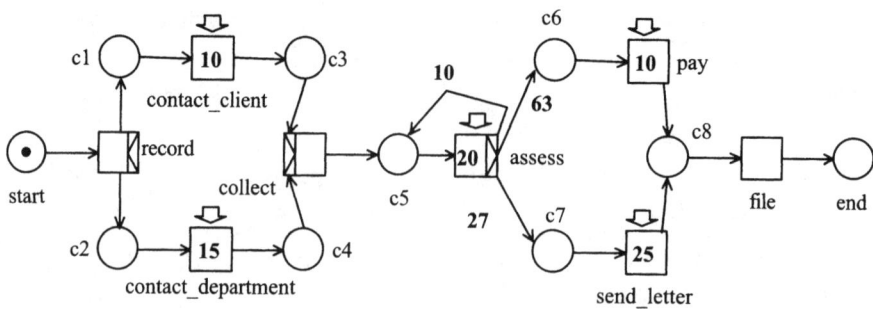

Figure 4.31
The process "handle complaint," showing the average processing time per task

number of staff may also vary according to seasonal factors. Consider, for example, travel insurance sales, which are clearly subject to seasonal influences. This needs to be taken into account when establishing staff allocation. In certain industries we also observe that the supply of new cases follows a clear pattern each week. So the *capacity plan* is always based upon a particular *capacity requirement*. The plan shows what resources, and of which type, are needed for each period. Capacity planning may be both short term and long term. In the short term, such factors as sick leave, small fluctuations in the supply of work, days off, overtime, and the hiring of temporary staff play an important role. In the longer term, demand forecasts, seasonal influence, machinery purchases, and staff recruitment policy enter the picture.

If we have a forecast of the supply of new cases, it is easy to estimate the capacity requirement. To illustrate this, we shall use a variant on the process *handle complaint* introduced in the previous chapter. Figure 4.31 shows the average processing time for each task.

It is assumed that the time taken to perform those tasks that require no resources is negligible. For the others, the average processing time in minutes is shown. For example, the task *assess* takes an average of 20 minutes. In general, 63% of the cases have been assessed positively at the end of this task, and 27% negatively. In the remaining 10% of cases a further assessment is required. Note that task *assess* may be executed an arbitrary number of times. The average number of times that asses is executed per complaint is 1.111 (see section 4.5.1). Eventually 70% are assessed positively, and 30% negatively. If we assume that 50 new cases

Task	Average number per day	Average processing time	Average number of minutes
record	50	0	0
contact_client	50	10	500
contact_dept.	50	15	750
collect	50	0	0
assess	56	20	1111
pay	35	10	350
send_letter	15	25	375
file	50	0	0

Figure 4.32
The capacity required per task

arrive each day, then we can calculate the capacity requirement for each task. Figure 4.32 shows that *assess* requires the most capacity.

A case is assessed an average of 1.111 times, because 10% of them require a second assessment. From an input of 50 cases, therefore, an average of approximately 56 assessments is required. The capacity requirement per task is easy to calculate in this case. In more extensive processes with a large number of iterations, this can be rather more complicated. Fortunately, based upon the process definition it is possible to automatically generate a Markov chain to calculate the capacity requirement for each task.

Based upon the capacity requirement per task, we can calculate the capacity requirement of each resource class. After all, we know from which resource class a required resource will come. As mentioned in the previous chapter, there are four resource classes in this case: *Employee, Assessor, Complaints,* and *Finances.* A resource belongs either to *Complaints* or to *Finances,* but not to both. Each resource that belongs to the resource class *Assessor* is automatically a member of the resource class *Employee.* The task *pay* is the only one requiring a resource from the resource class *Finances.* The other tasks always require a resource from the resource class *Complaints.* Moreover, the task *assess* is the only one that requires a resource from the resource class *Assessor.* Based upon this information, figure 4.33 shows the capacity requirement per resource class.

Figure 4.33 also shows the number of resources required at two particular levels of capacity utilization. When this is 80%, the complaints

Resource class	Average number of minutes	Number of resources at 80% of capacity	Number of resources at 60% of capacity
Employee	1975	5.14	6.86
Assessor	1111	2.90	3.86
Complaints	2736	7.13	9.50
Finances	350	0.91	1.22

Figure 4.33
The capacity requirement per resource class

department requires 8 people. Of these, at least 3 must be assessors. Because resource classes overlap, we must interpret the figures in figure 4.33 carefully. For example, every resource in the resource class *Assessor* also belongs to the resource class *Employee*. However, the figures in the row for the category *Employee* only refer to those employees who do not work as assessors. If we compare the numbers in figure 4.33 with the resources specified in the previous chapter, we see that the complaints department is understaffed for an inflow of 50 cases per day. On the other hand, the finance department has excess capacity.

4.5.1   Method to calculate capacity requirement

For figure 4.31 it is straightforward to calculate the capacity requirements listed in figures 4.32 and 4.33. For complex workflow processes this may be more involved. Therefore we provide more concrete guidelines. To determine the capacity required it is important to know the average number of times each task is executed. In figure 4.31 the tasks *record, contact_client, contact_department, collect,* and *file* are executed precisely one time. Task *pay* is executed 0.7 times, task *send_letter* is executed 0.3 times, and task *assess* is executed 1.111 times on average. How to calculate the average number of times each task is executed? One way is to construct a Markov chain that is isomorphic with the reachability graph and add the appropriate cost functions. The drawback of this approach is that the construction of such a Markov chain requires computer support and may be time-consuming. There is also a more pragmatic approach based on the design patterns described in figure 4.11. These patterns can be used to construct safe and sound workflow nets. However, as figure 4.34 shows, the patterns can also be used to determine the average number of times each task is executed.

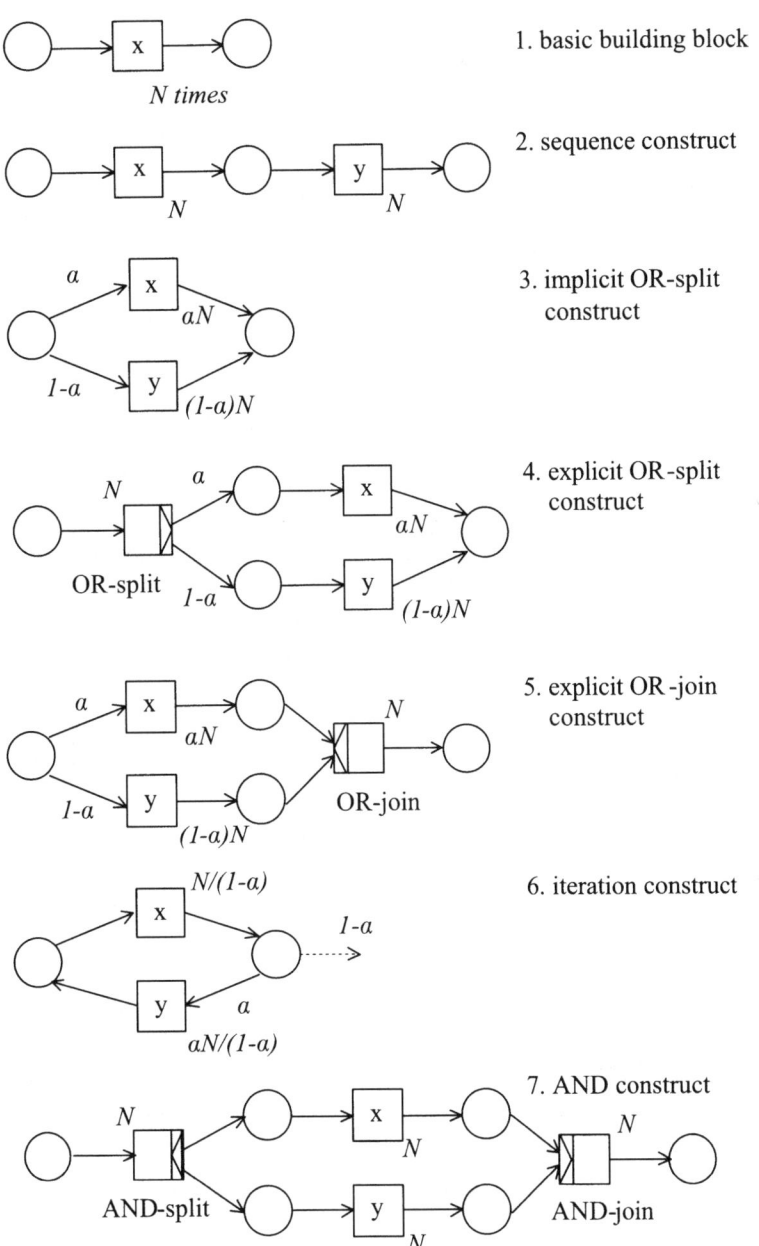

1. basic building block

2. sequence construct

3. implicit OR-split construct

4. explicit OR-split construct

5. explicit OR-join construct

6. iteration construct

7. AND construct

Figure 4.34
The number of times each task executed relative to the number of times task x is executed in the original situation

Compared to figure 4.11, the design patterns in figure 4.34 have been extended with numbers. Assume that task x is executed N times in the original situation, that is, before applying the pattern. If the sequence construct is used, then both x and y are executed N times in the new situation. If one of the three OR constructs is applied, then x is executed αN times and y is executed $(1-\alpha)N$ times (on average). Note that α is the probability that x is executed in the new situation. If the AND construct is used, then both x and y are executed N times in the new situation. The iteration construct is a bit more involved. Let α be the probability that after processing x a new iteration is needed. Using calculus one can calculate that in the new situation x is executed $N/(1-\alpha)$ times and y is executed $\alpha N(1-\alpha)$ times. To understand these figures consider the iteration construct in figure 4.34. Let v be the expected number of times x is executed for *one* case starting in place p. Then the following equation should hold: $v = 1 + \alpha v$, since it happens once and with probability α we return to place p. Solving this equation gives $v = 1/(1-\alpha)$. Task y is executed $v - 1 = \alpha(1-\alpha)$ times. Therefore, if place p is marked N times, x is executed $N/(1-\alpha)$ times and y is executed $\alpha N(1-\alpha)$ times.

Note that the workflow net shown in figure 4.31 cannot be constructed using the design patterns shown in figure 4.34. The standard iteration construct cannot be used to make the loop involving $c5$ and *assess*. However a similar iteration construct can be added to the list of constructs shown in figure 4.34. If α is the probability that *assess* is executed *again*, then the total number of times *assess* is executed equals $N/(1-\alpha)$.

If the average number of new cases per time unit and the average number each task is executed are known, then the average number of times a given task is executed can be calculated by taking the product of these two figures. If the average processing time and corresponding resource class of each task are known, it is straightforward to derive the total number of capacity per time unit per role (assuming a utilization of 100%).

4.5.2   Some basic queueing theory to take variability into account

Because there are always fluctuations in the supply of cases and the processing times, it is not always possible to make full use of the capacity available. It therefore is not sensible to assume that the resources will be utilized to their full capacity. To illustrate this, let us examine a process consisting of one task. During each time unit, λ new cases arrive that need to be processed by one resource. This resource is able to complete μ cases per time unit. The utilized capacity, ρ, of this resource is therefore:

$\rho = \lambda/\mu$

If we assume that processing times and case interarrival times are distributed in a negative exponential way, the average number of cases in progress is L, where:

$L = \rho/(1 - \rho)$

The average waiting time, W—that is, the completion time minus the processing time—is:

$W = L/\mu = \rho/(\mu - \lambda)$

The average system time, S—that is, the total completion time (waiting time and processing time)—is:

$S = W + 1/\mu = 1/(\mu - \lambda)$

Say an average of 8 new cases arrive per hour, and that an average of 10 cases can be processed per hour. The capacity utilization is therefore 80% ($\rho = 8/10 = 0.8$). On average, there are 4 cases in progress ($L = 4$) and the average waiting time is 24 minutes ($W = 0.4$ hours). With a capacity utilization of 80 percent, the average completion time is thus 30 $(24 + 6)$ minutes. At a capacity utilization of 95 percent and an average processing time of 6 minutes, the average completion time would rise to no less than 2 hours. This small example shows that when the arrival process is irregular, it is not at all sensible to seek a capacity utilization of more than 80 percent.

Figure 4.35 shows the impact of utilization on the average number of cases in progress. The impact resulting from the duplication of utilization from 0.25 to 0.50 (+0.66 cases) is much smaller than the impact from the small increase from 0.98 to 0.99 (+50 cases).

The situation just described corresponds with the $M/M/1$ *queue*. The first M shows that the interarrival times are distributed in a negative exponential way. The second M shows that the processing times are also distributed in this way. The number 1 indicates that there is only one

Utilization (ρ)	Average number in progress (L)	Utilization (ρ)	Average number in progress (L)	Utilization (ρ)	Average number in progress (L)
0.10	0.11	0.80	4.00	0.98	49
0.25	0.33	0.85	5.66	0.99	99
0.50	1.00	0.90	9.00	0.999	999
0.75	3.00	0.95	19.00	0.9999	9999

Figure 4.35
The average number of cases in progress given a utilization ratio

resource. To show just how sensitive the waiting times are to the variability of the processing times, we can consider the $M/G/1$ queue. In this the processing times are distributed randomly (G = general). The only things we know are that the average processing time is $1/\mu$ and that the standard deviation is σ. Based upon these two parameters, we can define the coefficient of variation, C:

$$C = \mu\sigma$$

The coefficient of variation is a measure of relative deviation from the average. The higher C is, the wider the spread of processing times will be. In the $M/G/1$ queue, capacity utilization is also equal to $\rho = \lambda/\mu$. However, the average number of cases in progress (L) now depends upon the coefficient of variation:

$$L = \rho + (\rho^2/(2(1 - \rho)))(1 + C^2)$$

(This is known as the Pollaczek-Khinchin formula.) The average waiting time, W, also strongly depends upon the value of C:

$$W = (\rho/(2\mu(1 - \rho)))(1 + C^2)$$

These formulae show that large variations in processing times can result in long completion times. Conversely, regular processing times will deliver shorter completion times. To illustrate this, let us assume a situation in which an average of 8 new cases arrive per hour, and the processing time for each is precisely 6 minutes. In this case, the coefficient of variation C is 0. By applying the formulae, we discover that the average waiting time is only 12 minutes. The completion times therefore depend strongly upon the variation in processing times. Note that in case of negative exponentially distributed processing times, C equals 1 and the Pollaczek-Khinchin formula reduces to the formula given earlier.

We have just made use of a number of simple formulae from the *queueing theory*, part of the discipline of *operations research* (OR). There are many results from the queueing theory that can be applied directly in the context of workflow management. As well as the $M/M/1$ and $M/G/1$ queues discussed earlier, $M/M/n$ queues (ones containing several identical resources) are also easy to analyze. For $M/G/n$ queues and $G/G/n$ queues, there exist formulae for approximating the average waiting time. One result that is applicable to every queue (regardless of interarrival pattern, distribution of processing times and number of resources) is *Little's formula*:

$$L = \lambda S$$

This establishes a link between the number of cases in progress, L, the intensity of the interarrival process, λ, and the average system time, S. If the average completion time for a case is 5 days ($S = 5$), and an average of 25 new cases arrive per day ($\lambda = 25$), then the average number of cases in progress is 125 ($L = 125$).

Given an expected supply of cases and a number of assumptions about their processing, we can use simulation and/or the queueing theory to determine the capacity requirement during a particular period. Based upon these capacity requirements, a capacity plan can be drawn up. When preparing a capacity plan, fluctuations in case supply, temporary loss of resources, and other problems should also be taken into account. The same applies to the desired level of service. To guarantee short completion times, it is sometimes necessary to substantially increase the number of resources.

There is a clear link between capacity planning in a workflow environment and in a production environment. Many concepts used in *manufacturing resources planning* (MRP-II) systems can be directly transferred into workflow management systems. Rather than the bill of material (BOM), however, it is now the process definition which is the starting point.

EXERCISES

Exercise 4.1   Optimize data usage
Consider the sequential process modeled in terms of a role/route diagram in figure 4.36.

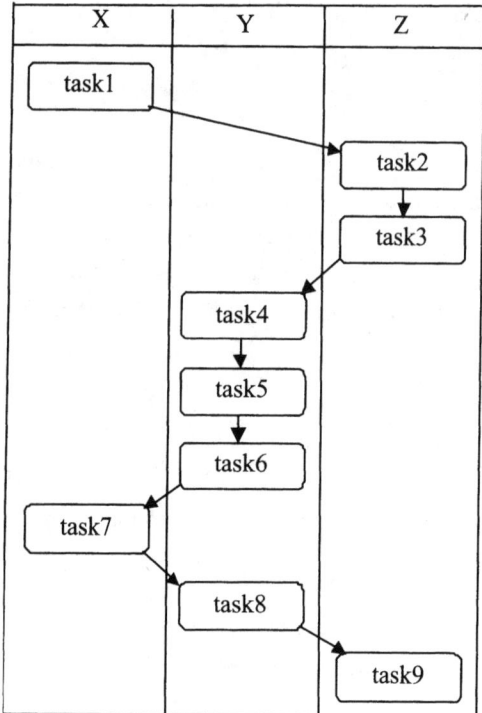

Figure 4.36
Process

There are nine tasks and the employees are divided into three resource classes (roles): X, Y, and Z. Each task needs to be executed by someone with the appropriate role.

(a) Model the process definition in terms of a Petri net.
(b) Is the role/route diagram appropriate for the specification of workflow processes?

For the execution of the workflow process the following nine data elements are relevant: $D1, D2, \ldots, D9$. The relationships between data elements and tasks are given in the CRUD matrix shown in figure 4.37.

Assume that only the data elements and their usage are relevant for the ordering of tasks. The sequential process shown in the role/route diagram is far from optimal, that is, task 4 can be executed directly after task 1; there is no need to wait for task 2 and task 3.

	D1	D2	D3	D4	D5	D6	D7	D8	D9
Task1	C	C							
Task2		R				C			
Task3						R	C		
Task4	R		C						
Task5	R	R		C					
Task6		R	R	R	C				
Task7	R	U			R		R		
Task8							R	C	
Task9	R	R						R	C

(C=Create, R=Read, U=Update, D=Delete)

Figure 4.37
CRUD matrix

(i)

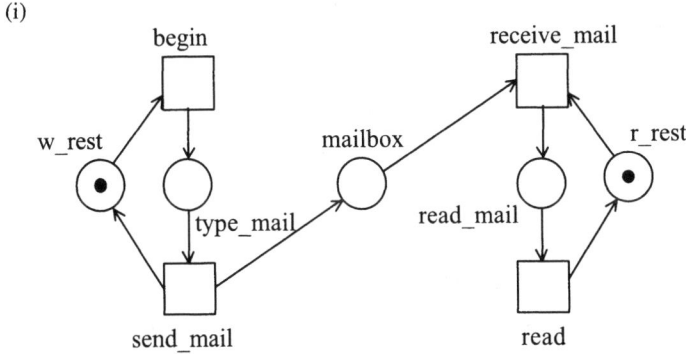

Figure 4.38
E-mail

(c) Improve the process by making it more parallel.

(d) Is it a good idea to combine tasks? If so, which tasks are proper candidates?

Exercise 4.2 Invariants

Consider the Petri nets shown in figure 4.38, figure 4.39, figure 4.40, and figure 4.41.

Answer for each Petri net the following questions (see appendix A):

(a) What are the place invariants (maximum 5)? What do they show?

(b) What are the transition invariants (maximum 5)? What do they show?

(ii)

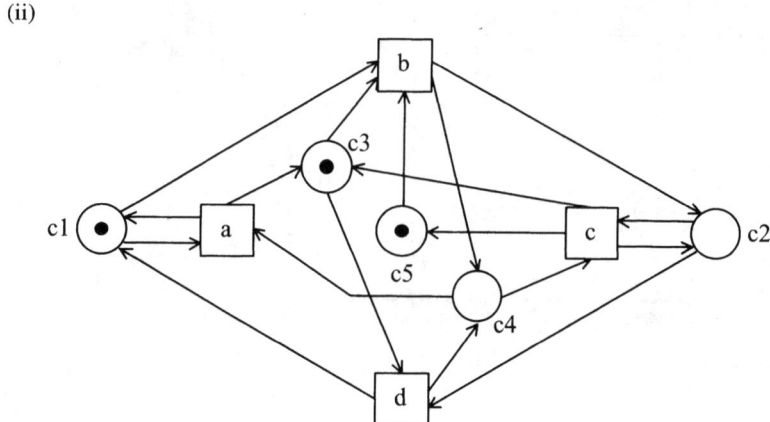

Figure 4.39
Network

(iii)

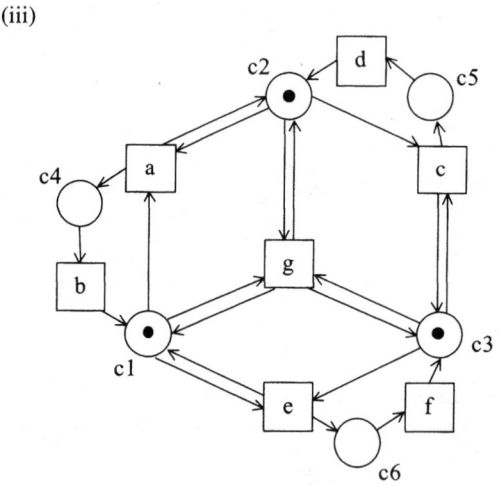

Figure 4.40
Network

(iv)

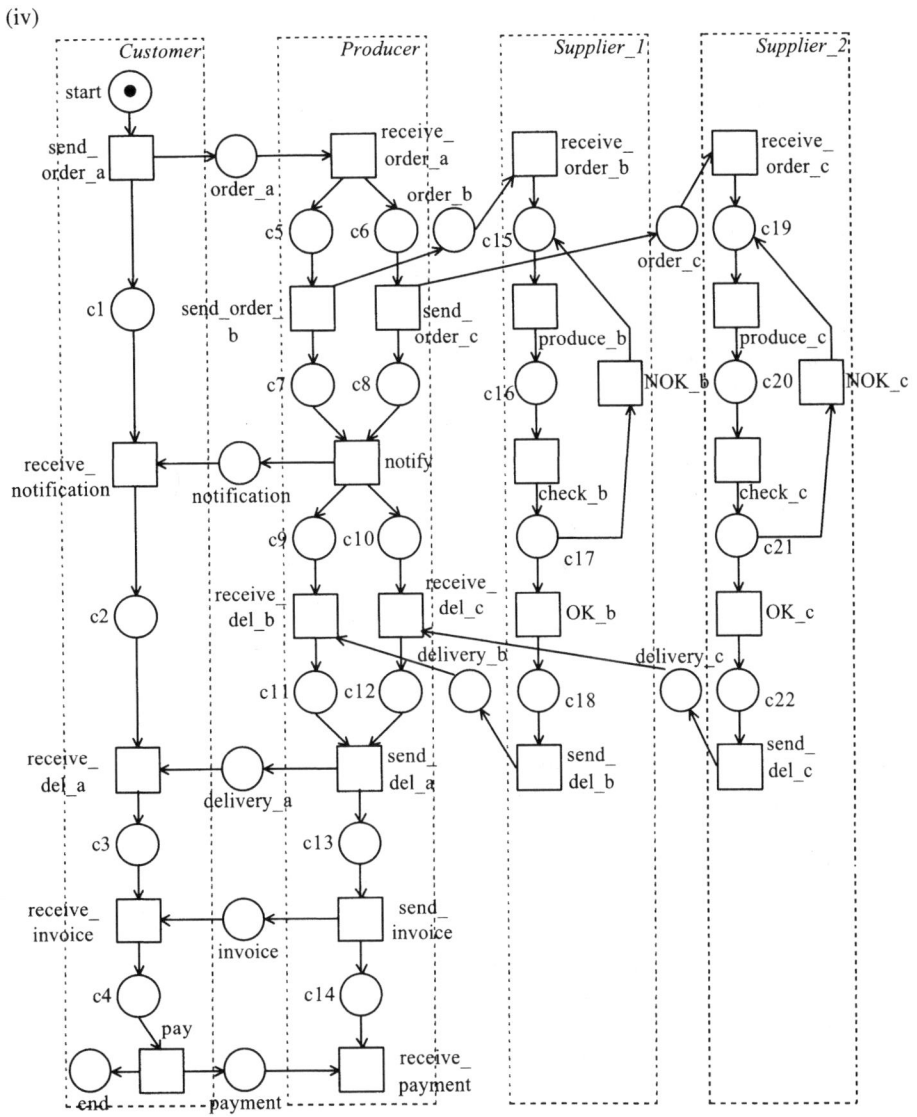

Figure 4.41
Supply chain

(c) Is the net bounded?

(d) Is the net live?

(e) Is the net free-choice?

(f) What are the S-components?

Exercise 4.3   Verification process definition

Consider the process definition shown in figure 4.42.

(a) Check, by constructing the reachability graph, the correctness.

(b) Estimate the number of states when condition c6 is removed.

(c) Prove by place invariants that the two sub-procedures ($t2 \ldots t6$ and $t7 \ldots t12$) are not active at the same time (mutual exclusion).

(d) Prove that there is a linear dependency between *start* and *ready* (give conservation laws in terms of place invariants).

Exercise 4.4   Search for errors

Consider the process definitions shown in figures 4.43, 4.44 and 4.45.

Answer for each process definition the following questions:

(a) Is the process definition correct?

(b) If not, show the error (reachability graph and/or place invariants).

Exercise 4.5   Performance analysis I

Consider the process in figure 4.46.

(a) Determine the following performance indicators:

· Occupation rate (utilization) for each resource,

· Average WIP (work in progress),

· Average flow time (throughput time), and

· Average waiting time for each task.

Task 2 is a check task. The management thinks about a selective execution of this task where only 25% of the cases are checked. The average service time of this new task is 6 minutes.

(b) Determine the performance indicators again:

· Occupation rate (utilization) for each resource,

· Average WIP (work in progress),

· Average flow time (throughput time), and

· Average waiting time for each task.

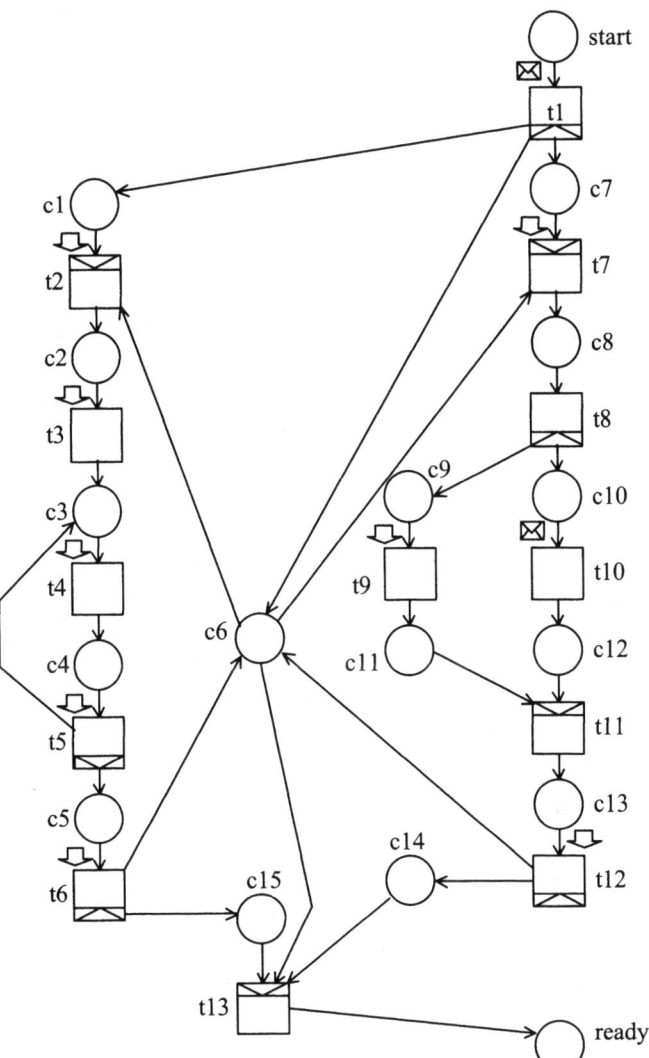

Figure 4.42
Network

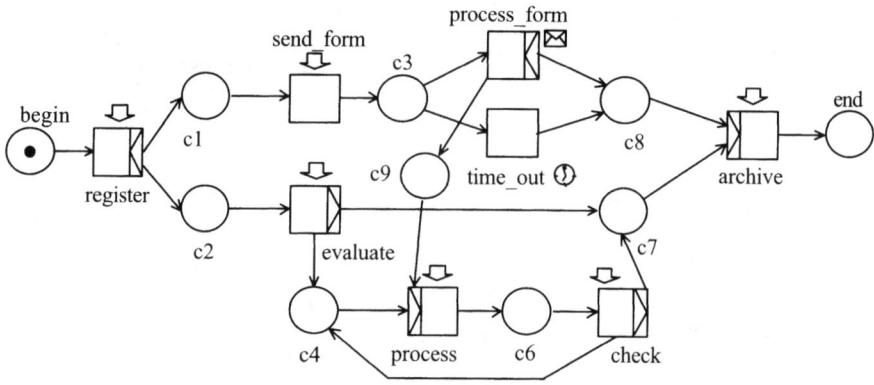

Figure 4.43
Complaint handling (1)

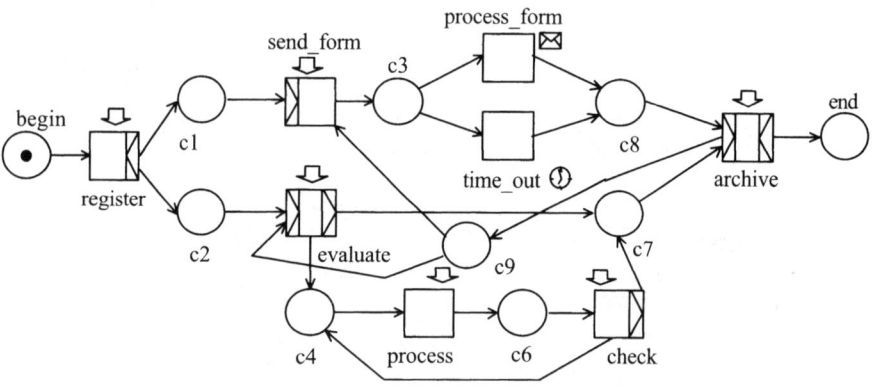

Figure 4.44
Complaint handling (2)

Exercise 4.6   Performance analysis II
Consider the process in figure 4.47.

(a) Determine the following performance indicators:
· Occupation rate (utilization) for each resource,
· Average WIP (work in progress),
· Average flow time (throughput time), and
· Average waiting time for each task.

The two resources working on task 1 join forces and work together on
both easy and difficult cases. As a result the average time to handle task 1
for one case is two minutes (i.e., a total of 4 minutes of capacity).

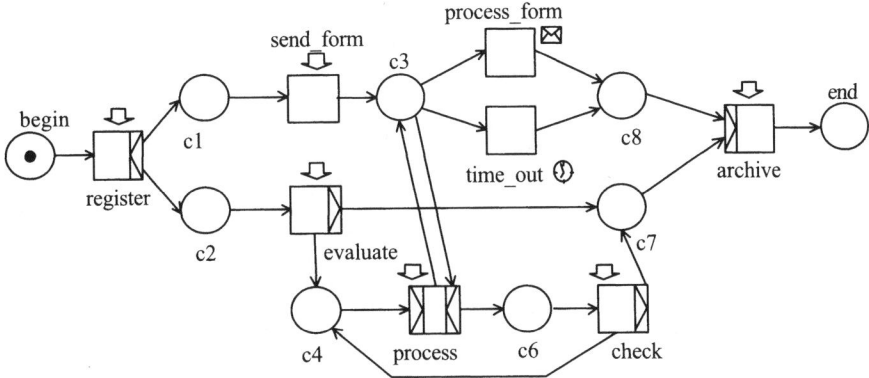

Figure 4.45
Complaint handling (3)

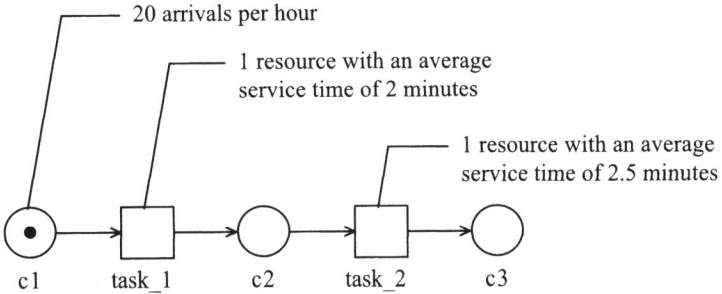

Figure 4.46
Process (1)

(b) Determine the performance indicators again:
· Occupation rate (utilization) for each resource,
· Average WIP (work in progress),
· Average flow time (throughput time), and
· Average waiting time for each task.

Exercise 4.7   Performance analysis III
Consider a process in which *ct1* and *ct2* are checks (see figure 4.48). If they are positive, task *bt* (e.g., pay damage) is executed. If one of them is negative, *bt* is skipped. The two check tasks are independent of each other.

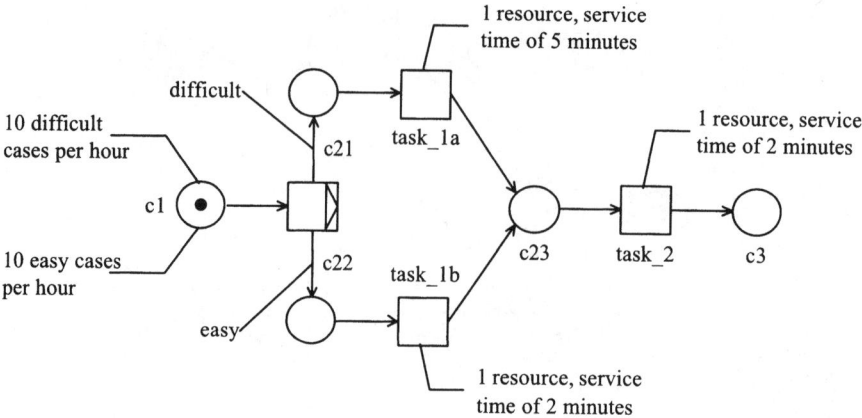

Figure 4.47
Process (2)

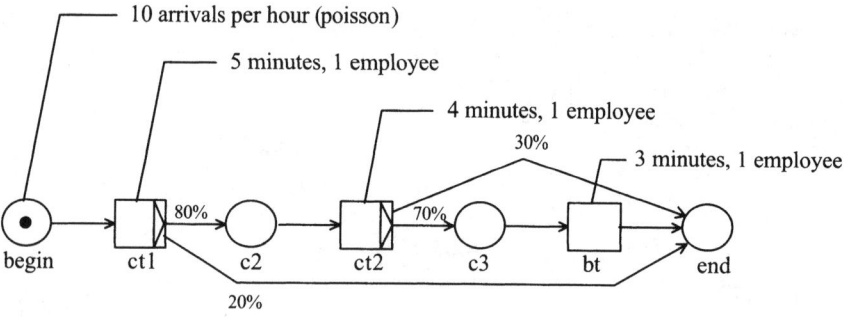

Figure 4.48
Process (3)

(a) Determine the following performance indicators:
• Occupation rate (utilization) for each resource,
• Average WIP (work in progress),
• Average flow time (throughput time), and
• Average waiting time for each task.

Give at least two alternatives, that is, improved workflow definitions.

(b) For each alternative answer the following questions:
• Why is it better?
• What is the utilization of resources?
• What is the maximal throughput?

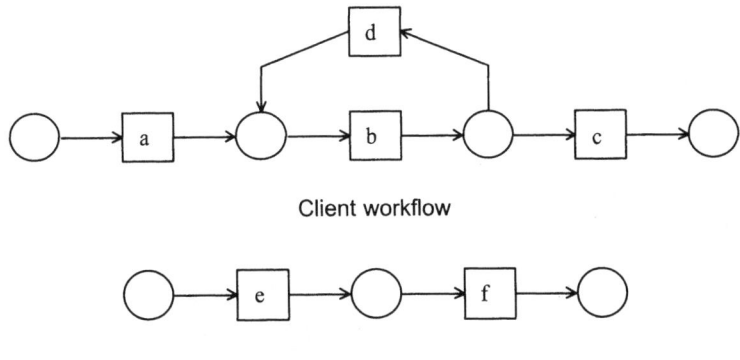

Client workflow

Server workflow

Coupled workflows

Figure 4.49
Workflows

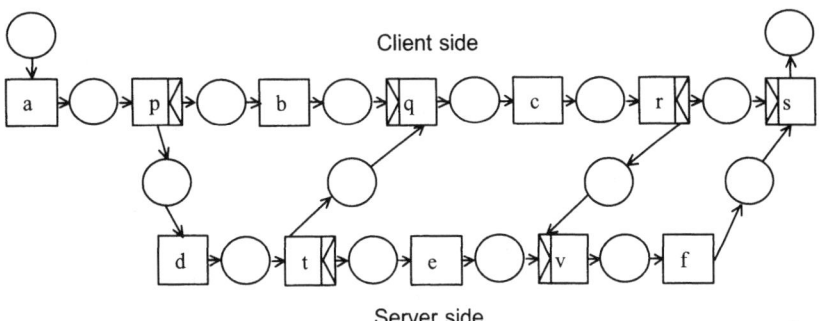

Figure 4.50
Client/server

Exercise 4.8   E-business

In electronic business workflows of different organizations are coupled. One of them plays the role of client and the other of server. These workflows are shown in figure 4.49.

(a) Give derivations for the client and the server.
(b) Use these derivations to obtain the derivation of the coupled work-flows. (Herewith we have proven that this coupling is sound and safe)

In figure 4.50 we see again the coupling between two processes: a client process and a server process. During the course of the server process there is some exchange of information between the server and the client: after task d has been done, a message is sent from t to q and later, when task c is done a message is sent from r to v.

(c) Is there a derivation with building blocks replacement possible?
(d) Is it a sound and safe workflow? Give arguments.

5

Functions and Architecture of Workflow Systems

5.1 Role of Workflow Management Systems

Extensive attention has been paid in the previous chapters to modeling and improving business processes. Techniques were presented for describing these in a structured way, for analyzing them, and for improving them. Clearly these techniques are the key to achieving drastic improvements in the efficiency and effectiveness of the organization and its work performance. One obvious question is how we can realize the desired business process using information technology. In doing so, we must not lose sight of the benefits of a process-oriented approach. The information system must be structured in such a way that it can respond to possible future changes. In practice, this means that information systems must meet a number of requirements:

· Information systems must be set up in such a way that the structure of the business processes is clearly reflected in them. This makes the process recognizable to the user and reduces the chances of errors occurring both during the development of the system and during the execution of the process.

· There should be an integrated approach, which also encompasses non-computerized tasks. Today's business processes now frequently extend far beyond what traditionally has been recorded in an information system.

· Information systems must be set up in such a way that the structure of the business processes can be modified easily. This enables organizations to respond flexibly to their changing environment and to restructure their business processes accordingly.

· It is important that the performance of a business process can be tracked properly so that any problems can be discovered at an early stage. Interventions should also be straightforward and possible at the moment when something goes wrong. To this end, the performance of the business process should be easy to measure, and it should be possible to refine that performance.

• The allocation of work to people is a point of particular interest. Good workload management is crucial to achieving effective and efficient business processes.

5.1.1   How information systems are traditionally structured

Traditionally, process management has not been separated from the application software in information systems. In other words, the process management has been hidden inside the information system. Because very little attention has been paid to process structure within the framework of traditional systems, it often has been difficult to actually recognize the business process. Even worse, the process contained in the system is often incorrect or incomplete.

5.1.2   Separation of management and execution

One important step towards achieving information systems that do fulfill the requirements listed above was their splitting into one subsystem that deals with the *management* of the business process (the "logistical system" or "management system") and one that supports the *execution* of tasks in a specific business process (the "application"; see figure 5.1). The management system deals with the logistical completion of cases, without actually performing tasks itself. It ensures that no steps are skipped, that they are carried out in the correct order, that tasks can be

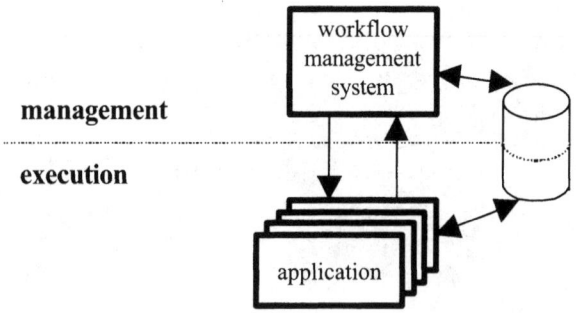

Figure 5.1
The separation between logistics and execution

performed in parallel where possible, that the correct applications are called in to support a task, and so on. It also makes sure that staff are assigned, considers their absence, supports the separation of functions and authorization levels, and so on.

Apart from the structure of the business process, the management system actually has no application-specific characteristics. To *differentiate* between management and execution, in this book we use the principle that management may only *consult* the case attributes in order to *make routing decisions.* We regard changing the case attributes as part of execution rather than management.

It is the task of the management system to bring the work (i.e., the work items) to the right person or application at the right time so that the tasks for a specific case can be carried out. The logistical management system interacts with the user, reacts to signals from its environment (for example, an incoming EDI message), or executes automatic or time-driven tasks. (In principle, a time-driven task also waits for a signal from the environment.) Once a supporting application for a particular step in the process has been defined, the management system starts this in the correct way. An application supports the user in performing the task. Management and applications communicate using case attributes. When an application is started, these can be passed on. When it closes again, any updated case attributes are passed back to the management level.

5.1.3 Advantages
Separating management from applications has a number of important advantages:

• It enables us to achieve uniform management functionality and to isolate this from the rest of the system. (Traditionally this functionality was spread throughout the information system.) This makes it possible to reuse the same functionality in more than one task.

• Applications no longer require any management functionality, and hence are simpler and completely independent of their context or place in the business process. This makes it possible to rearrange the business process at a later stage.

• The management layer makes it possible to integrate wide-ranging applications. In this way, it is even possible to integrate new applications with legacy systems.

• At the management level, the business process is identifiable and the state of a particular case within it is easy to establish. The process therefore is more tracable. Because it is clear at the management level which tasks have to be carried out, it is easy to determine who should be doing what for a particular case. The process execution is more manageable, with progress and bottlenecks more easy to check.

5.1.4   Workflow management software

Given that the process management functionality should, in principle, be widely applicable rather than intended for a specific application, it becomes attractive to use generic software: workflow management systems. These can interpret and apply the process structure and work allocation rules.

There is a large number of standard workflow management systems currently on the market. These vary widely in the functionality they offer. In this chapter, we shall try to indicate—in general terms—the functionality that one should or could expect from a workflow management system. In addition, we shall examine the technical aspects that are important in selecting and introducing such a system.

5.2   A Reference Model

As we saw in chapter 1, workflow management systems enable the "extraction" of process management from the application software. To a certain extent, we can compare such systems with a database management system. After all, database management systems make it possible to extract data management from the application software. Both types of systems support a piece of generic functionality. Because—unlike database management systems—workflow management systems have only been available for a short time, in many respects it is unclear which components are part of the systems' basic functionality. The technology is still young and not yet fully formed.

Moreover workflow management has many "faces." Workflow management systems may be implemented in order to achieve flexbility, system integration, process optimization, organizational change, improved maintainability, evolutionary development, and so on. All this means that confusion may easily arise as to what actually can be expected from

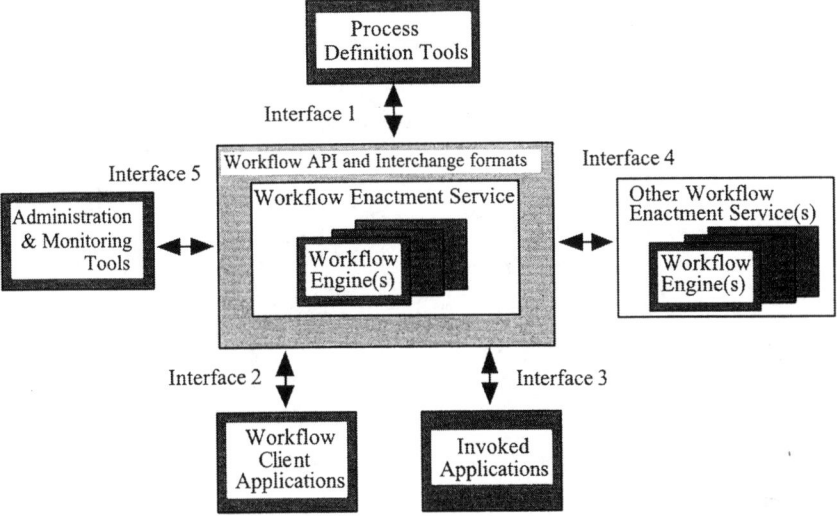

Figure 5.2
The Workflow Management Coalition's reference model (© WFMC)

the functionality of a workflow management system. This danger was recognized at an early stage by the *Workflow Management Coalition* (WFMC)—an organization whose role includes standardizing workflow management terminology and defining standards for the exchange of data between workflow management systems and applications. In 1996, the WFMC had already two hundred members (including many suppliers of workflow management products).

One of the many principles used by the WFMC is the so-called *workflow reference model*. This is a general description of the architecture of a workflow management system, in which the main components and the associated interfaces are summarized. Figure 5.2 illustrates the workflow reference model.

The model shows that the heart of a workflow system is the so-called *workflow enactment service*. This part of the system pumps—as it were—the cases through the organization. The enactment service ensures that the right activities are carried out in the right order and by the right people. In order to achieve this, use is made of process definitions and resource classifications produced by the so-called *process definition tools*. As well as illustrating the process and the organization, these tools frequently offer facilities for analysis techniques such as simulation. Work items are offered to the employees through *workflow client applications*. By selecting a work item, an employee can begin performing a specific task for a specific case. When carrying out a task it may be necessary to start an application. All the application software that can be started from the workflow system is known as *invoked applications* in the reference model. Workflow tracking, case control, and staff management are supported by the so-called *administration and monitoring tools*.

Five interfaces are also shown in figure 5.2. The WFMC is striving to standardize these. In creating an information system based upon a workflow management system, *Interface 3* and *Interface 4* are of particular significance. The former is associated with the control of applications from the workflow system, the latter with the exchange of cases (or parts of cases) between autonomous workflow systems. The other interfaces are mainly used by the workflow management system itself.

Figure 5.2 provides only a rough impression of the functionality of a workflow management system. We therefore shall further refine the definition of each component.

5.2.1 Workflow enactment service

The so-called *workflow enactment service* is the heart of a workflow system. This component creates new cases, generates work items based upon the process description, matches resources and work items, supports the performance of activities, and enables the recording of particular aspects of the workflow. For technical reasons, the enactment service may consist of several *workflow engines*. Their use can, for example, improve the scalability of the entire system. In an enactment service with more than one workflow engine, the work is distributed amongst them. This distribution may be based upon the characteristics of the case, the task, and/or the resource. In general, the user will not notice when a workflow system is using more than one engine.

Workflow engine A workflow engine provides those facilities which are required for the logistical completion of cases. In certain cases, several workflow engines operate alongside one another. Each then handles a portion of the cases and/or processes. The duties of a workflow engine include:

- creating new cases and removing completed ones;
- routing cases, using the interpretation of the appropriate process definition;
- managing case attributes;
- submitting work items to the correct resources (employees), based upon resource classification;
- managing and handling triggers;
- starting up application software during the execution of an activity;
- recording historical data;
- providing a summary of the workflow; and
- monitoring the consistency of the workflow.

The workflow engines are therefore the "core" of the workflow system, without which it would not operate.

5.2.2   Process definition tools

A workflow engine is based upon one or more workflow definitions. In chapters 2 and 3, we saw that the definition of a workflow is divided into two important parts: the process definition (chapter 2) and the resource classification (chapter 3). In the workflow reference model, the tools for constructing these are known as *process definition tools*. As well as tools for illustrating workflows, it is often also possible to make use of analysis tools. In chapter 4, we showed which analysis techniques are applicable in the context of workflow management. In principle, we thus can differentiate between three types of tools: (1) *process definition tools*, (2) *resource classification tools*, and (3) *analysis tools*. In a number of workflow management systems, these three tools are integrated into a single workflow definition and analysis tool. Please note that the term "process definition tools" used by the WFMC is slightly confusing, since it entails not only the tools for modeling process definitions, but also resource classification tools and analysis tools.

The process definition tool   A process is specified using the process definition tool. Chapter 2 examined processes defined in terms of a Petri net. In many workflow management systems, however, processes are formulated in a different way. Nevertheless in most cases it is easy to map the used routing constructs onto Petri net elements. The expressive power of these alternative methods of modeling is typically weaker because certain routing structures are excluded. For example, many workflow management systems abstract from the explicit modeling of states, and, this does not allow for forms of routing such as the implicit OR-split to be modeled. The basic functionality of the process definition tool consists of the following elements:

• the ability to establish process definitions (name, description, date, version, components, and so on);
• the ability to model sequential, parallel, selective, and iterative routing by means of such graphic components as the AND-split, AND-join, OR-split and OR-join;
• version management support (after all, there may be several versions of the same process);
• the definition of case attributes used in the process;
• task specification; and
• the checking of the (syntactical) correctness of a process definition and the tracing of any omissions or inconsistencies.

A number of characteristics need to be established for each task within a process. These determine the conditions under which that task may be carried out, and what operations should be performed. The following is established for each task:

• the name and description of the task;
• task information—in other words, any instructions and supporting information for the employee performing the task;
• the requirements with respect to the resource carrying out the task (for example, a specification of its role and organizational unit, or information about the separation of functions);
• the task's routing characteristics (AND-split, AND-join, OR-split, OR-join);
• the specification of any triggers required;
• instructions for the workflow engine (for example, priorities, case management, and resource management);
• the applications that may be started, plus the conditions and order in which this should be done;
• a specification of the case attributes that are used and adjusted by the application; and
• decision rules that determine the subsequent tasks based upon the case attributes, when there is an OR-split or mixed OR/AND-split.

The process established using the process definition tool is the crux of the workflow.

The resource classification tool   As well as defining the process, the resources needed to carry out the workflow must be classified so that the tasks can be decoupled from specific employees. Most workflow management systems provide a resource classification tool in which the relationship between the various resource classes can be shown graphically. In doing so, the following items are established:

- a list of the resource classes, often subdivided into roles (based upon qualifications, functions, and skills) and organizational units (based upon arrangement into teams, branches, and/or departments);
- any specific characteristics of a resource class; and
- the relationship between the various resource classes (for example, a hierarchy of roles or organizational units).

The analysis tool   Before a workflow that has been defined can go "into production," it is useful first to analyze it. Such analysis can encompass checking the semantic correctness of a process definition as well as performing a simulation in order to gain insight into the expected completion times for cases. In general we can state that the current generation of workflow management systems only offers limited analysis possibilities. In most systems it is therefore possible to define workflows that could have disastrous consequences if actually put into effect. However, as described in chapter 4, it is possible to apply advanced analysis techniques. Future workflow management systems therefore will offer more and more analysis possibilities.

5.2.3 Workflow client applications

Those employees who are only involved in the actual execution of a process will never use the process definition tools. The only contact they have with the workflow system is through the *workflow client applications*. Each employee has a *worklist* (also known as in-tray or in-basket) which forms part of the workflow client applications. The workflow engine uses this worklist to show which work items need to be carried out. By selecting a work item, an employee can begin performing a task for a specific case. In principle, therefore, every employee has a personal worklist which shows all the work to be performed by him, or by his group. The worklist therefore forms the ultimate link between the work and the employee.

As shown in chapter 3, the allocation of work may be push or pull-driven. It is the former when the workflow engine allocates work items to individual employees. It is the latter when work items are allocated to groups of staff. This may result in a work item appearing in several worklists. The basic functionality that should be offered by a worklist handler encompasses the following:

• the presentation of the work items that may be performed by an employee;
• the provision of relevant properties of a work item, such as case and task information;
• the ability to sort and select, based upon these properties;
• the provision of state information pertaining to the state of the workflow engine;
• the starting of a task for a specific case when a work item is selected; and
• the ability to report the completion of an activity (i.e., a selected work item).

In addition, the worklist handler may allow for locking or passing on a work item. It must also be able to deal with system faults. Figure 5.3 shows a worklist handler of the COSA workflow management system.

Most workflow management systems offer a so-called *standard worklist handler*. In some cases, though, it is necessary to create a customized worklist handler for a specific environment.

The standard worklist handler   The standard worklist handler offers the functionality just described. Because it is not customized to suit a specific business situation, the functions available are generic. In many cases, however, it is possible to use parameters for the standard worklist handler. It may, for example, be possible to influence the layout and content of the window. Some standard worklist handlers have facilities for showing the (logistical) state of a case graphically.

The integrated worklist handler   The only way in which a typical end user can access the workflow system is through the worklist handler. When such a system is supporting the work of, say, one hundred mem-

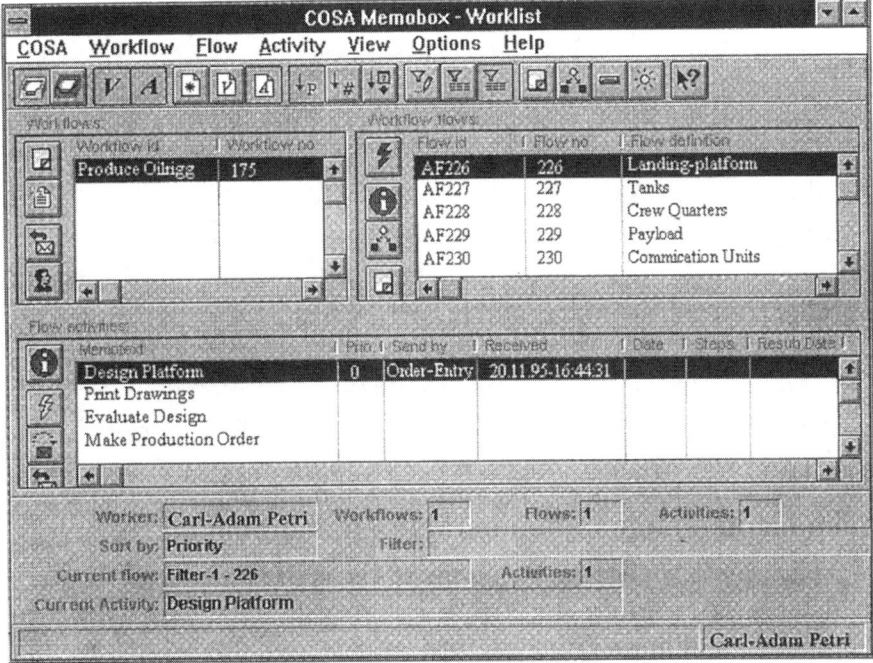

Figure 5.3
An example of a worklist handler (COSA, © Software-Ley)

bers of staff, the presentation of this component deserves particular attention. This may justify developing a customized worklist handler adapted to the specific business situation rather than using the standard one. This specific worklist handler would contain supporting facilities alongside the standard functionality described above. This is why it is referred to as an *integrated worklist handler*. It may, for example, use background data to provide additional support. Security and quality assurance considerations may also prompt the development of an integrated worklist handler. The same applies to the need for batch or chained processing of work items.

Batch processing is when an employee is able to perform a number of work items of the same type (in other words, repeat the same task) without switching back to the worklist handler. This enables her to carry out a particular task in routine several times in succession. *Chained processing* is when an employee is able to perform a number of successive tasks for a specific case. In this way, she does not have to get used to a new case repeatedly. *Batch* and *chained processing* avoid continually and unnecessarily switching between the worklist handler and the applications. This can provide considerable returns in terms of efficiency.

5.2.4   Invoked applications

The performance of a task may result in the starting up of one or more applications. These do not form part of the workflow management system because they are associated with the actual performance of work, not to its logistical management. Such applications do belong to the workflow system, though. This, after all, encompasses the applications, configuration files, workflow management system, database, and so on. Applications are started by the workflow engine in order to perform a specific task. In doing so, information about the case may be submitted. The application may, for example, make use of a particular case-attribute value. The case's identification is frequently used to find the appropriate information in the database. Conversely, the application may change the case-attribute values. These modified attributes are often used to decide the routing of the case. In general, a clear distinction is drawn between *interactive* and *fully automatic applications*.

Interactive application   An interactive application is always initiated as a result of the selection of a work item from the worklist handler. It may be a standard office tool such as a word processor or a spreadsheet, or a program developed especially for the business process (for example, an electronic form which needs to be completed).

Fully automatic application   A fully automatic application requires no interaction with the user. It thus may be a part of a task that can be performed without a user intervening. One example could be a program which performs a complicated calculation (such as establishing the amount of an installment payment).

5.2.5   Other workflow enactment services

A workflow system may contain several workflow engines. These come under the same management and use the same workflow definitions. Such engines are said to belong to the same *workflow domain*. However it is also possible to link several autonomous workflow systems with one another. In this way, cases (or parts of cases) can be transferred from one system to another. This means that the workflow enactment services of each system are linked. We refer to this as *workflow interoperability*. In the future, more and more workflow systems are expected to be linked. These may be in different branches of the same company or those of separate firms.

5.2.6 Administration and monitoring tools

The workflow enactment service ensures the processing of cases based upon workflow definitions. The supervision and operational management of these flows (including the resources) are done using *administration* and *monitoring tools*. These can be divided into those used for operational management of the workflows and those used for recording and reporting. In many workflow management systems they are integrated into a single tool.

The operational management tool   Operational management covers all operations pertaining to the management of the workflow. So it is not possible to use the *operational management tool* to change the structure of a business process. We can subdivide the information related to operational management into that which is case related and that which is not (i.e., resource or system related). The operational management tool functions for resource-related information include:

• addition or removal of staff; and
• input/revision of an employee's details (name, address, telephone number, role, organizational unit, authorization, and availability).

Additional operational management tool functions are:

• implementation of new workflow definitions; and
• reconfiguration of the workflow system (setting of technical system parameters).

Note that an employee's individual details fall under operational management. The adjustment of employee availability information as a result of a revised schedule, holiday, or sick leave is one example of resource-related operational management. Functions for performing case-related operational management are also required:

• inspection of the logistical state of a case; and

• manipulation of the logistical state of a case due to problems and exceptional circumstances.

The operational management tool thus is also used to provide ad hoc solutions to problems resulting from system faults and bottlenecks in the process.

The recording and reporting tool   Many aspects can be recorded and stored during the performance of a workflow. These are historical data which may be useful for management. For example, the following interesting *performance indicators* may be distilled from the data:

• average completion time for a case;

• average waiting time and processing time (possibly subdivided per task);

• percentage of cases completed within a fixed standard period; and

• average level of resource capacity utilization.

Note that in many situations not only the averages but also the variances of these performance indicators are of prime importance.

Information about the properties of completed workflows is crucial to management. Prompt warnings about bottlenecks and overcapacity can lead to the process being revised. The raw data is supplied by the workflow enactment service. It is then administered by the *recording and reporting tool*. This can, for example, decide at information should be stored. It also frequently offers reporting facilities. Some workflow management systems use predefined reports that are produced at regular intervals. Others offer an integrated report generator. This enables the user to define reports based upon the information recorded. And yet others deliberately do not provide reporting facilities. In this way, the recorded data can be found with the use of a standard database management system or a generic report generator. Often a huge amount of data needs to be translated in order to produce the information that is of interest to management. Clearly there is a link here with *data mining*, *data warehousing*, and *OLAP* (on-line analytical processing).

Figure 5.4 shows the relationship between the tools described. In fact, this illustrates a more detailed version of the workflow reference model given in figure 5.2. It does not, though, state that the analysis tool and

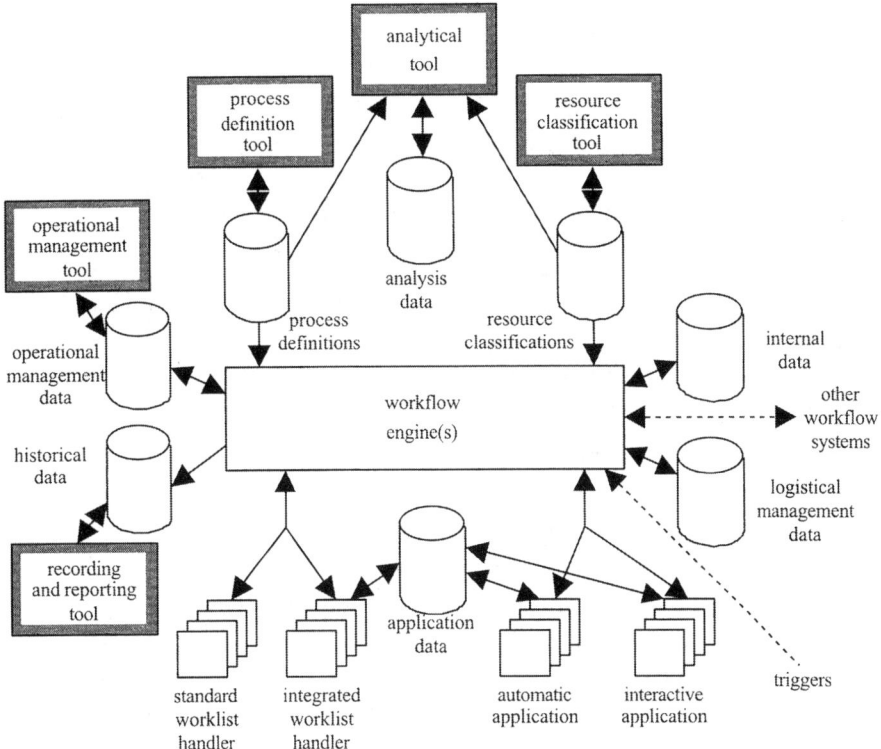

Figure 5.4
The various components of a workflow system

the recording and reporting tool often make use of one another's information. For example, historical data can be used in analyzing a workflow (through, say, simulation). Analytical results can also be used in dedicated searches for useful management information.

5.2.7   Roles of people involved

Figure 5.4 clearly shows that a workflow system is constructed from many components that are used by a wide range of people. In theory, there are four types of users:

• *The Workflow Designer*. The workflow designer uses the process definition tools (in other words, the process definition tool, the resource classification tool, and the analysis tools). This designer works on the structure of the workflow.

• *The Administrator.* The administrator uses the operational management tool. His typical activities include adding employees, issuing and withdrawing authorizations, implementing new processes, monitoring workflows, and solving problems and bottlenecks.

• *The Process Analyst.* The process analyst uses the recording and reporting tool to inform the management about the performance of the workflows. By aggregating detailed data into performance indicators, it is possible to provide insight into the operation of the business processes that are supported by the workflow management system.

• *The Employee.* The execution of work is carried out by employees. In this book, they are also referred to as resources. Such resources are the scarce means of production which need to be employed in the best way possible.

As well as the four types of users, other people are often involved in the structuring, management, and performance of the workflows. The users of the workflow management system are usually led by a *manager.* New and/or revised workflows often require new or updated applications. Information requirements may also be changed by the introduction of a new process. This is why *database designers/programmers* and *application designers/programmers* are also involved in the (re)structuring of a workflow. Figure 5.5 shows the various types of people involved in workflow design, implementation, and enactment.

It goes without saying that, in practice, the distinction between people and roles is not always as clear-cut as shown in figure 5.5. The process

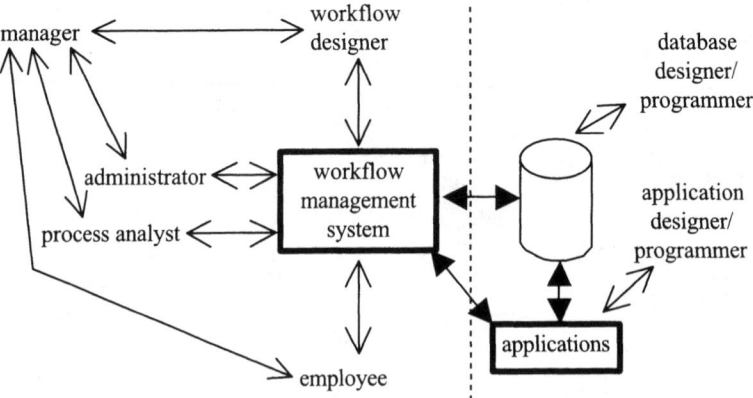

Figure 5.5
The users of a workflow management system

analyst may also be a manager, an employee also an Administrator—and there may be several types of administrators. In chapter 6, we shall examine in more detail the various types of people involved in implementing and managing workflow systems.

5.3   Storage and Exchange of Data

A workflow system consists of a large number of components. For the whole system to operate properly, these components must exchange information with one another. Furthermore it is important that different sorts of data are stored. Using figure 5.4 we shall show which data is administered within the workflow system. We shall then examine the links between the various components.

5.3.1   Data in a workflow system

Figure 5.4 shows which data is of significance to the workflow system. In most cases the workflow management system and the applications make use of the same database system. The workflow system thus "contracts out" data administration to a database management system. The following data sets are involved:

1. *Process definitions*. The definitions of processes and tasks. The name, description, routing, tasks, and conditions of each process are recorded. For each task, its name, description, decision rules, content, and allocation rules are recorded.

2. *Resource classifications*. The structuring of the various types of resources. As well as a list of resource classes (roles or organizational units), the relationships between them are recorded.

3. *Analysis data*. The results of any analyses carried out. In the case of simulations, for example, subrun results. (A simulation also sometimes makes use of historical data.)

4. *Operational management data*. The data that are important to the administrator of the workflow system. For example, information about the technical configuration of the system (system parameters), information about staff, and case-related data.

5. *Historical data*. The data that are stored in order to be able to retrace the progress of an individual case, trace the cause of a problem, or assess the performance of the business process.

6. *Application data.* The data that can be accessed by an application but not by the workflow management system. There are two types of application data: case data and master data. Case data are directly related to individual cases; master data are not. The latter includes general information about customers and suppliers.

7. *Internal data.* All the data that are maintained by the workflow management system but are not directly related to the workflow as such. For example, information about worklists that are active, the state of each engine, and network addresses. Unlike the operational management data, the internal data are technical in nature and therefore are only accessed by the enactment service.

8. *Logistical management data.* The state of each workflow is embedded in the logistical management data, which encompass information about case states (including case attributes), the state of each resource, and the triggers available. It is preferable that these are accessible only by the workflow engine. However, it is for technical reasons sometimes unavoidable that these are also consulted, and even revised, by external applications.

5.3.2   Interfacing problems

A workflow system consists of a large number of components. Some of these are the workflow management system tools themselves, while others are the applications used when carrying out the actual tasks. In order for these components to work together, they must exchange information. Agreements have therefore been reached within the WFMC about the standardization of interfaces between the various components. As shown in figure 5.6, the WFMC recognizes five such interfaces.

The objective of interface standardization is threefold. First, generally accepted standards will improve the exchange of data between (parts of) workflow management systems. Second, it will become possible to create links between different manufacturers' enactment servers in a simple way. Finally, the standards will enable the development of applications that are entirely independent of the chosen workflow management system.

A number of interfaces are currently achieved using files or databases. For example, in figure 5.4, we have assumed that Interface 1 and Interface 5 are realized using a database. Within the WFMC, however, it is assumed that every interface will be achieved using a so-called *application programming interface* (API). In the context of workflow management, the term WAPI (workflow application programming interface) is

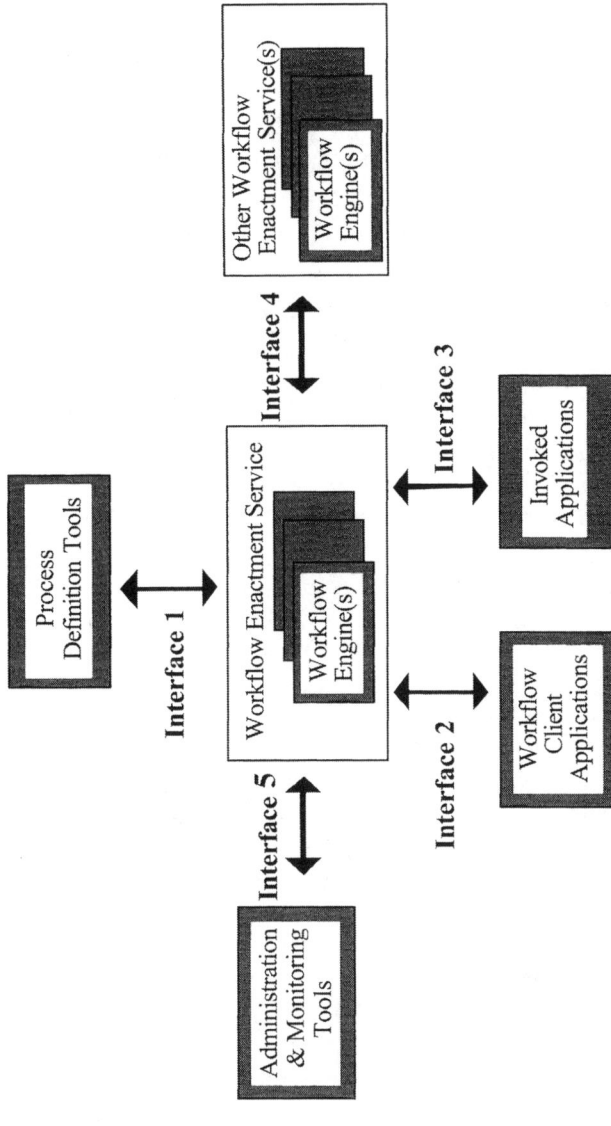

Figure 5.6
The interfaces between the various elements (© WFMC)

also used. An API is a group of *services* that are offered to a *client* via a *server*. These services can best be compared with procedure calls in a conventional programming language. The word client can refer to an application. An operating system such as UNIX is an example of a server. We can consider the copying of a file as a service offered by UNIX via an API (cp). In the specific case of workflows (WAPI), the workflow enactment service acts as the server and the tools and applications as clients. To provide an impression of the WAPIs recognized by the WFMC, we shall briefly describe the content of each interface:

1. *Interface 1 (process definition tools)*. Interface 1 provides the link between the tools designed for creating and modifying the workflow definitions (process definition tools) and the workflow enactment service. This WAPI contains functions for opening and closing a connection (connect/disconnect), obtaining a summary of the workflow definitions (process definitions and resource classifications), and opening, creating, and saving a process definition.

2. *Interface 2 (workflow client applications)*. The second interface is dedicated to communication between the worklist handler and the enactment service. The WAPI that enables this supports, among others, the following functions: opening and closing of a connection, production of case and work item state summaries, generation of new cases, and the beginning, interruption, and completion of activities.

3. *Interface 3 (invoked applications)*. An application is opened from the workflow management system through Interface 3. Figure 5.6 suggests that every application is opened directly from the workflow enactment service, but this is not always the case. An interactive application such as a word processor will generally be opened from the worklist handler.

4. *Interface 4 (other workflow enactment services)*. Interface 4 enables the exchange of work between several autonomous workflow systems (for example, case transfers and the outsourcing of work items). This WAPI thus facilitates workflow interoperability.

5. *Interface 5 (administration and monitoring tools)*. Interface 5 is concerned with the link between administration and monitoring tools and the workflow enactment service. It is subdivided into two parts: workflow system management functions and workflow tracking functions. The former could include the addition of an employee, the permission of authorization, and the execution of a process definition. To track a workflow, the enactment service records a wide variety of events in a logfile. Specific questions about this historical data can be posed via Interface 5. These could cover waiting times, completion times, processing times, routing, and staff utilization.

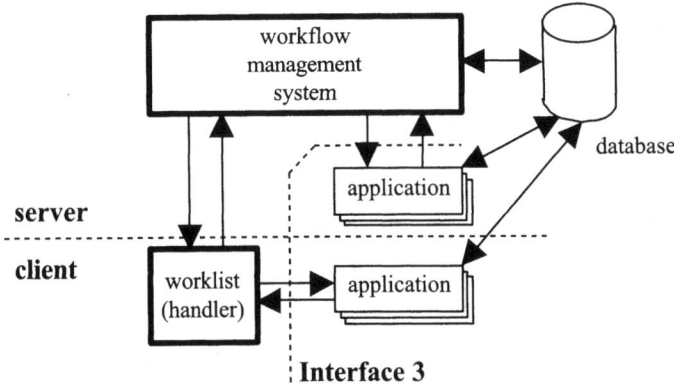

Figure 5.7
Potential problems around Interface 3

The WFMC is still working on standardizing the WAPIs. For example, little progress has been made thus far in agreeing on standards for Interfaces 3 and 5. Nevertheless the discussion about the five interfaces provides a good impression of the functionality desired of a workflow management system.

For those involved in the introduction of a workflow management system, Interface 3 is of particular importance. Interface 4 only becomes significant when one wishes to link more than one workflow system. Interface 2 enters the picture when the standard worklist handler is no longer adequate and an integrated application needs to be developed. Interface 5 becomes significant when one wishes to compile management information from the events recorded by the enactment service. In practice, Interfaces 3 and 4 appear to cause most problems. We therefore shall consider their potential difficulties in more detail.

Figure 5.7 shows diagrammatically how an application can be started (Interface 3). This may be done by an engine and/or from a worklist handler. An application is called to perform a task. Say the engine begins the performance of a task and so starts up an application. This application probably will modify application data in the database. If the workflow engine does not become accessible following the execution of the application due to a system error, then the engine and the application will be "out of synch." Once the system has been corrected, the engine will have no choice but to rollback the task. After all, it has no way of knowing that the application has completed the task successfully, and any changes in the case attributes have not been passed on. This results in the logistical data (case state) and application data no longer matching. Disastrous consequences may follow. Consider, for example, a payment by a bank: if the application has made the payment but the workflow management system is not aware of this because of a fault, then the same payment may be made again.

Similar problems may occur when an application is opened from the worklist handler. Assume that an error in the worklist handler occurs while the application is running. Again the workflow system and the application become "out of synch." The fact that the engine, database, worklist handler, and application can all operate on different systems only makes these problems worse. In a client/server environment, for example, the worklist handler and part of the applications run locally (client), but the rest operates centrally (server). To solve such problems effectively, it is vital that the engine, the database, the worklist handler, and the application all regard a task (or a part of a task) as a *common logical unit of work* (LUW). This means that the so-called *ACID* properties (atomicity, consistency, isolation, and durability) apply:

• *Atomicity*. A task either is completed successfully in full (commit) or restarts from the very beginning (rollback).
• *Consistency*. The result of an activity (in other words, the performance of a task) leads to a consistent state.
• *Isolation*. If several tasks are carried out simultaneously, the result is the same as if they had been carried out entirely separately. In other words, tasks performed at the same time should not influence one another. This property is also referred to as "serializability."
• *Durability*. Once a task is successfully completed, the result must be saved. A task therefore must be completed with a commit that ensures that the result cannot be lost.

Within classic *transaction processing* environments like those we encounter in the financial world, we frequently have to "pass the ACID test." In practice, though, with the current generation of workflow management systems, it appears not to be easy to address the ACID properties in full. This aspect therefore deserves to be taken fully into account at an early stage.

We encounter similar problems when linking two or more workflow systems (Interface 4). In addition, in most workflow management systems it is not always entirely clear what the state of a case is. In terms of Petri nets, the state of a case corresponds with the distribution of tokens amongst places (conditions) and the values of case attributes. The transfer of a case between two workflow systems based upon Petri nets therefore is equivalent to transferring tokens and case attributes. In many other workflow systems the situation is not so simple, because they often abstract from the state of a case at the conceptual level. (The places are omitted from the definition of the process.) In such cases, complicated "translation" work is required to transfer a case from one system to another. Note that, in addition to transferring cases, the outsourcing of work items and the generation of new cases in a different system also fall within the scope of workflow interoperability.

5.3.3   Interoperability standards

The presentation in this chapter is based on the reference model of the WFMC. This model was chosen as a starting point since it provides a nice introduction to workflow technology. Many authors have criticized the reference model as being too naïve or emphasizing the wrong issues. In this chapter we will not compare the reference model to alternative architectures: These more technical discussions are outside the scope of this book. However, we will point out recent efforts to resolve the interoperability problems identified in this chapter.

In the last couple of years several interoperability standards, that is, specifications for the exchanging information between workflow products, have been proposed. We can classify these interoperability specifications into two categories: specifications for workflow modeling and workflow description (i.e., design-time) and specifications for run-time interoperability.

The first category corresponds to Interface 1 of the reference model of the WFMC. The *WFMC's process definition language (WPDL)* falls into this category. Another example is *PIF (process interchange format)*. PIF is an interchange format designed to help automatically exchange process descriptions among a wide variety of process tools such as process modelers, workflow systems, process repositories, etc. These tools can interoperate by translating their native process description format to PIF, and vice versa. In this way, process descriptions can be exchanged automatically without using different translators for each pair of systems. If a translation to or from PIF cannot be achieved automatically, human efforts are needed. The PIF format did not gain sufficient momentum to become an industry standard. However, many of the ideas have been adopted by a new initiative: the *process specification language (PSL)*. PSL is promoted by NIST (U.S. National Institute of Standards and Technology) and has a scope which is much broader than the WPDL of the WFMC. There are several even more general standards emphasizing different aspects, that is, the standardization efforts in the context of *UML* (statechart diagrams, sequence diagrams, collaboration diagrams, and activity diagrams), the *ISO standard for (high-level) Petri nets* (ISO/ IEC JTC1/SC7/WG11), and the well-known *IDEF0* standard (also supported by NIST). These standardization efforts are relevant but clearly provide no solution for today's design-time interoperability problems. This is a result of the absence of a common conceptual or formal core model, as was mentioned before.

The second category of interoperability specifications is concerned with run-time interoperability. This category corresponds to Interface 2, Interface 3, and Interface 4, with a focus on Interface 4. The focal point is on the support of exchanging process enactment information at run-time. Clearly, Interface 4 is of the utmost significance when exchanging enactment information between systems of different vendors. The most notable initiatives with respect to run-time interoperability are the Interoperability Specification of the WFMC, SWAP, WF-XML, and OMG's jointFlow. Already in 1996, the WFMC released the *Interoperability Abstract Specification* (WFMC-TC-1012). This was followed by the so-called *Interoperability Internet e-mail MIME Binding* (WFMC-TC-1018). Recently (May 2000), the WFMC released the so-called *Interoperability Wf-XML Binding* (WFMC-TC-1023). The latter describes a realization of the Interoperability Abstract Specification using XML and is based on SWAP. *SWAP (Simple Workflow Access Protocol)* is an Internet-based standard and supported by multiple workflow vendors. SWAP heavily uses the HTTP protocol and can be used to control and monitor workflow processes. OMG's jointFlow is an initiative based on the CORBA architecture and also uses the Interoperability Abstract Specification of the WFMC as a starting point. The jointFlow standard is formed by a set of IDL specifications. The standards concerned with run-time interoperability are very relevant for the realization of workflow systems. In the context of electronic commerce, these standards will become even more

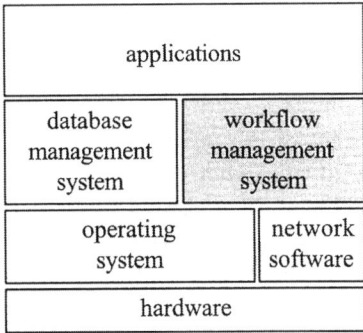

Figure 5.8
A summary of the technical components

important. Unfortunately, the standards are at a rather technical level and do not really deal with issues at a business level. It is possible to connect systems of different vendors using for example Wf-XML. However, this does not imply that the process is executed as intended.

5.4   Required Technical Infrastructure

In achieving a functional workflow system, it is not sufficient simply to purchase a workflow management system. As shown in figure 5.8, this is only one of the components required.

The successful introduction of a workflow system requires a suitable technical infrastructure. Most operate within a *client/server environment*. Such an environment typically consists of a central server operating in Windows NT/2000 or UNIX and a number of clients using MS-DOS/ Windows 3.1, OS/2 or Windows 95/98/2000. As we have already seen in figure 5.7, the workflow engine operates on the server side. The worklist handler, and hence the user interface, operates on the client side. The applications may operate on either side. The database of management and application data is administered by the server. Without becoming mired in a technical explanation, we shall briefly consider the main components:

1. *Hardware*. The server is usually a powerful microcomputer, or a mini or mainframe computer. Reduced instruction set computers (RISCs) are often used. Clients are generally choosing complex instruction set com-

puters (CISCs): for example, personal computers (PCs) based upon Intel 80x86 processors. The server is linked to the clients using coax, (un)shielded twisted pair or fiber-optic cable. Bridges, routers, hubs, and/ or gateways are also required when building large networks.

2. *Operating system.* The operating system of the server should allow for multiple users and multitasking. One obvious choice is UNIX; other possibilities are OS/2, Windows NT/2000, or Linux. Mainframes are seldom used· for workflow management. Operating systems like VMS, MVS, and AS400 are also rarely supported by the current generation of workflow management systems. The client's operating system is usually Windows 95/98/2000. However, it could also use UNIX, OS/2, or Linux. One characteristic of modern operating systems is that they support user interfacing.

3. *Network software.* The network plays a crucial role in the operation of a workflow system. It links the clients with the server. Common choices of network technology are the Ethernet and the Token Ring protocol. The communications software uses such a protocol to exchange messages. TCP/IP (Transmission Control Protocol/Internet Protocol) is currently the most widely-used standard in client/server environments. Other possibilities are NetWare, SNA, OSI, and AppleTalk.

4. *Database management system.* Many information systems are constructed around a database system. In a workflow system, too, the database plays a major role. Usually the applications and the workflow management system use the same database system. This means that the workflow management system must be able to make use of a database management system that has already been chosen. Most workflow management systems therefore support the most common relational database management systems such as Oracle, Sybase, and SQLserver. Using ODBC (open database connectivity) it is, in theory, even possible to make the workflow management system independent of the underlying database management system. However, the selection of an incompatible combination can result in poor performance by the entire workflow system.

5. *Applications.* The applications support the performance of tasks. They may be either standard software packages, such as a word processor or a spreadsheet, or customized software written in a script language, a third-generation language (such as C++ or Java), or a fourth-generation one (like Powerbuilder or Oracle Designer/2000). Various mechanisms are conceivable for starting up an application. Firstly, a command line can be used (in other words, it is started directly from the operating system). The case attributes can be exchanged through a WAPI or the database. The drawback to this is that a new program must be

started for each activity. It therefore is sometimes better to start the application only once. In such a case, the application is not closed when an activity is completed. So starting it a second, third, or fourth time is no longer necessary. In Windows, for example, DDE (Dynamic Data Exchange) is used to achieve this.

6. *Workflow management system.* The workflow management system has to deal with each of the components listed above. It must be able to exchange information with the applications and the database system. Moreover, it must be able to cope efficiently with the available processing and network capacity.

The above shows that technical as well as functional aspects need to be taken into account when selecting a workflow management system. Such a system uses the hardware, operating system, network software, database management system, and applications already in place. It therefore is vital that the chosen workflow management system suits those components. A poor combination can result in an unreliable system with long response time and a low processing speed.

5.5 Current Generation of Workflow Products

Today, many workflow management systems are available. Figure 5.9 lists some of them. This list is just a snapshot: It is far from complete and the support for some of the products listed has been discontinued. The number of suppliers offering workflow management software is estimated at two hundred—which indicates that such systems are expected to play a major role in the near future. Besides the specialized workflow management systems, most ERP-systems such as SAP, Baan, and JD Edwards have a workflow engine incorporated. In most cases these workflow engines cannot be used as standalone workflow management systems.

The information in this chapter is based upon the situation in early 2000. Due to the rapid pace of developments in the workflow market, this picture is likely to change completely within a few years. The rest of this book is, however, less time-dependent and will therefore remain current for many years to come.

Despite the large number of suppliers, some of which are listed in figure 5.9, the number of workflow systems actually in production is

ActionWorkflow	Action Technologies Inc.
Computron Workflow	Computron
COSA	Ley GmbH
CSE/WorkFlow	CSE
Documetrix Workflow	Universal Systems Inc.
FloWare	BancTec-Plexus
FLOWBuilder	PowerCerv
FlowMark/MQ Series Workflow	IBM
FormFlow	Delrina
HICOS	Empirica
InConcert	TIBCO/InConcert
Income	Promatis
JetForm Server	JetForm Corporation
KI Shell	UES Inc.
NAVIGATOR 2000/Workflow	I. Levy & Associates
Open Workflow	Wang
OPEN IMAGE	SNS Systems
PowerFlow	Optika Imaging Systems Inc.
Process Weaver	Cap Gemini Innovation
SAP Business Workflow	SAP AG
Staffware	Staffware
TeamWARE	TeamWARE
Ultimus	Ultimus
Verve	Verve Inc.
ViewStar	ViewStar
Visual WorkFlo	FileNet Corp.
WebFlow	Cap Gemini Innovation
Workflow Factory	Delphi Consulting Group
WorkFLOW SQL	Optical Image Technology Inc.
WorkParty	Siemens Nixdorf IS-AG
WorkVision	IA Corporation

Figure 5.9
A number of workflow management systems and their suppliers

relatively limited. There are several reasons for this. First, the technology is quite new, so systems developers often are insufficiently aware of the possibilities offered by a workflow management system. Also many workflow management systems still are not fully developed, resulting in limited functionality and unsatisfactory reliability. And it is currently not easy to opt for a specific workflow management system. The large number of systems available and the high degree of uncertainty about the future make the choice even more difficult. Finally, despite the efforts of the WFMC, standards with respect of functionality and system linking are lacking. For example, many workflow management systems use an ad hoc drawing technique to specify processes. One of the drawbacks of this is that it is difficult to exchange process descriptions between different suppliers' systems. (A conceptual standard based upon Petri nets would make a significant contribution in this respect.) Despite these obstacles, the importance of workflow management will only increase in the future.

In order to gain an impression of the current generation of workflow management systems, we shall briefly examine three products: Staffware® (Staffware Plc), COSA® (Ley GmbH), and ActionWorkflow® (Action Technologies Inc.). Staffware is one of the leading workflow products with an estimated market share of twenty-five percent. Therefore it serves as a nice illustration of the capabilities of today's workflow management systems. The latter two products have been chosen because they represent extremes in the broad spectrum of workflow management systems. COSA is a robust product with extensive possibilities for managing complex business processes. It also closely shadows the process modeling technique used in this book. ActionWorkflow represents an entirely different approach, in which the emphasis is placed upon coordinating the parties involved rather than managing the process. Staffware will be discussed in some detail. The other two are discussed only briefly. We will also present some tools for workflow analysis and BPR and mention some criteria for selecting a workflow management system.

5.5.1 Staffware

Staffware® is one of the most widespread workflow management systems in the world. In 1998, it was estimated by Gartner Group that Staffware has twenty-five percent of the global market. Staffware Plc, the company that develops and distributes Staffware, is headquartered in Maidenhead, U.K. In this section we describe the current version of Staffware: *Staffware 2000*. Staffware 2000, the successor of Staffware 97, was launched at the end of 1999.

Staffware consists of the following components:

1. *Graphical Workflow Definer (GWD)*. The GWD is the process definition tool of Staffware. It does not support any form of analysis.
2. *Graphical Form Designer (GFD)*. The GFD is used to define the interface that is presented to the end-user or, in case of an automatic task, the interface that is presented to the external application.
3. *Work Queue Manager (WQM)*. The WQM is the client tool of Staffware which is used to offer work to end-users.

4. *Staffware Server (SS)*. The server component of Staffware takes care of the run-time enactment of the workflow.

5. *Staffware Administration Managers (SAM)*. The SAM consists of a set of tools to support the workflow administrators. The following tools are included: user manager, backup manager, table manager, case manager, list manager, network manager, and sysinfo.

6. *Audit Trail (AT)*. The AT facility is used to monitor the execution of individual cases.

The Staffware components can be mapped onto the reference model of the WFMC quite easily: GWD and GFD correspond to the process definition tools (Interface 1), WQM corresponds to the workflow client applications (Interface 2), SAM and AT correspond to the administration and monitoring tools (Interface 5), and SS provides the workflow enactment service of Staffware.

Figure 5.10 shows a screenshot of the GWD. The modeling language used is specific for Staffware. The tasks are called *steps*. There are several kinds of steps: automatic steps (offered to an application instead of an end-user), normal steps (executed by an end-user), and event steps (triggered by some external event). The semantics of a step are *OR-join/ AND-split*; that is, a step becomes enabled if *one* of the preceding steps is completed and the completion of step will trigger *all* subsequent steps. Since the OR-join/AND-split semantics is fixed, two additional building blocks are needed: the *wait step* and the *condition*. The wait step can be used to synchronize flows and has AND-join/AND-split semantics. To model choices, that is, OR-splits, the condition building block can be used. Staffware only allows for binary choices, that is, just two possible outcomes (e.g., YES and NO). Staffware processes always start with a start step that is denoted by a symbol representing a traffic light. Termination in Staffware is implicit; it is possible to start multiple parallel threads that end concurrently. Therefore there is no need to have one sink node representing the completion of a case. The end of a thread is denoted by a stop symbol. Conditions are modeled by diamond-shaped symbols. Wait steps are modeled by symbols in the shape of a sand timer. The basic semantics of a step, a condition, and a wait are shown in figure 5.11.

The translation shown in figure 5.11 does not consider two additional features available for steps. First of all, it is possible to withdraw steps.

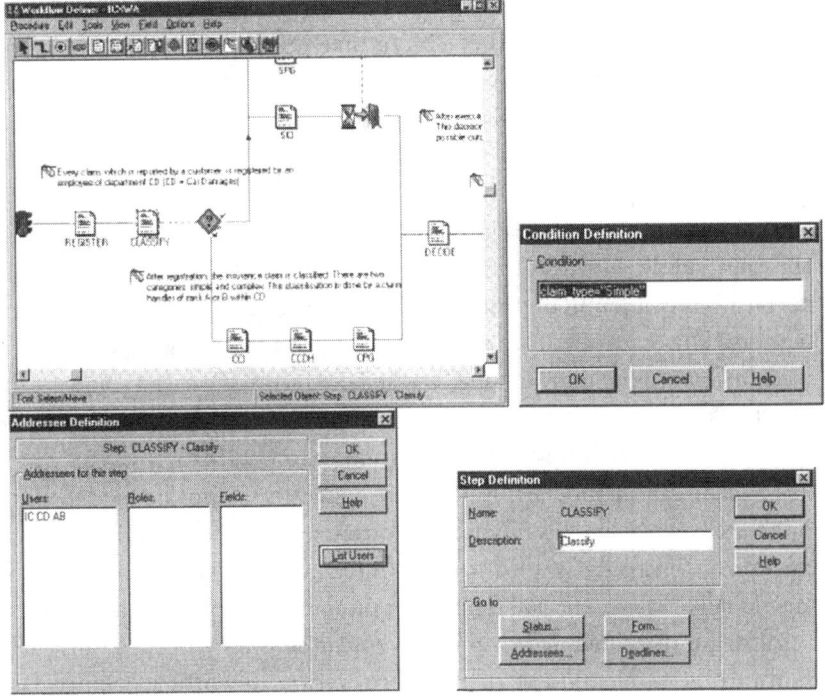

Figure 5.10
The graphical Workflow Definer (GWD): The design tool of Staffware

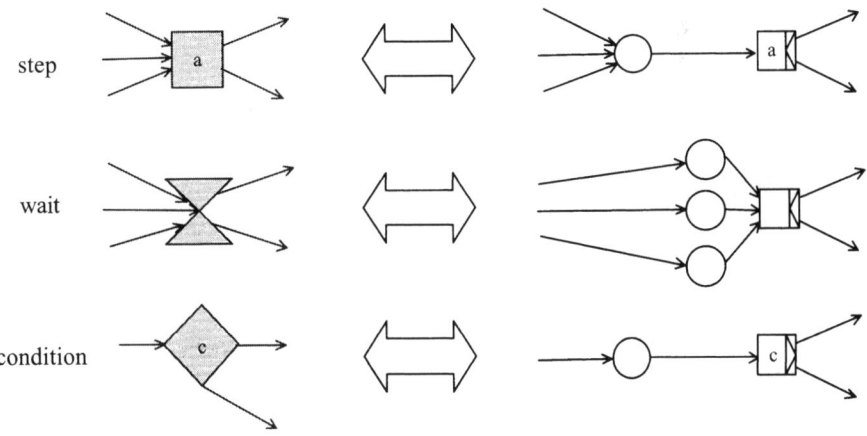

step

wait

condition

Figure 5.11
The semantics of some of the Staffware constructs (left) expressed in Petri nets (right)

Second, it is possible to model a time-out, that is, a step triggering other steps if it is not executed within a given time period.

Figure 5.12 shows the process of handling insurance claims used in chapter 2 modeled with the Staffware GWD. Figures 5.11 and 5.12 show that the modeling language used by Staffware is quite similar to the technique used throughout this book: concepts such as AND/OR-split/join play an important role in both types of models. Nevertheless there are some subtle, but relevant, differences. One of the core differences is the fact that the notion of states, that is, a concept similar to places, is not supported by Staffware. As a result, some models may appear to be more straightforward in Staffware (e.g., a simple sequential process). However, other models become larger as a result of the binary choice and the need to introduce wait steps for synchronization purposes. In fact, several constructs that can be modeled in terms of Petri nets cannot be modeled in Staffware, such as implicit choices, milestones, and other non-free-choice constructs. The only way to support these constructs is to encode the functionality in an external application or accept different semantics.

Staffware does not offer a tool for organizational modeling. Instead Staffware uses the concept of the *work queue*. A work queue can be compared to a resource class. Every queue is associated with a *group* of *users*. A user can be a member of many work queues and a work queue can be associated with many users. Each user sees the work queues for which she is a member of the associated group. Work items can be put into one or more work queues. If a work item is put into a work queue, one of the associated members has to execute the work item. When a user wants to process a work item, she selects it from its queue. While the user is processing the work item, the work item remains locked for all other members of the group. After processing, the user can either release the item (i.e., tell the system the work item is done), or put it back into the queue.

Figure 5.13 shows the WQM of Staffware. This tool is used to offer the work to end-users. On the lefthand side the work queues are shown. Note that each user has one personal work queue and several group queues. Figure 5.13 shows four group queues. On the righthand side some of the work items are shown. By selecting a specific queue, the user can see all work items corresponding to this queue. In figure 5.13 there are three work times corresponding to the work queue *IC CD Employee*.

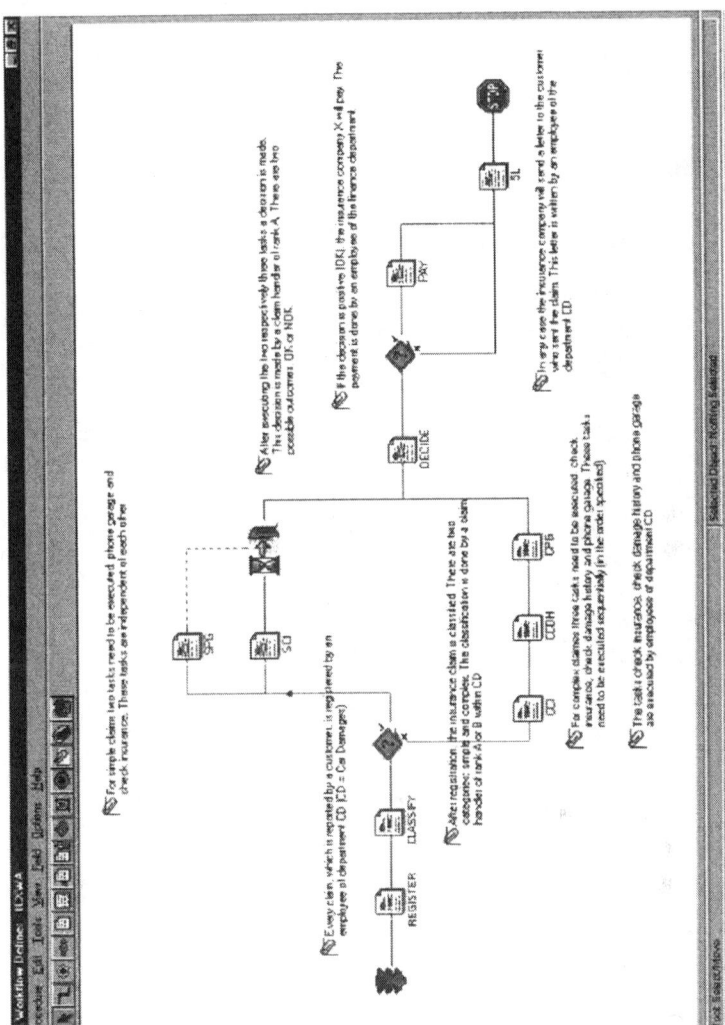

Figure 5.12
A Staffware process for handling insurance claims

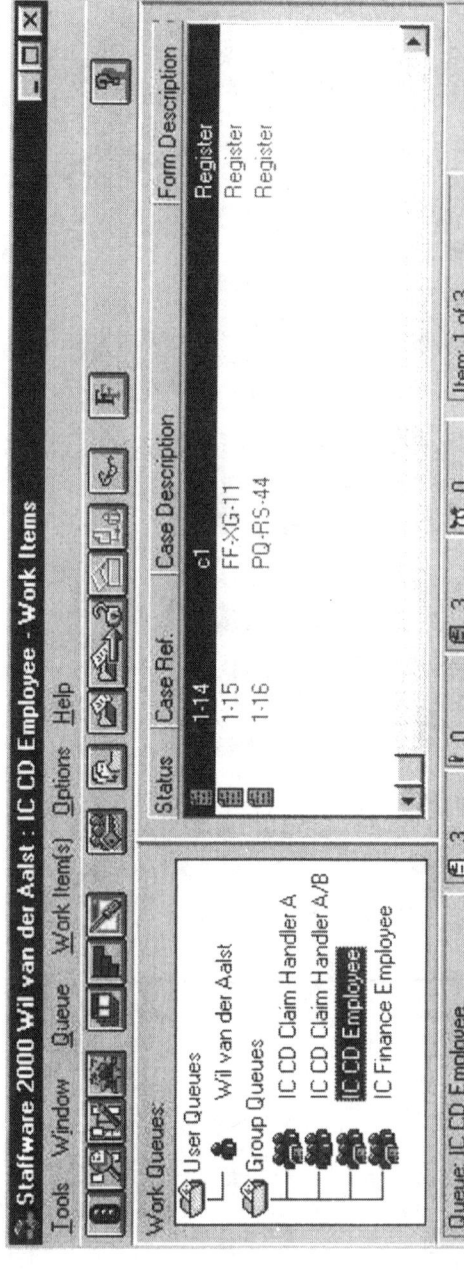

Figure 5.13
The Work Queue Manager (WQM) of Staffware

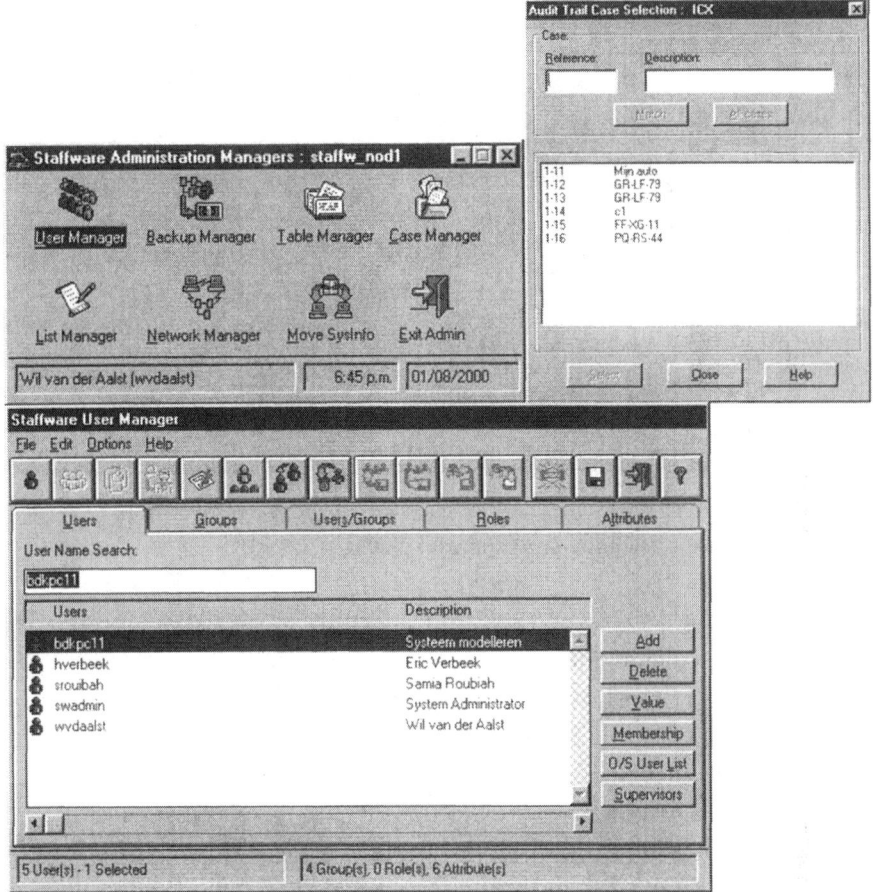

Figure 5.14
The Audit Trail and the User Manager (one of the Staffware Administration Managers tools)

Figure 5.14 shows some other tools offered by Staffware 2000. The Audit Trail tool (top right) shows a trace of all occurrences for a given case or process. The User Manager (bottom) is used to maintain a list of end-users, privileges, queue membership, etc. The User Manager is just one of the Staffware Administration Managers (SAM) tools.

This concludes our introduction to Staffware 2000. It nicely illustrates the features of the current generation of workflow management systems. The description of the two other workflow management systems (COSA and ActionWorkflow) will be less elaborate.

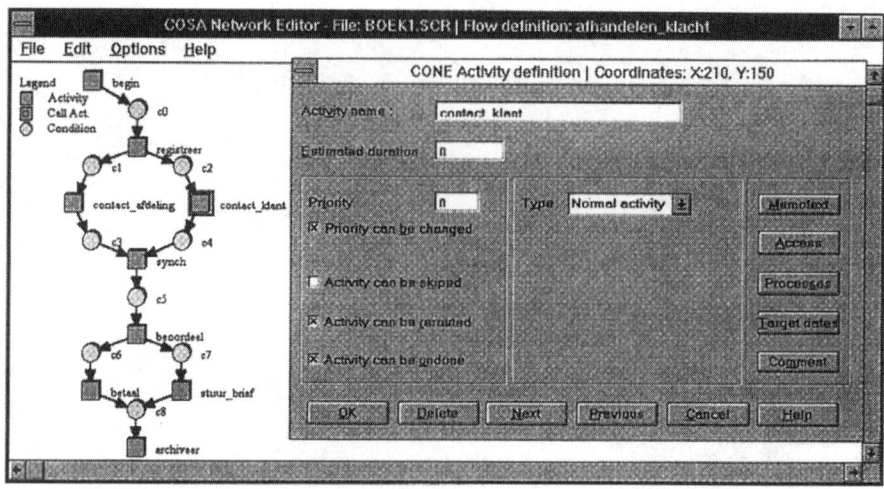

Figure 5.15
A COSA process definition produced with CONE

5.5.2   COSA

COSA® (COmputerunterstütze SAchbearbeitung) is produced by Software-Ley GmbH. It is a workflow management system based upon Petri nets. COSA can be described as a traditional workflow management system that closely follows the WFMC reference model. It is also characterized by very extensive functionality and a somewhat dated user interface. The figures shown in this section exhibit COSA 1.4. The user interface of COSA 2.0 and the recently released COSA 3.0 looks quite different but—in essence—offers the same functionality.

COSA consists of the following components:

1. *COSA Network Editor (CONE).* CONE is a process definition tool for defining and revising processes. As shown in figure 5.15, Petri nets are used to illustrate processes.

2. *COSA User Editor (COUE).* COUE is a resource classification tool for defining roles and organizational units. Figure 5.16 shows how resource classes can be structured hierarchically.

3. *COSA MemoBox (COMB).* COMB is a standard worklist handler for offering and starting work items (see figure 5.3). Every employee is provided with her own worklist handler.

4. *COSA Networkstate Displayer (COND).* COND is a graphic tool for presenting the state of a case. Because an employee can see the state of a case, she is aware of the business process.

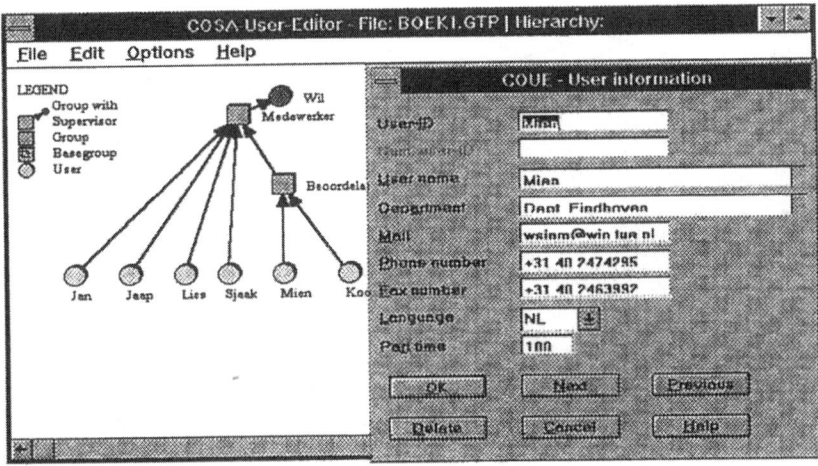

Figure 5.16
A subdivision into roles produced by COUE

5. COSA Runtime Server (CORS). The COSA Runtime Server is a workflow enactment service which consists of one or more engines.

6. COSA Simulator (COSI). COSA offers a primitive tool for simulating business processes. There is also a link available between COSA and the analysis tool ExSpect.

7. COSA Administrator (COAD). COAD is used to manage the workflows. COSA does not offer a recording and reporting tool. However standard reporting tools (such as Management Information Systems, OLAP, and Extraction tools) can read and process the information required from the COSA database.

COSA's architecture can easily be mapped onto the WFMC reference model (see figure 5.2). CONE, COUE, and COSI form the process definition tools (Interface 1). COMB and COAD respectively correspond with the workflow client applications (Interface 2) and the administration and monitoring tools (Interface 5). COND can be regarded as supplementing COMB.

COSA supports many technical platforms, including UNIX, Windows NT/2000, and OS/2 on the server side and OS/2, Windows NT/2000, Windows 3.1, Windows 95/98/2000, and UNIX on the client side. The following database management systems are supported: Oracle, Infomix, Sybase, Ingres, and DB2. It is also possible to communicate with running workflows via the Internet using COSA Portal; that is, it is possible to access the memobox functionality via a web browser.

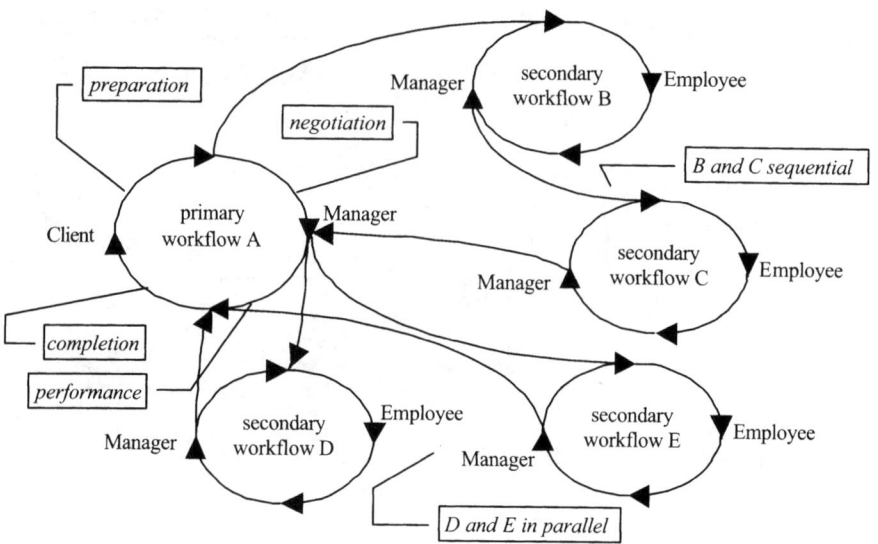

Figure 5.17
A Business Process Map with one primary and four secondary workflows

5.5.3 ActionWorkflow

ActionWorkflow® is produced by Action Technologies Inc., and focuses upon supporting processes in which communication between people and/or parties plays a major role. In this sense, ActionWorkflow is very different from more traditional workflow management systems like COSA and Staffware. Unlike COSA and Staffware, which concentrate upon the process, ActionWorkflow centers on coordination. Action-Workflow uses so-called *Business Process Maps* (BPM). These are constructed from a number of *workflows* (see figure 5.17). Each workflow corresponds with a transaction that passes through the following stages: (1) *preparation*, (2) *negotiation*, (3) *performance*, and (4) *completion*. Transitions between these stages take place using so-called *speech acts* (communication between the people/parties involved in the transaction). Workflows can be linked with one another to illustrate the connections between the transactions. In this way, refinements and various types of routing can be shown. In the BPM illustrated in figure 5.17, workflows D and E are carried out in parallel. Workflow C is performed after workflow B.

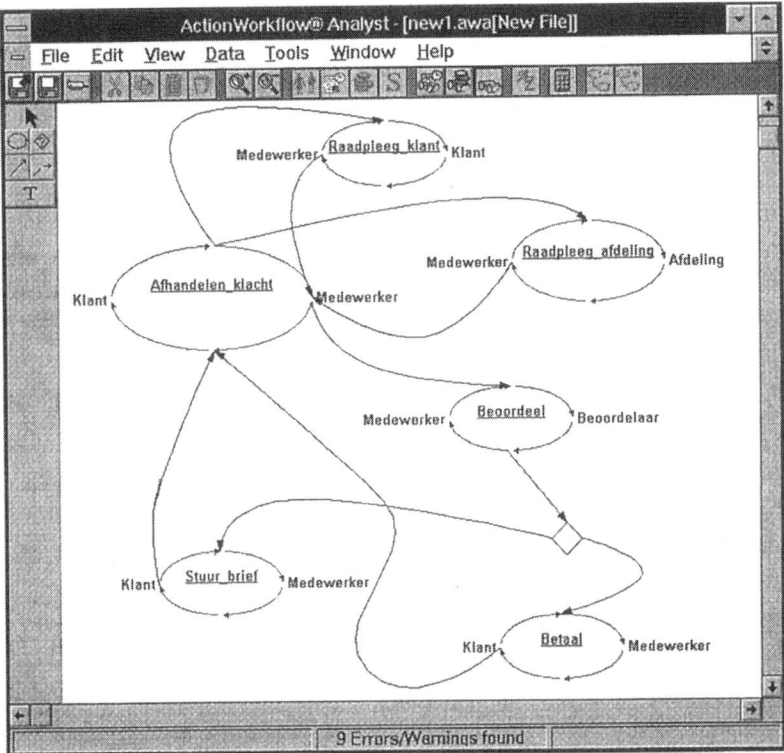

Figure 5.18
A Business Process Map (BPM) constructed using ActionWorkflow 2.0

In this section we discuss the functionality of ActionWorkflow 3.0. This is not the current workflow product of Action Technologies Inc. The focus of Action Technologies Inc. shifted from pure workflow management to complete business solutions. However, their latest product, called ActionWorks Metro (a so-called "e-process application platform"), includes the functionality of ActionWorkflow 3.0.

ActionWorkflow 3.0, also known as the ActionWorkflow Enterprise Series, consists of the following components:

1. *ActionWorkflow Process Builder.* The Process Builder is used to illustrate workflows, with the aid of Business Process Maps. There are two versions: an Analyst Edition for the process designer and a Developer Edition for the actual realization.

2. *ActionWorkflow Process Manager*. The Process Manager is at the heart of ActionWorkflow. It is both a workflow engine and a tool for managing the workflow. In addition it offers advanced possibilities for analyzing workflows which are in progress.

3. *Action DocRoute*. DocRoute is based upon the Process Manager and offers the ability to integrate document management and imaging applications seamlessly.

4. *Action Metro*. Action Metro offers the opportunity to create workflow systems which make use of the Internet. Web browsers such as Netscape Navigator and Microsoft Internet Explorer hence can be used as worklist handlers.

We can also illustrate the ActionWorkflow components using the WFMC reference model. ActionWorkflow Process Builder is the only process definition tool (Interface 1). ActionWorkflow Process Manager corresponds with the workflow enactment service, the administration and monitoring tools (Interface 5) and part of the workflow client applications (Interface 2). Action DocRoute is difficult to place in the reference model. Action Metro can be treated as an alternative to Interface 2; a Web browser acts as the Workflow Client Application.

ActionWorkflow is only available for a limited range of platforms. ActionWorkflow 3.0 is only available for Windows NT/2000 on the server side. The Process Builder also operates under Windows 95/98/2000. Through the use of the Internet, the client software is suitable for almost every system. Data management makes use of Microsoft SQLserver.

The above shows that COSA (or Staffware) and ActionWorkflow are two very different workflow management systems. COSA is traditional and thorough, enabling the support of most routine production processes within administrative organizations. ActionWorkflow differs in many respects from standard workflow management systems, and appears to be best suited to supporting processes in which coordination is crucial.

5.5.4 Analysis tools

As was pointed out in the previous chapter, there are several techniques for analyzing workflow systems. Unfortunately contemporary workflow management systems hardly support any form of analysis. In chapter 4 we differentiated between qualitative analysis (concerned with the logical correctness) and quantitative analysis (concerned with the performance and capacity requirements). Only a few workflow tools focus on qualitative analysis. Most of the workflow management systems have only trivial correctness checks, such as: is the workflow graph connected? More advanced checks like the absence of deadlocks, guaranteed termination, and proper termination are not supported. A few research tools have been developed to tackle the problem of qualitative analysis. Most notable are *Woflan* (SMIS/I&T, Eindhoven University of Technology, The Netherlands) and *FlowMake* (DSTC Pty Ltd, The University of Queensland, Australia). Both tools are capable of analyzing properties similar to the soundness property defined in chapter 4. Many of the workflow management systems available today support some export facility to simulation tools. This export facility is used to analyze the quantitative aspects of a workflow process. An example is the link between *Staffware* and *Structware/BusinessSpecs* (IvyTeam, Zug, Switzerland). Another example is the link between *COSA* and *ExSpect* (Deloitte & Touche Bakkenist, The Netherlands).

To illustrate the functionality of these analysis tools we briefly describe two products: Woflan and ExSpect.

Woflan   *Woflan* (WOrkFLow Analyzer) is a tool that analyzes workflow process definitions specified in terms of Petri nets. It has been designed to verify process definitions that are downloaded from a workflow management system such as Staffware and COSA. As indicated in chapter 4, there is a clear need for such a verification tool. Today's workflow management systems do not verify the correctness of workflow process definitions. Therefore errors made at design time such as deadlocks and livelocks may remain undetected. This means that an erroneous workflow may go into production, thus causing dramatic problems for the organization. To avoid these costly problems, it is important to verify the correctness of a workflow process definition before it becomes operational.

The development of the tool Woflan started at the end of 1996, and the first version was released in 1997. Basically, Woflan takes a workflow process definition imported from some workflow product, translates it into a Petri net, and tells whether or not the net is a sound workflow net. Furthermore using some standard Petri-net analysis techniques as well as those tailored to workflow nets, the tool provides diagnostic information about the net in case it is not a sound workflow net. Version 2.0 of Woflan has an import facility for COSA, Staffware, METEOR, and Protos. Figure 5.19 shows a screenshot of Woflan. A trial version of Woflan can be downloaded from http://www.tm.tue.nl/it/woflan.

ExSpect   *ExSpect* (Executable Simulation Tool) is a full-fledged simulation tool based on Petri nets. The development of ExSpect started in 1988 at Eindhoven University of Technology as a research prototype. In the mid-1990s the development moved to the Dutch consultancy company Bakkenist. At the moment ExSpect is supported by Deloitte & Touche Bakkenist, The Netherlands. The application of ExSpect is not limited to workflow analysis. ExSpect can also be used to simulate production processes, transportation networks, software components, embedded systems, etc. In fact, ExSpect can be used to prototype simple systems and can interact with run-time systems via the Microsoft COM standard. However, for this book, the link between ExSpect and several workflow products is most relevant. ExSpect can download workflow processes from workflow management systems such as COSA and BPR tools such as Protos. Figure 5.20 shows a screenshot of ExSpect. The screenshot shows that ExSpect supports graphical animation of the workflow processes. In addition ExSpect calculates confidence intervals for all kinds of metrics (flow time, utilization, etc.). It is also possible to modify automatically-created simulation models of the workflow to support management games. A trial version of ExSpect can be downloaded from http://www.exspect.com.

5.5.5   BPR tools
In chapter 3 it was shown that there is a close relationship between Business Process Re-engineering (BPR) and workflow management. Therefore there are also links between tools to support BPR efforts and workflow management systems. Some of the tools supporting BPR efforts focus exclusively on simulation. ExSpect is an example of such a tool. Other tools focus on the modeling of business processes without any real support for analysis. Examples of tools that focus exclusively on modeling are Protos (Pallas Athena BV, Plasmolen, The Netherlands) and ARIS (IDS Scheer AG, Saarbrücken, Germany). Some tools offer both simulation and extensive modeling capabilities tailored towards business

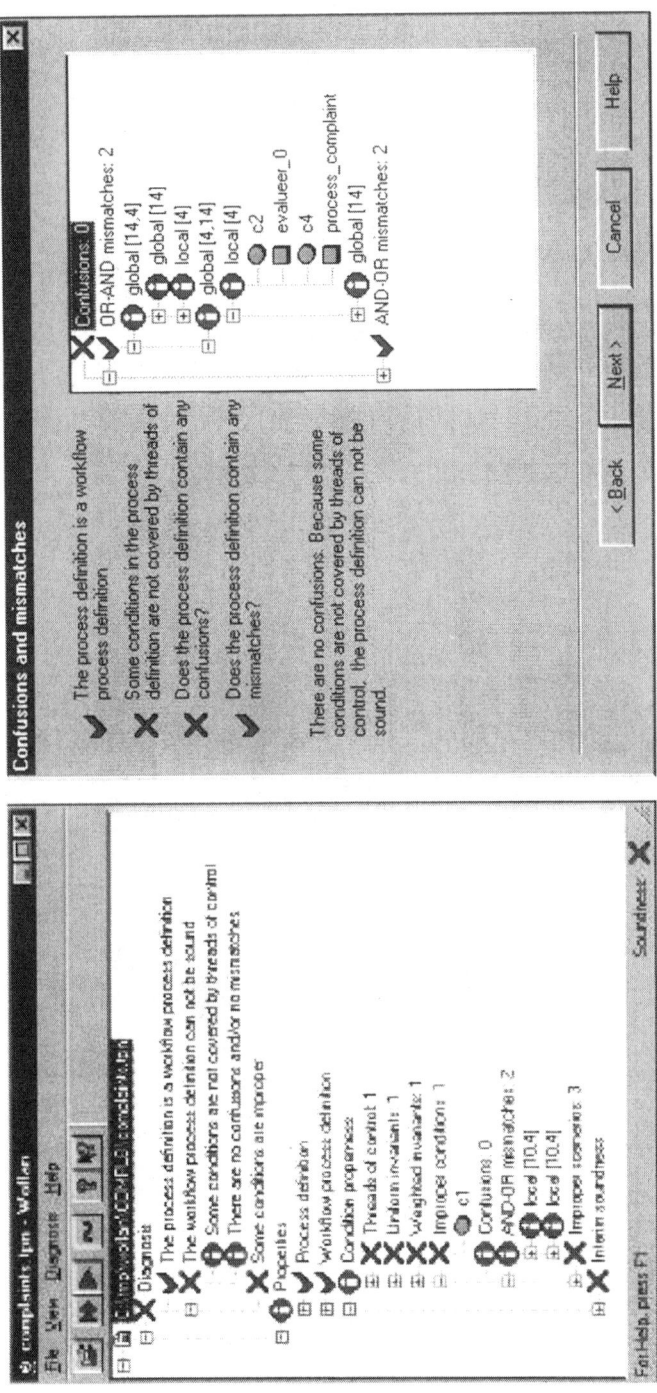

Figure 5.19
Woflan 2.0 analyzing an erroneous workflow process developed using COSA

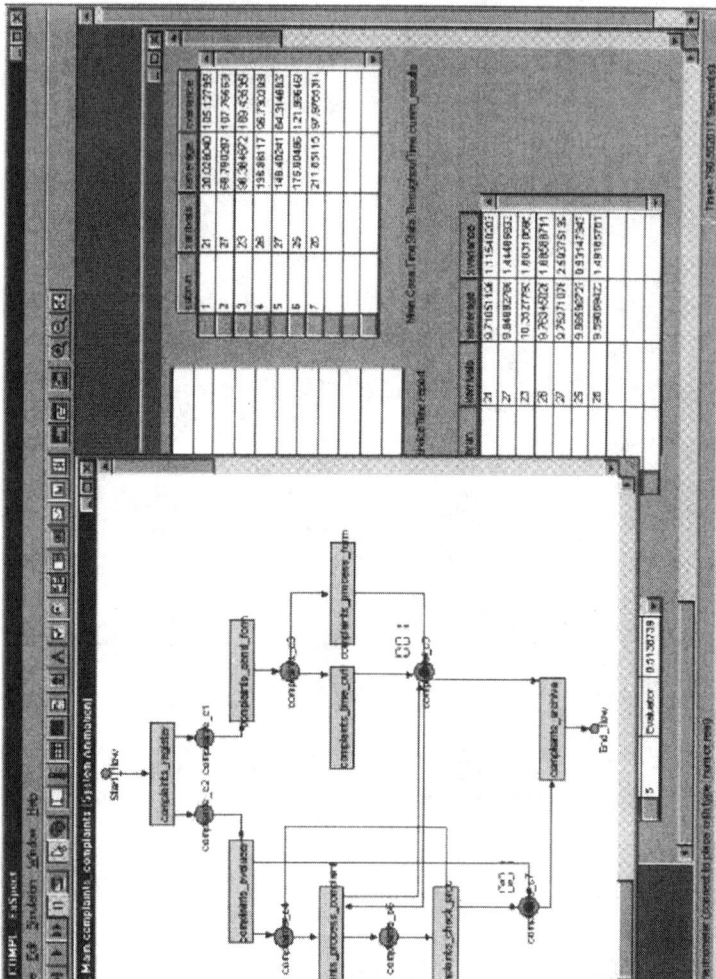

Figure 5.20
ExSpect simulating a workflow process developed using COSA

processes, such as BusinessSpecs (IvyTeam, Zug, Switzerland), Income (Promatis AG, Karlsbad, Germany), and Meta WorkflowAnalyzer (Meta Software, Cambridge, MA., U.S.A.). To illustrate the functionality of these tools we briefly introduce Protos.

Protos   Protos is a tool that can be used to model and document business processes. The tool is easy to use and is particularly useful for modeling workflow processes, that is, case-driven processes. Although Protos is not based on Petri nets it can support the diagramming technique used in this book. Protos supports the graphical modeling of processes, documents, applications, roles, groups, and teams. The analysis capabilities of Protos are limited: only very basic static dependencies can be analyzed (e.g., a role/route analysis comparable to the swim lanes in UML). Protos has excellent reporting facilities. It is possible to automatically generate RTF documents and HTML pages with hyperlinks. Protos supports an export facility to the simulation tool ExSpect. There also are interfaces with workflow management systems such as COSA (Ley GmbH), Corsa (BCT), and FLOWer (Pallas Athena). Figure 5.21 shows a screenshot of Protos. For more information we refer to http://www.pallas-athena.com.

5.5.6   Selecting a workflow management system

Selecting a workflow management system is not an easy matter. There are many aspects that need to be borne in mind. The selection process begins with the listing of the requirements that the system must meet. Based upon these, a *shortlist* is then compiled. When doing so, consideration is given to characteristics which are easy to check, such as the reliability of the supplier and whether the desired operating system and database management system are supported. The shortlist should preferably contain about five systems.

Each package on the shortlist is then subjected to closer scrutiny. One way to gain a good impression of a workflow management system quickly is to work through a *sample process* chosen *in advance*. Most suppliers are prepared to cooperate with a potential purchaser in doing this. It is very important that the sample process is representative of the relevant business processes. For example, one should ensure that all the

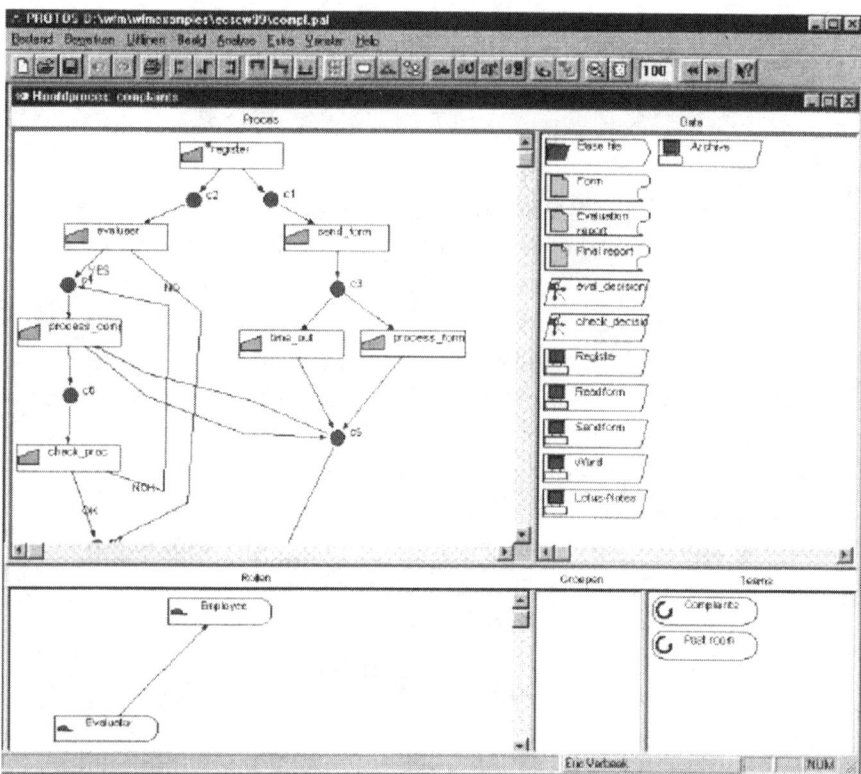

Figure 5.21
A Protos model of the complaints handling process

desired routing constructs are included. The sample process can be used to test both functional and performance requirements.

Figure 5.22 illustrates a possible sample process that, for the sake of convenience, we shall call *P*. Process *P* can be used to check functional requirements. All forms of routing are included, and a range of different triggers is used. The process is rather small for studying the performance of a workflow management system. However, if we produce a process in which *P* recurs four times as a subprocess, then we create something with far greater scope. By comparing the performance of the system when the four subprocesses run in parallel (linked by an AND-split and an AND-join) with that when there is selective routing between them (the four subprocesses are linked using an OR-split and an OR-join), one

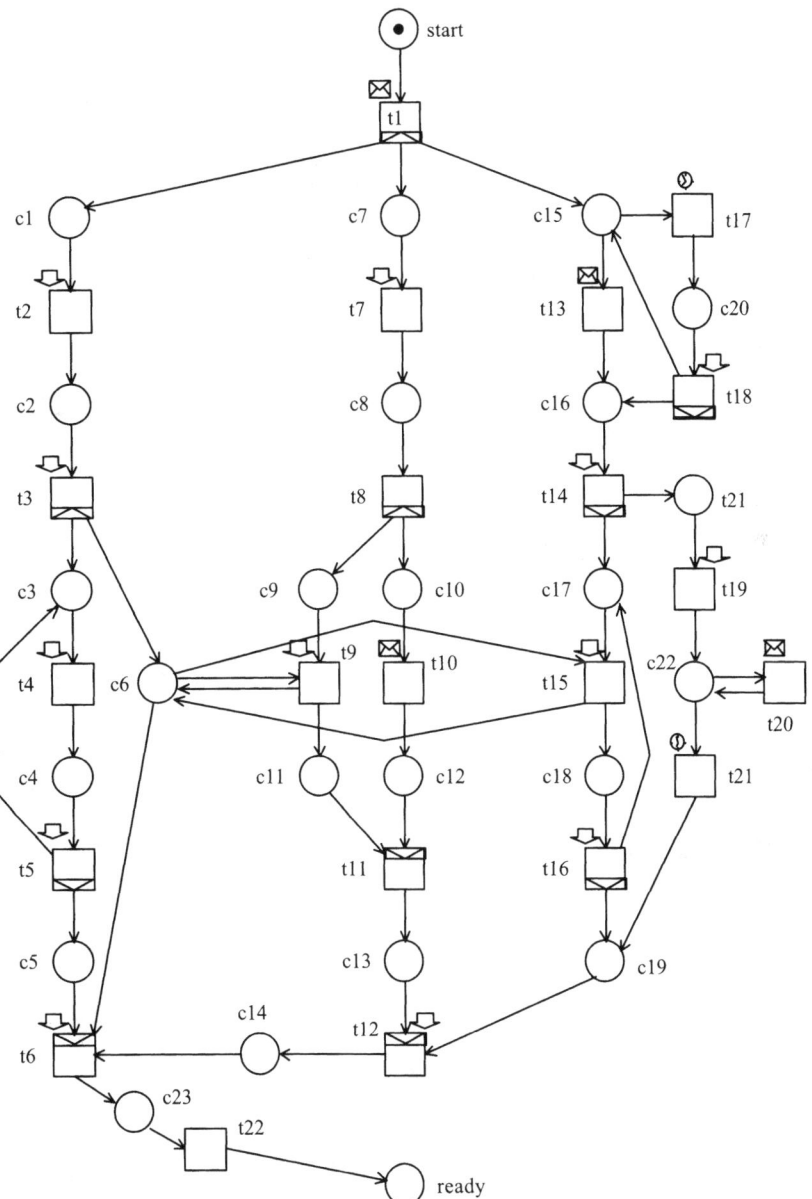

Figure 5.22
Sample process for evaluating a workflow management system

can gain a good insight into the speed of the workflow engine. In both cases the full process consists of ninety tasks. This is sufficient for most applications.

Once the workflow management systems on the shortlist have been put on trial in this way, it usually becomes clear which package is the best choice.

5.6   Adaptive Workflow

5.6.1   Workflow management and CSCW

At the moment, there are more than two hundred workflow products commercially available, and many organizations are introducing work-flow technology to support their business processes. It is widely recognized that workflow management systems should provide *flexibility*. However today's workflow management systems have problems dealing with *changes*. New technology, new laws, and new market requirements may lead to (structural) modifications of the workflow process definition at hand. In addition, ad hoc changes may be necessary because of exceptions. The inability to deal with various changes limits the application of today's workflow management systems.

Figure 5.23 shows the different fields of support for collaborative work. We distinguish between unstructured, information centric approaches (computer-supported, cooperative work or CSCW) and structured, process-centric ones (production workflow). Existing tools are typically in one of the two extremes of the spectrum: groupware products such as Lotus Notes and Exchange are typical CSCW tools, not providing much process support, whereas commercially available (production) WFMSs such as Staffware, COSA, and MQ Series are not able to cope with unstructuredness.

Linking production workflow management systems to groupware products does not really solve the problem, as the process logic then is still handled by the same inflexible workflow engine. To bridge the gap between CSCW and production workflow, several research groups are working on the problems associated with *adaptive workflow*. Adaptive workflow aims at providing process support like normal workflow systems do, but in such a way that the system is able to deal with certain changes. These changes may range from ad hoc changes such as changing

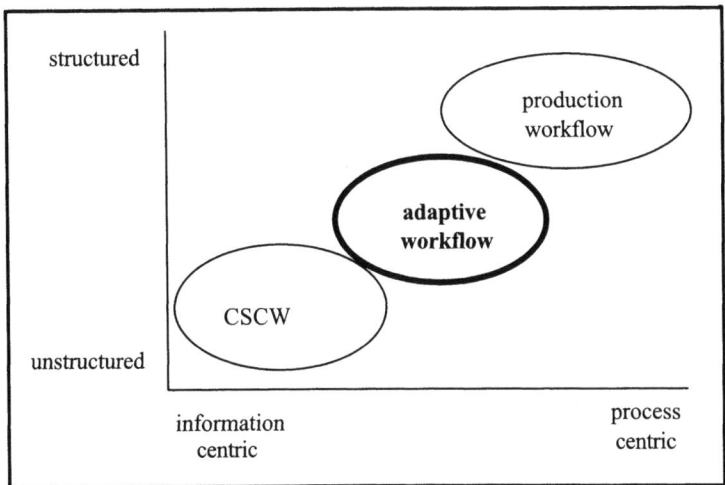

Figure 5.23
The collaborative work spectrum

the order of two tasks for an individual case (often called *exceptions*) to the redesign of a workflow process as the result of a business process redesign (BPR) project.

Typical issues related to adaptive workflow are:

• *Correctness.* What kind of changes are allowed and is the resulting workflow process definition correct with respect to the criteria specified? We distinguish syntactic correctness (e.g., are there any unconnected nodes in the graph?) and semantic correctness (e.g., can existing cases in the system be finished in a proper way?).

• *Dynamic change.* What is done with running instances (cases) of a workflow of which the definition has been changed? The term dynamic change refers to the problems that occur when running cases have to migrate from one process definition to another.

• *Management information.* How to provide a manager with aggregated information about the actual state of the workflow processes?

Taking these issues into account, a classification of the types of changes is presented.

5.6.2   Classification of change

This section deals with the different kinds of change and their consequences. Some of the perspectives relevant for change are:

• *process perspective*, that is, tasks are added or deleted or their ordering is changed,

• *resource perspective*, that is, resources are classified in a different way or new classes are introduced,

• *control perspective*, that is, changing the way resources are allocated to processes and tasks,

• *task perspective*, that is, upgrading or downgrading tasks, and

• *system perspective*, that is, changes to the infrastructure or the configuration of the engines in the enactment service.

For workflow management systems, the process perspective is dominant. Therefore we focus on the process perspective when classifying the different types of workflow change.

First of all, we can classify change based on the scope or impact of the change. Using this criterion, two kinds of change are identified:

• *Individual (ad hoc) changes.* Ad hoc adaptation of the workflow process: a single case (or a limited set of cases) is affected. A good example is that of a hospital: if someone enters the hospital with a cardiac arrest, the doctor is not going to ask him for his ID, although the workflow process may prescribe this. Within the class of ad hoc changes it is possible to distinguish between *entry time changes* (changes that occur when a case is not yet in the system) and *on-the-fly changes* (while in the system, the process definition for a case changes).

• *Structural (evolutionary) changes.* Evolution of the workflow process: all new cases benefit from the adaptation. A structural change is typically the result of a BPR effort. An example of such a change is the change of a four-year curriculum at a university to a five-year one.

There are three different ways in which a workflow can be changed:

• the process definition is *extended* (e.g., by adding new tasks to cover process extensions),

• tasks are *replaced* by other tasks (e.g., a task is refined into a subprocess), and

• tasks in the process are *reordered* (e.g., two sequential tasks are put in parallel).

If a change occurs, it may affect running cases. Handling existing cases in the system when a process definition changes poses potential problems. Dealing with existing cases is only relevant in the case of a structural change because individual changes will always be (similar to) exceptions and as such will be dealt with by the one who initiated the change explicitly. For structural changes there are three alternatives: (a) *restart*: running cases are rolled back and restarted at the beginning of the new process, (b) *proceed*: changes do not affect running cases by allowing for multiple versions of the process, and (c) *transfer*: a case is transferred to the new process. The term *dynamic change* is used to refer to the latter policy.

5.6.3 InConcert

Currently many researchers are working on problems related to adaptive workflow. Few commercial systems provide support for adaptive workflow. The problems related to dynamic change are difficult to tackle and not addressed by any of today's systems. Only for individual change there are some systems available. These systems are *ad hoc workflow* systems. In this section we describe one of these systems.

InConcert (TIBCO Software Inc.) is a workflow management system designed to develop flexible workflows. The tool has two unique features. First of all, the system supports "workflow design by discovery." This feature allows for the creation of templates based on the actual execution of workflow tasks for a given case. Second, InConcert supports a notion of class hierarchies that enables one InConcert object to inherit functionality of another InConcert object; in other words, the attributes of a parent workflow process definition can be inherited by child workflow process definitions.

Using the InConcert client software it is possible to bring into play the following tools:

1. *Process Designer*. The Process Designer is the tool used to design workflow process definitions. This tool can also be used to modify workflow process definitions on the fly.

2. *Task User Interface Designer*. The Task User Interface Designer is used to design the graphical interface presented to users when executing tasks.

3. *Work Group Manager*. The Work Group Manager is used to define new work groups and to monitor the workload of groups.

4. *Process Manager*. The Process Manager is used to start and manage cases (workflow instances).

5. *Document Organizer*. The Document Organizer is used to organize and create InConcert documents.

6. *Task Organizer*. The Task Organizer is used to display and execute work items.

Figure 5.24 shows the Process Designer of InConcert. The modeling language used by InConcert corresponds to a subclass of Petri nets: Acyclic Marked Graphs (AMG). This is the class of Petri nets without any cycles, and each place can have neither multiple input transitions nor multiple output transitions. InConcert does not provide any explicit OR-splits and OR-joins. Every task is considered to be an AND-split and an AND-join. To enable conditional routing each task has a Boolean condition associated to it: the so-called *perform condition*. The perform condition can be used to skip tasks. The workflow design shown in figure 5.24 shows the process of handling insurance claims. The task *pay* has a perform condition indicating that it should only be executed if the outcome of task *decide* was positive. The check tasks in figure 5.24 also have a perform condition: either the two parallel checks (top) or the three sequential checks (bottom) are executed.

The fact that InConcert does not allow for OR-splits, OR-joins, and iteration simplifies the modeling process. Workflow designers cannot make workflow models that deadlock or never end: The workflow process definition is guaranteed to be sound (cf. chapter 4). This makes InConcert a system where end-users can design or modify process definitions. Unlike production workflow management systems, InConcert associates a unique process definition to each individual case (i.e., workflow instance). There are several ways to create a new workflow instance:

1. Instantiate an existing workflow process definition: a copy is made of the process definition, and the first task is enabled without changing the workflow.

2. Instantiate a customized version of an existing workflow process definition: a copy is made of the process definition and is changed to allow for ad hoc routing.

3. Instantiate an ad hoc workflow process by specifying a sequence of tasks and users.

4. Instantiate a so-called "free routing process," that is, an empty ad hoc workflow process. There is no explicit workflow process definition: the workflow is created on the fly.

Instantiating an existing workflow process definition corresponds to the way cases are handled in traditional production workflow systems. The

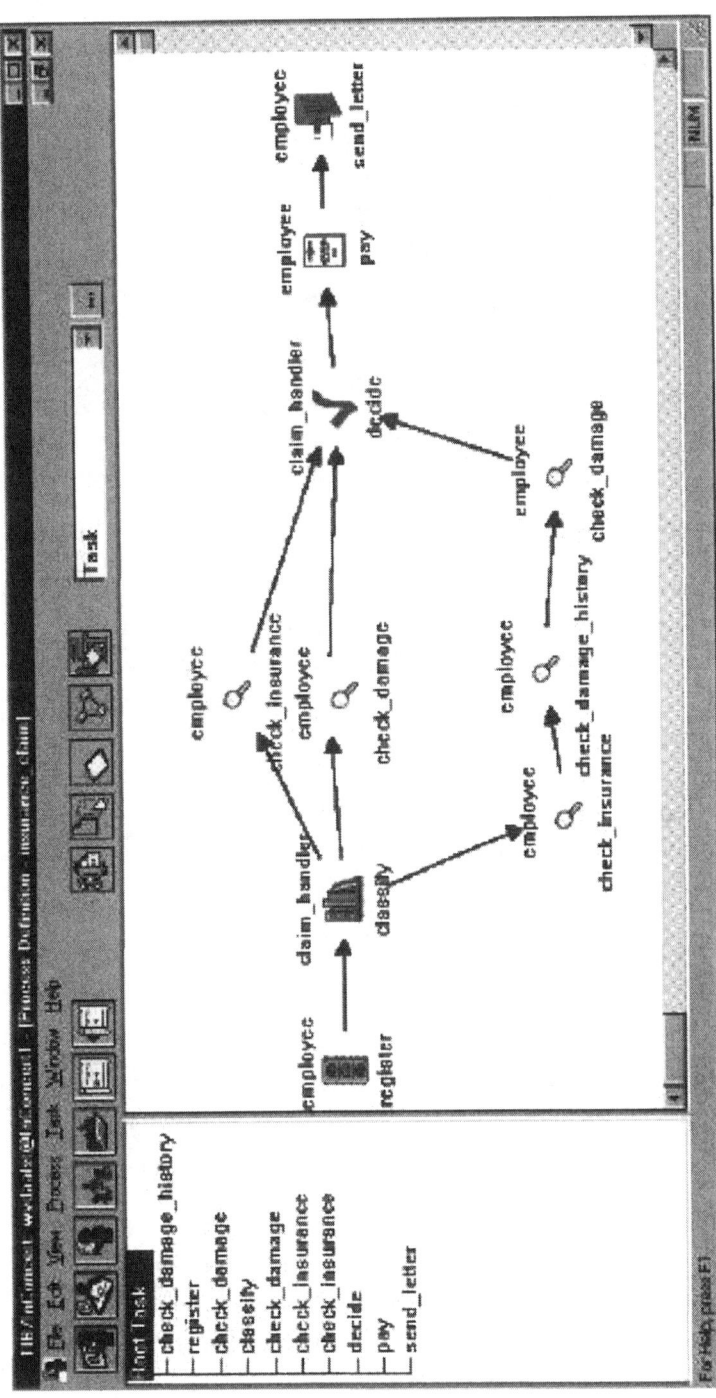

Figure 5.24
The Process Definition tool of InConcert

only difference is that the case does not refer to a common workflow process definition but to a private copy of the definition. By creating a copy and the possibility to change that copy, either at creation time or on the fly, the workflow process definition serves as a template. Instead of creating a copy of such a template, it is also possible to create an ad hoc process from scratch. The fact that each workflow instance has its own workflow process definition allows for on-the-fly changes. In principle, it is possible to modify the routing of a case at any point in time. This way ad hoc changes are supported completely. In addition, InConcert supports "workflow design by discovery." The routing of any completed workflow instance can be used to create a new template. This way actual workflow executions can be used to create workflow process definitions. Figure 5.25 shows a screenshot of InConcert while changing the process definition of a running instance.

InConcert also supports a class concept. There are three types of classes: process classes, task classes, and document classes. These classes are grouped into a class hierarchy and a child class inherits the attributes of its parent class. The class *Job* is the parent class of any process definition. By defining a child class *Activity_based_costing_processes*, all standard attributes are inherited and new costs attributes can be added. Any process definition of this new class is equipped with these new attributes. Similarly it is possible to define task and document classes. The class concept encourages reuse and a uniform way of realizing workflow support.

5.7 Workflow Management Trends

At present there are many suppliers of workflow management systems. The products they market are still developing at a rapid pace. It is a trait seen with all generic software: the manufacturers are, as it were, in a race. Each one tries to incorporate its competitors' successful functions into a new version of its own product as soon as possible, as well as devise some new features of its own as *unique selling points*. Thanks to these developments, we can see the packages converging with one another—although there are still differences. It is clear that the functionality desired by the WFMC is still far from being achieved. Nor is there enough practical experience as yet for us to know precisely what

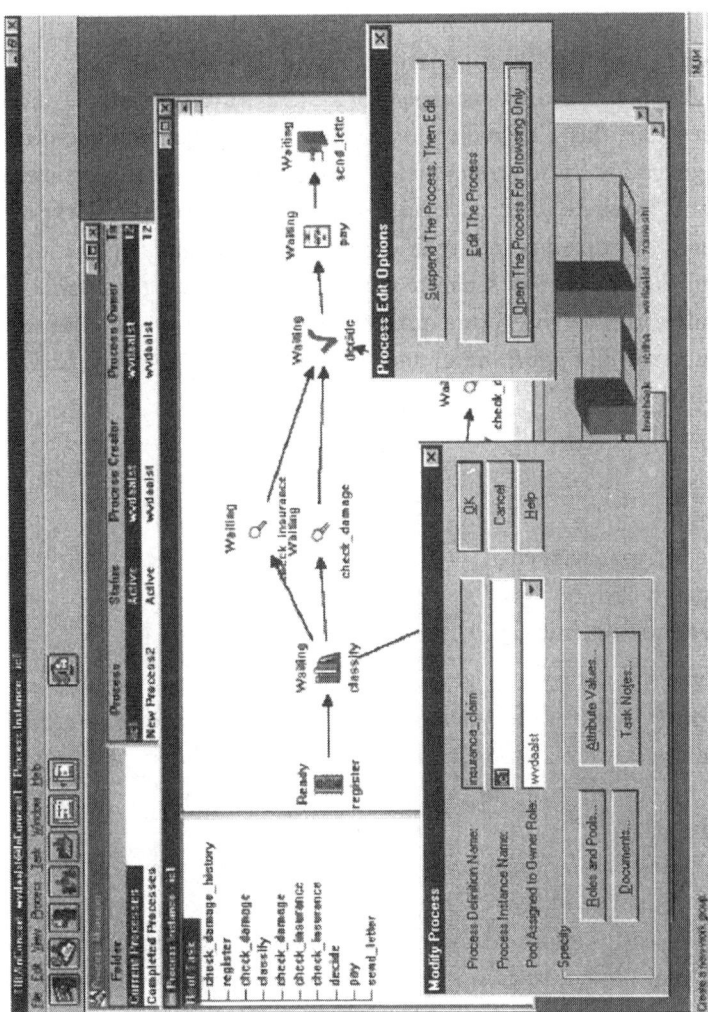

Figure 5.25
Changing the process definition of an instance on the fly

functionality workflow management systems will eventually encompass. It therefore is interesting to summarize their future potential.

As we shall see, workflow management systems have many application possibilities. But this also represents a threat, since the manufacturers of other generic software components—such as database management systems and logistical/ERP packages—will also incorporate workflow management functionality into their own products, eliminating the justification for the existence of separate workflow management systems.

We shall examine the future prospects for workflow management systems, in terms of *opportunities* and *threats*, in terms of seven areas of functionality:

1. modeling;
2. analysis;
3. planning;
4. transaction management;
5. interoperability;
6. Internet/Intranet; and
7. logistical management.

Because specific software for each of the above is also available, we shall consider threats alongside opportunities (i.e., application possibilities).

5.7.1   Modeling

One of the most important functions of a workflow management system is the modeling of workflows. This ability means that such a system can be regarded as a *repository* for *metabusiness data*: an organization's structural information, such as its processes and organizational diagram. Such tools have been given the name *orgware* (from "organization-ware"). However, there are specific repositories in which much more of an organization's data can be recorded: for example, all kinds of *performance indicators* of business processes, a *corporate data model* of the organization (a "data dictionary" of all the databases which it uses), and a *roadmap* of its information systems.

The advantage of such repositories is that they offer good query opportunities through which all the connections relevant to the management of the organization can be analyzed. They are often developed using a database management system and/or an OLAP tool (on-line analytical processing). One essential difference between these is that OLAP tools enable hierarchical structures to be searched through recursively (known as "downdrilling"), which is not possible in SQL (the query language used in relational database management systems). It therefore is obvious that workflow management systems will acquire more repository functions in the future, or improved interfacing with such tools.

Another important aspect is the *expressive power* of the modeling function in the current generation of workflow management systems. Many of the existing systems do not have a good process model. This means that certain common constructions in business processes are not handled well. This problem will certainly be solved, and one can expect that eventually all workflow management systems will model their processes in a way concomitant with the Petri-net theory.

One final aspect of modeling is that today's workflow management systems are mainly suited to *standard* processes. In other words, the process definition tool describes a number of business processes, by which many cases are performed. Because the number of cases is in general relatively large compared with the number of processes, we refer to this as *production workflow*. In the future, however, we should also expect systems which offer functionality for so-called *one-of-a-kind* processes (*ad hoc workflow*), with a separate process defined for each case.

An additional complication is that processes may change while a case is being processed. One encounters examples of this in the transport industry (when decisions to change route are made on the road) and in healthcare (when the appropriate treatment can only be decided after the diagnosis phase). In present-day workflow management systems, this can be partially overcome by defining a process with very generic tasks—but this is only really shifting the problem. The use of generic tasks results in much of the management having to be done within the applications. Solving the problem will mean further integrating the process definition functionality with the workflow engine.

5.7.2 Analysis

New business processes are analyzed in order to establish whether they will perform well in both the quantitative (completion times, resource utilization, and so on) and qualitative sense (are they correct, i.e., sound, and workable for the people in the organization?). When existing processes are improved, analysis of the modified processes is also desirable before the changes are put into effect. To perform analyses, we can use simulation and several formal verification techniques. Further expansion of these abilities is an obvious future development. For simulation, this means that it will be made easier to use historical data from the workflow management system to test modified business processes, and more opportunities for "games" will appear. In other words, people who play a part in the processes seek out weaknesses in the workflow management system using a business simulation game. This function can also be used to train new staff. Several existing workflow management systems already offer some game facilities, but there is much scope for improvement—for example, supporting rollback capabilities.

There are many simulation tools on the market, and it is not unthinkable that these will develop in the direction of workflow management systems. After all, it is not such a great leap from simulating workflows to coordinating real ones. It therefore is possible that some simulation tools may evolve into workflow engines. As well as simulation, there are also the formal analysis methods, which still leave a lot to be desired. Those available have mainly been developed for Petri nets and are not geared to specific business-process structures. It is likely that several correctness tests, like the ones offered by Woflan, will be incorporated into the process definition tools in the future. These will "rap the designer's knuckles" if he makes an error, without him having to understand the theory underlying the tests.

5.7.3 Planning

The current generation of workflow management systems sometimes offers only a limited ability to allocate resources to tasks and to decide the order in which tasks using the same resources should be carried out. (This type of planning is known as *scheduling*.) Existing systems pay virtually no attention to the *timetabling problems* that occur when organizing human resources. And owing to increasing labor flexibility and organizations' lengthening hours of business, this problem is becoming more and more significant. Functionality is required which is at present not sufficiently supported by workflow management systems.

Better planning support may be offered by the application of modern operations research and artificial intelligence methods in the preparation of rosters and schedules. Such methods as *simulated annealing, taboo search*, and *constraint satisfaction* have proven themselves in practice in recent years. Alongside these *operational* planning problems there are also *tactical* ones that pertain to decisions about how much of the *capacity* of particular resources (not just human ones) will be required during the period being planned for. Although a workflow management system does in fact contain all the relevant information needed to solve such problems, none yet actually offers the facility to do so. Also at issue is whether the producers of these systems should develop such functionality themselves, or whether it would be better for them to try to integrate propriety planning software into their programs.

5.7.4   Transaction management

Thus far most workflow management systems have confined themselves to work processes within a single organization. In doing so, they assume that the (human) resources are employed exclusively by that organization and can be allocated at will by the resource management (the boss or the workflow management system). Consequently it is assumed that all the human resources have the same client software and that all information exchange with them occurs in a uniform way. If we wish to apply workflow management systems to coordinate business processes in virtual companies or network organizations, then various problems arise that cannot be tackled by the current systems. Note that workflow management systems are very relevant for supporting e-business transaction processing. However they need additional functionality to support inter-organizational processes.

As described in chapter 1 using an example from the transport industry, finding a suitable resource will require a *communications process*. In doing so, a transaction tree is passed through until an actor is found who is willing to perform as a resource. An additional complication is that we can no longer assume that all the resources are able to interpret the same information. Messaging standards and conversion software like those commonly used in the EDI world therefore will become vital in inter-company workflow. XML offers a very promising standard for this. The communications process between the parties involved will not only cover the time within which the task can be completed, but also the amount of money associated with it. So workflow management systems will also have to provide functionality for the financial settlement of the work performed by resources.

One interesting complication of workflow management within network organizations is that the term "task" changes. It is not an atomic piece of work for everybody. What is a task for the principal is a process definition for the contractor. This is why it is so good that we use hierarchical Petri nets, because they can model such situations with ease. If the transaction trees (see chapter 1) for finding suitable actors to perform the case become very high, and each actor will only offer an upward commitment (a confirmation of order to its contractor) once it has obtained such a commitment from its subcontractors, then acceptance of an order at the highest level can become an extremely time-consuming business. This forms a "natural threshold" for the effectiveness of network organizations. In some situations, they will be practicable only if the communications process can be made largely automatic. As well as messaging standards, comprehensive agreements between the actors are also required to achieve this. Moreover, the additional functions for workflow management systems in network organizations also will bear fruit for hierarchical ones. After all, they provide an opportunity for controlled decentralization and so empower employees.

5.7.5   Interoperability

One of the interesting properties of a workflow management system is that human resources and computer applications are treated in a uniform way. The system organizes all the work that needs to be carried out on a case. In other words, it deals with the scheduling of resources and ensures that they have the correct information when they begin performing the task. In short, the workflow management system provides the logistical management of the work, and so closely resembles a computer operating system. After all, the operating system also performs tasks for the various user transactions and batch jobs. The difference is that a workflow management system also controls the work of human resources that are outside the computer system.

A workflow management system thus can be regarded as a kind of operating system for an organization. In theory, it could also be used to link various computer applications, since the order of tasks is described by the work process as some kind of flow chart. Such a system therefore could perform the control flow of a large information system, with the application programs carrying out its data transformations. However, although possible in principle, the current generation of workflow management systems is not yet suited to this type of usage. First, the existing standard application programming interfaces (APIs) are too limited. Second, the workflow management system would have to be able to function as a kind of *software bus* between various applications—a role for which its performance is still quite inadequate. It also would have to be possible to monitor protocols between communicating applications and to support data conversion between them. Moreover, there is often no functionality for rolling back transactions and coping with hardware failures. If these restrictions could be overcome, a workflow management system would become an ideal tool for bridging interoperability problems.

5.7.6   Internet/Intranet

A limited number of workflow management systems allow the use of a web browser such as Netscape Navigator or Microsoft Internet Explorer as a workflow client application (Interface 2). In such cases, a system-specific worklist handler is not used; instead the browser acts as the worklist handler. This makes it possible for us to access the workflow system through the *Internet*, also known as the *World Wide Web* (WWW). This has a number of significant advantages. First, one is no longer confined to a particular workplace. If the workflow management system is linked to the WWW, then in principle it is possible to perform work anywhere. Even from Australia, for example, there is no problem accessing a workflow system in Europe.

Another important advantage is the fact that one can employ widely accepted standards such as HTTP (HyperText Transfer Protocol), HTML (HyperText Markup Language), XML (eXtendible Markup Language), and CGI (Common Gateway Interface). As a result, there is no dependence upon exchange protocols specifically developed for a particular workflow management system. The use of XML/HTML pages is sufficient. The combination of workflow and the World Wide Web opens up new application opportunities: e-business. Many services offered on the Web can be supported by a workflow management system. Consider for example the processing of orders, complaints, applications, and so on. Interestingly, these applications blur the distinction between customer and employee: both access the workflow system in the same way. However there are also some problems associated with the use of the World Wide Web as a workflow client application. First, its speed may leave much to be desired; it often takes some time before a task can be opened or closed. Nor is the security perfect. Confidential information is difficult to protect. These problems can be solved to a large extent by using an *Intranet*. This has the same structure as the World Wide Web, but is limited in extent. Consequently a company can "shield" its network from the outside world and speeds are not limited by the "traffic jams" on the World Wide Web. Nevertheless it remains possible to use the standards and products mentioned above.

One problem that cannot be solved by an Intranet is the ponderous use of applications. Interactive applications such as word processors can only be started up through additional facilities, and data-intensive applications result in high loading of the network. New development environments (such as Java and CORBA) can only partially solve these problems. It therefore remains unclear what perspectives the World Wide Web can offer the future generation of workflow management systems.

5.7.7 Logistical management

One of the most successful categories of generic applications is that of logistical management systems, also known as *ERP Systems* (enterprise resource planning systems). Some of these packages have evolved from financial software and developed further through the extension of the stock-administration functionality. They enable the support of a large number of business functions in production (e.g., the automotive industry), distribution, transportation, discrete manufacturing, banking, insurance, and government. One of their most important functions is the calculation of materials requirements, based upon the planned lead-time of a product. Conversely the materials requirements are used to generate a detailed schedule. The basis for this is a products *component list*, also known as the "bill of material" (BOM). If a product must be ready on a certain date and it is known how long it takes to put together its largest subassemblies and finish the product (for example, paint), then one can calculate when the subassemblies must be ready. If they are also made in house, a similar schedule can be drawn up for the subassemblies. If they are purchased externally, a delivery deadline can be set.

The current generation of logistical management software does not use the term "business process" as generically and flexibly as today's workflow management systems do. Naturally their vendors follow developments in workflow management systems closely and are likely to incorporate some of the workflow functions in new generations of their products. Whether, given the structure of their products (legacy), they are able to do this effectively is difficult to foresee. Certainly such products have many other very interesting functions—particularly for production companies—and could probably compensate effectively for rather weak workflow support.

This threat again has an opportunity as its "flip side": it is quite possible to incorporate a number of functions from logistics packages into workflow management systems. The bill of material is of particular interest. Workflow management systems are always based upon a process made up of a number of tasks. The precise content of these tasks is entirely ignored, as is the information required to carry them out. Drawing up a bill of material for each type of case showing what information is required to complete it would in theory enable one to *deduce* what the tasks are. We can illustrate the use of such a list using the insurance claim example from chapter 1. The case can be closed when the level of payment is known and when the policyholder has agreed to a settlement (which may be zero). The amount therefore is required, and for this the value of the claim must be established, as well as whether it meets the policy conditions. (And so we can go on.) In this way, one can deduce the process from the information needs and have the format of the data required for each task immediately at hand. By beginning with a bill of material, the process designer can start her work at a higher level. This list can also be useful for the workflow engine, by enabling it to gather the information it requires in advance and to submit this to the resource at the appropriate moment.

We now have seen seven groups of functions that will be of importance to the workflow management systems of the future. Some already are being incorporated into the latest generation of systems. It is unlikely,

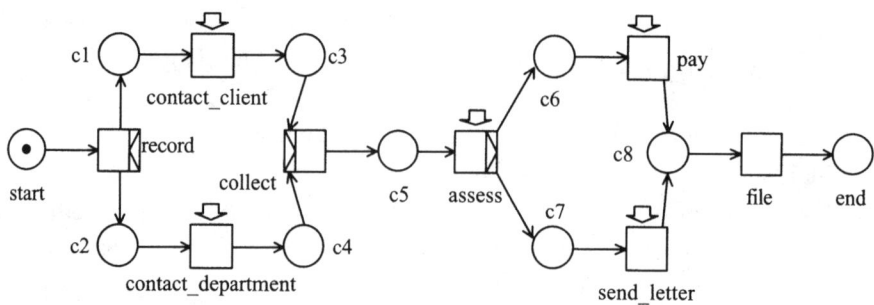

Figure 5.26
Process "handle complaint"

though, that manufacturers will incorporate all this functionality. This would not be sensible, because they would never be able to remain up to date in every one of these fields. A better solution is for the architecture of their systems to be left sufficiently open so that it is easy to integrate other manufacturers' software packages—with specific functions from the range described—into them. But for this a great deal of standardization is required.

EXERCISES

Exercise 5.1
Describe the reference model of the WfMC; that is, provide a graphical model of the components and interfaces. Describe each component in detail. Also discuss the functionality of each of the five interfaces.

Exercise 5.2
Answer the following short questions:

(a) What are the ACID properties?

(b) Which interface typically causes technical problems?

(c) What are the four roles of people involved in the design and deployment of a workflow management system?

(d) Name some examples of workflow interoperability standards focusing on run-time aspects.

(e) Characterize the following workflow management systems: Staffware, COSA, and ActionWorkflow.

(f) What is the functionality of analysis tools such as Woflan and ExSpect?

(g) Name some BPR tools.

Exercise 5.3

Model the process shown in figure 5.26 using the modeling languages supported by Staffware and COSA.

Exercise 5.4

Model the traveling agency described in chapter 2 using the modeling languages supported by Staffware and COSA.

6

Roadmap for Workflow System Development

6.1 Development Methods

The previous chapters have set out what workflows are, how you can model them, and the ways in which workflow management systems can play a part in the realization and management of business processes. Using these elements, we can develop specific systems to support workflows in organizations.

In this chapter, we describe a specific development method or a "roadmap" for developing workflow systems based upon workflow management software. A roadmap is a plan for developing systems, so it describes a sequence of phases and per phase the activities to be carried out and the deliverables. It tells us *what* to do but not *how* we should do it. Therefore a roadmap is used in combination with specific methods for each activity. For process modeling we have introduced these methods in the foregoing chapters. We call this method IPSD, standing for *interactive, process-oriented system development*.

6.1.1 Why a specific method for WFM?

Of course, various proven development methods already exist that can also be used to build workflow support systems. Why, then, should a specific method be needed for developing workflow systems?

The existing methods for the development of information systems place a strong emphasis upon defining data structures and the way in which the application is presented to its users (the user interface). Organizational change and the (re)design of processes receive limited attention in these methods. The development of a new generation of workflow systems usually goes hand in hand with a radical reorganization of the business processes. Moreover the opportunities which workflow management software provides for organizing and managing flows have far-reaching consequences for the relationships within an organization, and for the ways in which people collaborate. A method for developing a workflow system therefore should focus upon the business process and embrace both the organization and the technology.

The way in which the development process is carried out should correspond with this by involving the "users" as much as possible in the design of processes and systems. The development process should preferably be an evolutionary one. This means that the system's functionality is improved, through the continuous assessment and revision of sample applications or prototypes, until it proves satisfactory. By using modern software instruments such as CASE tools and software generators, rough prototypes can be produced based upon broad specifications. These then can be continuously readjusted with the help of user experiences. Configurable software, such as that for workflow management, also allows for this type of prototyping.

The fact that we are talking here about a new method does not mean, though, that we wish to completely "reinvent the wheel" from scratch. As a basis we use established ideas such as *business process re-engineering* (BPR) and *rapid application development* (RAD). The integration of RAD techniques within the BPR cycle provides an excellent context for the development of workflow systems, in which the development of work processes and support systems is completely integrated. An evolutionary approach supported by modern tools to enable prototyping and experimentation is an essential element in this development effort.

6.1.2   Business process re-engineering

Following several decades of computerization, many organizations have come to the conclusion that more is required to achieve actual improvements. Many information technology systems are still based upon methods of working that date from the age of the quill pen. A radical approach is therefore required to obtain a greater yield from IT.

BPR can, in short, be described as an effort to achieve the most effective and efficient possible business-process structure, without taking the existing "old processes" as a starting point. Information and communi-

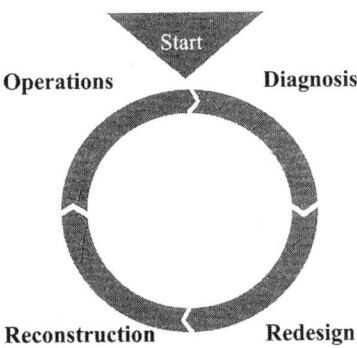

Operations   **Diagnosis**

Reconstruction   **Redesign**

Figure 6.1
BPR lifecycle

cations technology are the most important "enablers" in achieving this (see also chapter 3 for a more detailed definition of BPR).

BPR follows a more or less fixed cycle: the so-called *BPR lifecycle*. This is illustrated diagrammatically in figure 6.1. The cycle starts with an initiative, mostly coming from the senior management.

The BPR lifecycle has a number of phases.

1. The lifecycle starts with the *diagnosis phase*. This begins with an analysis of the current situation, and in particular of the problems caused by the existing way of working. Using this, objectives can be set by which the success of the improvements can be measured. The existing processes are analyzed and a diagnosis, as it were, is made of where problems arise or have arisen. Among other things, this shows us where the existing working methods are not producing the desired result.

2. Once the diagnosis has been made, the *redesign phase* follows. The new design developed during this starts with a "blank sheet of paper." In other words, the existing ways of working are not used as a basis. Instead an entirely new description of the process is produced—independent of such limitations as organizational structure and available resources, and determined solely by input and output.

3. The redesign phase is followed by a *reconstruction phase*. During this, a new system of process definitions, IT systems, and organization structure is created to support the processes previously identified.

4. During the *operational phase* the performance of the processes is measured and assessed using predefined performance criteria. Through these, potential bottlenecks can quickly be identified. These may well justify the launch of a new re-engineering cycle, quite possibly involving modifications of a less radical nature than during the original one.

The above provides a general overview of the activities involved in a BPR project. The crucial activities are those during the redesign and reconstruction phases. In 6.2 we encounter the same phases and there we will discuss the activities in more detail.

6.1.3   Rapid application development

Rapid application development is a method for developing systems which is characterized by a cyclical development process, close collaboration with users, and the use of modern rapid-development tools. Its main objectives are speed, cost reduction, and quality improvement, thanks to a high degree of user participation. In this book, we shall base our approach upon the rapid application development (RAD) method introduced by James Martin in 1991.

In general terms, the phasing used in RAD corresponds with the approaches used in more traditional methods. The difference lies not so much in the sequencing of activities but in the way in which they are carried out during each phase. Before we examine RAD's phases and methodology, let us first look at a number of terms and techniques that are crucial to it.

RAD is based upon a *cyclical*, or *iterative*, *development process*. In other words, the analysis, design, and construction phases are passed through repeatedly, in small steps which succeed one another rapidly. Each cycle results in a tangible end product which is used as the basis for starting the next. Newly acquired insights thus can make an immediate contribution through design updates, so benefiting quality and acceptability. *Prototyping* is an important instrument in establishing efficient and effective communication with users. The specifications of (a part of) a system, or of individual components, are assessed using the prototypes developed. This places less demand upon the imagination than would the assessment of paper specifications. We refer to *evolutionary development* when such a method results in the prototype development, through gradual improvement, into the final application. The specifications and the system "evolve" simultaneously into the operational system.

A system often is too large to be assessed in its entirety by the user, and its development and enactment at a single stroke entail too many risks. Therefore, it can be useful to develop *and* implement the system in a number of separate stages or "increments." We call this *incremental de-*

velopment. Each stage of development ends with the delivery and enactment of a new version of the system that is an improvement/expansion of the previous one. Evolutionary and incremental development are different strategies, but ones that can be combined very effectively. This, however, is not the same as *phased delivery and enactment*, which is based upon a single overall design for the system as a whole being followed by the phased construction, delivery, and enactment of modules of the complete application. This is only possible when the sections being implemented are not directly dependent—at least for the time being—upon other parts of the system that are to be delivered later on.

Such techniques as evolutionary development and prototyping can only be applied successfully when a very close working relationship can be established between developers and users. We call this *joint development*, because of the close collaboration and the subsequent collective responsibility for the result. Organizing such cooperation is an art in itself. Most information technologists are used to the "parliamentary" model, under which the users may only submit amendments to the developers' proposals (the draft final report). In joint development, *interactive workshops* play a major role. In principle, all the participants have an equal say during these joint sessions. Brainstorming, decision making, selection, and elaboration are fostered using special techniques. Because all those involved are present and play an active part, the communication gap is bridged and well-founded decisions can be made. Specification, prototyping, and testing all take place during these workshops.

The RAD approach consists of four directly successive phases: *requirements planning, user design, construction* and *delivery*. Figure 6.2 illustrates the relationship between these.

During the *requirements planning phase*, the intended results of the project are defined. Guidelines for the functionality of the system are set, as are the requirements to be met by the products delivered. Based upon the results to be achieved, the subsequent development route is planned.

During the *user design phase*, the system's functionality is blueprinted. Its specifications are drawn up interactively at *joint application design* (JAD) workshops. The users provide the input, which is recorded by the designers—in the form of specifications—in a CASE tool. Prototypes are created with the aid of a program generator. The users then can test the

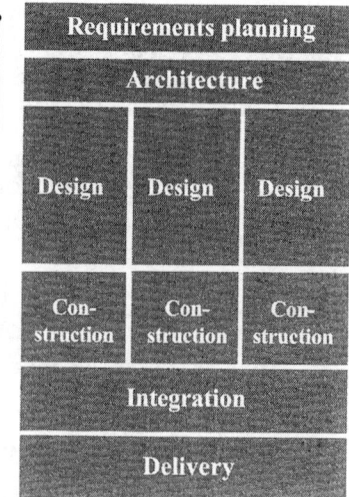

Figure 6.2
The phases of RAD

specifications directly against the prototypes. In traditional development methods, the design phase is clearly distinct from the construction phase. In RAD, this is not the case: the software to a large extent can be generated from the specifications laid down in the CASE tool.

During the *construction phase*, the generated software is perfected and elements which could not be produced automatically are made "by hand." Validation of the design by the users continues during this phase. During the *delivery phase*, the acceptance test is carried out and the system is then prepared for production. This involves such things as installation, any conversion that is necessary, and user training. For more extensive applications, a limited number of parallel design and construction paths may be taken, bearing project management in mind.

In order to integrate the system's individual components with one another, a technical architecture for their relationship is designed during a separate *architecture phase*, prior to the start of the user-design phase.

Once construction is complete, the operation of the separate components is tested during the *integration phase*. This is a preparatory test—mainly devoted to the technical compatibility between the separate components—carried out prior to the system being handed over to the user for an acceptance test and enactment.

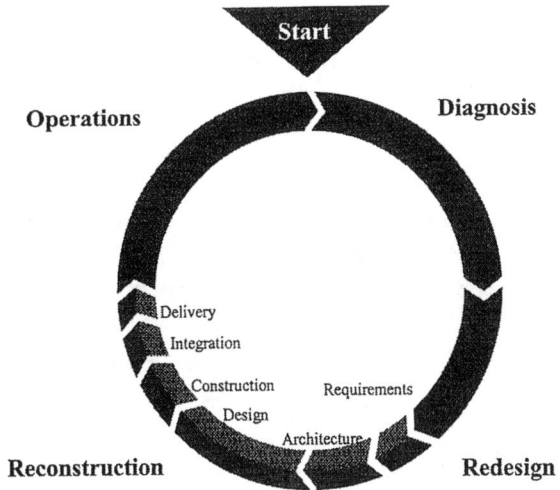

Figure 6.3
Lifecycle

6.2   The "IPSD" Method

IPSD stands for *interactive, process-oriented system development*. The design of efficient business processes and the development of information systems to support them are combined in an interactive approach by which complete workflow systems can be developed interactively in a BPR context. Moreover this model is also applicable in situations where no workflow system is being developed and so no workflow management software is used. In our discussion, however, we shall assume a situation in which workflows do exist, as described in this book.

If we project the RAD phases onto the BPR lifecycle, then the IPSD lifecycle of a workflow system is generated. This is illustrated diagrammatically in figure 6.3. Note that here the phases given in figure 6.2 (RAD) are superimposed onto those given in figure 6.1 (BPR).

In the rest of the chapter, we shall refine this lifecycle further. Ultimately we shall identify the following phases:

1. preparation;
2. diagnosis;
3. process redesign;
4. requirements;

5. architecture;
6. component design;
7. construction;
8. integration;
9. delivery;
10. enactment; and
11. monitor and improve.

A project conducted according to the IPSD method will pass through these eleven phases.

In the following sections we shall examine in more detail the activities carried out during the various phases. In doing so, we shall assume the complete redesign of a process and the development and enactment of a new information system supported by workflow management software in conjunction with "traditional" data-processing applications. In section 6.2.13, we shall turn our attention to situations in which workflow management software is integrated with existing (legacy) systems.

6.2.1 Basic principles

The IPSD method focuses upon the development of the best business processes possible. Good interaction between information technologists and users contributes to their quality and their acceptance within the organization. It also ensures that their development proceeds quickly and efficiently. Based upon these preconditions, we derive a number of basic principles that are essential to the successful application of the method:

1. The focus is on the business process. Throughout the entire development cycle, efforts concentrate upon achieving the best possible process structure. Amongst other things, this means that a solid process design is created at an early stage—with opportunities for improvement to it continually being sought as development continues.

2. By definition, radical change will occur that has consequences for the entire organization—or, at least, for parts of it. Success is only guaranteed if (senior) management supports the project and conveys this commitment unequivocally to the organization.

3. As far as possible, decisions are taken within the development team. This results in the progress of the project being disturbed as little as possible. The managers responsible therefore must either be part of the team or delegate their responsibility.

4. The developers and (representatives of) the user organization work as a team to improve processes and develop the information systems. Together they are responsible for the result. All the participants respect one another's expertise, and the input by each is treated equally.

5. When planning and organizing the development path, the emphasis is placed upon (project) targets and not so much upon performing (or assigning) activities.

6. The system's specifications are not defined and "frozen" in advance, but evolve during development. The specifications are laid down in the workflow system and a CASE tool, and tested with the aid of prototypes and (practical) simulations.

7. Errors are permissible during development. Because of the iterative nature of the approach, the system's functionality is continually tested. Whenever an error is made, it can be corrected during a later iteration.

8. Experience shows that no system is ever perfect the first time. Rather than devoting too much time to seeking out (technically) perfect solutions, it is better to achieve a tangible result that is considered "good enough" within a short time.

9. At the end of each phase the overall planning is updated according to the latest information.

6.2.2 Preparation

To prepare the project, a project team is established. The scope and composition of this team may vary during the course of the project, but initially it is desirable to begin with a "core" group of people who will remain involved until completion. In addition to a project manager, this team consists of representatives from those organizational units involved. These include people from the "user organization" and the IT department, as well as experts in the field of business-process analysis and modeling. The person appointed as project manager should be someone with sufficient authority within the organization. This may be someone from senior management, although there may be arguments against such an appointment (such as time pressure, availability, and lack of required knowledge and skills). Because a good line manager does not necessarily make a good project manager, and internal (IT) project managers may not have sufficient seniority, it is quite common to recruit a project manager externally.

Given the importance of the project and its consequences for the organization as a whole, the precise purpose of the re-engineering project must be made clear—preferably by the organization's highest level of management. It also must be absolutely clear that the management stands squarely behind the project manager and his or her work.

At the beginning of the project, the project manager draws up a project plan. This describes the approach to be taken and contains a rough timetable. The objective of the project must be clearly stated in the plan, and there should be a visible relationship between the approach chosen and the achievement of the objective. In other words, it must be absolutely clear how each activity will contribute to the project objective. At this stage, the project timetable is still very approximate; it only will be fixed definitively during the diagnosis phase. The project plan will be issued to all those in the organization who are involved in the project.

Activities
• Appointing the (core) project team;
• drafting the project plan;
• obtaining approval for the project; and
• communication of the mission statement, approach and timetable.

Deliverables
• Overall project plan

6.2.3 Diagnosis
A project should begin with an analysis of the existing situation. Understanding the existing strategy of the organization is an important first step. *Diagnosis* has three groups of activities: analysis, scoping, and visioning. They are interwoven and therefore we consider them as one phase. *Analysis* is concerned with the existing situation and understanding the reasons for change. *Scoping* is the clear identification of which parts of the organization, processes, and systems should be considered in the project and which should not. Also a timetable for the project and a rough budget should be determined. *Visioning* is focused on the possible directions for improvement.

The *analysis* starts with looking for the reasons for change. Change means transformation or re-engineering of the business processes, the organization, and the supporting information systems. Often there exist some bottlenecks in the performance of the existing processes or supporting information systems. These bottlenecks can be of a quantitative nature, which means that the processes have too little capacity to deliver enough products or services to fulfil the customer's demand. It also is possible that the bottlenecks are of a qualitative nature, which means that the products or services that are generated by the processes do not fulfil the customer's needs. Of course both causes may occur simultaneously. It is also possible that the production process is too expensive. Yet another possibility is that there are no bottlenecks but that they are expected in the near future if nothing is done. All these reasons are symptoms of some "illness." When analyzing a process, particular attention has to be paid to the following aspects:

· unnecessary sequential and bureaucratic activities;
· the formation of "island computerization";
· the need for excessive forms and approvals;
· paper usage and redundant stipulations; and
· policy guidelines and rules (either formal or informal) that are not being observed or do not appear to work.

In case an organization is in good shape, there can still be a need for change if there are some good opportunities to extend the business or to improve quality or efficiency by introducing some new technology.

A clear understanding of the reasons for the project as well as the existing strategy and the *critical success factors* (CSFs) of the organization are essential for a re-engineering project. Which factors determine its success or failure? A clear understanding of the value of the various processes—in other words, the extent to which they contribute to the organization's performance—is important when choosing which of them should be re-engineered. This requires knowledge of the organization, of the market, and of the competition. After all, what is the point of streamlining the administration procedure for processing orders and invoicing within a commercial firm if that company is losing orders as a result of inefficient inventory management and a poor distribution structure?

Analysis of the reasons for change will result in the formulation of *objectives* to be met. First this will be done in qualitative terms, such as "the clients should be served better" or "the production cost should be diminished."

In order to be able to translate the objectives into concrete targets the next step is the formulation and definition of *key performance indicators* (KPIs). They should be measurable and they should express all relevant aspects of the performance of the processes and information systems. For example, the objective that the clients should be served better could be expressed by two performance indicators: the time it takes to fulfil a customer's order and the quality of the product or service expressed by a rating by the customers. The relationship between the CSFs and the KPIs is that the KPIs are quantifiable and that they express the CSFs. There might be more KPIs to express one CSF and there might be KPIs that are only indirectly related to a CSF.

The final step of the analysis phase is the *null measurement*: the determination of the KPIs in the existing situation. This is extremely important because it is the only way to see later if the project caused real improvements. The null measurement will also be used in the redesign phase where the new processes will be modeled and analyzed to see if the targeted improvements will be realized. The null measurement might be laborious because the existing administration does not have the required data or it is not easy to obtain from existing information systems. It is always possible to use sampling techniques to obtain at least some estimates of the KPIs, for example by tracing a sample of customer orders through the processes and systems. In fact, this sample can be used later as use cases to test models and systems so they can be reused. Use cases, also referred to as business cases, should cover the most important types of cases, including the exceptions and errors that occur in practice.

During the analysis it becomes clear which parts of the organization, processes, and information systems have to be transformed in order to meet the objectives. So the *scoping* of the project is going hand in hand with the analysis. Often there are very good reasons to limit the scope of a project, although this could imply that relevant parts are left out. This means that we might not find the best solution, but this may counterbalance the risk that the project becomes unmanageable or that the continuity of the existing operations is at risk. Finally time and money limits are often given in advance and they require scope limits.

The analysis process often has the side effect that ideas for better solutions are generated. Here the vision for the "to be" situation is born.

Visioning starts with an artist's view of the "to be" situation. Once the processes that need re-engineering have been identified, the next question to be answered is how the best result can be achieved by applying information and communications technology. Modern technologies such as imaging, workgroup automation, workflow management, and expert and decision support systems offer opportunities for structuring the processes within an organization in an entirely different way. It is also often useful to look beyond the boundaries of the organization itself. The use of the internet infrastructure with technologies such as Web technology, electronic data interchange with XML, e-mail, and smart cards can result in dramatic improvements. Research into the opportunities that they offer for process re-engineering requires knowledge of these technologies and an insight into their applicability. Consideration needs to be given to such things as the extent to which such technology can be incorporated into the existing infrastructure.

The development of a vision of the re-engineering of business process requires a multidisciplinary team comprising representatives of the organization's management and IT experts. Moreover it is clear that a high degree of commitment on the part of senior management is an important precondition. In order to achieve the radical change intended, "wild" and controversial ideas must get a chance.

The null measurement is done by the project team and it often requires desk research. Most of the other activities are done during joint workshops with representatives of the relevant organizational units and if possible with management.

Activities

Analysis
• Analyze the reasons for change, the strategy, and the critical success factors;
• objectives to be met after transformation, formulated in a qualitative way;
• definition of key performance indicators to be able to quantify the objectives and to measure the intended improvements; and
• null measurement: determination of the performance indicators in the existing situation.

Scoping
• Identification of parts of the organization, processes, and systems that should remain unchanged and which fall in the scope of the project; and
• determination of boundary conditions on time frame and money to be spend.

Visioning
• Artist view of the new organization, processes, and systems;
• specification of the targets to be realized in the project, that is, the quantification of the objectives in terms of the key performance indicators; and
• generation of ideas and guidelines for redesign.

Deliverables
• Document describing the reasons for change, objectives, and the KPIs;
• a set of use cases;
• the null measurement;
• a list of processes, parts of the organization, and information systems to be re-engineered;
• boundary conditions on time and money; and
• artist's view of the new situation, ideas for improvement;
• specification of the targets in terms of KPIs.

6.2.4   Process redesign
The redesign phase starts with the modeling of the existing processes. This has two reasons: it is a way to understand the existing processes better, and it gives us the opportunity to calibrate the model of the existing situation with the null measurement. In this way we are able to estimate parameters of the processes that will not be affected by the redesign. They will be used in the models for the redesigned processes. It is also a check: if the bottlenecks and the KPIs computed by the model differ too much from the values in the null measurement there is something wrong: either the null measurement is wrong or the model is wrong, which means that we don't understand the existing situation properly. We advocate the use of Petri-net modeling. Simulation tools can assist us in the computation of KPIs, although sometimes analytical methods are available.

Since the targets of the re-engineering project have been formulated and the existing situation is assessed, the next step in the project can be taken: the new process can be designed. At this point, the project broadens. The project team is expanded to include end users with a detailed knowledge of the existing work processes and the requirements attached to them. Intensive involvement by these users will prepare the way for the acceptance of the forthcoming changes and enable risks to be identified at an early stage. Moreover expertise in the field of workflow management software configuration is also brought into the project team.

The redesign phase continues with a series of joint workshops to establish the basis for the redesign. Representatives of the organizational units involved in the project participate in these, together with the organization's management. Usually, two or three such workshops are sufficient to deal with all relevant topics. Using the improvement principles of chapter 3, various alternative scenarios for the organization of the business process are designed and assessed. These scenarios are not (minor) variations on a single process model, but variations that differ fundamentally from one another in the approach they take. Examples include centralized versus decentralized control, far-reaching forms of outsourcing, use of EDI, internet applications, and so on. At this stage, the description of the alternative process models will be at an abstract level.

To make an assessment of the alternatives as efficient as possible, some kind of visualization or prototyping is desirable. For this we make use of specific tools for modeling business processes. Those based upon Petri-net modeling are naturally preferable, but other tools could also be used. Many workflow management systems include a modeling tool which supports a simple form of animation. Given the degree of abstraction in the process model, tools that use some form of animation are the most suitable. At this stage a set of characteristic cases is designed. They should represent the most important types of cases, including errors and exceptions. These cases are called *use cases* and will also be used in the next phases.

Based upon the discussion and arguments put forward during the workshop(s), one of the alternatives is selected. This choice then is modeled in as much detail as possible during the next stage. Such development is done using the principle of iteration. An initial proposal is designed by an expert in the field of process modeling, preferably using a tool which supports Petri-net modeling. This model is iteratively improved and refined during a series of workshops where uses cases are used for manual testing. There exist tools to support verification of the correctness of the process. The KPIs of the new processes that express the logistical performance, such as throughput or waiting times and resource utilization, can be computed by means of simulation. They are compared to the targets and the simulations of the model of the existing situation. It is also possible to determine how sensitive the designed process is to internal disruption (for example, staff sickness).

Simulation shows only the logistical KPIs of the new processes, not the functional ones. The functional KPIs may be determined by means of life experiments, or *games* with the help of a workflow management system. In this case the process model is implemented into the workflow management system, and the participants in the game play out the practical situation that would apply following the enactment of the new process. Such an approach requires a great deal of preparation and, due to its structure, is often limited in how far it can simulate all the possible exceptions and bulk-processing effects. It is, however, a particularly good instrument for involving users in development and for encouraging support for future changes. For these reasons, it can be a very effective complement to the use of simulation.

The result is a new process model that forms the basis for further development and enactment. As the model is improved, all sorts of requirements and preconditions pertaining to data-processing systems are generated. As far as possible, these are recorded. They will be used during a later phase, when the systems which have to support the process are being designed and built.

The redesign of processes will usually have far-reaching consequences for the structure of the organization. The traditional boundaries between departments and business units may shift or disappear. Responsibilities change and decision making is relocated.

During the redesign phase, attention therefore also must be paid to the consequences for the organizational structure and human resource management (HRM). Issues to be addressed in this respect are:

• the redefinition of tasks and functions;
• self-managing teams and the associated management skills;

- appraisal systems;
- salary structures; and
- education and training.

These aspects are recorded in an organizational model and in a description of the measures that would be required to achieve this model.

Activities
- Modeling and calibration of the existing situation;
- development of alternatives for the new business process;
- analysis of the selected alternative: determination of correctness properties and logistical KPIs (by simulation);
- analysis of functional KPIs by means of gaming workshops using a workflow management system (optional); and
- description of the consequences for the organization.

Deliverables
- Calibrated model of existing processes;
- set of use cases;
- models for the preferred new processes;
- test results of simulations and gaming;
- requirements for data-processing applications; and
- organizational model.

6.2.5 Requirements

The core of the new workflow system—the newly designed business process—now has largely been established. Now the data-processing systems which have to support the process can be designed and constructed. Before we can do this we have to establish carefully what functionality the data-processing systems have to encompass in order to be able to plan and to budget the subsequent phases. We again achieve this in a series of (two or three) workshops. These cover the following topics:

- The data model of the systems. We distinguish case data and noncase data. The case data is best modeled as a dossier that is filled during the process. The noncase data can be divided into support data and management information. Support data is data that is used in the case handling processes such as addresses, rates, and instructions. Management information concerns the quality and the efficiency of case handling.

• Interaction between process steps and data-processing applications. The starting point is the process model: each task requires some data and produces some data for the dossier. The relationship with the process developed during the previous phase is established in a matrix of process steps and the system functions they use.

• Supplementary data processing functions for such matters as (application) management and data exchange with others.

• Requirements to be made of the systems in terms of speed, processing capacity, flexibility, and so on.

• The development and enactment strategy, and the schedule. It is established whether all the functionality can be achieved and introduced at a single stroke, or whether an incremental development strategy needs to be adopted.

• Risks and risk management strategy.

The results from the process redesign phase, in particular, and those from these workshops provide a good foundation for further development. Certainly not all the details are yet known, but the picture now available of the process and systems to be developed, and of the requirements that they must meet, is clear. Given the subjects addressed during this phase, the project team at this stage is expanded to include one or more experienced developers who will be involved in the actual establishment of the new system during the design and construction phases.

Based upon the requirements workshops, the overall project plan drawn up during the preparatory phase can be further developed.

The project plan incorporates all the topics raised during the requirements-planning workshops, including a detailed schedule for the subsequent course of action.

Activities
• Preparation and staging of requirements workshops;
• development of risk-management measures;
• development of the project schedule and budget; and
• drawing up of a detailed project plan.

Deliverables
• Rough data model (entities and relationships);
• rough functional model of the applications to be developed;
• matrix of functions for each process (step); and
• detailed project plan for the subsequent course of action.

6.2.6 Architecture

Before we begin the actual development of the systems themselves, a number of largely technical choices now need to be made. A workflow system is a complex one, which by its nature and structure is distributed. A good architecture is necessary in order that the system's various *components* work as well as possible with one another. This "architecture" describes the various components in the system, and indicates the way in which they communicate with one another (*interface* descriptions). In this respect, we distinguish between the *functional architecture* and the *technical architecture*. The former subdivides the system into a number of functionally interdependent components. This functional structuring enables different teams to work on different components in parallel. The technical architecture subdivides the system into software and/or hardware components. This structure to a large extent is dictated by existing technology and the shape of database management systems, operating systems, and so on. The functional and technical architecture are often closely linked with one another. A complete description of the architecture therefore consists of descriptions of both the functional and the technical architecture, and illustrates the relationship between them. The following are examples of matters addressed in the description of the architecture:

- technical infrastructure (hardware, networks, OS, and communication protocols);
- workflow management software;
- development tools;
- interface descriptions (workflow management system versus components, components versus one another, and components versus databases); and
- standard graphical user interface.

In this way, a kind of "framework" is defined within which the various elements in the workflow system fit. Figure 6.4 shows diagrammatically how the description of the architecture can assist in relating the different elements to one another.

The best results are achieved when the architecture is based upon (open) industry standards. This provides the greatest likelihood that the tools used (WFMS, DBMS, and development tools) will provide the

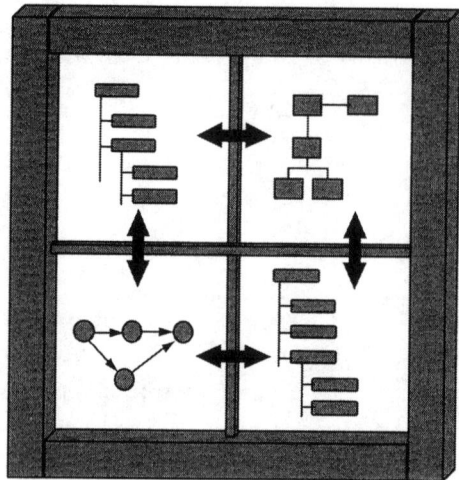

Figure 6.4
Integration framework

support required and ensures continuity for the future. In particular, the interface descriptions mentioned earlier include the way in which the workflow management software communicates with data-processing applications, as well as how the data-processing applications communicate with one another (see chapter 5). By translating the architecture into a set of development guidelines, it becomes possible to integrate more or less independently developed components without too many problems. These guidelines cover the programming of interfaces between the various components, as well as the design of the system—in particular, its subdivision into separately usable modules or objects.

The architecture phase is predominantly technical in nature. During this phase, therefore, staff need to be called in with an in-depth technical knowledge of the integration aspects of workflow management systems containing database management systems and application software in a distributed environment. It may well be that specific software routines need to be developed during this phase in order to enable the integration of the architecture's various components.

During the architecture phase, it is recommended that several components be developed as prototypes in order that the architecture selected— and in particular its interfaces and integration—can be tested in practice for feasibility and, where necessary, refined. This prototype can also act as a reference model during further development.

Activities
- Description of the functional architecture;
- description of the technical architecture;
- illustration of the functional and technical architecture;
- establishment and description of standards and guidelines; and
- development and testing of prototypes.

Deliverables
- Description of architecture;
- prototype; and
- standards and requirements for components.

6.2.7 Component design

During this phase, the specifications of the data-processing components are developed iteratively, using prototyping. The processes specified during the redesign phase are—insofar as this has not already been done—implemented in a workflow management system. The result is a working prototype of the process management. The fastest way to achieve this is if there exists an automatic link between the modeling tool used during the redesign phase and the workflow management system.

The data-processing components are largely created using CASE tools and generators, and can therefore be adjusted quickly and easily. Based upon the models defined during the requirements phase, and with the aid of software generators, prototypes of the new components are produced by the developers involved in the project. Integrated with the process model implemented in the workflow management system, these prototypes are submitted to the users for assessment during so-called prototyping workshops. They are refined in a series of cycles (usually three) until they fulfill the users' needs. Workflow management (in the WFMS) and data-processing components are fully tested and, where necessary, adjusted.

Several series of workshops are planned, each session covering a range of functionality limited enough to enable its thorough review and assessment by the users. The time required to prepare and adjust the prototypes also needs to be taken into account. During the initial workshops, the main emphasis is placed upon the data model and the general standards for the user interface. The number of workshops held depends upon the overall size of the system. When scheduling the preparatory activities and workshops, a completed part of the process must always be selected: one that consists of several process steps which form a logical whole. This is necessary in order for a representative rendering to be given of the workflow in practice. The workshops must be thoroughly prepared, with attention paid to such matters as a clear division of roles and a simulation structure based upon case studies.

Thanks to this method of prototyping, it is not only the correctness of the data-processing component and process-definition specifications that are tested, but also the practical feasibility of the process.

At the end of the design phase, the users in the team give their formal approval to the functionality. This encompasses all the specifications already implemented in the workflow management system and the CASE tool (represented by prototypes), as well as a list of further refinements and/or links with other components. The latter is realized during the next phase: construction.

Activities
• Harmonization of the data model and the user interface;
• design/generation/harmonization of the functionality of the data-processing component and workflow definitions using prototyping and simulations of use cases; and
• establishment of specifications for specific links with office systems and/or other components.

Deliverables
• Standard for the user interface;
• specification of the workflow within the workflow management system;
• specification of the data-processing components in a CASE tool;
• final system prototype(s) and list of components to be completed; and
• description of links which still need to be made with office systems and/or other components.

6.2.8   Construction
A large part of the system has already been created (in an evolutionary way) during the system design phase. Specific functionality, which can be created using generators or which requires additional programming, is added during the construction phase. Examples of this include complex

checks, batch processing, and data exchange with other (external) \
systems.

The remaining parts of the system are thus constructed in a traditional way, based upon unambiguous specifications.

Finally, various aspects of the system are optimized for use in the operational environment. These include:

- the specific integration of the workflow management system with data-processing and general office applications (word processors, spread-sheets, e-mail, and so on);
- extension and optimization for large-scale use;
- performance optimization;
- management-information functions (insofar as these are not incorpo-rated as standard);
- technical-management functions; and
- conversion software.

Although the construction phase mainly involves technical aspects, the users should continue to be involved. Especially when testing and assessing the results, active user input remains highly desirable. The users concerned are also closely involved in preparing for the acceptance test and enactment.

Activities
- Integration and optimization of the workflow management system;
- setting up of the test environment;
- completion of the system documentation;
- system test; and
- preparation of the integration and acceptance test.

Deliverables
- Components ready for the integration test;
- system documentation;
- integration and acceptance-test plan (including use cases); and
- conversion software.

6.2.9 Integration

By definition, a workflow system consists of several components. The process management implemented within the workflow management software is an independently operating unit with its own dynamics and management environment, and in many cases its own hardware environment. This generally also applies to the data-processing components. The separate components communicate via interfaces. The blueprint for these components and their interrelationship is produced during the architecture phase. Especially in larger applications, program development will be carried out in more or less independent subprojects. A certain amount of autonomy for these is important to hasten their completion. The degree to which the components work properly with one another therefore is strongly dependent upon the quality and detail of the architecture defined. The integration test is the moment when the separate components are checked for their full mutual compatibility.

This test focuses primarily upon the operation of the functions in (technical) combination with one another, and in particular upon the interaction between the various components. Here the use cases, designed in the redesign phase, are reused. This set is extended and forms the basis for test scripts.

The most wide-ranging activity is to establish whether the functions created work properly and provide predictable results under all circumstances. The emphasis is placed upon the points of contact between the different components: the interfaces. In addition, such matters as security and authorization, performance (peak loads, long-term loads), and recovery are tested. Naturally any faults or errors which come to light during testing should be rectified as soon as possible.

In order to assess the behavior of the components properly, it is vital that the integration test be carried out on a hardware and software infrastructure that is identical to the final production environment, or as close to it as possible. This will prevent unwelcome surprises and unexpected setbacks when the production systems themselves are established.

In fact, the integration test is the first step in the acceptance of the system, with the main emphasis being placed upon technical compatibility and robustness. During this phase, information technologists and users work closely together with the objective of delivering a properly operating system that can be subjected to a (functional) acceptance test by the users alone.

Activities
• Test conversion;
• performance of integration test;

- rectification of faults; and
- production of test report.

Deliverables
- Environment and software prepared for acceptance test;
- test scripts (for future regression tests); and
- test report.

6.2.10 Delivery

The workflow system is now so far advanced that it can be formally handed over to the users. The objective of the acceptance test is to establish whether the system operates in accordance with the specifications and fulfills all the requirements made of it to support the day-to-day business process in the best way possible. This includes the condition that the user organization must, as far as possible, be able to perform the acceptance test on the workflow system independently.

For this reason, the developers involved in the project remain in the background at this stage, only providing support when absolutely necessary—for example, because one or more components are not functioning as they should.

An acceptance test addresses the following matters:

- functionality (user interfaces, input, internal processing, output);
- everyday use of the system by means of use cases chosen in the redesign phase;
- (day-to-day) management; and
- the system documentation supplied.

The vast majority of the functionality and general management functions of the workflow systems already have been tested by the users during earlier phases. Such testing is an integral part of the development process, with the users always remaining closely involved in the creation and ongoing assessment of prototypes. The backbone of the system already has been thoroughly checked during the integration test. The acceptance test therefore should concentrate mainly upon the day-to-day use and management of the workflow system, as well as the technical and user documentation supplied with it.

The best approach in such a situation is a systematic one in which a process is tracked step by step using predefined use cases. For each stage in the process, a test script is written describing the operations that the user should carry out and the expected results of the test. In this way, everyday use is simulated as closely as possible and the operation of the process can be assessed.

In addition to the functional acceptance described above, a technical acceptance test must be performed by the future managers of the system. During this, checks are made as to whether the software produced meets the standards and general quality norms set for the project.

Activities
- Performance of the acceptance test using scenarios;
- rectification of faults; and
- production of an acceptance-test report.

Deliverables
- Environment and software ready for use and management;
- formal acceptance by the user organization;
- formal acceptance by the management organization; and
- acceptance-test report.

6.2.12   Enactment

The restructuring of entire business processes and the enactment of new technology have consequences for the way in which people work (together). Traditional hierarchical relationships change or disappear, and responsibilities shift. This places demands not only upon the processes and the information systems, but also upon the people who work with them. Requirements with respect to knowledge and skills change in both the technical and social fields.

The enactment of a workflow system in an organization therefore is at least as important as its design and construction. Do staff know what to expect, and are they well prepared for their new tasks? Do they possess the necessary knowledge and skills? Are there enough tools available? And have all the necessary agreements been reached?

Enactment requires thorough preparation and explicit interest in the project. Preferably a special team should be set up within the project organization to deal with both its preparation and subsequent supervision. This implies that a considerable part of the project budget must be allocated to enactment activities.

The activities of the enactment team to some extent "shadow" the other phases of the IPSD approach. As early as the redesign phase, it should concern itself with analyzing the project's implications for the organization and its human resource management aspects. As the project progresses, attention is paid to everything required to prepare for successful enactment. This includes providing information about the project and its results (in particular, the changes that the organization should expect), as well as preparing training materials, providing courses, and continuing to monitor the organization once the system has been implemented.

The enactment team preferably should consist of staff who know the organization well and have good contacts. In order to carry out the activities described above, it should contain people who are able to perform the following functions:

- communications expert;
- technical copywriter;
- organizational expert;
- infrastructure expert;
- trainer; and
- process supervisor.

Ideally, such a team will comprise representatives from both the user organization and the IT organization, plus executive staff and—possibly —outside experts.

Activities
- Communication about the progress of the project;
- communication about forthcoming changes;
- description of the organizational structure;
- preparation of case descriptions;
- preparation of manuals;
- preparation of training materials;
- provision of training;
- planning and enactment of the technical infrastructure;
- preparation and supervision of conversion; and
- supervision of the change process.

Deliverables
- Enactment plan;
- communications plan;

- conversion plan;
- organizational model;
- case descriptions;
- manuals;
- information and training materials; and
- infrastructure.

6.2.12   Monitor and improve

Once the workflow system has been successfully implemented, attention turns to whether the intended improvements are actually being achieved and sustained. This requires the permanent monitoring of the processes using the predefined performance criteria. These are the so-called *key performance indicators* (KPIs) established during the diagnosis phase. The workflow management system can be of assistance in measuring and assessing a number of these. Because it records a great deal of information about the process and individual cases, it is easy to gain an overview of the behavior and performance of the process in practice. These indicators are mainly "hard" ones such as system usage, processing times, workloads, supplies of work, and productivity. In addition research can be carried out into such matters as level of service, customer satisfaction, and quality. This can be regarded as an ongoing continuation of the diagnosis phase with the objective of identifying potential improvements. It may prompt adjustments to the processes and systems linked to it— not radical changes as in BPR, but usually minor improvements to the processes.

We call this approach *continuous process improvement* (CPI). Because the changes are not so large, the frequency with which they can be implemented is much higher. Figure 6.5 illustrates the relative positioning of CPI and BPR.

The use of workflow management software has clear advantages in this respect. Because the process definitions are established in terms of parameters, adjusting the process requires relatively little effort and so makes decisions to do so easier to take. Consequently a virtually continuous process of measurement, redesign, and enactment develops. The IPSD approach also can be used as the guiding principle in CPI, providing the activities are more limited in scope and performed in quick suc-

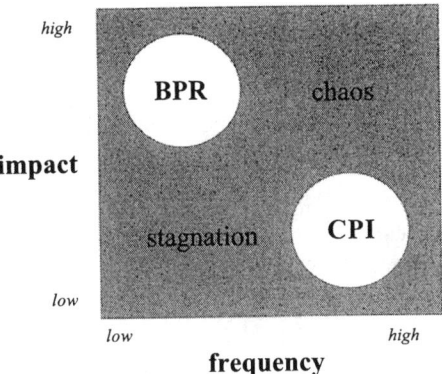

Figure 6.5
BPR versus CPI

cession. Sometimes activities can be "skipped," and there is no need to seek a clear delineation between phases. But the lists of activities and products used in the IPSD method do make a good checklist for planning and implementing such projects.

6.2.13   Integrating WFMS with legacy systems

The above description of the IPSD method assumes that entirely new information systems will be developed alongside the new processes. In many cases, however, existing systems must (also) be integrated with workflow management software to create a workflow system. In fact, this provides a very good opportunity for giving old, hard-to-maintain "legacy" systems a new lease on life.

In general terms, the IPSD method is well suited to such situations. However, some specific problems do arise, which need to be addressed.

When integrating an existing system, one needs to maintain established components rather than to create new ones. Instead of generating prototypes, intensive upgrading of existing (and often old) software needs to be carried out. The development environment in which these programs were constructed does not lend itself very well to the type of prototyping that we use in the IPSD method. As a result the design and construction phases, in particular, should be structured in a somewhat different way. The existing components may, in fact, act as the initial prototype, but good interaction in which prototypes rapidly succeed one another is not possible. Nevertheless some form or other of evolutionary development can often be used. If the adaptations to the user interface are limited, then rather old-fashioned software is no great obstacle. If the modifications are more far-reaching in nature, one may decide to install a more modern programming environment for the interface part. Rebuilding parts of the system from scratch often proves cheaper than making extensive changes to existing software—especially when long-term maintenance is included in the calculation.

Another aspect of working with existing systems is the elimination of old workflow aspects from legacy applications. Many older programs contain functionality that supports some kind of workflow. It is well worth removing such functionality as far as possible from the legacy applications and implementing it in the workflow management system. This reduces the amount of effort required to maintain the legacy system, and enables one to take immediate advantage of the flexibility offered by the workflow management system. Which parts of the existing system are to be removed and how the workflow management system and the legacy application communicate with one another need to be carefully established during the architecture phase.

A more serious problem is the "mismatch" between the process steps and the system architecture of the existing applications. The modularity of these programs does not correspond with the steps in the newly designed process, which complicates interaction between the workflow management system and the data-processing applications. Separate process steps are defined in the process. Although each of these relates to different functions, they are all implemented through a single, wide-reaching COBOL program. In such cases, it is virtually impossible to call up functionality from the existing applications in the workflow management system, even when that functionality does exist. Figure 6.6 illustrates this situation diagrammatically.

The solution to this problem needs to be sought in the way in which existing code can be "rewrapped"—preferably in smaller units that enable supported interaction between process steps and the functionality in the legacy system. This technique is called *object wrapping*. By defining straightforward interfaces, the development of standards for distributed

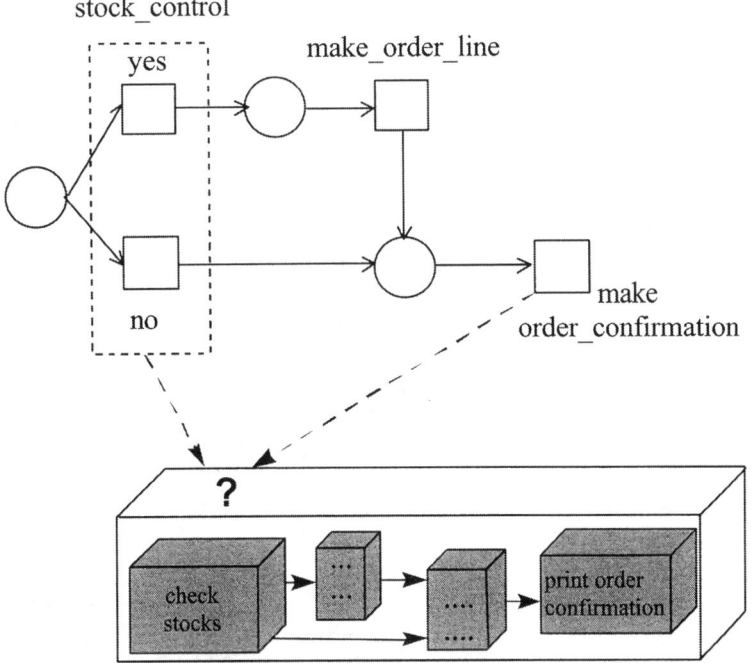

Figure 6.6
Modularity of legacy applications

environments and object architectures such as DCE and CORBA contributes to the reuse of existing software. Consideration of the use of products based upon such standards forms part of the architecture phase. The existing system's code can then—in a separate step between the architecture and design phases—be restructured and rewrapped in such a way that flexible reuse of that existing code becomes possible.

Enterprise application integration (EAI) has emerged as the latest information management trend. EAI identifies and links user workflow and application functions through sophisticated message queuing and Web-based technologies. EAI tools identify, capture, integrate, and deliver data and system functionality to users under a series of cross-functional, multi-platform interfaces. Message queuing technologies from various vendors have matured to the point where they can support the integration of these functions without major retooling of complex legacy environments.

EXERCISES

Exercise 6.1

(a) Give two good reasons for involvement of (potential) users in the activities of the IPSD lifecycle.

(b) Give the three criteria for selection of users to become part of the redesign team.

Exercise 6.2

Use cases play an important role in the ISPD lifecycle. Indicate where they are used and why they are important.

Exercise 6.3

Requirements and Architecture are two separated phases in the ISPD lifecycle. They could be integrated into one phase, normally also called "architecture." In that case both the functional and technical aspects are considered in one phase. Give advantages and give also disadvantages of having them separated.

7

Sagitta 2000 Case Study

7.1 Background Information

The concepts introduced in this book can only be "brought to life" when they are illustrated using an actual case study. The development of the Sagitta 2000 declaration-processing system of the Dutch Customs Service, part of the Dutch Tax Authority, provides an excellent opportunity for doing this. The design of the new system began in early 1995, and it has now reached the beginning of the construction phase. One of the fundamental principles in the development of Sagitta 2000 always has been that—throughout the design and construction procedure—the management of the Customs Service's complex administrative business processes, which the system will handle, be kept separate from the applications that support them. For this reason a great deal of attention was paid to the explicit modeling of the process structure during the design of Sagitta 2000. In doing so, it always was envisioned that the business processes should eventually be incorporated into a separate layer of management.

This chapter begins with a short description of the task of the customs organization and the particular role of declaration processing in this. This makes it clear what issues the Customs Service faces and what major developments have occurred to result in the need for an overhaul of the business processes in declaration procedures. We shall also examine the way in which the business processes are described in Sagitta 2000, and the management ideas underlying these descriptions. We shall then discuss the description of a part of the Customs Service's business process. Within the Sagitta 2000 project, intensive research into how the management concept should be achieved technically was carried out alongside the design phase. This also makes it possible to examine the enactment of the process diagrams in a workflow management system, and the technical problems which arise when integrating a workflow management system with the application software. We end the chapter with a review of some of the experiences gained thus far from the project and some ideas for the future.

7.2   Customs Service Business Process

The Dutch Customs Service performs a number of tasks that are closely linked with flows of goods into and out of the Netherlands. These include the levying and collecting of the Dutch and European taxes and duties that must be paid when importing goods into the European Union. The Customs Service also ensures that no goods enter the country that would endanger the health and safety of society in general. In performing all these tasks, it is vital that the Customs Service be able to track the flow of goods and carry out selective checks. This is done mainly using customs declarations that must be submitted to the Customs Service by the various parties involved in flows of goods. The Customs Service's business processes focus primarily upon the processing of these declarations.

Why redesign the business processes?
The internal processing of declarations by the Customs Service has long been heavily concentrated upon just one of the many types of declarations submitted. The Customs Service's current information systems also are configured mainly to deal with one particular type of declaration. Two significant developments are now changing this traditional picture. On the one hand, the Customs Service is attempting to base its tracking of and checks on the flow of goods, as well as the processing of declarations, more emphatically upon its opinion of the parties involved in those flows. On the other hand, a new law (the Community Customs Code, or CCC) has come into effect that, more than ever before, requires a clear system for the way in which declarations relate to one another (the "tracking of goods") and how they can be made. These two developments prompted the redesign of the business process within the Sagitta 2000 project, with the objective of creating a uniform procedure that can be used to deal with every type of declaration.

Why separate management and application?

The handling of customs declarations is a process that involves a huge amount of data. Controlling and managing such large quantities of information requires great attention to detail. By consciously separating business-process management in Sagitta 2000 from the supporting applications, the following is achieved:

• An opportunity is created for improved control of the business processes (management and monitoring). By making this explicit, it becomes possible to define the way in which process control should be structured. Consider, for example authorization; work allocation and workload management; separation of functions; and progress monitoring. Moreover it becomes possible to perform both process management and process monitoring using a workflow management system.

• A guarantee that a number of formal steps that must be taken in the business process do indeed take place in accordance with the law. It is also desirable that, on the one hand, these steps can be taken in a uniform way throughout the country and, on the other, that the various organizational units are free to structure the process as they wish within the legal framework.

• The ability to adapt the business process to new organizational wishes and changes in the law more easily than was possible so far (all this, of course, without incurring higher maintenance costs).

Petri nets for the design of business processes

As mentioned above, the Sagitta 2000 project involved a redesign of the business processes for processing customs declarations. At the start of the project, however, it was not yet clear how the separation of management and application would be achieved, nor how the redesign of the business processes would be structured. Eventually it was decided to use Petri nets to establish the business processes. This enabled a number of important characteristics of declaration processing to be modeled in an appropriate way:

• The Customs Service's business processes consist of a large number of individual tasks or steps. In other words, the task is either considered to be carried out at a single stroke or not at all. Some tasks are performed by a customs officer, possibly with the support of a system, whereas others are fully computerized.

• There is no fixed procedure for the processing of every type of customs declaration. Each declaration must be routed along the correct route through the process according to its individual content (its case attributes). Sometimes a choice between alternative options of processing needs to be made, after which the process returns to a common path.

• Because many tasks are initiated by events in the Customs Service's environment, it is difficult to predict in advance which will be performed. This means that the correct step to be taken can only be determined once a particular event has occurred. This aspect can be modeled properly only if the "pending" states in which the process may be held, while awaiting a particular event, can be modeled explicitly.

• The steps in the business process may be activated by various types of triggers. It therefore is necessary to differentiate between these when modeling.

• "Parallelization" is possible in declaration processing. In other words, two or more subprocesses may be performed independently of one another, with subsequent synchronization as the process returns to a common path.

Sagitta 2000 methodology

Sagitta 2000 uses Petri nets very similar to those described earlier in this book. There are, however, a few minor differences in the symbols used in the Sagitta 2000 methodology. Moreover the number of "nesting" levels is limited to two, and no use is made of preconditions. The task (called the "process task" in the Sagitta 2000 project) is at the heart of the system, and is shown by a rectangle. "The principle of unity of time, place and operation" applies to each task. The states in which a case can be held between the various tasks are illustrated in Sagitta 2000 by an inverted triangle. However, the meaning of this is no different to that of the conditions (places) which we saw earlier in this book. Sagitta 2000 also differentiates between different types of triggering: an incoming message ("envelope" symbol), a fixed moment in time ("clock" symbol), automatic ("cogs" symbol), or user activation. In fact, six types of triggers have been identified. An example of a Petri net used in Sagitta 2000 is shown in figure 7.1.

Relationship with application software

As mentioned earlier, the process tasks within the business process may be supported by application software. In other words, once a task is activated, an application that performs it—or assists the user in performing it—must be started. Such a task-supporting application is called

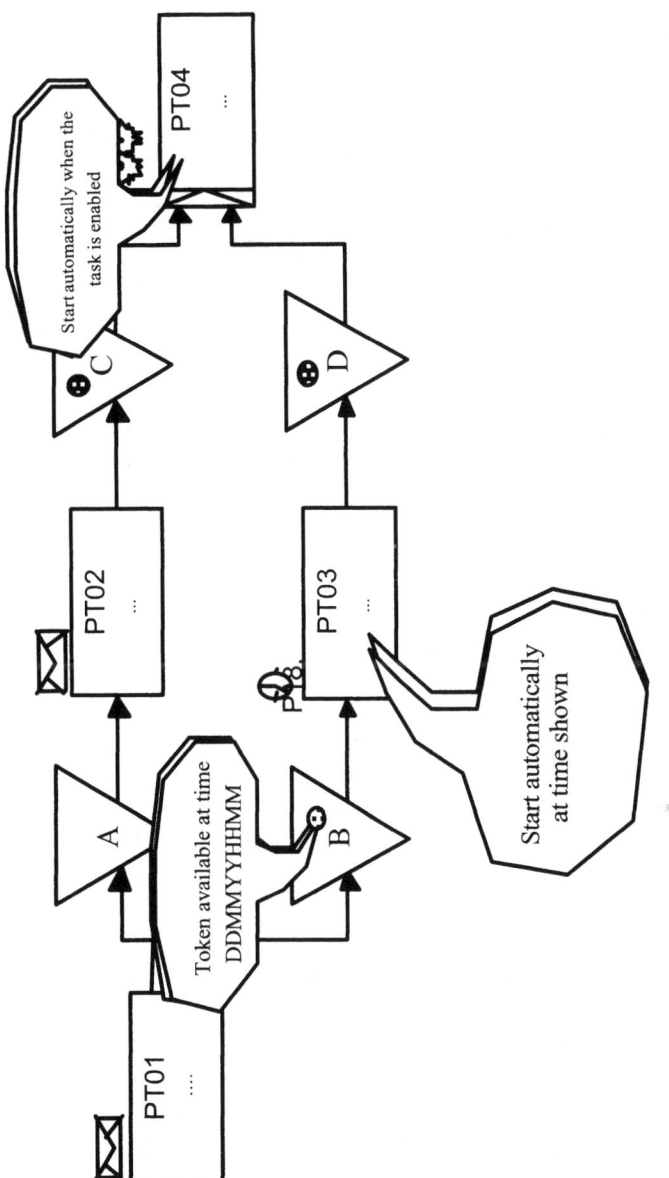

Figure 7.1
Example of a Petri net used in Sagitta 2000

an application task. Most Sagitta process tasks have an application task, but some are entirely manual and so have no associated application task.

The management layer, which we are creating with a workflow management system, tells the application layer which application must work on which case. The application then works on the case regarding the content and—once its task is completed—informs the management layer of the (possibly) adjusted values of the case attributes, so that management can decide which follow-up states the case should proceed to, and possibly what subsequent tasks can begin. This principle is illustrated in figure 7.2.

A task, possibly together with an application task, is regarded as one "logical unit of work" (LUW), which is either carried out in full ("commit") or not carried out at all ("rollback"). If a task is interrupted halfway through, the case state must be "rolled back" to that which existed at the moment when the task was begun.

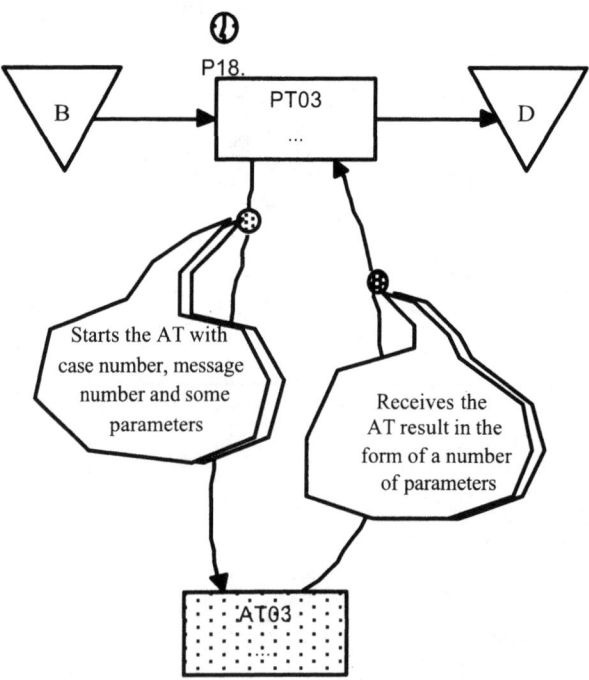

Figure 7.2
Communication between management and application

7.3   Working Methods

The Sagitta 2000 business processes always focus upon processing one kind of case. The project therefore began by determining the different types of cases which could be identified under the heading "declaration processing." Then business processes were designed for each of these case types. A business process is a sequence of steps (process tasks) designed to process a case of *one particular type*. Each step must add value to the sequence and carry out a necessary operation affecting the case attributes.

The criteria for designing a business process are always strictly applied. In other words, if it is established, when performing a task on one case, that—due to the content of that case—operations need to be carried out on another case of the same or different type, then these operations are never modeled as part of this task. Such situations are modeled by generating triggers from the processing of other cases; they lead to the activation of other process tasks that deal with the related cases. The relationship between two business processes thus is *never* shown by creating common conditions (i.e., places) or process tasks for them. If there is interdependency between different cases, then these are made through the application level. In this way, the execution of an application for one particular case may lead to the generation of a number of triggers for other cases. These triggers are not generated by the workflow management system, because knowledge of the content of the declarations is required to determine the relationships between cases.

7.3.1   Iterative design

The design of a business process is done iteratively. In other words, it is not possible to design a process at a single stroke. The initial, rudimentary process design is gradually refined through close interaction between customs experts and designers. The customs experts, whose background is purely in Customs Service techniques, appear to be highly capable of considering their business processes in Petri-net terms. The initial, rudimentary process design is produced following an analysis of the current procedure and customs law. A brainstorming session also is held to establish what events occur in the lifecycle of a case. The new customs law, the Community Customs Code (CCC), provided a very good starting point. The CCC explicitly states what procedures are available for processing declarations, and what major "states" and "operations" can be identified in the lifecycle of a declaration.

7.3.2   What is a task?

Within the business processes, the task is the smallest unit of work. The most important criterion for decomposing a task is that there must exist *unity of time, place, and operation*. During the design of the processes, however, this principle does not always provide sufficient grounding. In fact, it acts as a sort of basic condition that subsequently allows several design decisions to be made. The criterion does not act as an imperative, in the sense that a collection of operations and system functions must be clustered into a single task when there exists at least one procedure in which the unity of time, place, and operation would apply to that collection. In such a situation, it is quite legitimate to split this task into two tasks to be carried out immediately after one another.

Proper consideration also requires other criteria to be taken into account:

• *Recognizability of the task*. To the organization, a task must be recognizable and involve a useful cluster of operations and system functions. A task therefore has a clear function and objective, and ultimately is also the unit of work allocated to the members of staff. The latter (in order to separate functions, for example) might be a motive for splitting a task into subtasks to be performed by different members of staff.

• *Sensible interim states*. All the interim states (conditions) in the business process should be given (reasonably) sensible names. If this proves impossible or very difficult, then it may perhaps indicate that a state has been defined that is not recognizable by, or important to, the users.

• *An acceptable "commit work" for each of the process tasks*. The splitting of process tasks and the introduction of an interim state result in the creation of a separate "commit work" for each task. On the one hand, this leads to flexibility for the user; on the other, in the operational situation, it is no longer possible to roll back the first task once the second has begun.

7.3.3   Dealing with complexity

The Customs Service's processes are too complicated to be shown in a single, flattened Petri net. A process description containing too many process tasks, conditions, and interconnecting paths—with a different set of requirements attached to each path—is no longer recognizable and comprehensible to analysts or customs experts. Moreover, the chance of modeling errors occurring in such a complex model is very high. In Sagitta 2000, decomposition has been used to overcome the complexity of the process. Given that too many levels of decomposition are also difficult to manage, the final design has only two such levels. In addition, "routing tasks" have been introduced. These are tasks in which various subprocesses come together, all the decision rules are evaluated at the same time, and the subsequent route is determined.

7.4   Example: A Customs Service Business Process

Various business processes are distinguishable within Sagitta 2000, each with totally different characteristics. Because of their close relationship with the physical flow of goods, some are highly time-critical. These include, for example, the processing of (standard) declarations. Given that a declaration needs to be made for every shipment, there is an enormous number of cases. On the other hand, some processes are not time-critical and involve far fewer cases, each of which may be very wide in scope. These include, for example, the processing of monthly declarations in which major declaring companies justify an entire month.

What the various types of processes in the declaration processing procedure have in common is that they are highly structured but complex. Given the fact that the Customs Service must constantly respond dynamically to events in its environment—which cannot always be predicted in advance—it is vital to include conditions in the process structure. Below we describe an example from customs practice concerning the processing of a standard declaration. First the main process diagram is presented, which shows the overall structure of the process. Then we show a subprocess containing a process description at the lowest level of decomposition: the process tasks.

Main process

The main declaration process is shown in figure 7.3. This is a generic process suitable for dealing with every type of declaration and declaration procedure. The declarations are routed correctly through the process using decision rules. Figure 7.3 does not show the most recent version of the process. Sagitta 2000 is an ongoing process and the declaration process is still subject to minor revisions.

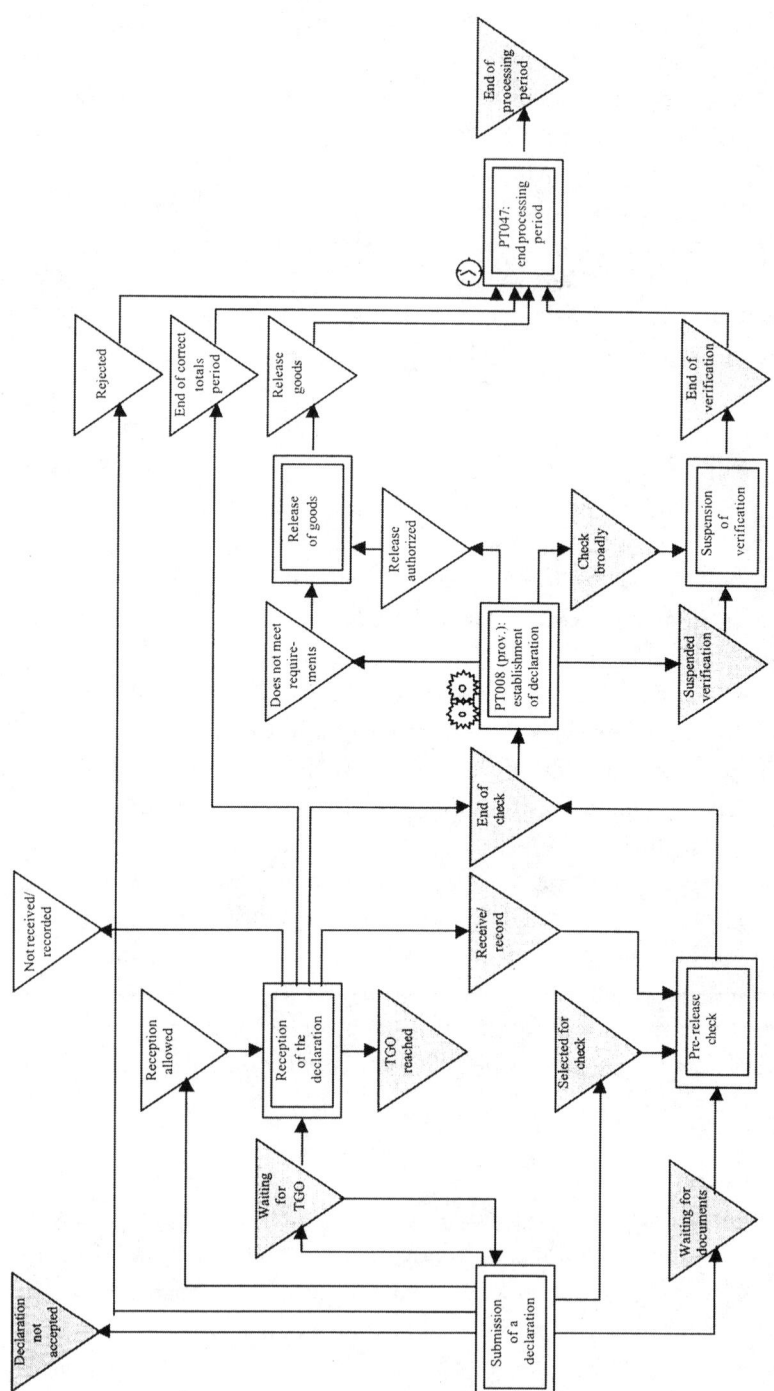

Figure 7.3
Example of the main Sagitta 2000 process

Several subprocesses can be identified within the main process:

• *Submission of a declaration.* The processing of the declaration begins with the submission and intake of a declaration form. This takes place before—or at the latest at—the moment when the goods become available for a physical check. The declaration form also contains all the data that determines how the declaration will proceed through the process. These characteristics are recorded as case attributes and play a very important role in the routing of the case through the process. The subprocess is suitable for both electronic and written declarations, as well as for both the initial version and new versions.

• *Acceptance of the declaration.* The declaration acceptance subprocess begins once the declaration has been submitted. This is a very explicit procedure, owing to the legal significance of the acceptance of a customs declaration in the CCC. The subprocess waits until the goods are physically present, after which Sagitta 2000 allocates the "accept" state. Even once the declaration has been accepted, its correction and cancellation by the declaring party is still possible. These are examples of events outside the Customs Service to which it must respond.

• *Pre-release check.* The checking process takes place in parallel with the acceptance process and is in theory conditional. Only when it is decided that a (physical) inspection must take place is the check subprocess activated. The thoroughness of the check is determined using the selection profiles contained in the "declaration submission" subprocess. Using the decision rules, the declaration is routed either to or around the "pre-release check" subprocess.

• *Release of the goods.* The release of the goods can take place once the declaration has been accepted and any check has taken place. *PT008* is the fully automatic task which releases goods. Release itself indicates to the declaring party that it is free to remove the goods covered by the declaration.

• *Suspension of verification.* The suspension of verification may be regarded as a state within Sagitta 2000 under which the goods can, in principle, be released but in which the check has not been or cannot be completed. In theory, suspension of verification occurs independently of the release of the goods. It therefore is modeled in parallel to the release task. Once verification has been completed and the goods released, the process ends. This is done by carrying out task *PT047*.

A case—that is, a declaration—eventually ends up in one of the conditions *Declaration not accepted, Not received/recorded,* or *End of processing period.*

Submission of a declaration

Figure 7.4 shows the content of the "submission of a declaration" subprocess. Again note that this is not the most recent version of the process: Sagitta is an ongoing project. We can see how a number of conditions from the highest level of the procedure are repeated. These make the link with the rest of the process at the higher level.

The subprocess is designed to check declarations (*PT000* and *PT001*) and new versions of the declaration (*PT039* and *PT040*) regarding their content, and—if they are in order—to record them (*PT007*). Declarations can be submitted either electronically (*PT001*, *PT040*a, and *PT040*b) or in writing (*PT000*, *PT039*a, and *PT039*b). The contents of tasks *PT039*a and *PT039*b are the same: in both cases, it means the correction of a written declaration. *PT039*a is performed when the goods to which the declaration pertains are not yet available (in other words, when there is still a token in *Waiting for TGO*); otherwise, *PT039*b is performed. Sometimes checks are required that the system cannot carry out automatically. It may be necessary, for example, to involve one of the Customs Service's external contacts in checking the declaration before it can be accepted by the system. Another example of a check that the system cannot perform is assessing whether the issue of a permit in a simplified procedure is permissible. In figure 7.3, *PT002*a corresponds with the assessment of a new declaration. This task determines whether the simplified procedure is permissible. *PT002*b and *PT002*c correspond with a similar assessment of a corrected declaration.

It has been decided to introduce six separate process tasks for the intake of new electronic and written declarations and subsequent versions of declarations. On the one hand, this is because the process tasks for declarations submitted in writing have a different trigger from those submitted electronically. On the other hand, in the business process we wish to explicitly differentiate between new declarations, new versions of accepted declarations and new versions of yet-to-be accepted declarations.

For many declarations, it is not necessary to carry out the additional, nonautomatic checks between the conditions "external organizations to be informed" and "acceptance possible" (these process tasks are not shown in the illustration). For these declarations, therefore, process tasks *PT000*, *PT001*, *PT039*a, *PT039*b, *PT040*a, and *PT040*b can be directly followed by *PT007*. Therefore these pairs of process tasks (*PT000*–*PT007*, *PT001*–*PT007*, *PT039*a–*PT007*, *PT039*b–*PT007*, *PT040*a–

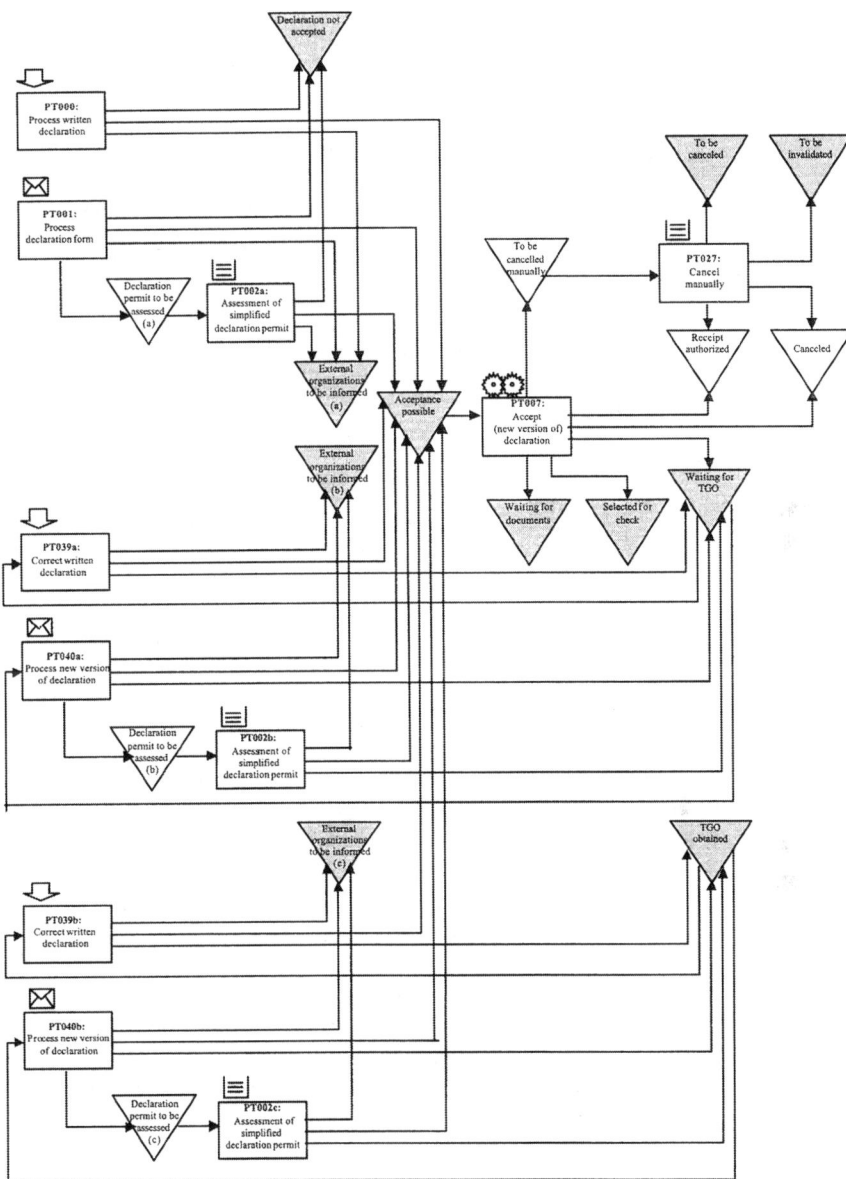

Figure 7.4
Example of the submission of a declaration

PT007, and *PT040b–PT007*) each could have been incorporated into a single task (with the *PT007* part as an optional subtask). Here, therefore, a modeling decision has clearly been made, with the principle of unity of time, place, and operation on the one hand, and the mapping of functionality onto a single task (that of *PT007*) on the other, being weighed against one another. Moreover the chosen solution has the advantage that all declarations pass through *PT007* and from there are routed as appropriate. *PT007* therefore acts as a routing task that increases the readability of the business process.

Figures 7.3 and 7.4 show only a part of the entire process. The declaration process contains more than fifty individual tasks. (In total, Sagitta 2000 will support more than two hundred tasks.) For each of these, its precise behavior is determined by a decision rule. Figure 7.5 shows the decision rules for a number of tasks.

7.5   Enactment of the Workflows in a Workflow Management System

Ultimately it is intended that the Sagitta 2000 business processes are incorporated into a workflow management system. Although there do exist other technical solutions in which the control of the business process is neatly separated from the application, it is the policy of the Dutch Tax Authority to implement standard software whenever possible. For this reason, a provisional workflow management product was selected at an early stage so as to test whether incorporation of the Sagitta 2000 business processes could be possible. This workflow product must not only provide the functionality required to deal with the Customs Service's complex business processes, but it also must meet the technical-infrastructure requirements set by the Tax Authority and be a solid and robust enough solution to cope with the large number of declarations and the high standards required by the Customs Service in terms of integrity and timing.

7.5.1   Selection of a workflow management system
In selecting a provisional workflow product, the main question addressed was whether it would allow enactment of the Customs Service's business processes. Particular study was made of the workflow management system's ability to meet, amongst others, the following requirements:

PT007: *Accept (new version of) declaration*

Process:

   IF manually_cancel
   THEN
      CASE → to_be_canceled_manually

     IF NOT   customs regime ∈ {Internal comm. customs traffic, External comm. customs
              traffic}
   OR
          procedure ∈ {'multiple procedure', 'domicile procedure'}
     THEN CASE → Receipt_authorized
   END
   OTHERWISE
      CASE → Canceled

      CASE → Receipt_authorized
   END

   CASE → Waiting_for_TGO
     ⏱ IF tgo <> <<empty>>
       THEN case time (PT00
     END

   IF selected_check_thoroughness ∈ {red, yellow}
   THEN
     IF documents_to_be_submitted = 'needed and reported' AND NOT documents_submitted
   AND
        procedure <> 'domicile procedure'
     THEN CASE → Wait_for_documents
     OTHERWISE CASE → selected_for_c
     END

PT002a: *Assessment of simplified declaration permit*

Process:

   IF permit = 'present'
   THEN
     IF import_or_export_permit
     THEN CASE → External_organizations_to_be_informed
     (a)
     OTHERWISE CASE → Acceptance_possible
     END
   OTHERWISE CASE → Declaration_not_accepted
   END

PT000: *Process written declaration*

Process:

   IF acceptance_possible
   THEN
     IF import_or_export_permit
     THEN CASE →
     External_organizations_to_be_informed (a)
     OTHERWISE CASE → Acceptance_possible
     END
   OTHERWISE CASE → Declaration_not_accepted
   END

Figure 7.5
Decision rules for PT000, PT002a, and PT007

- it must be possible to explicitly model states from the business processes in the workflow management system;
- all forms of routing must be supported;
- various forms of triggering must be supported;
- it must be possible to specify a hierarchy in the business process;
- it must be possible to extract a case from the workflow management system and load it into another workflow management system (export/import functionality); and
- there must be sufficient support for case attributes and decision rules.

In addition, a short survey was carried out into the requirements that the product must meet in respect to work allocation and workload management, so that these aspects could be taken into account during selection. Matters covered included work allocation rules, separation of function and authorization requirements, opportunities for chained and batched processing, and so on.

The aspects listed are best tested by running through part of the business process and allocation rules, together with an expert of the product being evaluated. This will rapidly make it clear whether that product provides a good solution for the explicit modeling of states, the various forms of triggering, the desired method of allocation, the complexity of the decision rules, and so on. In many of the workflow products, it turned out to be necessary to translate the Sagitta 2000 Petri nets into that product's own language before the processes could be introduced. During this translation it was not always possible to find a suitable solution in the product language for all the constructions used in the process.

In 1998, the COSA product (see chapter 5) was selected as the workflow management system for Sagitta. The decision to select COSA as the standard workflow product for the Dutch Tax Authority was a result of a European-wide tender. COSA is used in several pilot projects within the Dutch Tax Authority. However, for Sagitta 2000, COSA is not used at this point in time (July 2000). A pilot is conducted using custom-made software and focusing on a small fragment of the whole process (involving about ten tasks).

7.5.2   Distribution aspects

Sagitta 2000 is a distributed system; its workstations are, after all, spread amongst dozens of customs posts. The system consists of a central hub and a number of local elements. The hub coordinates the entire system, and is also the place where many noninteractive tasks are performed. The interactive tasks are carried out locally by customs officers. Staff allocation is arranged locally, at each customs post. The management-application and central-local separation results in the four-part structure shown in figure 7.6.

A mainframe environment is used centrally. The environment is client/server-based locally. In 1998, the COSA workflow management system

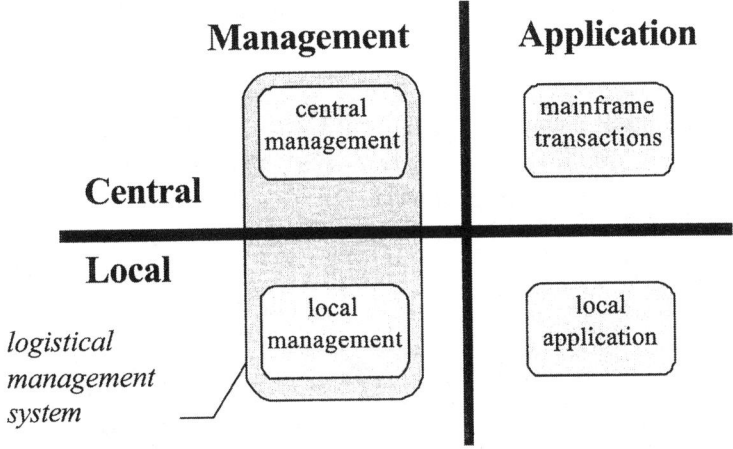

Figure 7.6
Division between central and local and between management and application

was selected for local management. At this point in time, it is not clear whether COSA will actually be used for the local system. For the central hub things are even more complicated, because there are no workflow management systems available for the mainframe computer used by the Tax Authority. In addition, high performance and reliability standards are set for the central hub. It is not (yet) clear how central management will be performed. The Tax Authority is experimenting with a number of prototype management systems (e.g., the *flowcontrol* system). These prototype systems are based upon Petri nets and the modeling technique presented in this book.

The starting point for Sagitta 2000's distributed management is the principle that a case (customs declaration) always is in one place only at any given time. The case therefore is either at the central hub or a local post, and cannot be worked upon simultaneously at two places. It is sometimes necessary to transfer a case from one place to another—that is, from one local post to another or from the central hub to a local post. Conceptually, we can compare the transfer of a case with the removal of all the tokens belonging to a declaration from one process diagram and their placing in another. When transferring cases, the state definition is also crucial. Workflow management systems not based upon Petri nets often abstract from the state and therefore prove inadequate in this respect.

7.5.3   Mapping of the process onto the WFMS

Although the workflow management system that has been selected (COSA) does support the Petri-net technique, even in this product it is not possible to transfer the processes one on one. Since the selected system does not accept all the constructions which are allowed in a high-level Petri net, it is necessary to devise standard solutions that do not detract from the desired functionality. All these solutions have been laid down in an enactment manual. This is followed strictly during enactment, so the differences between the high-level Petri nets and the language used by the selected workflow system are always resolved in a consistent way. Some examples of the agreements included in the enactment manual are:

• the way in which case attributes must be dealt with, and the names given to these attributes;
• the way in which decision rules are established;
• the way in which automatic processes are established;
• the way in which time-based triggering is dealt with;
• inspection of a condition by a task, or the enactment of iteration (examination of a case and its return to the same condition);
• the creation of a case as a result of a message from outside; and
• the enactment of triggering between two processes.

Figure 7.7 shows a small part of one of the Sagitta 2000 process definitions. For enactment in COSA, the decision rules are translated into conditions for the arcs between transitions and places. As the illustration shows, these conditions can become extremely complex.

As required by the IPSD methodology described in the previous chapter, interactive workshops have played a major role in the validation of the business processes. These workshops have stimulated and supported customs experts in carefully testing the specified business processes during simulations of the process using the workflow management system.

Please note that figure 7.7 has just been added for illustration purposes. COSA was selected as a workflow system in 1998. However at this point in time it is not clear whether COSA will actually be used as

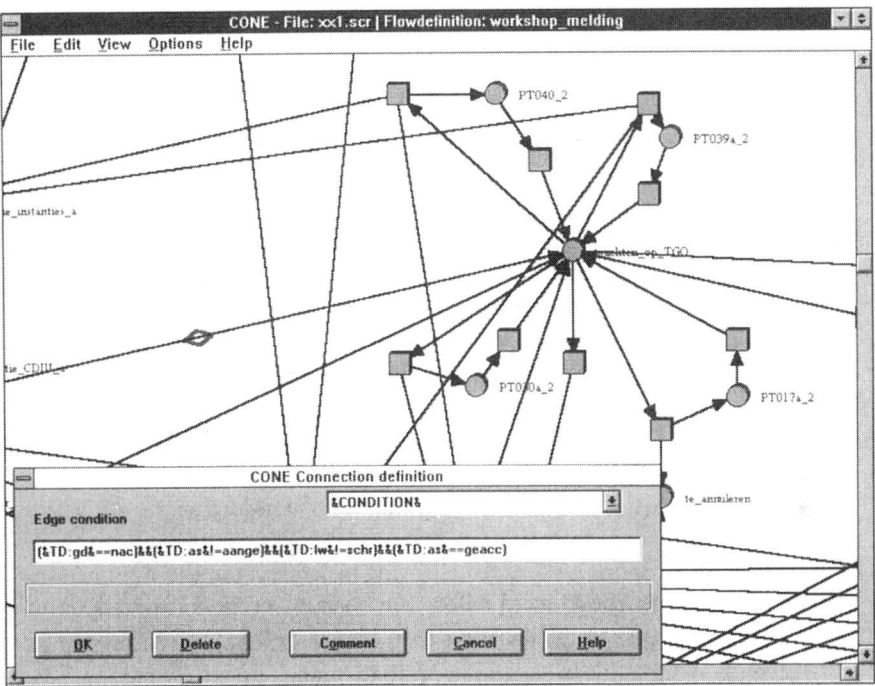

Figure 7.7
Part of the process definition in COSA

the basis for Sagitta. The first production version of Sagitta, supporting only a small part of the total process, will use custom-made software.

7.6   Some Experiences Thus Far

Although opportunities to put workflow-management ideas into practice in various sections of the Dutch Tax Authority have previously been sought, Sagitta 2000 is the first project that has actually succeeded in separating application and logistics (management) in its design. To achieve this, extensive investigation into the (types of) building blocks from which the system is constructed and into methods for modeling and specifying business processes has been carried out. Eventually a methodology based upon Petri nets was chosen. Some aspects of methodology and architecture have been tested in a so-called feasibility project. During this pilot project, the business processes were incorporated into the selected workflow management system.

The most important experiences thus far are as follows:

• Petri nets are a suitable way of specifying Customs Service procedures. No situations arose in which Petri nets were incapable of modeling the desired procedure.

• Petri nets also are, in principle, very well understood by the Customs Service's customs experts. The explicit representation of a case's state contributes to a better understanding of the workflow being modeled.

• It is vitally important for a team of process architects (information technologists) and customs experts to work together.

• A formal way of describing the business processes and incorporating them into a workflow management system enables them to be carried out. In Sagitta 2000, workshops have been used to test the business process by (other) customs experts. By calling up a standard application for each task that shows the user a textual description of the task rather than the actual application task itself, it is not necessary for the application tasks to have been constructed before the business process is tested.

• Thus far little attention has been paid to the functional requirements concerning work allocation and workload management. A survey has been conducted into these aspects. Initial experiences show that the user organization still finds it difficult to appreciate the opportunities created by workflow management. Consideration is given to the formulation of an initial version of the requirements, in which minimal use is made of workflow management's opportunities. Further research into the opportunities and new potential offered by workflow management is now under way. This research is addressing the following aspects:

(1) user authorization for tasks: user's competences, separation of functions;

(2) workload management: efficient distribution of work among the available users; and

(3) ensuring that the process progresses, and warnings when stagnation occurs.

• At present, most "headaches" are being caused by technological problems. The introduction of workflow management within an environment that sets very high standards for its technical infrastructure requires a great deal of attention to be paid to technology. The Customs Service demands the *round-the-clock* availability of certain subprocesses, a very high level of robustness, and complete integrity of the system and its associated databases. These high standards make it hard to introduce workflow technology.

Conclusion

With Sagitta 2000, a good start has been made in improving the way in which systems can be created and workflow management can be integrated into a new information system. However, the battle is far from over: on both the technical and organizational fronts, there are still plenty of obstacles to be overcome. Nevertheless there is a great deal of confidence that this will be done, and expectations within the user organization are high. Quite apart from the workflow management aspect, Sagitta 2000 has already proven very fruitful in thoroughly reconsidering and explicitly defining the Customs Service's business processes. The new process tackles the inefficiencies and inconsistencies of the existing ones, and fulfils the latest requirements made by the Customs Service to its business processes (CCC and the Client Concept).

EXERCISES

Exercise 7.1   Traveling at Somewhere University

Apply the modeling technique described in this book to the workflow process of the following travel agency.

Some time ago the board of Somewhere University (SU) decided to open a travel agency at the campus. The new agency is supposed to organize both business and private trips for employees of SU. However the service is not as the board expected. The most important complaint is that both the organization of a trip and the financial settlement take too long. Therefore the board has started an investigation. Interviews with several people involved have provided the following process description. (To avoid confusion between employees of SU who want to book a trip and employees who are involved in the organization of the trip, in the remainder, the former are called clients.)

The whole process starts when someone drops in at the travel agency to book a trip. An employee of the agency registers all the relevant information of the client. The agency maintains a separate file for each trip. An important issue is whether the client wants to book a private trip, a business trip, or a combination of both. Approximately twenty percent of all the trips organized by the agency is private.

Private trips are easy. The agency has one employee dedicated to the organization of private trips. As soon as the wishes of a client are registered, she can start with the organization of the trip.

Business trips are more complicated. The agency has two employees for the organization of business trips (although one of them works only three days a week). For each trip, there is always a single employee responsible who also carries out as many tasks as possible for this trip. In this way the service to clients should be guaranteed. For business trips a client needs a travel permit. Usually clients that are familiar with the process have already filled out a permit. Clients who arrive without a permit are given a blank permit that they can fill out later, after which they must return the permit to the agency. Travel permits are always checked before any other action is taken. If a permit is not filled out properly, it is returned to the client with the request to provide the missing information and send the permit back as soon as possible. In case a permit is not returned in time, the travel agency can no longer guarantee a timely organization of the trip. In the rare occasion that this happens, a notification is sent to the client and the file is closed. If a travel permit is okay, it is filed and the actual organization of the trip can start. First, however, a copy of the file is sent to the finance department of SU, because this department is responsible for the financial aspects of the trip.

An employee of the finance department of SU checks whether the client is allowed to make business trips paid by SU. The results of this check are sent to the travel agency in an internal memo. If the result is negative for the client, which is hardly ever the case because clients usually know when they are permitted to make business trips, the finance department does not make any payments. If the result is positive, the finance department makes an advance payment on the bank account of the client. It also pays any registration fees that might need to be paid in case of conference visits. Finally it pays those flights of the trip that are made for business purposes. However, these payments only can be made after the finance department has received detailed pricing information from the travel agency. After all the necessary payments have been made, the finance department is no longer involved in the preparations of the trip. However, after the client returns, the finance department handles the client's declaration (see below).

To prepare a trip (private or business), the travel agency always starts with flight arrangements. If a trip involves one or more flights, the responsible employee of the travel agency starts by preparing a flight schedule that includes departure and arrival times of all flights as well as pricing information. Then the client is called to approve the schedule. If the client does not approve the schedule, a new proposal is prepared and the client is contacted again. When a client approves the schedule, arrangements must be made to pay the flight(s). In case the trip is private, an appointment is made with the client to pay cash or by credit card. In case the trip is (partly) business, the travel agency has to wait for the memo of the finance department that states whether or not the client is allowed to make business trips for SU. If the memo is negative, the employee of the travel agency responsible for the trip calls the client to explain the problem. If the client still wants to make the trip, he or she has to pay all the costs and an appointment is made to pay for the flights. Often the client decides to cancel the trip, in which case the file is closed. If the memo is positive, the travel agency determines the costs of business flights and, if applicable, the costs of private flights. Relevant information on business flights is sent to the finance department, which handles the actual payment. In case of private flights, the client is contacted to make an appointment to arrange the payment.

The internal memo that the travel agency receives from the finance department is also used to determine whether a request must be sent to the in-house bank office (which is situated at the campus close to the travel agency) to prepare cash and travel cheques for the client. Such a request is always made when a business trip is allowed. (In case of private trips, the client has to take care of acquiring cash and cheques herself.)

The task of the bank in the process is very straightforward. Upon receipt of a request, a bank employee prepares cash and travel cheques and sends them to the travel agency. If a client returns cash and/or cheques after the trip, information about the exact amount that is used by the client is sent to the finance department. The finance department needs this information to process the client's declaration. In case a client does not return cash or cheques in time, the amount supposedly spent by the client is fixed to the value of the cash and cheques handed out to the client before the trip.

After flight arrangements have been made and any private flights have been paid, the responsible employee of the travel agency books hotels and makes reservations for local transportation (train, car, etc.). She also prints vouchers for any hotels that are booked. When cash and cheques have been received from the bank and all flight tickets have been received from the central office of the travel agency in Somewhere Else where they are printed, the employee puts all the documents together in a handy folder for the client. The agency has to make sure that everything is ready at least three working days before the trip starts because, then, the client picks up the documents. At that point, the involvement of the agency with the trip is finished. In case of a private trip, this also means that the process is complete. In case of a business trip, however, the declaration of the client still needs to be processed.

As mentioned, the finance department takes care of processing declarations. When it has received a client's declaration and the necessary information of the bank, an employee of the finance department processes the declaration and calculates the balance. The result must be approved by the director of the finance department. In case of mistakes, the employee must make the necessary corrections. After the declaration has been approved by the director, the balance is settled with the next salary payment of the client. In addition, the total cost of the trip is deducted from the travel budget of the faculty or other unit where the client is employed. If a client does not hand in his or her declaration in time (within a month after completion of the trip), the finance department assumes that the total cost of the trip equals the sum of the advance payment and the value of the cash and cheques given to the client.

The board of SU thinks that the main reason the above process takes so long is that the coordination between the three departments involved is poor. It believes that a workflow system might provide a solution. As a starting point, it would like to receive a report covering the following subjects.

(a) A resource classification of all the resources involved in the current process, distinguishing roles, and groups.
(b) A process model of the current situation, including information about roles, groups, and triggers.
(c) An analysis of the resource classification and the process model, using the guidelines for process (re)design discussed in earlier chapters.
(d) An improved resource classification/process model, based on the results of the analysis.

Appendix A: Workflow Theory

This book offers concrete techniques and guidelines for designing complex workflow processes. Although the need for a theoretical foundation was emphasized, formal definitions and notations have been avoided as much as possible to improve the readability. This appendix introduces the theoretical basis for the modeling technique used throughout this book.

Today's situation with respect to workflow management software is comparable to the situation as regards to database management software in the early 1970s. In the beginning of the '70s most of the pioneers in the field of database management systems (DBMSs) were using their own ad hoc concepts. This situation of disorder and lack of consensus resulted in an incomprehensive set of DBMSs. However, emerging standards such as the relational data model and the entity-relationship model led to a common formal basis for many DBMSs. As a result the use of these DBMSs boosted. There are many similarities between today's workflow management systems (WFMSs) and the DBMSs of the early '70s. Despite the efforts of the Workflow Management Coalition, a real conceptual standard is missing. As a result many organizations are reluctant to use existing workflow management software.

The relational data model and the entity-relationship model served as a catalyst for the use and functionality of DBMSs. Comparable models are missing for WFMSs. A WFMS addresses many perspectives and it is utopian to assume that a straightforward model comparable to the relational data model or the entity-relationship model can capture all relevant aspects. However for the most dominant perspective, that is, the process (control-flow) perspective, there seems to be consensus on the main concepts. In our opinion Petri nets constitute a good basis for the standardization of this perspective. Inspired by practical experiences, we have come to realize that many of the features of Petri-net formalism are useful in the context of workflow management.

In chapter 2 of this book we motivated the use of Petri nets as a design language. In our opinion, Petri nets constitute a good starting point for a *workflow theory*. In this appendix we focus on the roots of such a theory. First, we introduce the Petri-net formalism. Then we formalize the notion of correctness used in chapter 4 (i.e., soundness). Finally we demonstrate that Petri-net theory can aid in finding structural characterizations (i.e., design patterns) of correctness and efficient analysis techniques.

A.1   Petri Nets

This section introduces the basic Petri-net terminology and notations. Readers familiar with Petri nets can skip this section.[1]

The classical Petri net is a directed bipartite graph with two node types called *places* and *transitions*. The nodes are connected via directed *arcs*. Connections between two nodes of the same type are not allowed. Places are represented by circles and transitions by rectangles.

DEFINITION 1 (Petri net).   A Petri net is a triple (P, T, F):

- P is a finite set of places;
- T is a finite set of transitions $(P \cap T = \emptyset)$; and
- $F \subseteq (P \times T) \cup (T \times P)$ is a set of arcs (flow relation).

A place p is called an *input place* of a transition t iff (if and only if) there exists a directed arc from p to t. Place p is called an *output place* of transition t iff there exists a directed arc from t to p. We use •t to denote the set of input places for a transition t. The notations t•, •p and p• have similar meanings, that is, p• is the set of transitions sharing p as an input place. Note that we do not consider multiple arcs from one node to another. In the context of workflow procedures it makes no sense to have other weights because places correspond to conditions.

At any time a place contains zero or more *tokens*, drawn as black dots. *State M*, often referred to as marking, is the distribution of tokens over

1. Note that states are represented by weighted sums and note the definition of (elementary) (conflict-free) paths.

places, that is, $M \in P \to IN$. We will represent a state as follows: $1p_1 + 2p_2 + 1p_3 + 0p_4$ *is* the state with one token in place p_1, two tokens in p_2, one token in p_3 and no tokens in p_4. We can also represent this state as follows: $p_1 + 2p_2 + p_3$. To compare states we define a partial ordering. For any two states M_1 and M_2, $M_1 \leq M_2$ iff for all $p \in P$: $M_1(p) \leq M_2(p)$, where $M(p)$ denotes the number of tokens in place p in state M.

The number of tokens may change during the execution of the net. Transitions are the active components in a Petri net: they change the state of the net according to the following *firing rule*:

(1) A transition t is said to be *enabled* iff each input place p of t contains at least one token.

(2) An enabled transition may *fire*. If transition t fires, then t *consumes* one token from each input place p of t and *produces* one token for each output place p of t.

Given a Petri net (P, T, F) and a state M_1, we have the following notations:

- $M_1 \xrightarrow{t} M_2$: transition t is enabled in state M_1 and firing t in M_1 results in state M_2

- $M_1 \to M_2$: there is a transition t such that $M_1 \xrightarrow{t} M_2$

- $M_1 \xrightarrow{\sigma} M_n$: the firing sequence $\sigma = t_1 t_2 t_3 \ldots t_{n-1}$ leads from state M_1 to state M_n via a (possibly empty) set of intermediate states $M_2, \ldots, M_{n-1}$, i.e., $M_1 \xrightarrow{t1} M_2 \xrightarrow{t2} \cdots \xrightarrow{tn-1} M_n$

A state M_n is called *reachable* from M_1 (notation $M_1 \xrightarrow{*} M_n$) iff there is a firing sequence σ such that $M_1 \xrightarrow{\sigma} M_n$. Note that the empty firing sequence is also allowed, i.e., $M_1 \xrightarrow{*} M_1$.

We use (PN, M) to denote a Petri net PN with an initial state M. A state M' is a *reachable state* of (PN, M) iff $M \xrightarrow{*} M'$.

Let us define some standard properties for Petri nets. First we define properties related to the dynamics of a Petri net, and then we give some structural properties.

DEFINITION 2 (Live).   A Petri net (PN, M) is live iff for every reachable state M' and every transition t there is a state M'' reachable from M' that enables t.

A Petri net is *structurally live* if there exists an initial state such that the net is live.

DEFINITION 3 (Bounded, Safe).   A Petri net (PN, M) is bounded iff for each place there is a natural number n such that for every reachable state the number of tokens in p is less than n. The net is safe iff for each place the maximum number of tokens does not exceed 1.

A Petri net is *structurally bounded* if the net is bounded for any initially state.

DEFINITION 4 (Well-formed).   A Petri net PN is well-formed iff there is a state M such that (PN, M) is live and bounded.

Paths connect nodes by a sequence of arcs.

DEFINITION 5 (Path, Elementary, Conflict-free).   Let PN be a Petri net. A path C from a node n_1 to a node n_k is a sequence $(n_1, n_2, \ldots, n_k)$ such that $(n_i, n_{i+1}) \in F$ for $1 \le i \le k - 1$. C is elementary iff, for any two nodes n_i and n_j on C, $i \ne j \Rightarrow n_i \ne n_j$. C is conflict-free iff, for any place n_j on C and any transition n_i on C, $j \ne i - 1 \Rightarrow n_j \notin \bullet n_i$.

For convenience, we introduce the alphabet operator α on paths. If $C = (n_1, n_2, \ldots, n_k)$, then $\alpha(C) = \{n_1, n_2, \ldots, n_k\}$.

DEFINITION 6 (Strongly connected).   A Petri net is strongly connected iff, for every pair of nodes (i.e., places and transitions) x and y, there is a path leading from x to y.

DEFINITION 7 (Free choice).   A Petri net is a free choice Petri net iff, for every two transitions t_1 and t_2, $\bullet t_1 \cap \bullet t_2 \ne \varnothing$ implies $\bullet t_1 = \bullet t_2$.

DEFINITION 8 (State machine).   A Petri net is a state machine iff each transition has exactly one input and one output place.

DEFINITION 9 (S-component).   A subnet $PN_s = (P_s, T_s, F_s)$ is called an S-component of a Petri net $PN = (P, T, F)$ if $P_s \subseteq P$, $T_s \subseteq T$, $F_s \subseteq F$, PN_s is strongly connected, PN_s is a state machine, and for every $q \in P_s$ and $t \in T$: $(q, t) \in F \Rightarrow (q, t) \in F_s$ and $(t, q) \in F \Rightarrow (t, q) \in F_s$.

DEFINITION 10 (S-coverable).   A Petri net is S-coverable iff for any node there exists an S-component that contains this node.

See references [9, 15] for a more elaborate introduction to these standard notations. The notion of S-coverability is related to the notions of place and transition invariants [9, 14, 15]. A *place invariant* assigns a weight to each place such that no transition can change the "weighted token sum." The weighted token sum is defined as the sum of all tokens multiplied by the weights of the corresponding places; that is, function w is a place invariant if for any state M_1 and any transition t such that $M_1 \xrightarrow{t} M_2$: $\sum_{p \in P} w(M_1(p)) = \sum_{p \in P} w(M_2(p))$. Note that place invariants are structural, that is, they do not depend on the initial state. Place invariants correspond to conservation laws. A place invariant is *semipositive* if it does not assign negative weights to transitions. Positive place invariants assign a positive weight to each place. Note that each S-component corresponds to a semipositive place invariant. Moreover, if the Petri net is S-coverable, then there is a positive invariant. *Transition invariants* are the dual of place invariants. A transition assigns a weight to each transition such that if every transition fires the specified number of times, the initial state is restored. Negative weights correspond to "backward firing." A Petri net that is live and S-coverable (or bounded) has a positive transition invariant.

A.2   WF-Nets

Workflow management has many perspectives. The process (i.e. control-flow) perspective is the most prominent one, because the core of any workflow system is formed by the processes it supports. In the control-flow dimension building blocks such as the AND-split, AND-join, OR-split, and OR-join are used to model sequential, conditional, parallel, and iterative routing. Clearly a Petri net can be used to specify the routing of cases. *Tasks* are modeled by transitions and causal dependencies are modeled by places and arcs. In fact, a place corresponds to a *condition* that can be used as pre- and/or post-condition for tasks. An AND-split corresponds to a transition with two or more output places, and an AND-join corresponds to a transition with two or more input places. OR-splits/OR-joins correspond to places with multiple outgoing/incoming arcs. Moreover in [1] it is shown that the Petri net approach also allows for useful routing constructs absent in many WFMSs.

A Petri net that models the control-flow dimension of a workflow is called a *workflow net* (WF-net). It should be noted that a WF-net specifies the dynamic behavior of a single case in isolation.

DEFINITION 11 (WF-net).   A Petri net $PN = (P, T, F)$ is a WF-net (Workflow net) if and only if:

(i) There is one source place $i \in P$ such that $\bullet i = \emptyset$;

(ii) there is one sink place $o \in P$ such that $o\bullet = \emptyset$; and

(iii) every node $x \in P \cup T$ is on a path from i to o.

A WF-net has one input place (i) and one output place (o) because any case handled by the procedure represented by the WF-net is created when it enters the WFMS and is deleted once it is completely handled by the WFMS; in other words, the WF-net specifies the lifecycle of a case. The third requirement in definition 11 has been added to avoid "dangling tasks and/or conditions," that is, tasks and conditions that do not contribute to the processing of cases.

Given the definition of a WF-net it is easy to derive the following properties.

PROPOSITION 1 (Properties of WF-nets).   Let $PN = (P, T, F)$ be a Petri net.

• If PN is a WF-net with source place i, then for any place $p \in P$: $\bullet p \neq \emptyset$ or $p = i$, i.e., i is the only source place;

• If PN is a WF-net with sink place o, then for any place $p \in P$: $p\bullet \neq \emptyset$ or $p = o$, i.e., o is the only sink place;

• If PN is a WF-net and we add a transition t^* to PN which connects sink place o with source place i (i.e., $\bullet t^* = \{o\}$ and $t^*\bullet = \{i\}$), then the resulting Petri net is strongly connected;

• If PN has a source place i and a sink place o and adding a transition t^* which connects sink place o with source place i yields a strongly connected net, then every node $x \in P \cup T$ is on a path from i to o in PN and PN is a WF-net.

Figure A.1 shows a WF-net that models the processing of complaints. First the complaint is registered (task *register*), then in parallel a questionnaire is sent to the complainant (task *send_questionnaire*) and the complaint is evaluated (task *evaluate*). If the complainant returns the questionnaire within two weeks, the task *process_questionnaire* is executed. If the questionnaire is not returned within two weeks, the result of the questionnaire is discarded (task *time_out*). Based on the result of the evaluation, the complaint is processed or not. The actual processing of the complaint (task *process_complaint*) is delayed until condition $c5$ is satisfied, that is, the questionnaire is processed or a time-out has occurred. The processing of the complaint is checked via task *check_processing*.

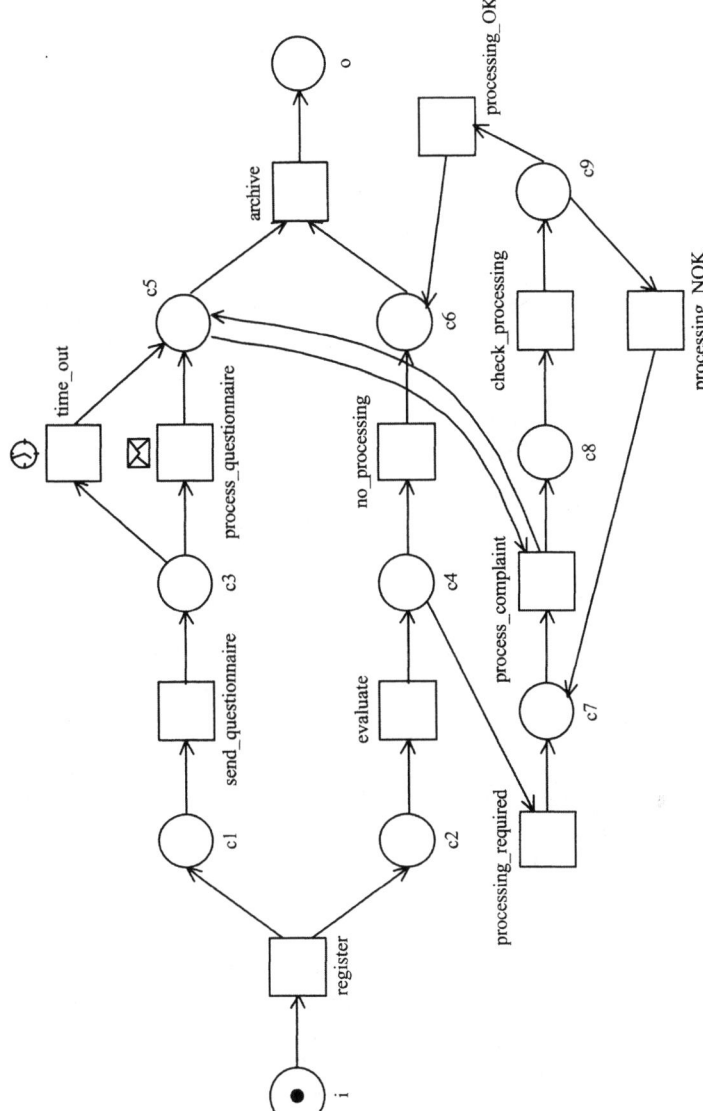

Figure A.1
A WF-net for the processing of complaints

Finally task *archive* is executed. Note that sequential, conditional, parallel, and iterative routing are present in this example.

The WF-net shown in figure A.1 clearly illustrates that we focus on the control-flow dimension. We abstract from resources, applications, and technical platforms. Moreover we also abstract from *case attributes* and *triggers*. Case attributes are used to resolve choices (OR-split); in other words, the choice between *processing_required* and *no_processing* is (partially) based on case attributes set during the execution of task *evaluate*. The choice between *processing_OK* and *processing_NOK* is resolved by testing case attributes set by *check_processing*. In the WF-net we abstract from case attributes by introducing nondeterministic choices in the Petri net. If we don't abstract from this information, we would have to model the (unknown) behavior of the applications used in each of the tasks and analysis would become intractable. In figure A.1 we have indicated that *time_out* and *process_questionnaire* require triggers. The clock symbol denotes a time trigger and the envelope symbol denotes an external trigger. Task *time_out* requires a time trigger ("two weeks have passed") and *process_questionnaire* requires a message trigger ("the questionnaire has been returned"). A trigger can be seen as an additional condition that needs to be satisfied. In the remainder of this chapter we abstract from these trigger conditions. We assume that the environment behaves fairly; that is, the liveness of a transition is not hindered by the continuous absence of a specific trigger. As a result, every trigger condition will be satisfied eventually.

A.3   Soundness

In this section we summarize some of the basic results for WF-nets presented in [2]. The remainder of this chapter will build on these results.

The three requirements stated in definition 11 can be verified statically; in other words, they only relate to the structure of the Petri net. However there is another requirement that should be satisfied:

For any case, the procedure will terminate eventually and the moment the procedure terminates there is a token in place o and all the other places are empty.

Moreover there should be no dead tasks; it should be possible to execute an arbitrary task by following the appropriate route through the WF-net. These two additional requirements correspond to the so-called *soundness property*.

DEFINITION 12 (Sound). A procedure modeled by a WF-net $PN = (P, T, F)$ is sound if and only if:

(i) For every state M reachable from state i, there exists a firing sequence leading from state M to state o. Formally:[2]

$$\forall_M (i \xrightarrow{*} M) \Rightarrow (M \xrightarrow{*} o);$$

(ii) State o is the only state reachable from state i with at least one token in place o. Formally:

$$\forall_M (i \xrightarrow{*} M \wedge M \geq o) \Rightarrow (M = o);$$

(iii) There are no dead transitions in (PN, i). Formally:

$$\forall_{t \in T} \exists_{M, M'} i \xrightarrow{*} M \xrightarrow{t} M'.$$

Note that the soundness property relates to the dynamics of a WF-net. The first requirement in definition 12 states that starting from the initial state (state i),[2] it is always possible to reach the state with one token in place o (state o). If we assume a strong notion of fairness, then the first requirement implies that eventually state o is reached. Strong fairness means in every infinite firing sequence, each transition fires infinitely often. The fairness assumption is reasonable in the context of workflow management: all choices are made (implicitly or explicitly) by applications, humans, or external actors. Clearly they should not introduce an infinite loop. Note that the traditional notions of fairness (i.e., weaker forms of fairness with just local conditions, e.g., if a transition is enabled infinitely often, it will fire eventually) are not sufficient. See [3, 13] for more details. The second requirement states that the moment a token is put in place o, all the other places should be empty. Sometimes the term *proper termination* is used to describe the first two requirements [12]. The last requirement states that there are no dead transitions (tasks) in the initial state i.

Figure A.2 shows a WF-net that is not sound. There are several deficiencies. If *time_out_1* and *processing_2* fire or *time_out_2* and

---

2. Note that there is an overloading of notation: the symbol i is used to denote both the *place i* and the *state i* with only one token in place i (see section 1).

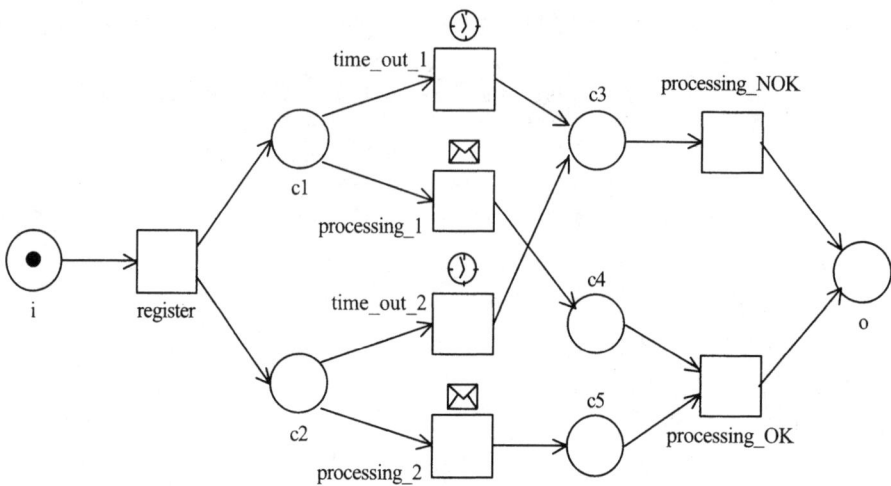

Figure A.2
Another WF-net for the processing of complaints

processing_1 fire, the WF-net will not terminate properly because a token gets stuck in *c4* or *c5*. If *time_out_1* and *time_out_2* fire, then the task *processing_NOK* will be executed twice and because of the presence of two tokens in *o* the moment of termination is not clear.

Given a WF-net $PN = (P, T, F)$, we want to decide whether PN is sound. In [2] we have shown that soundness corresponds to liveness and boundedness. To link soundness to liveness and boundedness, we define an extended net $\underline{PN} = (\underline{P}, \underline{T}, \underline{F})$. $\underline{PN}$ is the Petri net obtained by adding an extra transition t^* which connects o and i. The extended Petri net $\underline{PN} = (\underline{P}, \underline{T}, \underline{F})$ is defined as follows: $\underline{P} = P$, $\underline{T} = T \cup \{t^*\}$, and $\underline{F} = F \cup \{\langle o, t^* \rangle, \langle t^*, i \rangle\}$. In the remainder we will call such an extended net the *short-circuited* net of PN. The short-circuited net allows for the formulation of the following theorem.

THEOREM 1. A WF-net PN is sound if and only if $(\underline{PN}, i)$ is live and bounded.

PROOF. See [2].

This theorem shows that standard Petri-net-based analysis techniques can be used to verify soundness.

A.4 Structural Characterization of Soundness

Theorem 1 gives a useful characterization of the quality of a workflow process definition. However, there are a number of problems:

• For a complex WF-net it may be intractable to decide soundness. (For arbitrary WF-nets liveness and boundedness are decidable but also EXPSPACE-hard, cf. Cheng, Esparza, and Palsberg [7].);

• Soundness is a minimal requirement. Readability and maintainability issues are not addressed by theorem 1; and

• Theorem 1 does not show how a non-sound WF-net should be modified; that is, it does not identify constructs that invalidate the soundness property.

These problems stem from the fact that the definition of soundness relates to the dynamics of a WF-net while the workflow designer is concerned with the static structure of the WF-net. Therefore it is interesting to investigate structural characterizations of sound WF-nets. For this purpose we introduce three interesting subclasses of WF-nets: free choice WF-nets, well-structured WF-nets, and S-coverable WF-nets.

A.4.1 Free choice WF-nets

Most of the WFMSs available at the moment, abstract from states between tasks; in other words, states are not represented explicitly. These WFMSs use building blocks such as the AND-split, AND-join, OR-split, and OR-join to specify workflow procedures. The AND-split and the AND-join are used for parallel routing. The OR-split and the OR-join are used for conditional routing. Because these systems abstract from states, every choice is made *inside* an OR-split building block. If we model an OR-split in terms of a Petri net, the OR-split corresponds to a number of transitions sharing the same set of input places. This means that for these WFMSs, a workflow procedure corresponds to a free choice Petri net (cf. definition 7).

It is easy to see that a process definition composed of AND-splits, AND-joins, OR-splits, and OR-joins is free choice. If two transitions t_1 and t_2 share an input place ($\bullet t_1 \cap \bullet t_2 \neq \varnothing$), then they are part of an OR-split, that is, a "free choice" between a number of alternatives. Therefore the sets of input places of t_1 and t_2 should match ($\bullet t_1 = \bullet t_2$). Figure A.2 shows a free choice WF-net. The WF-net shown in figure A.1

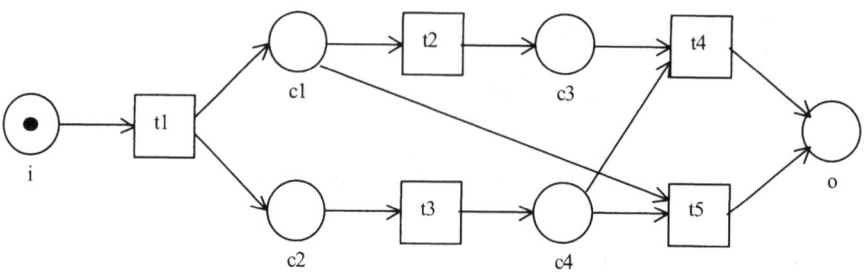

Figure A.3
A non-free choice WF-net containing a mixture of parallelism and choice

is not free choice; *archive* and *process_complaint* share an input place but the two corresponding input sets differ.

We have evaluated many WFMSs and just one of these systems (COSA [18]) allows for a construct that is comparable to a non-free choice WF-net. Therefore it makes sense to consider free choice Petri nets in more detail. Clearly parallelism, sequential routing, conditional routing, and iteration can be modeled without violating the free choice property. Another reason for restricting WF-nets to free choice Petri nets is the following. If we allow non-free choice Petri nets, then the choice between conflicting tasks *may* be influenced by the order in which the preceding tasks are executed. The routing of a case should be independent of the order in which tasks are executed. A situation where the free choice property is violated is often a mixture of parallelism and choice. Figure A.3 shows such a situation. Firing transition *t1* introduces parallelism. Although there is no real choice between *t2* and *t5* (*t5* is not enabled), the parallel execution of *t2* and *t3* results in a situation where *t5* is not allowed to occur. However, if the execution of *t2* is delayed until *t3* has been executed, then there is a real choice between *t2* and *t5*. In our opinion parallelism itself should be separated from the choice between two or more alternatives. Therefore we consider the non-free choice construct shown in figure A.3 to be improper. In literature, the term *confusion* is often used to refer to the situation shown in figure A.3.

Free choice Petri nets have been studied extensively (cf. [9]) because they seem to be a good compromise between expressive power and analyzability. It is a class of Petri nets for which strong theoretical results and efficient analysis techniques exist. For example, the well-known Rank Theorem ([8]) enables us to formulate the following corollary.

COROLLARY 1. The following problem can be solved in polynomial time: given a free choice WF-net, decide if it is sound.

PROOF. Let PN be a free choice WF-net. The short-circuited net $\underline{PN}$ is also free choice. Therefore the problem of deciding whether $(\underline{PN}, i)$ is live and bounded can be solved in polynomial time (Rank theorem [8]). By theorem 1, this corresponds to soundness.

Corollary 1 shows that, for free choice nets, there are efficient algorithms to decide soundness. Moreover a sound free choice WF-net is guaranteed to be safe (given an initial state with just one token in i).

LEMMA 1. A sound free choice WF-net is safe.

PROOF. Let PN be a sound free choice WF-net. $\underline{PN}$ is the Petri net PN extended with a transition connecting o and i. $\underline{PN}$ is free choice and well-formed. Hence $\underline{PN}$ is S-coverable [9] (i.e., each place is part of an embedded strongly connected state-machine component). Since initially there is just one token, $(\underline{PN}, i)$ is safe and so is (PN, i).

Safeness is a desirable property because it makes no sense to have multiple tokens in a place representing a condition. A condition is either true (1 token) or false (no tokens).

Although most WFMSs only allow for free choice workflows, free choice WF-nets are not a completely satisfactory structural characterization of "good" workflows. On the one hand, there are non-free choice WF-nets that correspond to sensible workflows (cf. figure A.1). On the other hand there are sound free choice WF-nets that make no sense. Nevertheless the free choice property is a desirable property. If a workflow can be modeled as a free choice WF-net, one should do so. A workflow specification based on a free choice WF-net can be enacted by most workflow systems. Moreover a free choice WF-net allows for efficient analysis techniques and is easier to understand. Non-free choice constructs such as the construct shown in figure A.3 are a potential source of anomalous behavior (e.g., deadlock) which is difficult to trace.

A.4.2 Well-structured WF-nets

Another approach to obtain a structural characterization of "good" workflows, is to balance AND/OR-splits and AND/OR-joins. Clearly two parallel flows initiated by an AND-split should not be joined by an OR-join. Two alternative flows created via an OR-split, should not be

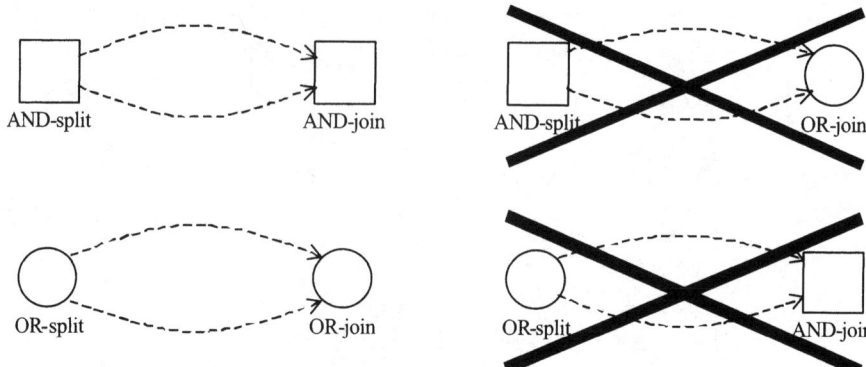

Figure A.4
Good and bad constructions

synchronized by an AND-join. As shown in figure A.4, an AND-split should be complemented by an AND-join and an OR-split should be complemented by an OR-join.

One of the deficiencies of the WF-net shown in figure A.2 is the fact that the AND-split *register* is complemented by the OR-join *c3* or the OR-join *o*. To formalize the concept illustrated in figure A.4 we give the following definition.

DEFINITION 13 (Well-handled).   A Petri net *PN* is well handled iff, for any pair of nodes x and y such that one of the nodes is a place and the other a transition and for any pair of elementary paths C_1 and C_2 leading from x to y, $\alpha(C_1) \cap \alpha(C_2) = \{x, y\} \Rightarrow C_1 = C_2$.

Note that the WF-net shown in figure A.2 is not well handled. Well-handledness can be decided in polynomial time by applying a modified version of the max-flow min-cut technique. A Petri net that is well handled has a number of nice properties such as strong connectedness and well-formedness coincide.

LEMMA 2.   A strongly connected, well-handled Petri net is well formed.

PROOF.   Let *PN* be a strongly connected well-handled Petri net. Clearly, there are no circuits that have PT-handles nor TP-handles [11]. Therefore the net is structurally bounded (see theorem 3.1 in [11]) and structurally live (see theorem 3.2 in [11]). Hence *PN* is well-formed.

Clearly well-handledness is a desirable property for any WF-net *PN*. Moreover we also require the short-circuited $\underline{PN}$ to be well handled. We impose this additional requirement for the following reason. Suppose we want to use *PN* as a part of a larger WF-net *PN′*.

PN′ is the original WF-net extended with an "undo task." See figure A.5. Transition undo corresponds to the undo task, transitions *t1* and *t2* have been added to make *PN′* a WF-net. It is undesirable that transition undo violates the well-handledness property of the original net. However *PN′* is well handled iff $\underline{PN}$ is well handled. Therefore we require $\underline{PN}$ to be well handled. We use the term *well-structured* to refer to WF-nets whose extension is well-handled.

DEFINITION 14 (Well-structured).   A WF-net *PN* is well-structured iff $\underline{PN}$ is well-handled.

Well-structured WF-nets have a number of desirable properties. Soundness can be verified in polynomial time and a sound, well-structured WF-net is safe. To prove these properties we use some of the results obtained for *elementary extended non-self-controlling nets*.

DEFINITION 15 (Elementary extended non-self-controlling).   A Petri net *PN* is elementary extended non-self-controlling (ENSC) iff, for every pair of transitions t_1 and t_2 such that $\bullet t_1 \cap \bullet t_2 \neq \varnothing$, there does not exist an elementary path C leading from t_1 to t_2 such that $\bullet t_1 \cap \alpha(C) = \varnothing$.

THEOREM 2.   Let *PN* be a WF-net. If *PN* is well-structured, then $\underline{PN}$ is elementary extended non-self-controlling.

PROOF.   Assume that $\underline{PN}$ is not elementary extended non-self-controlling. This means that there is a pair of transitions t_1 and t_k such that $\bullet t_1 \cap \bullet t_k \neq \varnothing$ and there exists an elementary path $C = \langle t_1, p_2, t_2, \ldots, p_k, t_k \rangle$ leading from t_1 to t_k and $\bullet t_1 \cap \alpha(C) = \varnothing$. Let $p_1 \in \bullet t_1 \cap \bullet t_k$. $C_1 = \langle p_1, t_k \rangle$ and $C_2 = \langle p_1, t_1, p_2, t_2, \ldots, p_k, t_k \rangle$ are paths leading from p_1 to t_k. (Note that C_2 is the concatenation of $\langle p_1 \rangle$ and C.) Clearly, C_1 is elementary. We will also show that C_2 is elementary. C is elementary, and $p_1 \notin \alpha(C)$ because $p_1 \in \bullet t_1$. Hence C_2 is also elementary. Since C_1 and C_2 are both elementary paths, $C_1 \neq C_2$ and $\alpha(C_1) \cap \alpha(C_2) = \{p_1, t_k\}$, we conclude that $\underline{PN}$ is not well-handled.

Consider for example the WF-net shown in figure A.6. The WF-net is well-structured and, therefore, also elementary extended non-self-

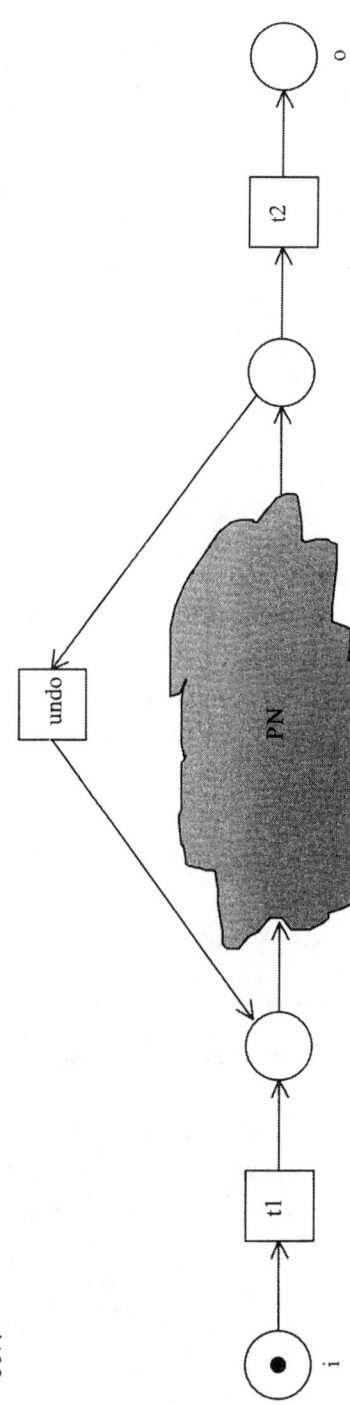

Figure A.5
The WF-net PN′ is well handled iff PN is well handled

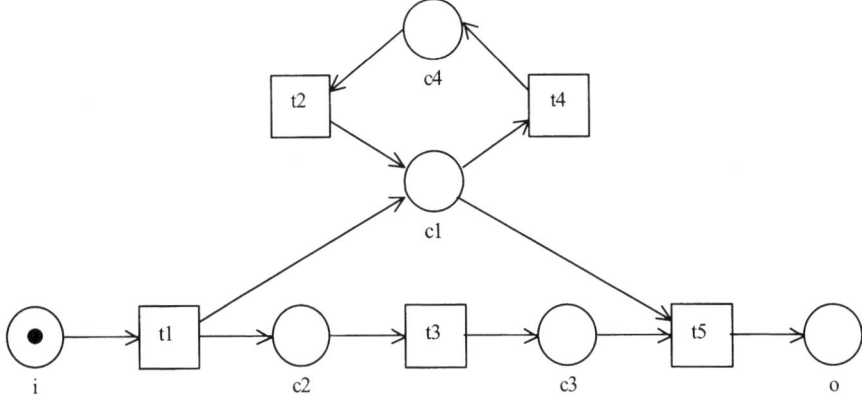

Figure A.6
A well-structured WF-net

controlling. However the net is not free choice. Nevertheless it is possible to verify soundness for such a WF-net very efficiently.

COROLLARY 2.   The following problem can be solved in polynomial time. Given a well-structured WF-net, to decide if it is sound.

PROOF.   Let PN be a well-structured WF-net. The short-circuited net $\underline{PN}$ is elementary extended non-self-controlling (theorem 2) and structurally bounded (see proof of lemma 2). For bounded elementary extended non-self-controlling nets, the problem of deciding whether a given marking is live can be solved in polynomial time (see [6]). Therefore the problem of deciding whether $(\underline{PN}, i)$ is live and bounded can be solved in polynomial time. By theorem 1, this corresponds to soundness.

LEMMA 3.   A sound well-structured WF-net is safe.

PROOF.   Let $\underline{PN}$ be the net PN extended with a transition connecting o and i. $\underline{PN}$ is extended non-self-controlling. $\underline{PN}$ is covered by state-machines (S-components), see corollary 5.3 in [6]. Hence $\underline{PN}$ is safe and so is PN (see proof of lemma 1).

Well-structured WF-nets and free choice WF-nets have similar properties. In both cases soundness can be verified very efficiently and soundness implies safeness. In spite of these similarities, there are sound well-structured WF-nets that are not free choice (figure A.6) and there are sound free choice WF-nets that are not well structured. In fact, it is possible to have a sound WF-net that is neither free choice nor well structured (figures A.1 and A.3).

A.4.3   S-coverable WF-nets

What about the sound WF-nets shown in figure A.1 and figure A.3? The WF-net shown in figure A.3 can be transformed into a free choice well-structured WF-net by separating choice and parallelism. The WF-net shown in figure A.1 cannot be transformed into a free choice or well-structured WF-net without yielding a much more complex WF-net. Place *c5* acts as some kind of milestone which is tested by the task *process_complaint*. Traditional workflow management systems that do not make the state of the case explicit are not able to handle the workflow specified by figure A.1. Only workflow management systems such as COSA [18] have the capability to enact such a state-based workflow. Nevertheless it is interesting to consider generalizations of free choice and well-structured WF-nets: *S-coverable WF-nets* can be seen as such a generalization.

DEFINITION 16 (S-coverable).   A WF-net is S-coverable if the short-circuited net *PN* is S-coverable.

The WF-nets shown in figure A.1 and figure A.3 are S-coverable. The WF-net shown in figure A.2 is not S-coverable. The following two corollaries show that S-coverability is a generalization of the free choice property and well-structuredness.

COROLLARY 3.   A sound free choice WF-net is S-coverable.

PROOF.   The short-circuited net *PN* is free choice and well-formed. Hence, *PN* is S-coverable (cf. [9]).

COROLLARY 4.   A sound well-structured WF-net is S-coverable.

PROOF.   *PN* is extended non-self-controlling (theorem 2). Hence, *PN* is S-coverable (cf. corollary 5.3 in [6]).

All the sound WF-nets presented in this appendix are S-coverable. Every S-coverable WF-net is safe. The only WF-net that is not sound, that is, the WF-net shown in figure A.2, is not S-coverable. These and other examples indicate that there is a high correlation between S-coverability and soundness. It seems that S-coverability is one of the basic requirements any workflow process definition should satisfy. From a formal point of view, it is possible to construct WF-nets that are sound but not S-coverable. Typically these nets contain places that do not restrict the firing of a transition, but that are not in any S-component. (See for example figure 65 in [14].) From a practical point of view, these WF-nets are to be avoided. WF-nets that are not S-coverable are difficult to interpret because the structural and dynamical properties do not match. For example, these nets can be live and bounded but not structurally bounded. There seems to be no practical need for using constructs which violate the S-coverability property. Therefore we consider S-coverability to be a basic requirement any WF-net should satisfy.

Another way of looking at S-coverability is the following interpretation: S-components correspond to *document flows*. To handle a workflow several pieces of information are created, used, and updated. One can think of these pieces of information as physical documents, insofar as at any point in time the document is in one place in the WF-net. Naturally the information in one document can be copied to another document while executing a task (i.e., transition) processing both documents. Initially all documents are present but a document can be empty (i.e., corresponds to a blank piece of paper). It is easy to see that the flow of one such document corresponds to a state machine (assuming the existence of a transition t^*). These document flows synchronize via joint tasks. Therefore the composition of these flows yields an S-coverable WF-net. One can think of the document flows as threads. Consider for example the short-circuited net of the WF-net shown in figure A.1. This net can be composed out of the following two threads: (1) a thread corresponding to the processing of the form (places i, $c2$, $c3$, $c5$, and o), and (2) a thread corresponding to the actual processing of the complaint (places i, $c2$, $c4$, $c5$, $c6$, $c7$, $c8$, and $c9$). Note that the tasks *register* and *archive* are used in both threads.

Although a WF-net can, in principle, have exponentially many S-components, they are quite easy to compute for workflows encountered in practice (see also the above interpretation of S-components as document flows or threads). Note that S-coverability only depends on the structure and the degree of connectedness is generally low (i.e., the incidence matrix of a WF-net typically has few non-zero entries). Unfortunately, in general, it is not possible to verify soundness of an S-coverable WF-net in polynomial time. The problem of deciding soundness for an S-coverable WF-net is PSPACE-complete. For most applications this is not a real problem. In most cases the number of tasks in one workflow process definition is less than 100 and the number of states is less than 200,000. Tools using standard techniques such as the construction of the coverability graph have no problems in coping with these workflow process definitions.

A.4.4 Summary

The three structural characterizations (free choice, well-structured and S-coverable) turn out to be very useful for the analysis of workflow process definitions. Based on our experience, we have good reasons to believe that S-coverability is a desirable property any workflow definition should satisfy. Constructs violating S-coverability can be detected easily and tools can be build to help the designer to construct an S-coverable WF-net. S-coverability is a generalization of well-structuredness and the free choice property (corollary 3 and 4). Both well-structuredness and the free choice property also correspond to desirable properties of a workflow. A WF-net satisfying at least one of these two properties can be analyzed very efficiently. However we have shown that there are workflows that are not free choice and not well-structured. Consider for example figure A.1. The fact that task *process_complaint* tests whether there is a token in $c5$, prevents the WF-net from being free choice or well-structured. Although this is a very sensible workflow, most workflow management systems do not support such an advanced routing construct. Even if one is able to use state-based workflows (e.g., COSA) allowing for constructs which violate well-structuredness and the free choice property, then the structural characterizations are still useful. If a WF-net is not free choice or not well-structured, one should locate the source that violates one of these properties and check whether it is really necessary to use a non-free choice or a non-well-structured construct. If the non-free choice or non-well-structured construct is really necessary, then the correctness of the construct should be double-checked, because it is a potential source of errors. This way the readability and maintainability of a workflow process definition can be improved.

A.5 Compositionality of WF-Nets

The WF-nets shown in this appendix are very simple compared to the workflows encountered in practice. For example, in a practical setting there are workflows consisting of more than one hundred tasks with a very complex interaction structure. For the designer of such workflows the complexity is overwhelming and communication with end-users using huge diagrams is difficult. In most cases hierarchical (de)composition is used to tackle this problem. A complex workflow is decomposed into subflows and each of the subflows is decomposed into smaller subflows until the desired level of detail is reached. Many WFMSs allow for such a hierarchical decomposition. In addition, this mechanism can be utilized for the reuse of existing workflows. Consider for example multiple workflows sharing a generic subflow. Some WFMS-vendors also supply reference models which correspond to typical workflows in insurance, banking, finance, marketing, purchase, procurement, logistics, and manufacturing.

Reference models, reuse, and the structuring of complex workflows require a hierarchy concept. The most common hierarchy concept supported by many WFMSs is *task refinement* (a task can be refined into a subflow). This concept is illustrated in figure A.7. The WF-net PN_1 contains a task t^+ that is refined by another WF-net PN_2; in other words, t^+ is no longer a task but a reference to a subflow. A WF-net that represents a subflow should satisfy the same requirements as an ordinary WF-net. The semantics of the hierarchy concept are straightforward; simply replace the refined transition by the corresponding subnet. Figure A.7 shows that the refinement of t^+ in PN_1 by PN_2 yields a WF-net PN_3.

The hierarchy concept can be exploited to establish the correctness of a workflow. Given a complex hierarchical workflow model, it is possible to verify soundness by analyzing each of the subflows separately. This is illustrated by the following theorem.

THEOREM 3. Let $PN_1 = (P_1, T_1, F_1)$ and $PN_2 = (P_2, T_2, F_2)$ be two WF-nets such that $T_1 \cap T_2 = \emptyset$, $P_1 \cap P_2 = \{i, o\}$, and $t^+ \in F_1$. Let $PN_3 = (P_3, T_3, F_3)$ be the WF-net obtained by replacing transition t^+ in PN_1 by PN_2, i.e., $P_3 = P_1 \cup P_2$, $T_3 = (T_1 \setminus \{t^+\}) \cup T_2$, and $F_3 = \{(x, y) \in F_1 \mid x \neq t^+ \wedge y \neq t^+\} \cup \{(x, y) \in F_2 \mid \{x, y\} \cap \{i, o\} = \emptyset\} \cup \{(x, y) \in P_1 \times T_2 \mid (x, t^+) \in F_1 \wedge (i, y) \in F_2\} \cup \{(x, y) \in T_2 \times P_1 \mid (t^+, y) \in F_1 \wedge (x, o) \in F_2\}$. (PN_1, i) and (PN_2, i) are safe and sound if and only if (PN_3, i) is safe and sound.

PROOF. The proof is a special case of the proof theorem 3 in [5]. The crux of the proof is the observation that every state in PN_3 can be

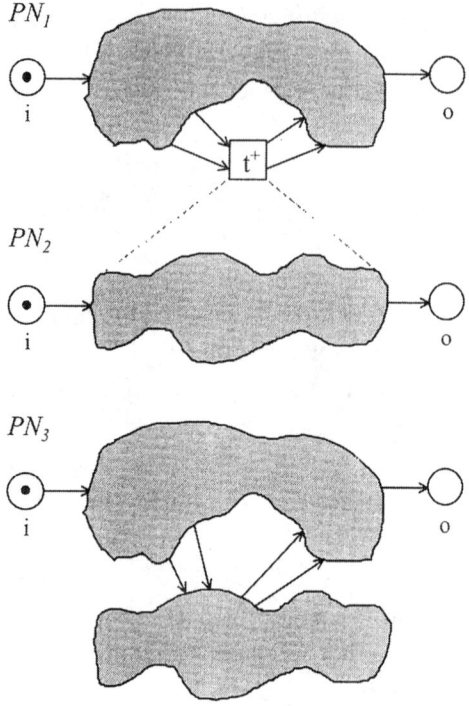

Figure A.7
Task refinement: WF-net PN3 is composed of PN1 and PN2

mapped onto a state in PN_1 and a state in PN_2 and vice versa. Moreover it is essential that the nets are safe: if the subnet PN_2 is activated multiple times, its behavior cannot be related to a single firing of t^+ in PN_1. For more details we refer to [5].

Theorem 3 is a generalization of the result given by Vallette in [16]. Figure A.8 shows a hierarchical workflow process with one main workflow and two subflows. Both of the subflows are safe and sound. If in the main workflow the two subflows are replaced by ordinary tasks, then the main workflow is also safe and sound. Therefore the overall workflow shown in figure A.8 is also safe and sound. Theorem 3 is of particular importance for the reuse of subflows. For the analysis of a complex workflow, every safe and sound subflow can be considered to be a single task. This allows for an efficient modular analysis of the soundness property.

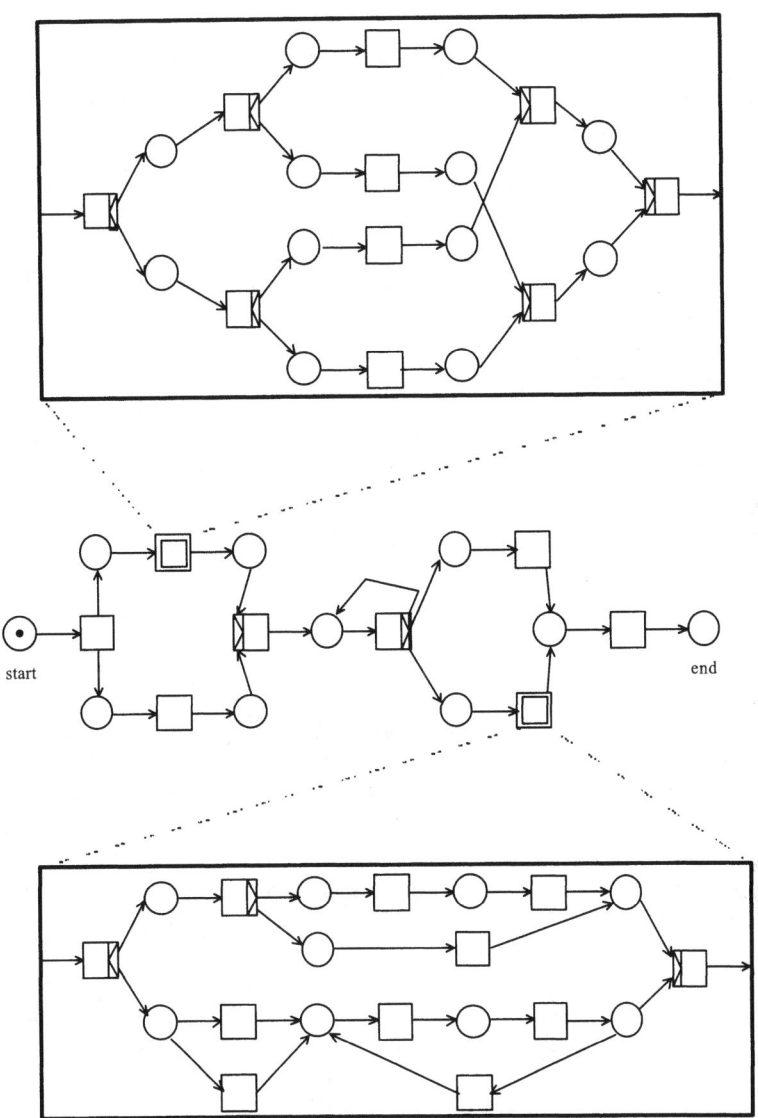

Figure A.8
Building complex workflows (that are safe and sound) out of safe and sound subflows

The results presented in this appendix give workflow designers a handle to construct correct workflows. Although it is possible to use standard Petri-net-based analysis tools, we have developed a workflow analyzer, called Woflan, which can be used by people not familiar with Petri-net theory [4, 17]. Woflan interfaces with existing workflow products such as Staffware, COSA, METEOR, and Protos.

References

[1] Aalst, W. M. P. van der. "Three Good Reasons for Using a Petri-net-based Workflow Management System." In *Proceedings of the International Working Conference on Information and Process Integration in Enterprises (IPIC'96)*, Edited by S. Navathe and T. Wakayama 179–201. Cambridge, Massachusetts, Nov. 1996.

[2] ———. "Verification of Workflow Nets." In *Application and Theory of Petri Nets 1997*, volume 1248 of *Lecture Notes in Computer Science*, Edited by P. Azéma and G. Balbo. 407–426. Berlin: Springer-Verlag, 1997.

[3] ———. "The Application of Petri Nets to Workflow Management." *The Journal of Circuits, Systems, and Computers*, 8:1(1998):21–66.

[4] ———. "Woflan: A Petri-Net-Based Workflow Analyzer." *Systems Analysis —Modelling—Simulation*, 35:3(1999):345–357.

[5] ———. "Finding Control-Flow Errors Using Petri-Net-Based Techniques." *Business Process Management: Models, Techniques, and Empirical Studies*, volume 1806 of *Lecture Notes in Computer Science*. 161–183. Berlin: Springer-Verlag, 2000.

[6] Barkaoui, K., J. M. Couvreur, and C. Dutheillet. "On Liveness in Extended Non Self-Controlling Nets." In *Application and Theory of Petri Nets 1995*, volume 935 of *Lecture Notes in Computer Science*, Edited by G. De Michelis and M. Diaz. 25–44. Berlin: Springer-Verlag, 1995.

[7] Cheng, A., J. Esparza, and J. Palsberg. "Complexity Results for 1-safe Nets." *Foundations of Software Technology and Theoretical Computer Science*, volume 761 of *Lecture Notes in Computer Science*, Edited by R. K. Shyamasunder. 326–337. Berlin: Springer-Verlag, 1993.

[8] Desel, J. "A Proof of the Rank Theorem for Extended Free-Choice Nets." *Application and Theory of Petri Nets 1992*, volume 616 of *Lecture Notes in Computer Science*, Edited by K. Jensen. 134–153. Berlin: Springer-Verlag, 1992.

[9] Desel, J. and J. Esparza. *Free Choice Petri Nets*, volume 40 of *Cambridge Tracts in Theoretical Computer Science*. Cambridge: Cambridge University Press, 1995.

[10] Esparza, J. "Synthesis Rules for Petri Nets, and How They Can Lead to New Results." In *Proceedings of CONCUR 1990*, volume 458 of *Lecture Notes*

in Computer Science, Edited by J. C. M. Baeten and J. W. Klop. 182–198. Berlin: Springer-Verlag, 1990.

[11] Esparza, J. and M. Silva. "Circuits, Handles, Bridges, and Nets." In *Advances in Petri Nets 1990*, volume 483 of *Lecture Notes in Computer Science*, Edited by G. Rozenberg. 210–242. Berlin: Springer-Verlag, 1990.

[12] Gostellow, K., V. Cerf, G. Estrin, and S. Volansky. "Proper Termination of Flow-of-control in Programs Involving Concurrent Processes." *ACM Sigplan*, 7:11(1972):15–27.

[13] Kindler, E. and W. M. P. van der Aalst. "Liveness, Fairness, and Recurrence." *Information Processing Letters*, 70(1999):269–274.

[14] Reisig, W. *Petri Nets: An Introduction*, volume 4 of *EATCS Monographs in Theoretical Computer Science*. Berlin: Springer-Verlag, 1985.

[15] Reisig, W. and G. Rozenberg, editors. *Lectures on Petri Nets I: Basic Models*, volume 1491 of *Lecture Notes in Computer Science*. Berlin: Springer-Verlag, 1998.

[16] Vallete, R. "Analysis of Petri Nets by Stepwise Refinements." *Journal of Computer and System Sciences*, 18(1979):35–46.

[17] Verbeek, H. M. W., T. Basten, and W. M. P. van der Aalst. "Diagnosing Workflow Processes using Woflan." *Computing Science Report 99/02*, Eindhoven: Eindhoven University of Technology, 1999.

[18] Software-Ley. *COSA User Manual*. Software-Ley GmbH, Pullheim, Germany, 1998.

Appendix B: Workflow Modeling Using UML

In recent years, the Unified Modeling Language (UML) has become the de facto standard for software development. UML is a graphical language for visualizing, specifying, constructing, and documenting the artifacts of a software intensive system. However, the use of UML is not restricted to software development. Some of its diagrams also are used for enterprise modeling, business engineering, process analysis, and system configuration. Given the widespread use of UML as an industry standard and the fact that UML offers four diagram types for process modeling, this appendix discusses the use of UML in the context of workflow management. The most relevant diagram types are introduced and the relationship with the modeling technique used in this book is discussed.

The development of UML started in 1994 when James Rumbough joined Grady Booch at Rational Software Corporation. Both had been working on object-oriented methods named OMT (Object Modeling Technique) and Booch. In 1994 there were about fifty object-oriented methods. Rumbough and Booch joined forces to unify their methods and to gain critical mass. In 1995, a third prominent author of object-oriented methods joined this initiative: Ivar Jacobson contributed his work on OOSE (Object-oriented Software Engineering) to the UML project within Rational. In January 1997, UML 1.0 was offered to the Object Management Group (OMG), in response to their request for a standard modeling language. Since this time, UML has been adopted by industry and academia as the standard language for object-oriented modeling. Moreover, the language was extended and refined in several iterations. This appendix is based on UML 1.3.

UML 1.3 defines the following diagram types:

- Use case diagram
- Class diagram
- Sequence diagram
- Collaboration diagram
- Statechart diagram
- Activity diagram
- Component diagram
- Deployment diagram

A *use case diagram* shows a set of cases and actors and their relationships. A *class diagram* shows a set of classes and their relationships. Both diagrams address the static view of a system. The use case diagram focuses on identifiable pieces of functionality and puts these pieces of functionality into context. The *class model* is mainly a structuring mechanism for objects. Both *sequence diagrams* and *collaboration diagrams* are essentially interaction diagrams, that is, diagrams focusing on the interaction (e.g., message passing) between objects and actors. A sequence diagram is an interaction diagram that emphasizes the time-ordering of messages. A collaboration diagram emphasizes the organizational structure rather than time-ordering. *Statechart diagrams* are typically used to model object lifecycles. A statechart diagrams emphasizes object states. *Activity diagrams* are typically used to describe the flow of control among objects. Compared to statechart diagrams the emphasis is moved from states to activities. Note that UML uses four types of diagrams to model the dynamic view of a system: sequence diagrams, collaboration diagrams, statechart diagrams, *and* activity diagrams model dynamic behavior. The remaining two diagram types model the implementation view of a system. In a *component diagram* sets of objects are grouped into components. A *deployment diagram* shows the configuration of run-time processing nodes and the components that live on them.

Workflow management systems focus on the process perspective. Since sequence diagrams, collaboration diagrams, statechart diagrams, and activity diagrams address the dynamic behavior of a system, these diagrams are very relevant for workflow management and will be discussed in more detail. Component diagrams and deployment diagrams are relevant for the architecture, implementation, and run-time configuration of the workflow system. Although relevant, a detailed discussion of these diagram types is outside the scope of this book. Use case diagrams are very useful in the early stages of workflow modeling. A use case diagram can be used to identify stakeholders and clarify the case types handled by the workflow system. The class diagram can be used to model the relationships between cases and case attributes.

B.1   Sequence Diagram

Figure B.1 shows two sequence diagrams. The diagram on the lefthand side models a scenario which corresponds to a customer successfully ordering a book. The righthand side diagram models the scenario where a customer order is rejected because the ordered book is not in stock. A sequence diagram shows for each object or actor a so-called lifeline. In both diagrams shown in figure B.1 there are three lifelines: the *customer* lifeline, the *bookshop* lifeline, and the *publisher* lifeline. Time is increasing along each lifeline from top to bottom. A sequence diagram also shows the messages exchanged. Consider for example the lefthand side diagram. First the customer orders a book by sending the message *Order_book*. Then the (on-line) bookshop sends a query to the publisher to see whether the book is available (message *Query*). The publisher responds by sending the message *In_stock* indicating that the book is available. The bookshop confirms the order (message *Confirm_order*) and pays for the book (message *Payment*). After receiving the payment, the publisher sends the book to the customer (message *Deliver_book*) and notifies the bookshop (message *Notify*). Triggered by this notification, the bookshop sends a bill (message *Bill*) and the customer pays for the book (message *Payment*).

Note that the lefthand side diagram does not specify a process but merely one scenario. This scenario corresponds to handling a customer order successfully. If the book is not in stock, the diagram on the righthand side applies. In the second scenario, the book is not available (message *Out_of_stock*) and the customer order is rejected (message *Reject_order*). Figure B.1 illustrates that sequence diagrams can only be used to model scenarios and are not suitable for making full-fledged process models. The basic sequence diagram has no provision for routing constructs such as choice, synchronization, iteration, etc. Sequence dia-

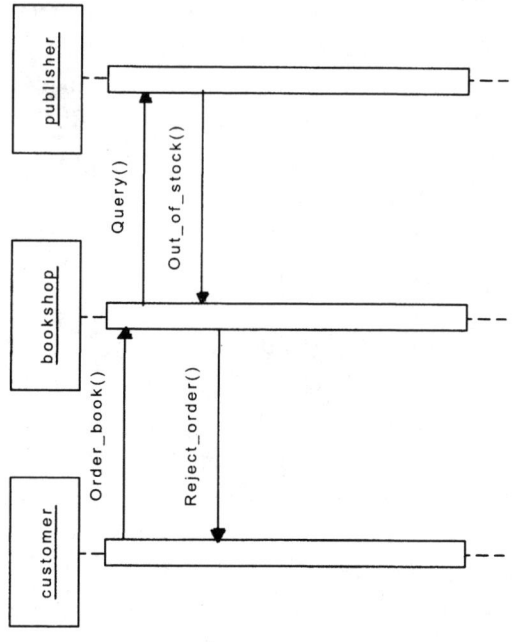

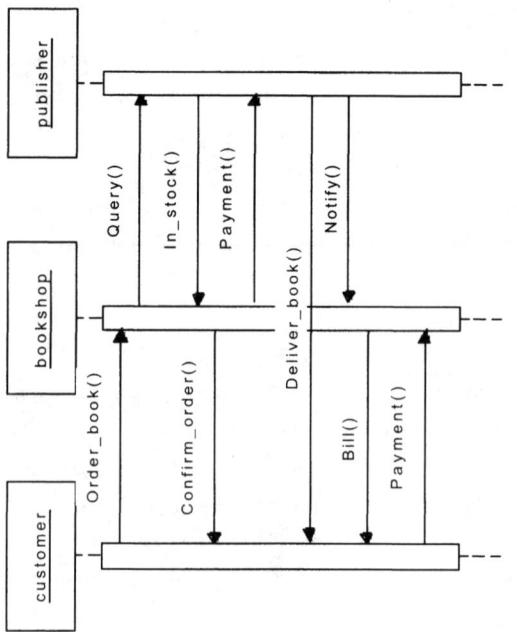

Figure B.1
Two sequence diagrams

grams have been extended with features to handle these routing constructs. However, these extended diagrams become difficult to read and difficult to interpret.

B.2   Collaboration Diagram

A collaboration diagram highlights the organization of objects that participate in an interaction. Compared to sequence diagrams the emphasis is shifted from temporal relations to organizational relations. From a semantical point of view collaboration diagrams and sequence diagrams are interchangeable, that is, semantically equivalent. The lifelines are replaced by numbered sequences. Consider figure B.2. The two collaboration diagrams correspond to the two sequence diagrams shown in figure B.1. One can translate a sequence diagram and translate it to a collaboration diagram without any loss of information (and vice-versa).

The order of the messages exchanged is captured by a numbering scheme. The numbers in figure B.2 indicate the order in which messages are exchanged among the customer, bookshop, and publisher. Collaboration diagrams can be extended with more complex constructs such as nesting, iteration, and branching. However, just like sequence diagrams, collaboration diagrams are particularly suited for modeling scenarios, that is, examples of straight sequential flows of control. For true process modeling one should use statecharts diagrams or activity diagrams.

B.3   Statechart Diagram

Statecharts are an extension of basic state machines. A basic state machine consists of states and transitions. At any point in time, the system (or object) resides in one of these states. A transition moves the system from one state to another. The basic state machine corresponds to the class of Petri nets where each transition has one input and one output place. In a statechart diagram one can have composite states, orthogonal regions, variables, events, conditions, and actions. Composite states can be used for nesting. Orthogonal regions can be used to model parallelism. Transitions can be augmented with so-called ECA (event-condition-action) rules. This means that a transition only takes place when a specified event occurs and a condition is satisfied. Both the event and condition are

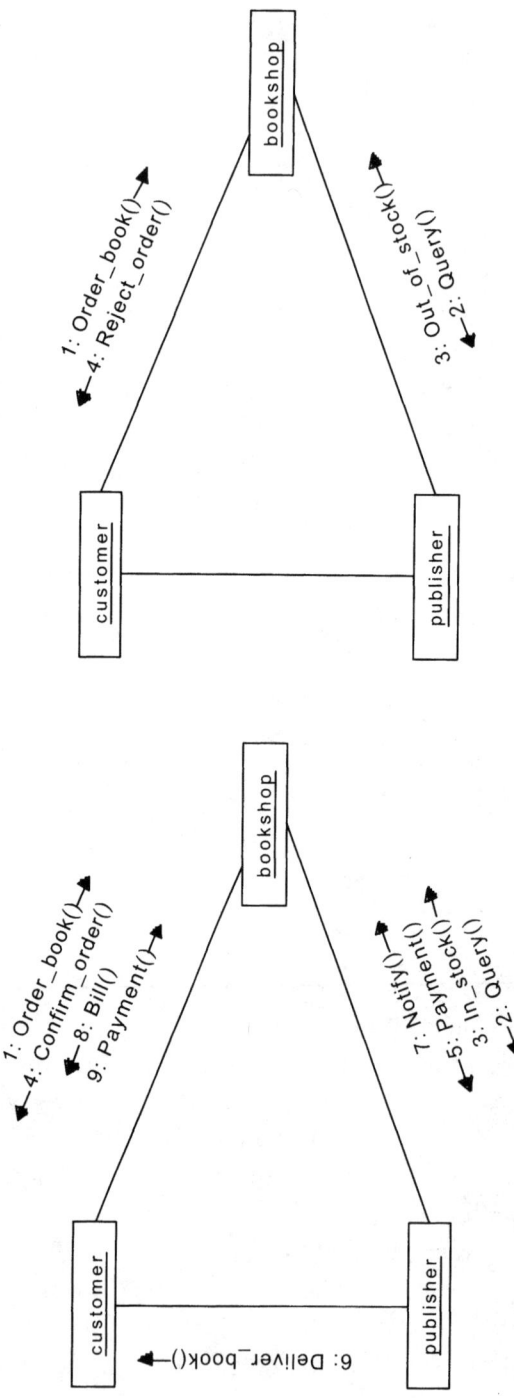

Figure B.2
Two collaboratin diagrams

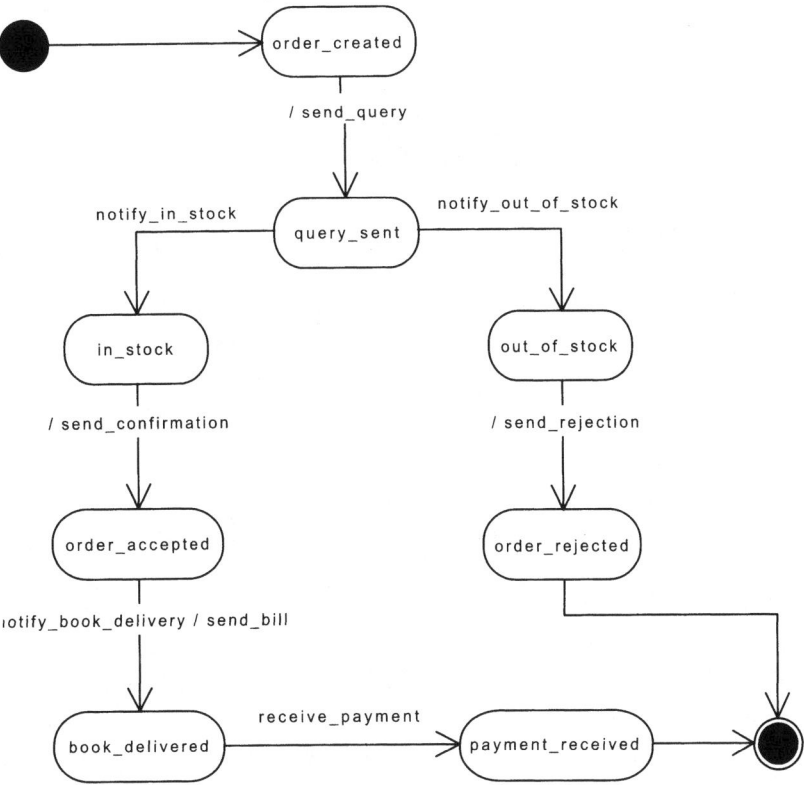

Figure B.3
A statechart diagram

optional. It is also possible to add an action to a transition. This means that the action is executed the moment the transition takes place. The standard notation for these ECA rules is "*event [condition]/action.*"

Figure B.3 shows a very simple statechart diagram. This statechart models the lifecycle of an order. The initial state is modeled by a black dot. The final state is modeled by a black dot within a circle. A state is modeled by a rounded rectangle. Transitions are modeled by arcs. The transition connected to states *order_created* to *query_sent* generates the action *send_query*. In state *query_sent* two potential transitions are enabled. One of them is triggered by the event *notify_in_stock* and leads to state *in_stock*. The other one is triggered by the event *notify_out_of_stock* and leads to state *out_of_stock*.

B.4   Activity Diagram

Statecharts are well-suited for modeling the lifecycle of one object. Unfortunately statecharts are less suitable to model the control flow among objects. For this purpose UML offers activity diagrams. Activity diagrams are close to the diagramming technique used in this book. Therefore it is no surprise to see that activity diagrams are used for enterprise modeling, workflow modeling, and business process re-engineering.

Consider figure B.4. This activity diagram models the process illustrated by the two sequence/collaboration diagrams. The diagram is divided into three main parts: customer, bookshop, and publisher. These parts are called *swimlanes*. A swimlane specifies a locus of activities and is particularly useful for business modeling. Using swimlanes it is possible to partition the process into roles or organizational units. Please note that the modeling technique used in this book can also be extended with swimlanes. Just like in a statechart diagram the initial and final state are indicated using black dots. Activities (also called activity states) are denoted by rounded rectangles. Solid lines correspond to control flow. Dashed lines correspond to object flow. The objects passed are modeled by rectangles. Consider for example the upper left corner of the activity diagram. Starting in the initial state the activity *send_order* is executed. After execution of *send_order* an object *order* is passed on to the bookshop which executes *handle_customer_order*. The thick horizontal lines in figure B.4 correspond to *synchronization bars*. A synchronization bar is either a *fork* or a *join*. Forks correspond to AND-splits. Joins correspond to AND-joins. An explicit OR-split is modeled by a so-called *branch* and is depicted by a diamond. The diamond symbol can also be used to model OR-joins. The activity diagram shown in figure B.4 has one branch. This branch makes the process dependent upon the availability of the book ordered by the customer. The remainder of the process is self-explanatory.

B.5   Other Process Modeling Techniques

Many process modeling techniques have been developed since the early sixties. Some of these techniques are *informal* in the sense that the diagrams used have no formally defined semantics. These models are typi-

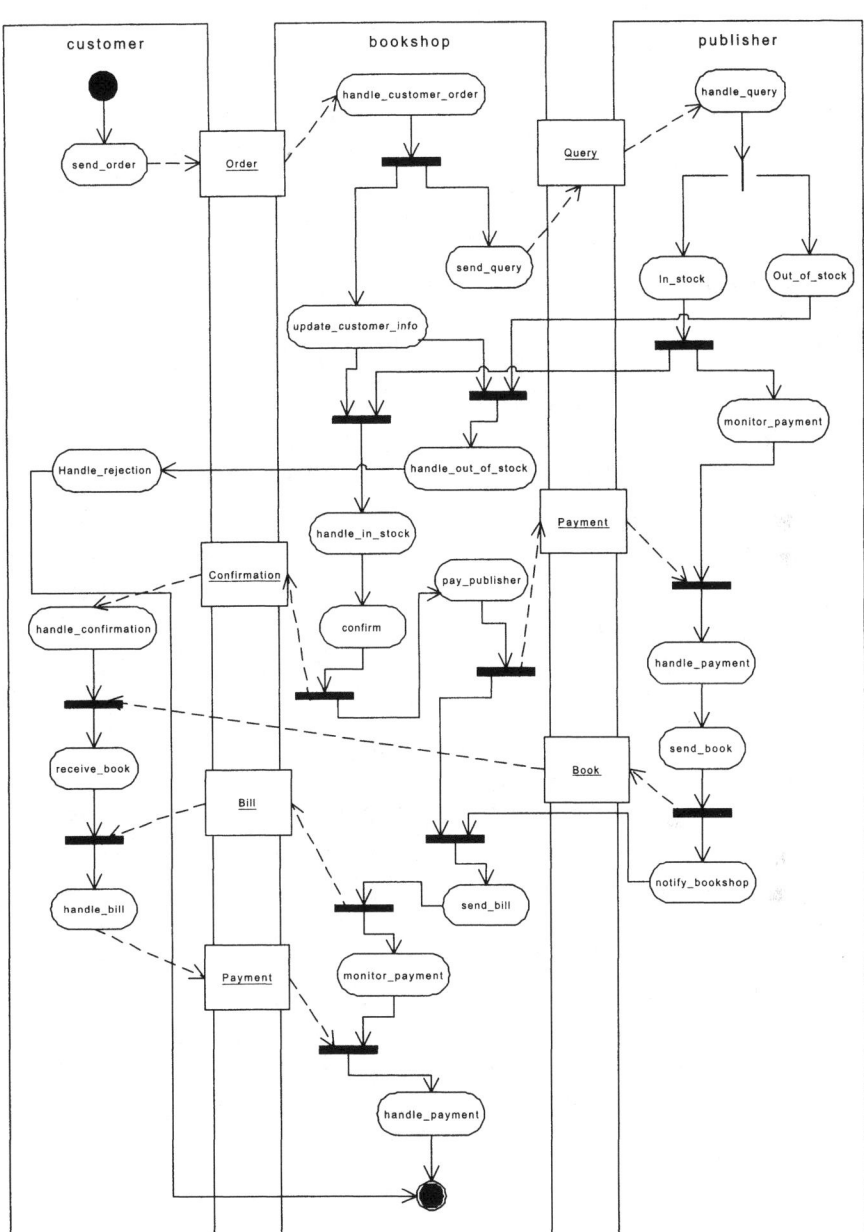

Figure B.4
An activity diagram

cally very intuitive and the interpretation shifts depending on the modeler, application domain, and characteristics of the business processes at hand. Examples of informal techniques are ISAC, DFD, SADT, and IDEF. SADT, and its military equivalent IDEF0, were developed to describe complex systems and control the development of complex software through a systematic approach to requirements definition. One of the aims was to develop a process that includes definition of human roles and interpersonal procedures as part of the technique. SADT (or IDEF) approaches requirements definition through a series of steps that determine *why* the system is needed, *what* the system features will serve, and *how* the system is to be constructed. Related and comparable techniques are the Structured Design approach of Yourdon, Structured Analysis of De Marco, Essential System Analysis of McMenamin and Palmer, and Information Systems Work and Analysis of Change (ISAC) developed by Lundeberg, Goldkuhl, and Nilson. These techniques have in common that they have no formal semantics. Although there have been efforts to provide formal semantics for most of these techniques (most notable IDEF0), these semantics typically use an interpretation that is different from the way these models are described in textbooks and applied in practice.

There are many formal process modeling techniques: for example, finite state machines, labeled transition systems, statecharts, Petri nets, and process algebra's such as ACP, CSP, and CCS. Finite state machines and labeled transition systems are basic models that have problems coping with concurrency and large state spaces. Both statecharts and Petri nets provide methods for coping with concurrency and large state spaces. Although statecharts and Petri nets are fundamentally different, they share the same characteristics. Both techniques are graphical, have formal semantics, and support concurrent processes. The focus of statecharts is on states and state transitions. The focus of Petri nets is on object flow (tokens) and activities (transitions). Process algebras such as ACP, CSP, and CCS are not graphical and are hardly used for business process modeling.

While UML reflects some of the best modeling experiences available, it suffers from a lack of precise semantics; this is necessary if one is to use the notations to precisely model systems and to rigorously reason about the models. One could argue that the syntax of UML is formalized.

However in many situations the interpretation of a syntactical construct is ambiguous or undefined. The precise UML (pUML) group aims to bring together international researchers and practitioners who share the aim of developing the Unified Modeling Language (UML) toward a precise (i.e., well-defined) modeling language. This initiative shows that UML is somewhere in between formal and informal process modeling techniques.

To conclude, we discuss the relationship between UML and the modeling technique used throughout this book. There is a clear relationship between activity diagrams and the Petri-net-based process definitions used in this book. An activity diagram can be translated into a Petri net by translating activities to transitions, object flows to places, and synchronization bars to transitions. Moreover additional places need to be added to connect the transitions. Similarly a rough translation from Petri nets to activity diagrams is possible. In an activity diagram there is no explicit marking (i.e., global state) concept and the moment of choice is not well defined. Therefore subtle constructs such as the implicit choice, the milestone, and non-free choice structures are difficult to handle. Interaction diagrams, that is, sequence diagrams and collaboration diagrams, can be translated easily to Petri nets. Consider for example a sequence diagram: each lifeline is represented by a sequence of places and transitions. Messages are represented by places connecting a transition from one lifeline to a transition of another lifeline. Translating a basic statechart diagram to a Petri net is also straightforward: each state in the statechart corresponds to a place in the Petri net, and each transition in the statechart corresponds to a transition in the Petri net. Translating more advanced concepts such as composite states (i.e., nesting of states), orthogonal regions (i.e., concurrent substates), and history states are more difficult to translate. Similarly certain Petri-net constructs are difficult to mimic using statecharts (e.g., unbounded places and non-free choice behavior). It should also be noted that most analysis techniques based on statecharts are brute force techniques that simply explore the state space. For Petri nets, as was demonstrated in appendix A, there are also structural techniques which analyze the process without exploring the state space.

Note that for each of the diagrams shown in this appendix there is a straightforward equivalent Petri-net-based process definition. This is left as an exercise for the interested reader.

Solutions to Exercises

SOLUTIONS TO EXERCISES, CHAPTER 1

Exercise 1.1

(a) The rules are:
- *sequencing:* one after the other;
- *selection of choice:* only one of the tasks will be performed, depending on some condition;
- *parallelism:* tasks may be performed at the same time or in any order; and
- *iteration:* one or more tasks have to be executed (potentially) multiple times.

(b) Iteration is not a basic construct: it can be expressed in terms of "selection of choice."

Exercise 1.2

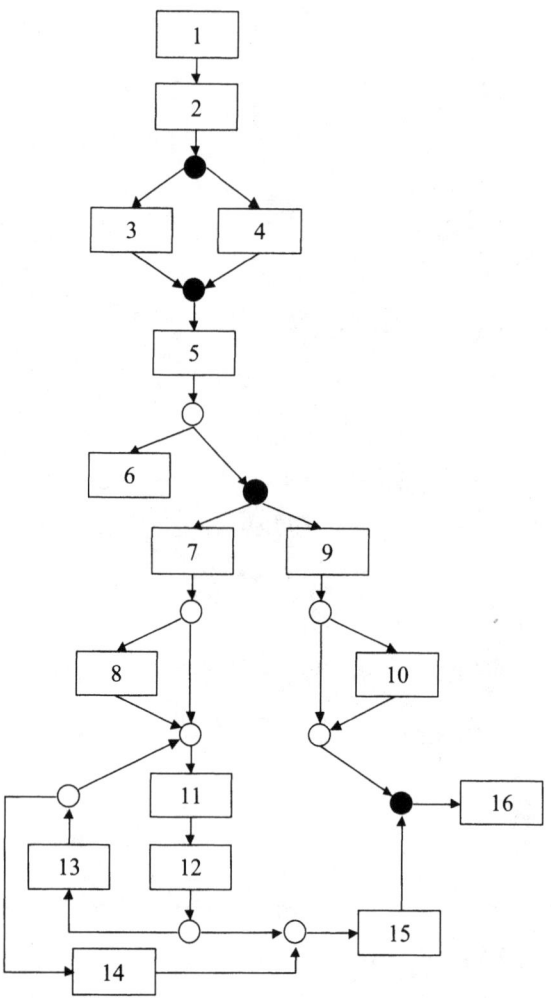

Figure S1.1
Insurance process

Exercise 1.3

Considered within one process a task is a logical unit of work that is performed by one resource. Considered from the point of view of a (sub)contractor a task is an order to be fulfilled. However, the fulfilment may require a process with several tasks.

Exercise 1.4

We can divide the personnel in *capacity groups, functional departments,* and *process teams.* An advantage of capacity groups is that persons with the same skills are in the same unit, which gives flexibility in resource planning. A disadvantage is that the units have no direct responsibility for a process or case handling. An advantage of process teams is that they are focused on the performance of processes and efficient case handling. A disadvantage is that the exchange of employees between process teams is more difficult. A functional department organization is a mixture of both: there is no responsibility for complete case handling, but there is responsibility for a set of tasks of possibly more than one process that require similar skills.

SOLUTIONS TO EXERCISES, CHAPTER 2

Classical Petri Nets

Exercise 2.1   German traffic light

(a) The possible states and transition system are as shown in figure S2.1.

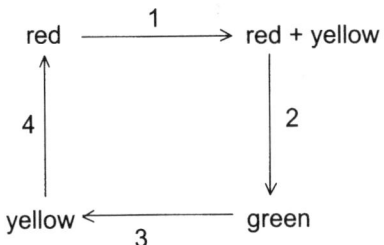

Figure S2.1
States and transitions

(b) The model constructed with the solid lines is able to behave like a German traffic light, i.e., ignore places *c1* and *c2*.

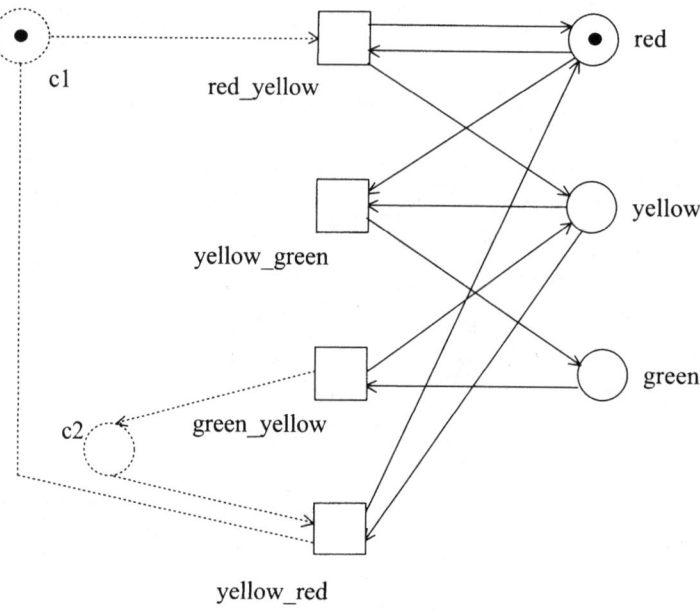

Figure S2.2
German traffic light model

(c) The addition of the dotted places and arcs is required to make the model work as a German traffic light. Without this, the traffic light *can* behave properly, but there are also potential anomalies such as:

• transition *red_yellow* fires repeatedly without switching to *yellow* or *green* and thus results in an accumulation of tokens in *yellow*.

• *yellow_red* can fire before *green_yellow* fires.

Exercise 2.2 Project X

(a)

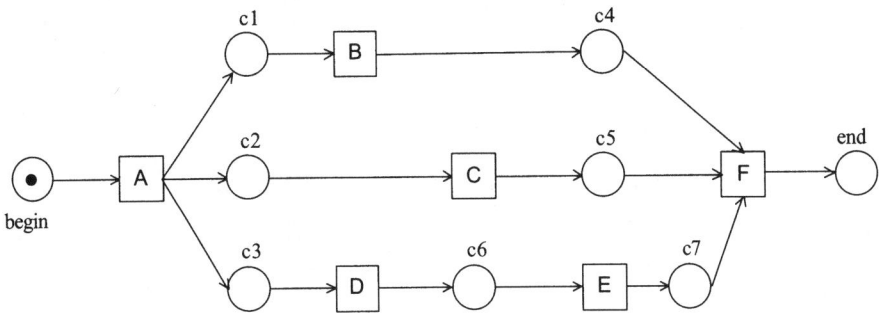

Figure S2.3
Project X

(b) To make *E* optional, a by-pass for this transition has to be made.

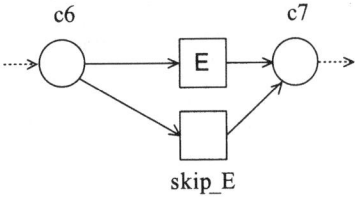

Figure S2.4
Bypass E

(c) Place *c8* is introduced to make sure that if transition *D* starts, *B* and *C* are not able to be executed because they also need a token in *c8*. When transition *E* is finished, a token is produced for *c8* to make new transitions possible.

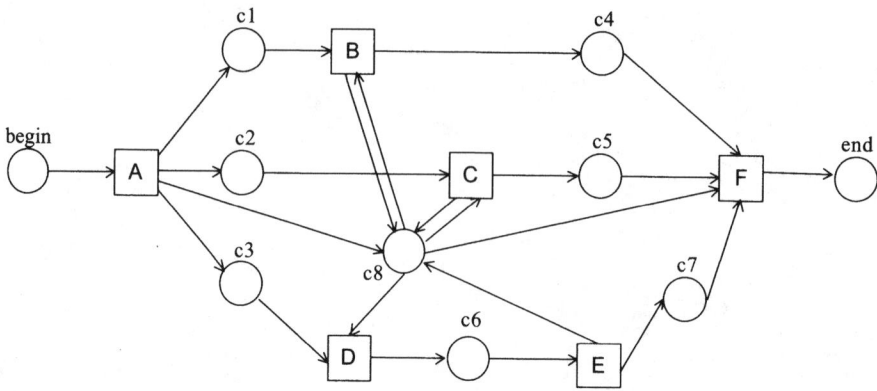

Figure S2.5
Extension c8

Exercise 2.3   Railnet

(a) One track can be modeled as shown in figure S2.6.

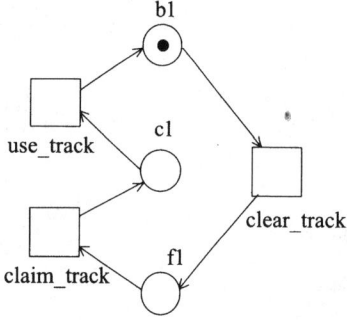

Figure S2.6
One railroad track

A track consists of three places (b = busy, c = claimed, and f = free) and the transitions between them. To make four tracks with two trains, we copy this track four times and place two tokens in a b-place and two tokens in an f-place.

We then have to make some additions. A train can move to another track only if it has successfully claimed another one. Therefore it has to check if the other track is free. These are the arcs between the *b*-places and the *use_track* transition.

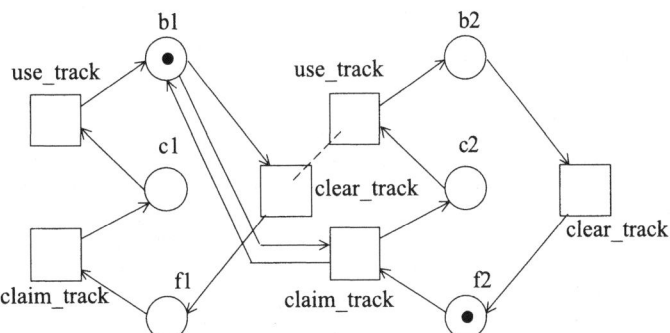

Figure S2.7
Two tracks

Also note that the transitions *use_track* and *clear_track* of two subsequent tracks are executed at the same time. Therefore, we fuse them in one transition: *transfer*.

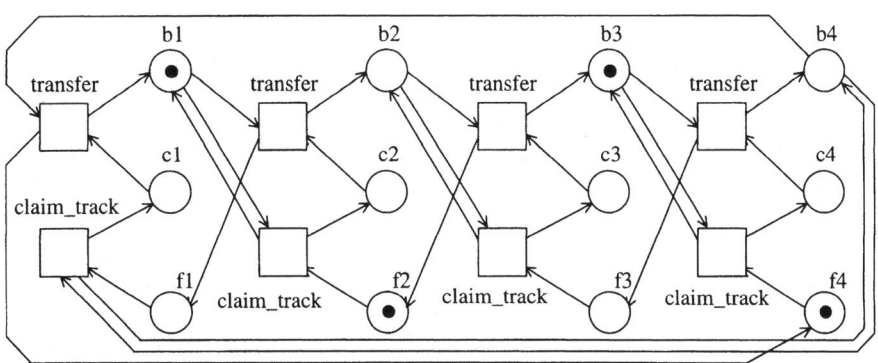

Figure S2.8
Complete system consisting of four tracks and two trains

(b) Just add new tracks. While the total number of states increases rapidly, the size of the Petri net is linear in the number of tracks. Note that the number of states is expressed by the following equation:

$$\frac{n^*(n-1)}{2} + (n^*(n-2)) + \frac{n^*(n-3)}{2} = 2n(n-2)$$

Exercise 2.4   Binary counter

The different states are of course as follows:

a	b	c			a	b	c		
0	0	0	=	0	1	0	0	=	4
0	0	1	=	1	1	0	1	=	5
0	1	0	=	2	1	1	0	=	6
0	1	1	=	3	1	1	1	=	7

This gives us the following model shown in figure S2.9.

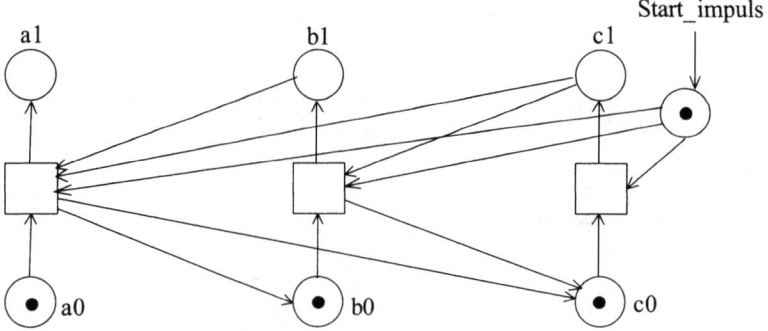

Figure S2.9
Binary counter

The places *a1* and *a0* represent the state of the first digit, *b1* and *b0* represent the state of the second digit, and *c1* and *c0* represent the state of the third digit.

High-Level Petri Nets

Exercise 2.5   Driving school

(a)

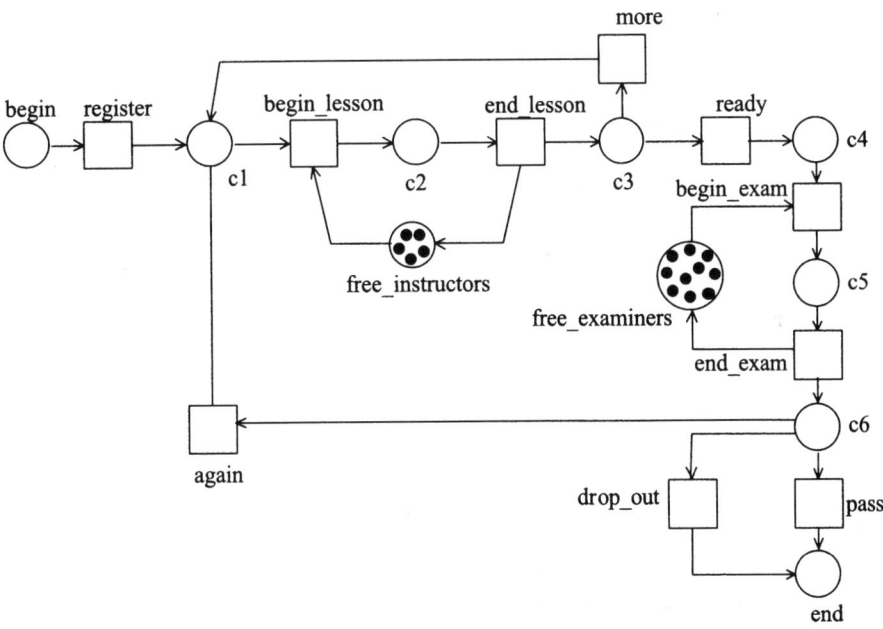

Figure S2.10
Driving school

(b) Every token in the places *begin, c1, c2, c3, c4, c5, c5, end* has a value now. For instance: A person named J. Walker, 18 years old who has taken no lessons and no exams yet, is represented as:

[id: 'X07'; name: 'J. Walker'; age: '18'; gender: 'male'; nof_lessons: '0'; nof_exams: '0']

The last two attributes are important to the exercise, because we want two know how many lessons and exams a person has already had.

The transitions are specified as follows:

register: nof_lessons: = 0
              nof_exams: = 0

The transition to *more* and *ready* can be fused in one transition: *more?* with the following behavior:

<u>if</u>

nof_lessons < 10

<u>then</u>

produce token for *c1*

<u>else</u>

produce token for *c4*

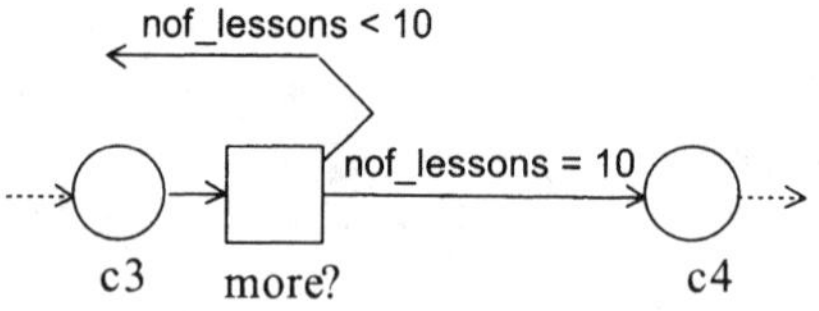

nof_lessons < 10

nof_lessons = 10

c3   more?   c4

Figure S2.11
Transitions *more* and *ready* combined into transition *more?*

end_lesson: nof_lessons: = nof_lessons + 1

end_exams: nof_exams: = nof_exams + 1

again has a precondition: nof_exams < 3
   set the attribute nof_lessons: = 0, because one has to take another ten
   lessons before the next exam.

(c) All delays are equal to zero except the one indicated in figure S2.12.

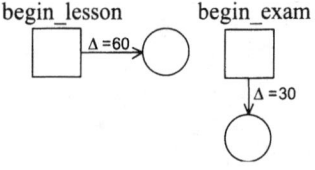

begin_lesson   begin_exam
          Δ=60   Δ=30

Figure S2.12
Addition of positive delays

Exercise 2.6 Bicycle factory

(a)

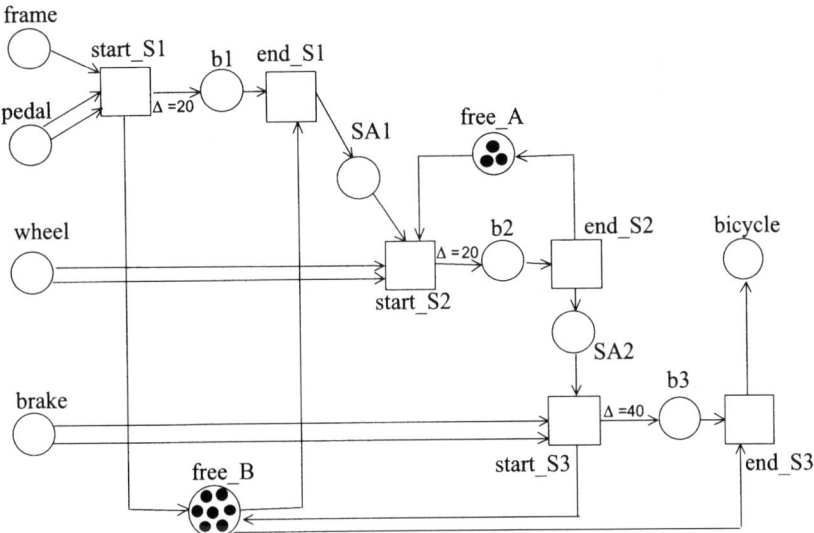

Figure S2.13
Bicycle factory

(b) Capacity A: $3^* (60 \text{ minutes}/20 \text{ minutes of action SA2}) = 9$ p/h
Capacity B: $7^* (60 \text{ minutes}/20 + 40 \text{ minutes of action SA1 and}$
$\text{SA3}) = 7$ p/h

We identify the capacity of machine B as the bottleneck and so the factory is capable of producing seven bicycles an hour.

Workflow Exercises

Exercise 2.7   Insurance company

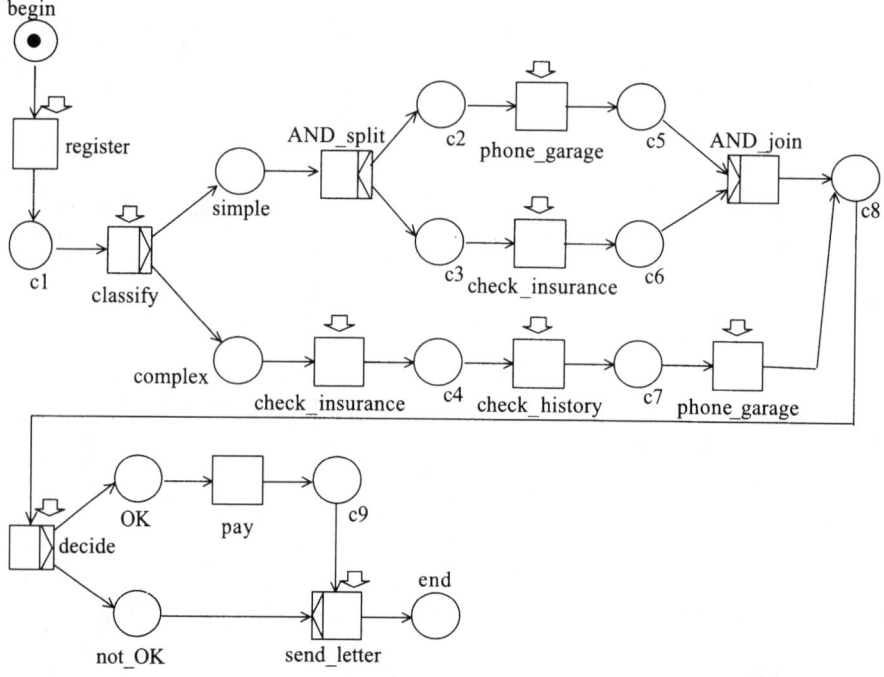

Figure S2.14
Insurance company

The choice between *OK* (and then *pay*) and *not_OK* can also be made with one place for the *not_OK* and the *c9* places. In this case *send_letter* has only one input place and does not require the OR-join notation.

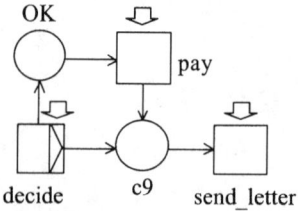

Figure S2.15
Removing the OR-join by merging places c9 and not_OK

Exercise 2.8   Complaints handling

The most difficult part to model is the relation between the handling of the form and the actual processing: Task process has to wait until the handling of the form is completed and may be executed an arbitrary number of times. In figure S2.16, this problem is resolved by having two tasks for the actual processing: *process* and *process_again*. In figure S2.17, there is just one task named *process*. Here *process* takes a token from $c9$ but also places one immediately back. As a result, *process* can be executed an arbitrary number of times without removing the token from $c9$.

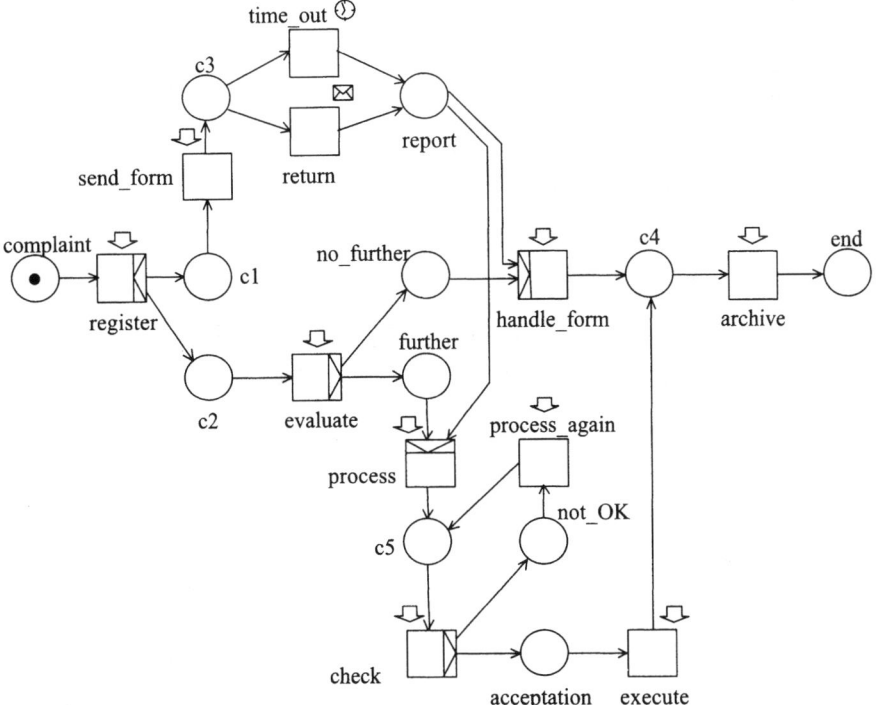

Figure S2.16
Complaints handling

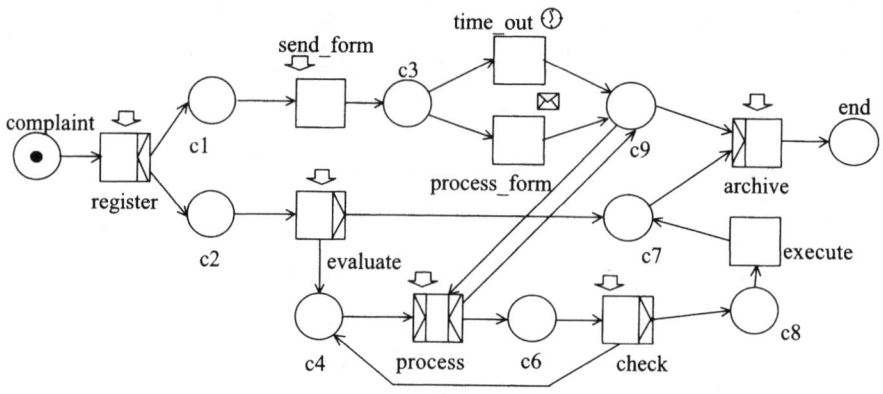

Figure S2.17
Complaints handling

Exercise 2.9   Let's have a party

(a) Three parts of the process can be identified:
· organizing the location
· organizing the music
· final arrangements (billing, food, drinks and visit)

The first two parts are executed in parallel followed by the third part. The second part (music) is the most complex part of the process. Two implicit OR-splits are needed to handle time-outs.

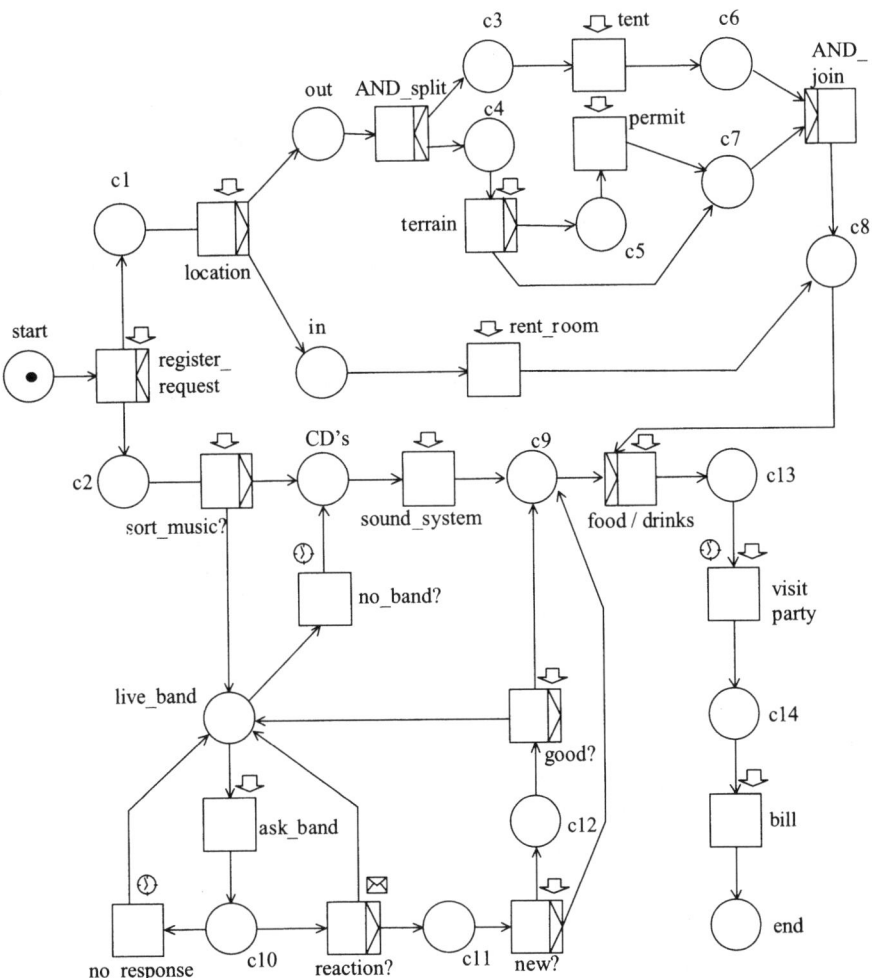

Figure S2.18
Party

(b) Improvement:
The most important bottleneck in the process is the selection of a band. This part of the process may take a longtime, particularly when one or two bands refuse or when the performance of a band is too poor. Therefore, the biggest improvement can be obtained when the process is split into two separate processes: one for handling requests for parties and one for evaluating bands. As a result, bands can be evaluated independent of specific requests for parties.

SOLUTIONS TO EXERCISES, CHAPTER 3

Exercise 3.1   Insurance company

The following roles are identified:

Employee	(E)
Claim handler	(CH)
Claim handler A	(CHA)
Claim handler B	(CHB)

The following organizational units are identified:

Department Car Damages	(CD)
Finance Department	(FN)

This results in the model shown in figure S3.1.

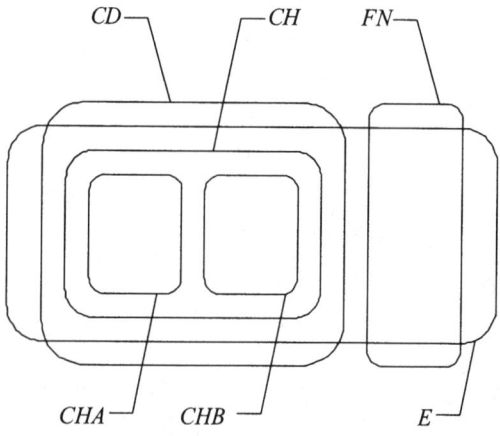

Figure S3.1
Resource classification insurance company

We assume that all claim handlers are also employees. This means that when an employee of the Car Damages department is required for a task, it doesn't matter whether he or she is a claim handler or not. If we assume instead that claim handlers cannot do the task of an "ordinary" employee, then figure S3.1 needs to be adapted (*CH*, *CHA*, and *CHB* will be outside *E*).

If we combine the resource classification with the process model, we obtain the model shown in figure S3.2.

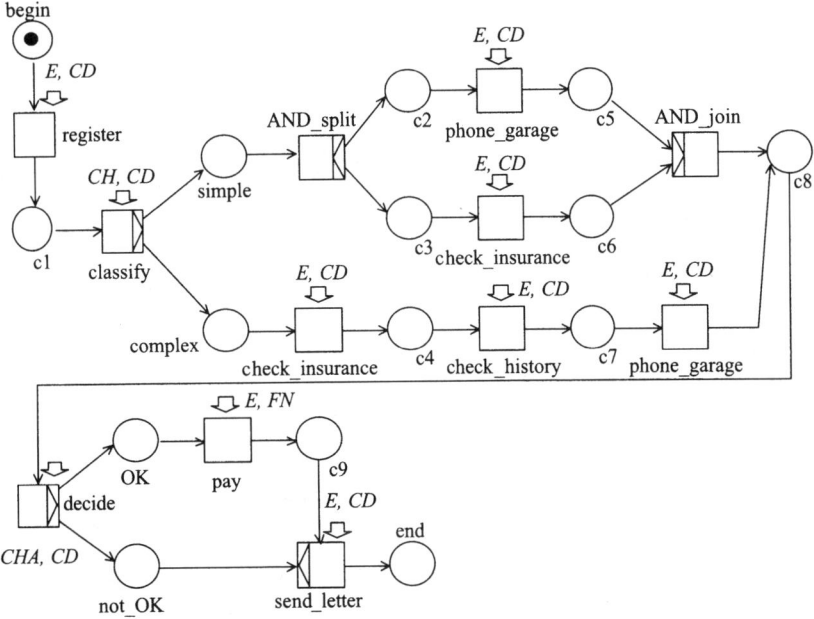

Figure S3.2
Resource classification in model insurance company

Exercise 3.2   Complaints handling
The following roles are identified:

Employee   (E)
Complaint manager   (CM)

The following organizational units are identified:

Department C   (DC)
Logistics department   (LD)

This results in the model shown in figure S3.3.

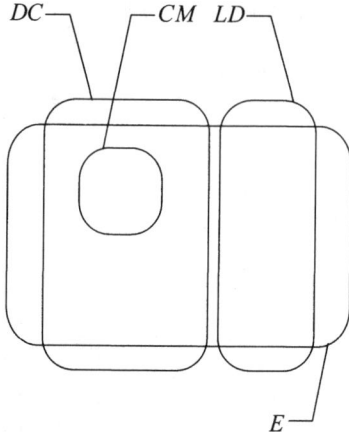

Figure S3.3
Resource classification complaints handling

Here we (also) assume that the complaint manager is an employee. This means that he is also available for work that could be done by an employee.

If we combine the resource classification with the process model, we obtain the model shown in figure S3.4.

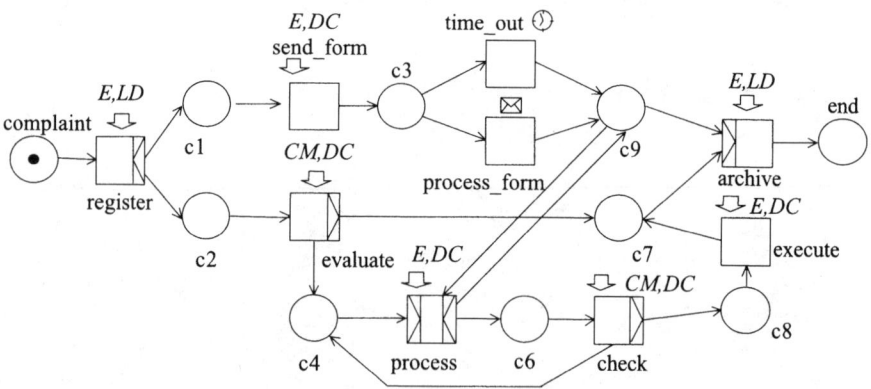

Figure S3.4
Resource classification in model complaints handling

Exercise 3.3   Employment office

(a) The following roles are identified:

Public Relations   (PR)
Business Relations   (BR)
Recruitment   (RC)
Manager   (MA)
IT-specialist   (IT)

The following organizational units are identified:

Job Shop   (JS)
Eindhoven   (EH)
Leeuwarden   (LW)

This results in the model shown in figure S3.5.

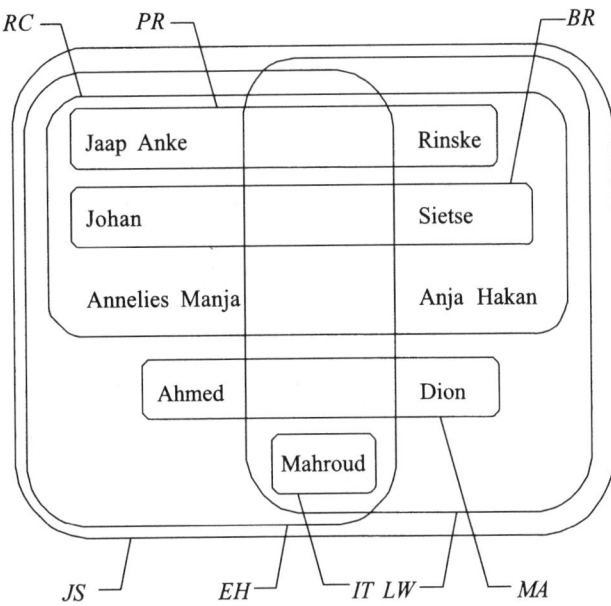

Figure S3.5
Resource classification employment agency

(b) Figure S3.6 shows the process model. It is important to add the right triggers. The time trigger added to task *stop_processing* for instance is crucial to keeping the flow moving and prevents cases residing forever in place *wait*.

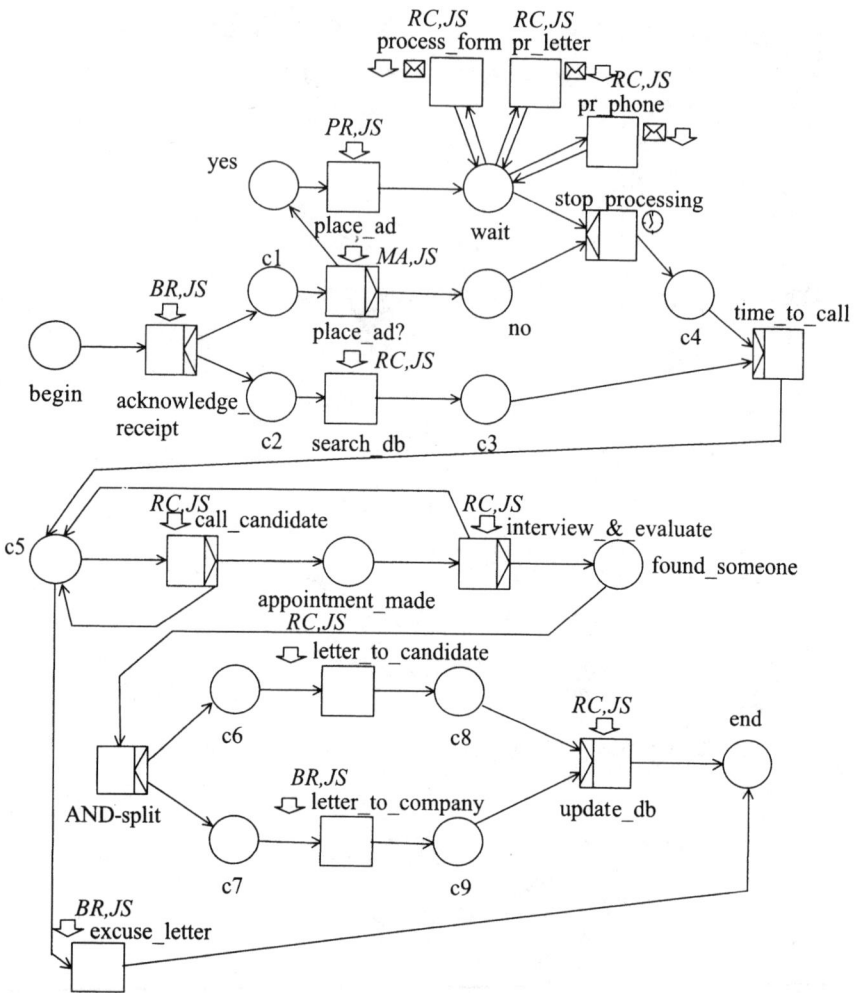

Figure S3.6
Process employment agency

Exercise 3.4   Have a nice flight with CRASH

(a) The following roles are identified:

Loadmaster   *(LM)*
Navigator   *(NV)*
Captain   *(CP)*
Meteo   *(MT)*

Director   *(DR)*
Logistics   *(LG)*
Secretary   *(SE)*
Courier   (CO)
The following organizational units are identified:
AIR   (AR)
KLM   (KL)
Support   (SP)
CRASH   (CR)
This results in the model shown in figure S3.7.

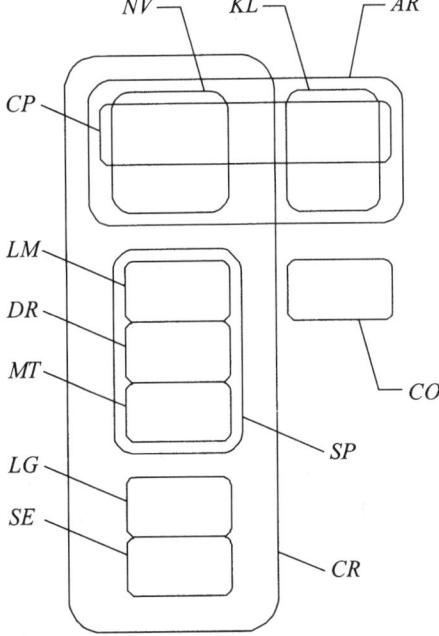

Figure S3.7
Resources *CRASH*

(b) The process is straightforward; simply apply the basic routings constructs. Task *discuss* requires two resources: a navigator and a load master. Therefore, two roles are attached to this task: *NV* and *LM* (see figure S3.8). Because they are both members of *CR* we use the *NV/LM*, *CR* notation. It is also possible to see them as independent members of a different organizational unit and use the notation *NV, AR/LM, CR*. This concept is also used in the other tasks where two different resources are required. Note that the current generation of workflow systems does not support multiple resources working on one work item. Therefore, we avoid tasks with multiple resources as much as possible.

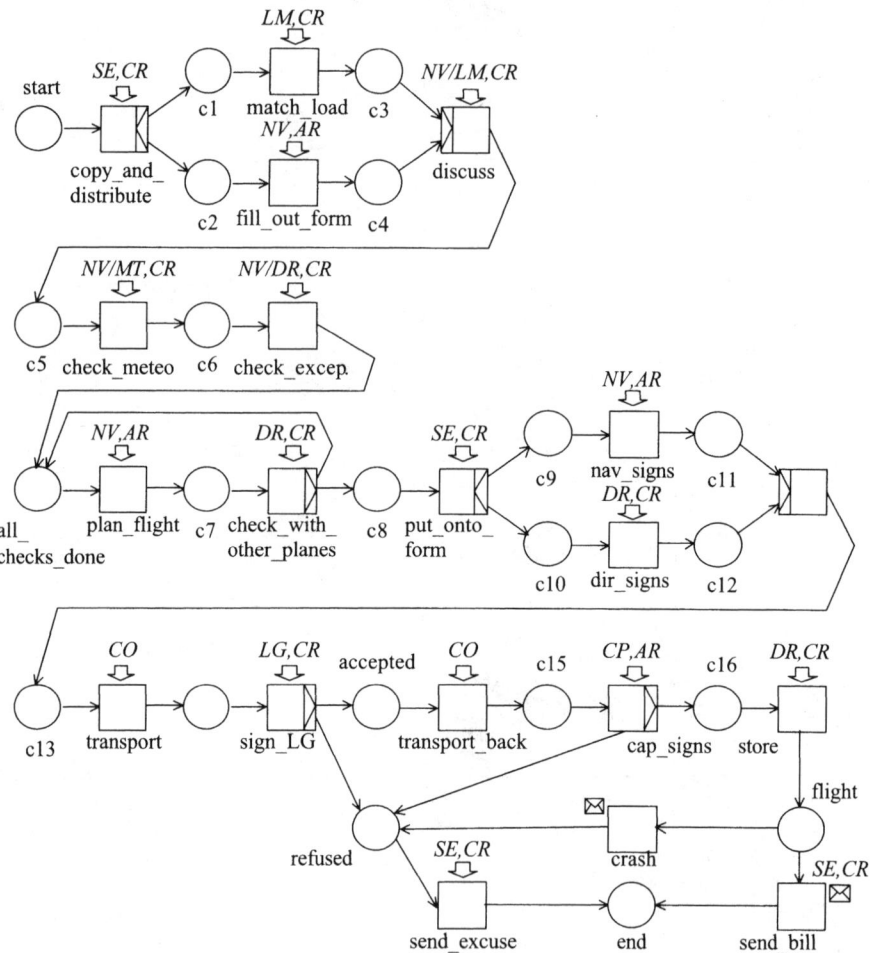

Figure S3.8
Process *CRASH*

(c) Possible improvements: The introduction of electronic documents (workflow system) can improve the throughput time. Several tasks become redundant (e.g. *copy_and_distribute, put_onto_form*) and the amount of parallelism can be increased. Moreover, the tasks *sign_LG* and *cap_signs* should be executed as early as possible, to avoid work for flights that are never really done.

SOLUTIONS TO EXERCISES, CHAPTER 4

Exercise 4.1   Optimize data usage

(a)

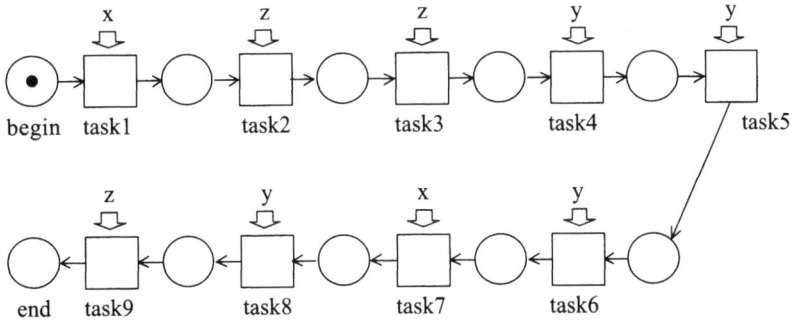

Figure S4.1
Sequential process

(b) No, it is not possible to represent various forms of routing such as selective and parallel routing.

(c) In figure S4.2 we see all the precedence relations. In figure S4.3 we skip the ones that can be derived, i.e., if *task1* has to be executed before *task2* and *task7* and *task2* also has to be executed before *task7*, the relation between *task1* and *task7* can be derived and therefore omitted. This will result in the Petri net shown in figure S4.4.

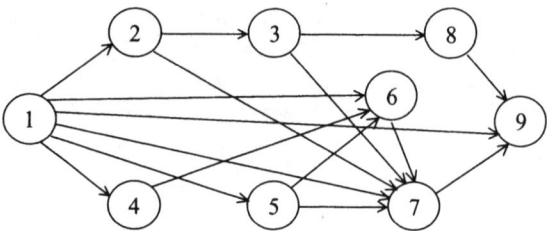

Figure S4.2
Total process

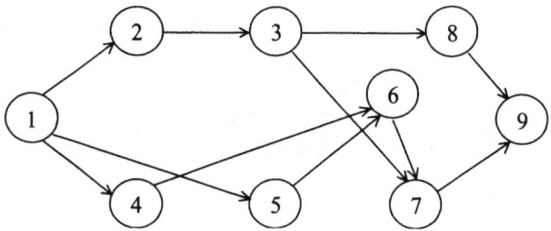

Figure S4.3
Stripped process

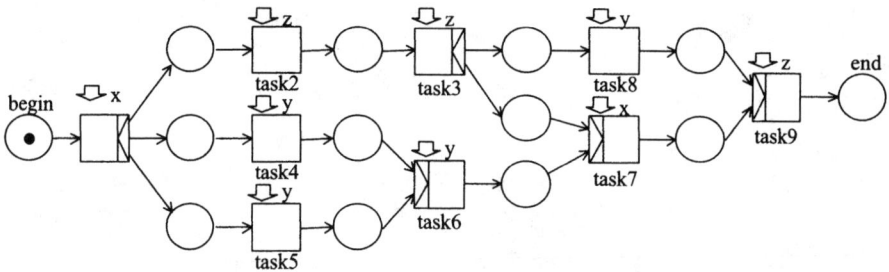

Figure S4.4
Petri net

(d) Yes. Tasks 2 and 3 and tasks 4, 5, and 6 are executed by one type of re-source and can be clustered. Therefore they can be combined into one task.

Exercise 4.2   Invariants

(i) First Petri net (figure 4.38)

(a) $w\_rest + type\_mail$ $(= 1)$
     $r\_rest + read\_mail$ $(= 1)$

(b) *begin + send_mail + receive_mail + read*

(c) No, there can be arbitrarily many tokens in place *mailbox*

(d) Yes

(e) Yes

(f) {*w_rest, type_mail, begin, send_mail*}, {*read_mail, r_rest, receive_ mail, read*}

(ii) Second Petri net (figure 4.39)

(a) $c1 + c2$ $(= 1)$
     $c3 + c4$ $(= 1)$

(b) $a + b + c + d$

(c) Yes

(d) Yes

(e) No

(f) {$c1, c2, a, b, c, d$}, {$c3, c4, a, b, c, d$}

(iii) Third Petri net (figure 4.40)

(a) $c1 + c4$ $(= 1)$
     $c2 + c5$ $(= 1)$
     $c3 + c6$ $(= 1)$

(b) g
     $a + b$
     $c + d$
     $e + f$

(c) Yes

(d) Yes

(e) No

(f) {c1, c4, a, b, g, e}, {c2, c5, a, c, d, g}, {c3, c6, e, f, c, g}

(iv) Fourth Petri net (figure 4.41)

(a) $start + c1 + c2 + c3 + c4 + end$ $(= 1)$
     $start + order\_a + c5 + c7 + c9 + c11 + c13 + invoice + c4 + end$ $(= 1)$
     $start + order\_a + c6 + c8 + notification + c2 + c3 + c4 + end$ $(= 1)$
     $c5 + c7 - c6 - c8$ $(= 0)$
     $c9 + c11 - c10 - c12$ $(= 0)$
     Etc.

(b) $produce\_b + check\_b + NOK\_b$
     $produce\_c + check\_c + NOK\_c$

(c) Yes

(d) No

(e) Yes

(f) None

Exercise 4.3   Verification process definition

(a)

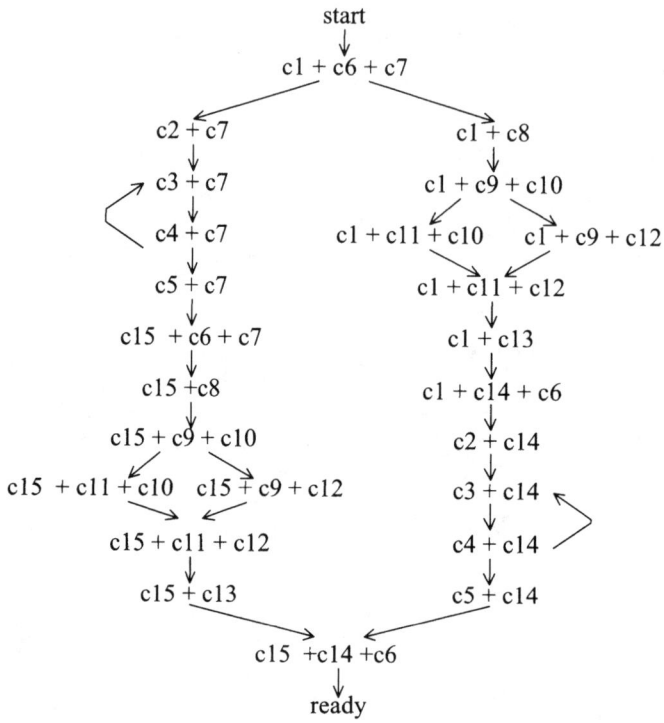

Figure S4.5
Reachability graph

(b) $1 + (6 * 8) + 1 = 50$. Note that the original process has only 26 states.

(c) $start + c6 + c2 + c3 + c4 + c5 + c8 + 1/2\,(c9 + c10 + c11 + c12) + c13 + ready$

(d) $start + c1 + c2 + c3 + c4 + c5 + c15 + ready$
$start + c7 + c8 + c9 + c11 + c13 + c14 + ready$
$start + c7 + c8 + c9 + c10 + c12 + c14 + ready$
$start + 1/2(c1 + c2 + c3 + c4 + c5 + c15) + 1/2(c7 + c8 + 1/2(c9 + c10 + c11 + c12) + c13 + c14) + ready$

Exercise 4.4 Search for errors

(i) If a form is processed and *evaluate* produces a token for c_7, a token will remain in c_9. When a *time_out* occurs and *evaluate* produces a token for c_4, the process deadlocks in the state marking c_8 and c_4.

(ii) Because c_9 begins as an empty place and remains empty, the process cannot continue when tokens are placed in c_1 and c_2.

(iii) If the upper part of the process reaches c_8 before a token in the process part below reaches c_4, *process* is unable to fire and the process deadlocks in the state marking c_8 and c_4.

Exercise 4.5 Performance analysis I

We use the following formulas:

$$L = \frac{\rho}{1 - \rho} \qquad S = \frac{1}{\mu - \lambda} \qquad W = \frac{\rho}{\mu - \lambda}$$

(a) Task 1:   Task 2:

$\quad \lambda = 20$ $\qquad\qquad\qquad\quad$ $\lambda = 20$

$\quad \mu = 60/2 = 30$ $\qquad\qquad$ $\mu = 60/2.5 = 24$

$\quad \rho = 0.67$ $\qquad\qquad\qquad$ $\rho = 0.83$

$\quad L = 2$ $\qquad\qquad\qquad\quad$ $L = 5$

$\quad S = 0.1$ (6 minutes) $\qquad$ $S = 0.25$ (15 minutes)

$\quad W = 0.066$ (4 minutes) $\quad$ $W = 0.208$ (12.5 minutes)

Total:

$L^T = 7$ $W^T = 0.274$ (16.5 minutes)

$S^T = 0.35$ (21 minutes)

(b) Task 1:   Task 2:

$\quad \lambda = 20$ $\qquad\qquad\qquad\quad$ $\lambda = 5$

$\quad \mu = 60/2 = 30$ $\qquad\qquad$ $\mu = 10$

$\quad \rho = 0.67$ $\qquad\qquad\qquad$ $\rho = 0.5$

$\quad L = 2$ $\qquad\qquad\qquad\quad$ $L = 1$

$\quad S = 0.1$ (6 minutes) $\qquad$ $S = 0.2$ (12 minutes)

$\quad W = 0.066$ (4 minutes) $\quad$ $W = 0.1$ (6 minutes)

Total:

$L^T = 3$

$S^T = 0.1 + 1/4 * 0.2 = 0.15$ (9 minutes) $\Delta = -12$ min., i.e., 12 minutes less than before.

Exercise 4.6   Performance analysis II

(a) Task 1a:

$\lambda = 10$ $\rho = 0.833$ $S = 0.5$

$\mu = 12$ $L = 5$ $W = 0.04167$

Task 1b:

$\lambda = 10$ $\rho = 0.33$ $S = 0.05$

$\mu = 30$ $L = 0.5$ $W = 0.0166$

Task 2:

$\lambda = 20$ $\rho = 0.66$ $S = 0.100$

$\mu = 30$ $L = 2$ $W = 0.066$

Total:

$L^{T} = 5 + 0.5 + 2 = 7.5$

$S^{T} = 1/2 * 0.5 + 1/2 * 0.05 + 0.100 = 0.375 \ (22.5 \text{ minutes})$

(b) Task 1:

$\lambda = 20$ $\rho = 0.66$ $S = 0.100$

$\mu = 30$ $L = 2$ $W = 0.066$

Task 2:

$\lambda = 20$ $\rho = 0.66$ $S = 0.100$

$\mu = 30$ $L = 2$ $W = 0.066$

Total:

$L^{T} = 2 + 2 = 4$

$S^{T} = 0.1 + 0.1 = 0.2 \ (12 \text{ minutes}) \ \Delta = -10.5 \text{ min.}$

Exercise 4.7   Performance analysis III

(a) ct1:   (% = 1.0)

$\lambda = 10$ $\rho = 0.833$ $S = 0.5$

$\mu = 12$ $L = 5$ $W = 0.04167$

ct2:   (% = 0.8)

$\lambda = 8$ $\rho = 0.533$ $S = 0.143$

$\mu = 15$ $L = 1.14$ $W = 0.076$

bt: (% = 0.56)

$\lambda = 5.6$ $\rho = 0.28$ $S = 0.0694$

$\mu = 20$ $L = 0.389$ $W = 0.0194$

Total:

$L^T = 6.53$

$S^T = 1 * 0.5 + 0.8 * 0.143 + 0.56 * 0.0694 = 0.5 + 0.114 + 0.0389 = 0.65$
(39.2 minutes)

(b) Alternative 1:

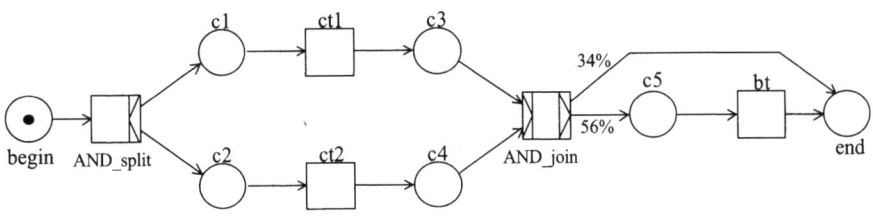

Figure S4.6
Alternative 1

It is possible to reduce flow time by executing things in parallel.

ct1:   (% = 1.0)

$\lambda = 10$ $\rho = 0.833$ $S = 0.5$

$\mu = 12$ $L = 5$

ct2:   (% = 1.0)

$\lambda = 10$ $\rho = 0.67$ $S = 0.2$

$\mu = 15$ $L = 2$

bt: (% = 0.56)

$\lambda = 5.6$ $\rho = 0.28$ $S = 0.07$

$\mu = 20$ $L = 0.389$

ct1 is the bottleneck in the parallel process.

Total:

$L^T > 5.39$

Maximal throughput $= \lambda * (1/\rho_{\text{bottleneck}}) = 10 * (1/0.833) = 12$

Alternative 2:

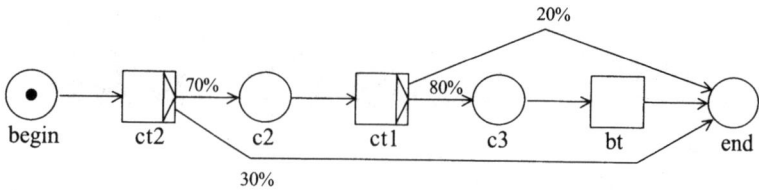

Figure S4.7
Alternative 2

In this case more tokens will go directly to end so the resources are used less.

ct1: $(\% = 0.7)$

$\lambda = 7$ $\rho = 0.583$

$\mu = 12$ $L = 1.4$

ct2: $(\% = 1.0)$

$\lambda = 10$ $\rho = 0.67$

$\mu = 15$ $L = 2$

bt: $(\% = 0.56)$

$\lambda = 5.6$ $\rho = 0.28$

$\mu = 20$ $L = 0.389$

ct2 has now become the bottleneck and there are fewer cases in the system.

Total:

$L^T = 3.79$

Maximal throughput $= \lambda * (1/\rho_{\text{bottleneck}}) = 10 * (1/0.67) = 15$

Other alternatives:

· Combine *ct1* and *ct2* into one task to save setup time.

· Make one pool of resources available for all tasks.

Exercise 4.8   E-business

(a)

step	set of tasks	selected task	used block	new task
1	a	a	sequence	b
2	a,b	b	sequence	c
3	a,b,c	b	iteration	d

client workflow

step	set of tasks	selected task	used block	new task
1	e	e	sequence	f

server workflow

(b)

step	set of tasks	selected task	used block	new task
1	a	a	sequence	b
2	a,b	b	sequence	c
3	a,b,c	b	iteration	d
4	a,b,c,d	b	and	e
5	a,b,c,d,e	e	sequence	f

coupled workflow

Steps 1, 2 and 3 of the coupled workflow are the same as for the client workflow. Step 4 is new and step 5 is step 1 of the server workflow.

(c) No, such a derivation is not possible. To verify this note that (p,q), (t,v), and (r,s) form pairs of and-splits and and-joins. So each of them must be made by one replacement of an and-block. However, then they would be nested (one enclosed in the other) or disjoint. This is not the case; in fact, they have the following sequence: p, t, q, r, v, s. So they cross each other.

(d) Yes, it is a sound and safe workflow. To see this note that without the message exchange, i.e., without q, t, r, and s, we have a sound and safe workflow (see exercise 1). Since b and d will fire, we see that t and later q will fire and so c and e will fire. Similarly r and later v will fire. So *f* and later *s* will fire. No tokens are left, so the net is sound. That the net is safe is a direct consequence of the fact that the net without message exchange is safe.

SOLUTIONS TO EXERCISES, CHAPTER 5

Exercise 5.1

Figure S5.1 shows a graphical representation of the reference model of the WfMC. For a detailed description of the components and interfaces see chapter 5.

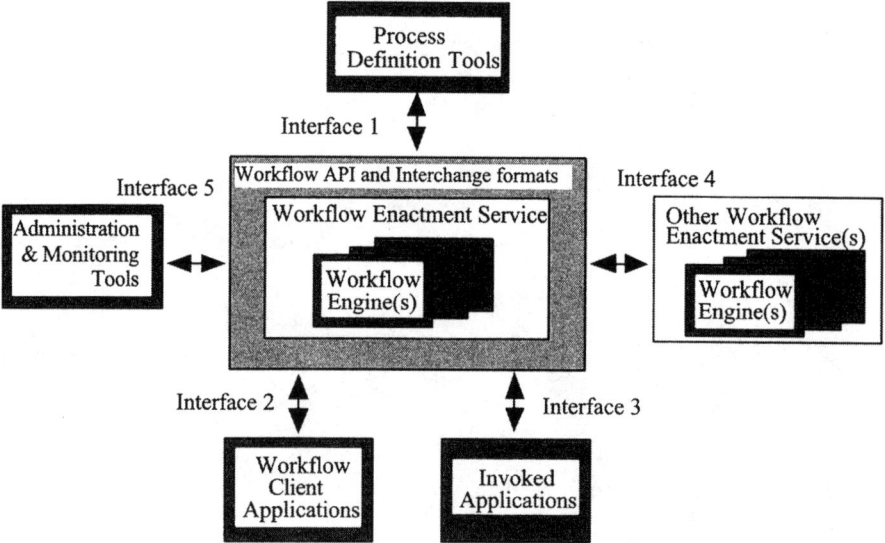

Figure S5.1
The Workflow Management Coalition's reference model (© WFMC)

Exercise 5.2

Answers to the short questions:

(a) Atomicity, Consistency, Isolation, and Durability

(b) Interface 3: Workflow management system and applications are out of sync.

(c) Workflow designer, Administrator, Process analyst, and Employee.

(d) Interoperability: Specification of the WFMC, SWAP, WF-XML, and OMG's jointFlow.

(e) Staffware: market leader aiming at production workflow. COSA: Petri-net-based workflow management system aiming at production workflow. ActionWorkflow: a system emphasizing collaboration and negotiation rather than routing, and quite different from typical production systems.

(f) Woflan: verification using state-of-the-art analysis techniques, i.e., qualitative analysis. ExSpect: simulation tool based on Petri nets. Both tools can be used in combination with several workflow products.

(g) Protos (Pallas Athena BV, Plasmolen, The Netherlands), ARIS (IDS Scheer AG, Saarbrücken, Germany), BusinessSpecs (IvyTeam, Zug, Switzerland), Income (Promatis AG, Karlsbad, Germany), and Meta WorkflowAnalyzer (Meta Software, Cambridge, MA, USA).

Exercise 5.3

COSA is based on Petri nets. Therefore, there is a one-to-one translation and we do not show the process using CONE. The translation of the process to Staffware is more involved. Figure S5.2 shows the corresponding workflow process definition in the GWD of Staffware. The model is straightforward given the description of the building blocks.

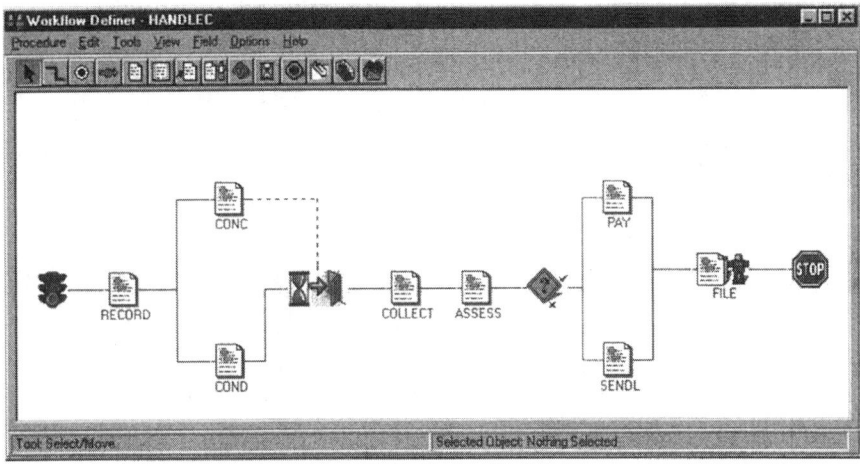

Figure S5.2
Process "handle complalint" modeled using the GWD of Staffware

Exercise 5.4

There is a one-to-one translation from the model shown in chapter 2 to COSA. The translation of the process to Staffware is more involved. Figure S5.3 shows the corresponding workflow process definition in the GWD of Staffware. The first part of model is straightforward given the description of the building blocks. To only thing that is less trivial to model is the cancel task. Typically, non-free-choice constructs are hard, if not impossible, to model using Staffware. In this case we can use a simple trick to model this: two cancel steps with a time-out. For simplicity we did not model triggers and simplified the choice for both types of insurances.

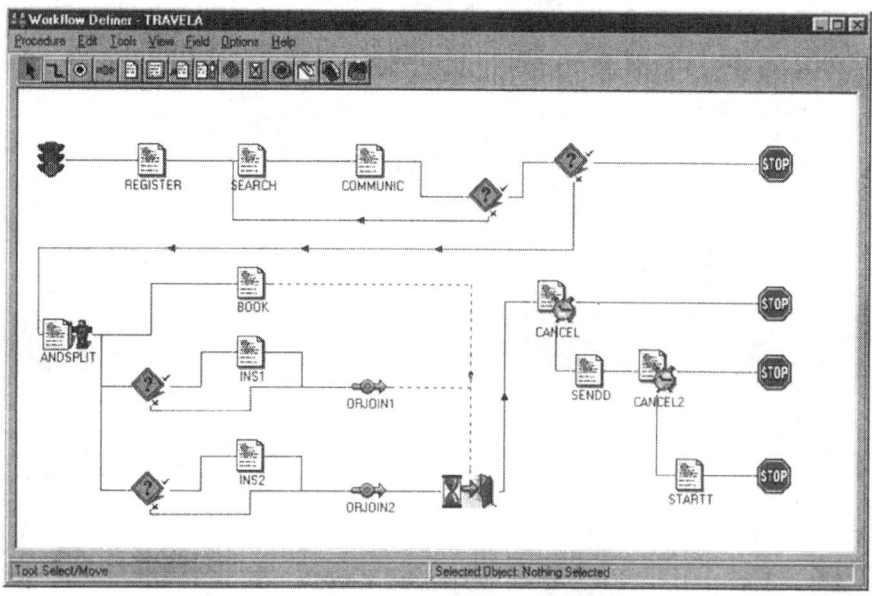

Figure S5.3
Process "travel agency" modeled using the GWD of Staffware

SOLUTIONS TO EXERCISES, CHAPTER 6

Exercise 6.1

(a) First, it is important to involve (potential) users because they have a lot of knowledge of the existing processes and systems. Often they also have good ideas for improvement. So their knowledge and creativity are of great value for the redesign team.

Second, their involvement is important to obtain commitment in the organization. Persons who have actively participated in the design of new processes and systems have the feeling that it is also their "baby." So they are willing to defend the new processes and systems to anyone, in particular their colleagues. So they become the key persons in the change process. This is essential because very often change operations create strong resistance with the sitting staff. Change is a very emotional process.

(b) It is very important to select persons with the following characteristics:

- Respected by their colleagues
- Knowledgeable about processes or systems
- Open-minded, i.e., possessing the ability to "think outside the box"

Exercise 6.2

In the *diagnosis phase*, business cases are used to determine the values of the Key Performance Indicators (KPIs) in the actual situation: the null measurement. It is sometimes easier to explain something by an example than to formulate the rule to which the example belongs. Business cases can be considered as examples while processes are the rules. For users it is therefore easier to "think" in terms of business cases rather than in more abstract terms of processes. The next phase where they are used is in the *process redesign phase*, i.e., in the simulation experiments and in the games. In specification of requirements they can be used as well. Finally business cases are used in the *integration phase* when the system is tested and for the *delivery phase* when the acceptance test has to be performed. Therefore, it is important to maintain the set of business cases carefully. This way they can also be used in the *monitor and improve phase* when an improvement is considered.

Exercise 6.3

Advantages of combining the phases are as follows. It is good to specify the conceptual data model and functional model together with the component structure because then the distribution of functionality over the components can be derived in an iterative way. If the requirement models and architecture are divided over two phases, iteration is more difficult. It can be an advantage to consider the functional and technical details in one phase, because it prevents technical infeasible requirements.

There are also disadvantages. In the requirements phase the users could make a significant contribution, while they are less useful in the specification of the technical architecture. Therefore it is natural to split the phases here. Another disadvantage is the violation of the "principal of separation of concerns," which says that it is better to concentrate on one aspect at a time, i.e., functional and technical details should be considered in separate phases.

SOLUTIONS TO EXERCISES, CHAPTER 7

Exercise 7.1

We provide the solution only to the question 7.1(b). Figure S7.1 shows the process model of the current situation. We did not model resource triggers: most of the tasks require a resource trigger.

Tasks

1. Register private client
2. Register business client
3. Check permit
4. Give blank permit
5. Return improper permit
6. Receive filled permit
7. File proper permit
8. Check proper permit
9. Start business trip
10. Send copy to fd
11. Start private trip
12. Check allowed
13. Prepare proposal
14. Prepare new proposal
15. Call client for approval
16. Send positive memo
17. Check approved proposal
18. Check private trip
19. Determine costs of flights
20. Call client
21. Send negative memo

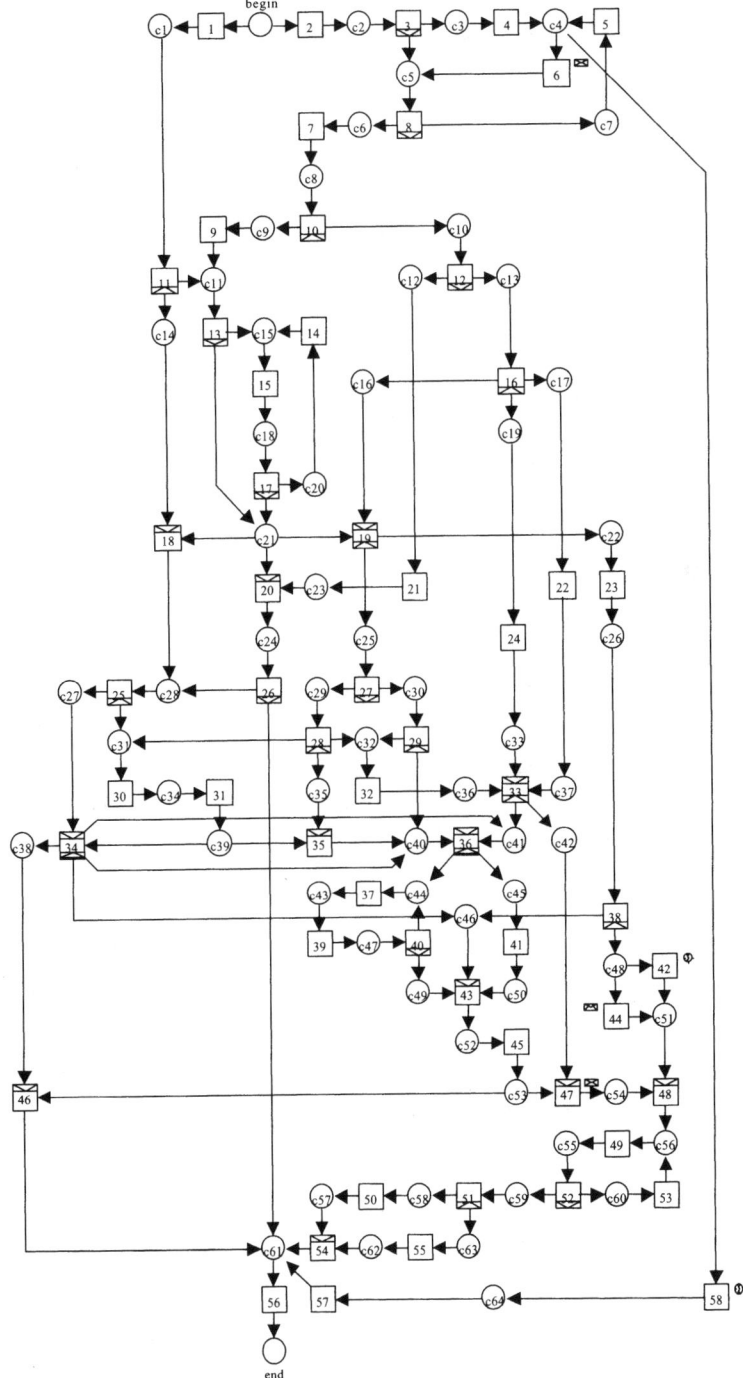

Figure S7.1
The travel agency process of Somewhere University

22. Make advanced payments
23. Prepare cash and checks
24. Pay registration fees
25. AND-split
26. Check decision
27. Check flight payments
28. AND-split
29. AND-split
30. Make appointment
31. Client pays
32. Send fd costs of business flights
33. Pay for flights
34. Check private trip paid for
35. Check business trip paid for
36. Check all paid for
37. Book hotel
38. Send cash and checks
39. Print voucher
40. Check all booked
41. Print tickets
42. Nothing returned
43. Make handy folder
44. Client returns cash or checks
45. Pick up
46. End private trip
47. Receive declaration
48. Process declaration
49. Calculate balance
50. Deduct from budget
51. AND-split
52. Check approved
53. Correct
54. End business trip
55. Settle balance
56. Close file
57. Send noticifation
58. Receive no filled permit

Conditions

c1. Private trip registered

c2. Business trip registered

c3. No permit

c4. Client fills permit

c5. Filled permit

c6. Proper permit

c7. Improper permit

c8. Permit filed

c9. Copy sent

c10. Copy of file sent

c11. Start trip organization

c12. Not allowed

c13. Allowed

c14. Organizing private trip

c15. Proposal

c16. Positive memo

c17. Advance payment

c18. Client (dis)approved

c19. Registration fee

c20. No schedule

c21. Schedule

c22. Request for cash and checks

c23. Negative memo

c24. Client decided

c25. Flight costs known

c26. Cash and checks

c27. Paying for private trip

c28. Paying for private trip and private flights to be paid for

c29. Some private flights

c30. All business flights

c31. Private flights to be paid for

c32. Business flights to be paid for

c33. Fee done

c34. Client to pay

c35. Paying for business trip

c36. Detailed price info

c37. Payments completed

c38. Private trip paid for

c39. Client payed

c40. Private flights paid for

c41. Business flights paid for

c42. Wait for declaration

c43. Hotels booked

c44. Book hotels

c45. Have tickets printed

c46. Cash and checks sent

c47. Voucher printed

c48. Wait for return

c49. Transport arranged

c50. Tickets printed

c51. Amount info

c52. Folder ready

c53. Picked up

c54. Declaration received

c55. Balance

c56. Processing declaration

c57. Deducted

c58. Amount to deduct

c59. Balance approved

c60. Balance not approved

c61. File to be closed

c62. Settled balance

c63. Approved balance

c64. Unable to guarantee trip

Glossary

ActionWorkflow   ActionWorkflow is a workflow management system that concentrates upon the coordination of people.

Activity   An activity is the carrying out of an assigned task. In contrast to a task, an activity is related to a specific case.
Synonyms
- task instance;
- transition firing; and
- operation.

Actor   An actor is a person, machine, or organizational unit that is directly or indirectly involved in carrying out work. An actor "performs" as a contractor and/or a subcontractor.
Synonyms
- player.

Ad hoc workflow   In general, many different cases involve the same business processes. However in certain cases it is necessary to modify the process for a specific case. We refer to this as an ad hoc workflow.

AND-join   An AND-join is a task that may only be carried out once certain conditions have been met. We can compare an AND-join with a stage in assembly that can only take place once all the necessary components are available. An AND-join is applied at the moment when several parallel workflows need to be synchronized. Using the AND-join, it is possible to coordinate various parallel workflows for a particular case.
Synonyms
- join;
- rendezvous; and
- synchronization task.

AND-split   An AND-split task is the logical opposite of an AND-join task. Carrying out an AND-split results in more than one parallel workflow being created for the same case. We can also say that an AND-split divides a case into various parts which can be worked upon simultaneously.

Synonyms
• split; and
• fork.

API   API stands for application programming interface. Most workflow management systems offer APIs for the integration of that system with other applications. In the workflow management context, we also sometimes refer to WAPI (workflow application programming interface) rather than API.

Application   A workflow management system only controls the logistical aspects of a case. Its content usually is supported by other tools such as word processors and calculation programs. We call these tools applications. The performance of a task for a particular case can lead to the initiation of an application. In this way separate applications can be integrated by the workflow management system to form a single whole.
Synonyms
• external program; and
• tool.

Application data   This is the data that is used by external programs, rather than being managed by the workflow system. The latter therefore cannot access this data directly. It can, however, be accessed indirectly through the case attributes and the applications themselves.

Architecture   The architecture of a (workflow) system is its structure in the form of components and the way in which they interact with one another (interfacing). This structure is often hierarchical with a distinction made between the functional and technical infrastructure. The functional architecture is based upon the structure of the logical components in the system. The technical architecture refers mainly to its hardware and software components.

Assignment   An assignment is described in a specification that clearly states which tasks must be carried out to complete a particular case, and in what order and within what timeframe they must be performed.
Synonyms
• commission; and
• order.

Audit trail   An audit trail is an electronic archive in which the history of a workflow is recorded. It contains various details about each case such as starting time, tasks performed, and resources allocated.
Synonyms
• log file; and
• trace.

Business process   A business process is one focused upon the production of particular products. These may be either physical products, such as an aircraft or bridge, or less tangible ones such as a design, a consultation paper, or an assessment. In other words, the "product" can also be a service.

Synonyms
• work process.

Business process re-engineering   Business process re-engineering is the fundamental reconsideration and radical restructuring of business processes in order to achieve drastic improvements in costs, quality, and service.
Synonyms
• BPR;
• business process redesign; and
• business regeneration.

Capacity planning   Capacity planning determines how many resources are allocated to which resource class during a particular period. Because the range of cases is often subject to seasonal influences, weekly patterns, and other fluctuations, capacity planning concentrates mainly upon finding a balance between the resources required and those available.

Case   A case is what a workflow management system is designed to control. We can also regard it as a "product in progress." Examples of a case could include an insurance claim, a mortgage application, a tax return, an order, or a course of treatment in a hospital. Each case has a unique identity. Moreover a case is always at a particular stage of development at any given moment.
Synonyms
• case;
• project;
• deal;
• product;
• service;
• process cycle;
• assignment; and
• workflow instance.

Case attribute   The way in which a case progresses through the workflow process depends upon its specific characteristics. Various attributes therefore can be identified for each case. An activity may change the value of these attributes. Naturally a case only draws upon its own attributes. These attributes are used to "route" a case. For example, a decision resulting from an OR-split may be based upon the associated case attributes.
Synonyms
• operational parameter; and
• case variable.

Case manager   A case manager is a person who is responsible for the handling of a whole case or a set of several tasks for the case.

Case state   At any point in time, a case has a particular state that is determined by those conditions that have been met and the values of the associated case attributes.

Case type   Similar cases belong to the same case type. There is a one-to-one correspondence between case types and processes. In other words, precisely one process definition belongs to each case type.

Computer-Supported Cooperative Work   Computer-supported cooperative work (CSCW) is the collective name for the methods, techniques and systems which support the cooperative performance of work. Groupware products as well as workflow management systems fall under this heading.

Condition   Before a task can be performed as part of a particular case, that case must fulfill certain conditions. A condition therefore is a necessary requirement that must be met before an activity can take place. Once all the conditions for a task in a particular case are met, that task can be carried out.
Synonym
• place.

Contract   A binding agreement between a contractor and a subcontractor.

Contractor   A (sub)contractor is a "resource" who is responsible for a process and carries out the activities ordered by the principal. Note that it is also possible for a contractor to act as a principal by subcontracting other resources.
Synonyms
• subcontractor; and
• process owner.

COSA   COSA is Software Ley's-Petri-net-based workflow management system. See http://www.cosa.de.

Critical success factor   A critical success factor is a (verbally expressed) parameter of a process or system that plays a key role in the performance of that system or process.

ExSpect   ExSpect is a Petri-net-based simulation tool. See http://www.exspect.com.

Groupware   Groupware is the collective name for software products that enable groups to cooperate. The term groupware is closely related to CSCW (computer-supported cooperative work). Groupware and workflow management software are often used in combination with one another. Typical groupware products focus mainly upon cooperation between people, whereas the emphasis of workflow systems is upon supporting business processes.

Hierarchical organization   In a hierarchical organization, the authority relationships have a treelike structure, which is often represented in an organization chart.

High-level Petri net   A high-level Petri net is a Petri net extended to include color, time, and hierarchy. This extension enables complex processes to be described in a simple way.

InConcert InConcert is one of the few ad hoc workflow management systems. Each case has a private process definition that enables on-the-fly changes and workflow design by discovery.

Interoperability The term interoperability refers to the ability to enable separate applications to communicate and cooperate with one another. Because a workflow system links and integrates different applications, the term interoperability certainly applies to it. The mutual interoperability between workflow systems is also crucial for the success of workflow management in large organizations.

IPSD method IPSD stands for interactive, process-oriented system development. The IPSD method combines RAD and BPR elements to produce one approach to the development of workflow systems.

Iteration Iteration is possible within a workflow if its structure permits one or more tasks to be performed repeatedly. An iteration may, for example, result from a quality control: as long as the result of the task is unsatisfactory, it must be repeated.
Synonyms
• workflow loop; and
• repetition.

JAD Joint application design (JAD) is an approach to the development of specifications during a RAD process by using interactive workshops.

Knowledge management Knowledge management is the process of collection, enrichment, and distribution of knowledge. The goal of knowledge management to make sure that the right knowledge is at the right time with the person who needs this knowledge to fulfil a task.

Matrix organization A matrix organization is structured along functional as well as hierarchical lines. The functional structure is based upon projects of a temporary nature.

Network organization A network organization consists of independent actors who together produce goods and/or provide services. Because there exists no mutual authority relationship between the actors, we also sometimes refer to a "virtual company."

Organizational chart An organizational chart is a treelike structure that graphically illustrates authority relationships. In other words, it shows the hierarchical structure of the positions within an organization.

Organizational unit Staff usually work in groups. The composition of such a group may be based upon the location of the work, upon common roles to be fulfilled, or upon a package of tasks. In such situations we refer respectively to a geographical, a functional, or a process-based group structure. A group of people working together under its own leadership, on its own tasks, and with its own responsibilities is called an organizational unit. An organization is often divided into organizational units in a hierarchical way, making it possible for one such unit to form part of another. It should be possible to identify the organizational unit responsible for performing every task. It is also possible for this to depend upon the case itself. For example, mortgage applications worth more than $200,000 are dealt with by unit A. Every resource is "owned" by a particular organizational unit. In fact, such a unit is none other than a resource class based upon organizational characteristics.

Synonyms
• department; and
• team.

OR-join   An OR-join is a task in which a number of alternative workflows reconverge. Unlike an AND-join, however, no synchronization occurs. In other words, the task can be performed as soon as just one single condition has been met.

Synonym
• asynchronous join.

OR-split   An OR-split is a task in which a choice is made. During the performance of an OR-split, one workflow is selected from a number of available options. Only the selected flow is initiated by the OR-split. The choice is often based upon the particular attributes of the case in hand. However it may also be a random one. The OR-split is the logical opposite of the OR-join: an OR-split can divide a workflow into a number of alternative streams that later reconverge at an OR-join. There are two types of OR-split tasks: implicit and explicit. The difference between the two is based upon the moment at which the choice is made.

Synonyms
• switch;
• conditional choice; and
• decision point.

Parallel routing   Two or more tasks related to a specific case may be carried out in parallel if, by definition, the process contains an AND-split and an AND-join. The AND-split allows more than one task to be initiated at the same time. Upon completion, the parallel workflows are resynchronized using the AND-join.

Performance indicator   A performance indicator is a (definition of a) quantity that is used to measure a critical success factor of a process or system. Examples of performance indicators are average flow time, utilzation, and service level.

Petri net   A Petri net is the description of a process in terms of places, transitions, and arcs. The semantics—the precise meaning—is always formally defined.

Synonym
• P/T net.

Place   Places are the passive components of a Petri net. A place may contain no, one, or more tokens. In workflow-process modeling, conditions are depicted by places.

Synonyms
- condition; and
- channel.

Primary process A process for dealing with customer-oriented cases. The process concentrates upon the delivery of products and/or services to the company's customers.
Synonym
- production process.

Principal A principal is an actor who wants an activity to be performed by a contractor: the principal contracts out work to a subcontractor. Under the terms of such a contract, the principal and contractor make agreements about the nature of the work, its scheduling, and the costs involved. Within an internal organizational context, the term principal also encompasses a "boss."
Synonyms
- customer;
- contractor;
- case owner; and
- flow owner.

Process The definition of a process indicates which tasks must be performed—and in what order—to successfully complete a case. In other words, all possible routes are mapped out. A process consists of tasks, conditions, and subprocesses. By using AND-splits, AND-joins, OR-splits, and OR-joins, parallel and alternative flows can be defined. Subprocesses also consist of tasks, conditions, and possible further subprocesses. The use of subprocesses can enable the hierarchical structuring of complex processes.
Synonyms
- workflow net;
- WF-net;
- flow chart;
- workflow script;
- procedure; and
- process diagram.

Process manager A process manager is responsible for a process: the completion of cases and the allocation of resources.
Synonym
- process supervisor.

Protos Protos is a BPR tool that facilitates the modeling and distribution of workflow models. See http://www.pallas-athena.com/.

Prototype A prototype is a software system whose functionality closely resembles a system that has yet to be produced. A prototype can also be compared with a scale model.

RAD Rapid application development (RAD) is a method of system development. RAD is characterized by a cyclical development process in which close cooperation with users is prioritized.

Synonym
• Rapid application development.

Reference model   The WFMC's reference model is an architectural definition in which the following components are distinguished: (1) workflow enactment service; (2) process definition tools; (3) workflow client applications; (4) invoked applications; and (5) administration and monitoring tools.

Resource   A resource is a means of production or a group of such means. It may include such actors as people, machines, means of transport, applications, departments, and business units. Resources can only perform certain tasks, and so are grouped into one or more resource classes. The inclusion of a resource in a particular category provides information about the place that a resource has in the organization or about a particular quality that it has.
Synonyms
• agent;
• participant;
• means of production;
• user;
• performer; and
• employee.

Resource class   Resources can only perform a limited number of tasks. In order to make it easy to indicate—when defining a process—which resources can carry out a certain task, they are grouped into so-called resource classes. One resource may belong to several resource classes. The grouping of resource is in general structured in two ways. First, resources are divided up on the basis of their place within the organization. This results in resource classes, which are also known as organizational units: for example, "Purchasing Department," "Team A," or "Atlanta Branch." Second, they may be divided up according to functional characteristics—also known as roles. Examples of roles are "Executive C," "Information Analyst" and "Cobol programmer." Each of these roles corresponds with a resource class. Those categories not based upon a role or an organizational unit are called free resource classes.
Synonyms
• resource category;
• group; and
• resource type.

Resource classification   Resources—both staff and automated devices—can only perform a limited number of tasks. What these are depends upon such factors as which roles a resource can fulfill and the location where this must be done. A resource classification divides the resources into subsets, also known as resource classes. Examples of resource classification include separation into roles or into organizational units. Resources with the same characteristics under a particular system of classification form a resource class. Some workflow management systems enable the relationships between the resource classes to be illustrated schematically.

Synonyms
- organizational diagram;
- organization chart; and
- role model.

Resource management For each case a number of tasks must be carried out. These are performed by resources. Because the number of resources is limited, it is necessary to harmonize the activities that need to be carried out with resource capacity available to do this. This is when we refer to resource management.
Synonyms
- allocation; and
- workload management.

Role In order to perform tasks, skills are required. Each resource—for example, a person—has certain skills. A role is a collection of complementary skills. It thus becomes possible to identify which role is necessary to perform which task. Which roles each resource can perform is also indicated. By using roles, it is possible to ensure that tasks are assigned to the correct people. In fact, a role is the same as a resource class based upon functional characteristics.
Synonyms
- function; and
- qualification.

Rollback A failure may occur during the performance of an activity. Once the workflow system has registered this failure, a rollback takes place. In other words, the workflow system returns to its state at the start of the activity. Once the failure has been rectified, the activity is performed again. As soon as the activity has been successfully completed, a "commit" takes place.

Routing The definition of a process determines how cases are routed through the various tasks. Four types of routing are often distinguished: sequencing, selection, parallelization, and iteration.

Sagitta 2000 Sagitta 2000 is the name of a new Dutch customs declarations system. Workflow management plays a major role in it.

Secondary process A process which supports the primary processes, in particular by providing resources.
Synonym
- support process.

Selective routing Because most processes need to be able to handle various types of cases, not all cases proceed through a given process in the same way. In other words, there may be various routes through a process. In order to ensure that—dependent upon a case's characteristics—a particular route is chosen, we can make use of the OR-split or the OR-join. For each case, an OR-split selects from a number of alternative tasks for each case. These different routes can be reconverged using an OR-join.

Synonyms
- alternative routing;
- conditional routing; and
- selection.

Sequential routing   We refer to sequential task execution when a number of tasks are performed one after the other. When two successive tasks are linked by a condition, then they must be performed sequentially.
Synonyms
- sequencing; and
- succession.

Sound   Soundness is a correctness criterion defined for workflow nets, that is, Petri nets that represent workflow processes. A workflow net is sound if, for any case, the procedure will terminate eventually and the moment the procedure terminates there is a token in the sink place and all the other places are empty. Moreover there should be no dead transitions; in other words, it should be possible to execute an arbitrary task by following the appropriate route though the workflow net.
Synonym
- correct.

Simulation   A simulation is the imitation (on a computer) of a process by running through it in sequence. In this way the process being simulated can be analyzed.
Synonym
- modeling.

Staffware   Staffware is one of the leading workflow management systems. See http://www.staffware.com/.

Task   A task is an "atomic" process: one that is not further subdivided into component processes. It thus is a logical unit of work; in other words, a task is either carried out in full or not at all. A task is not itself linked to a specific case. When a task is carried out for a specific case, we refer to it as an activity. We also differentiate between manual, automatic, and semi-automatic tasks. A manual task is performed by a person, without any intervention by an application (for example, the signing of a document). An automatic task is one performed by an application without any human intervention. A semi-automatic task involves the use of an interactive application (for example, a word processor).
Synonyms
- process task;
- process step;
- work step; and
- transition.

Tertiary process   Tertiary processes are those managerial processes that control the primary and secondary processes.

Synonyms
- managerial process; and
- executive process.

Token The state of a Petri net is determined by the distribution of tokens amongst the places. If workflows are mapped onto Petri nets, the state of a case will correspond to one or more tokens.
Synonym
- object.

Transaction A transaction is the exchange protocol which results in a contract being issued for an activity.

Transaction processing system A transaction processing system is an information system that registers, transforms, and communicates relevant details of the flow of states of a system.

Transition Transitions are the active components of a Petri net. The triggering of a transition results in the state of the network being changed. In workflow-process modeling, a transition often coincides with a task.
Synonyms
- event; and
- processor.

Triage Triage is the selection and prioritization of cases in the performance of a task, based upon easy-to-identify characteristics. (One example of triage is the fast lane in a supermarket, where cases are split into large cases—cases that require a lot of work—and small cases—cases that require less work.) The objective of triage is to reduce average completion time.

Trigger A work item can only be carried out once the state of the case in question allows it. But the actual performance of a task often requires more. If the work item is to be carried out by a person, she must first "retrieve" it from his in-tray before it can become an activity. In other words, the work item is only performed once a resource has taken an initiative. In such cases, we refer to "triggering": the work item is triggered by a resource. Other forms of triggering are also possible, though: by an external event (for example, the arrival of an EDI message) or a particular time (such as the generation of an order list at six o'clock). We therefore differentiate between three types of triggers: (1) resource-initiated, (2) externally-generated, and (3) time-based. Work items that must always be carried out immediately—without the intervention of a resource or other prompt—do not require a trigger.
Synonyms
- activation; and
- prompt.

UML UML (Unified Modeling Language) is the de facto standard for software development. UML is a graphical language for visualizing, specifying, constructing, and documenting the artifacts of a software intensive system. However the use of UML is not restricted to software development. Some of its diagrams are also used for enterprise modeling, business engineering, process analysis, and system configuration.

Use case   A use case is a case of a workflow process that is used to describe, demonstrate, specify, or test a process or system. The set of use cases should cover the most characteristic cases, including errors and exceptions.
Synonyms
• business case; and
• scenario.

Woflan   Woflan is a Petri-net-based workflow analyzer. See http://www.tm. tue.nl/it/woflan.

Work item   A work item is the combination of a case and a task which is about to be carried out. Just like an activity, therefore, a work item is linked to a specific case. The work item disappears at the moment that it begins to be acted upon— the moment that performance of the task itself starts. It then becomes an activity. Note that it is possible, based upon the case's state, to determine which work items are waiting to be handled.
Synonyms
• work assignment; and
• work item.

Workflow   A workflow comprises cases, resources, and triggers that relate to a particular process.

Workflow definition   A workflow definition consists of the definition of a process, a summary of the resources required, and the classification of those resources into classes.

Workflow definition tool   The tool used to define processes and resource classifications.
Synonym
• workflow modeler.

Workflow engine   The workflow engine takes care of the actual management of the workflow. Amongst other things, it is concerned with task-assignment generation, resource allocation, activity performance, case preparation and modification, the launching of applications, and the recording of logistical information.
Synonyms
• enactment service; and
• run-time executor.

Workflow interoperability   Workflow interoperability is the degree to which two or more workflow engines are able to work together in dealing with a common workflow. This encompasses, for example, the exchange of cases and the contracting out of work items.

Workflow management   The term workflow management refers to the ideas, methods, techniques, and software used to support structured business processes. The objective of workflow management is to achieve streamlined and easy-to-maintain work processes.
Synonyms
- workflow support; and
- WFM.

Workflow Management Coalition   The Workflow Management Coalition is an international organization consisting of users, suppliers, and developers of workflow products. The most important objective of this organization is to develop standards in the workflow field. The results achieved are published through such media as the World Wide Web (http://www.aiim.org/WfMC/).
Synonym
- WFMC.

Workflow management system   A workflow management system is a software package for the implementation of a workflow system. The term refers to a universally applicable system; in other words, a workflow management system is not customized to a specific business situation. By configuring such a system, it is turned into one which supports specific workflows. Unlike a workflow system, a workflow management system is thus a generic application.
Synonym
- WFMS.

Workflow net   A workflow net is a Petri net which respresents a workflow process. Such a workflow net has one source place and one sink place. Every node (i.e., place/condition or transition/task) is on a path from the source place to the sink place. A workflow net is sound if, for any case, the procedure will terminate eventually and the moment the procedure terminates there is a token in sink place and all the other places are empty. Moreover there should be no dead transitions; it should be possible to execute an arbitrary task by following the appropriate route though the workflow net.
Synonym
- WF-net.

Workflow state   The state of a workflow is the "sum" of the state of each case, the state of each of the resources concerned, and the triggers.

Workflow system   A workflow system is one that supports the workflows in a specific business situation. Unlike a workflow management system, a workflow system is adapted to a particular application. A workflow system usually consists of a workflow management system plus process and resource classification definitions, applications, a database system, and so on. We can compare the difference between a workflow management system and a workflow system to that between a database management system and a database system.
Synonym
- WFS.

Worklist handler   A workflow management system ensures that work items are allocated to resources. If a work item is allocated to a person, it appears in her (actual or metaphorical) in-tray. This always contains a list of those tasks still to be performed. By selecting a work item from the in-tray, the person can carry out that task. Note that a work item may appear in more than one in-tray.

Synonyms

- work tray;
- in-tray;
- worklist; and
- to-do list.

Bibliography

Workflow Management

Aalst, W. M. P. van der and K. M. van Hee. *Workflow Management: Modellen, Methoden en Systemen.* (in Dutch) Schoonhoven: Academic Service, 1997.

Georgakopoulos, D., M. Hornick, and A. Sheth. "An Overview of Workflow Management: From Process Modeling to Workflow Automation Infrastructure." *Distributed and Parallel Databases,* 3(1995):119–153.

Jablonski, S. and C. Bussler. *Workflow Management: Modeling Concepts, Architecture, and Implementation.* London: International Thomson Computer Press, 1996.

Koulopoulos, T. M. *The Workflow Imperative.* New York: Van Nostrand Reinhold, 1995.

Leymann, F. and D. Roller. *Production Workflow: Concepts and Techniques.* New Jersey: Prentice-Hall, 2000.

Schäl, T. *Workflow Management for Process Organizations,* volume 1096 of *Lecture Notes in Computer Science.* Berlin: Springer-Verlag, 1996.

Sheth, A. P., W. M. P. van der Aalst, and I. B. Arpinar. "Processes Driving the Networked Economy: ProcessPortals, ProcessVortex, and Dynamically Trading Processes." (special issue on Workflow Management Systems) *IEEE Concurrency,* 7:3(1999):18–31.

Workflow Management Coalition

Lawrence, P. Editor. *Workflow Handbook 1997, Workflow Management Coalition.* New York: John Wiley and Sons, 1997.

WFMC. Workflow Management Coalition Terminology and Glossary (WFMC–TC–1011). Technical report. Brussels: Workflow Management Coalition, 1996.

Workflow Management Coalition. WFMC Home Page. http://www.wfmc.org.

Business Process Management/Re-engineering

Aalst, W. M. P. van der, J. Desel, and A. Oberweis, Editors. *Business Process Management: Models, Techniques, and Empirical Studies*, volume 1806 of *Lecture Notes in Computer Science*. Berlin: Springer-Verlag, 2000.

Aalst, W. M. P. van der. "On the Automatic Generation of Workflow Processes Based on Product Structures." *Computers in Industry*, 39(1999):97–111.

Aalst, W. M. P. van der and K. M. van Hee. "Business Process Redesign: A Petri-Net-Based Approach." *Computers in Industry*, 29:1–2(1996):15–26.

Davenport, T. H. *Process Innovation : Re-engineering Work Through Information Technology*. Boston: Harvard Business School Press, 1993.

Hammer, M. Re-engineering Work: Don't automate, Obliterate. *Harvard Business review*, pages 104–112, July/August 1990.

Hammer, M. and J. Champy. *Re-engineering the Corporation*. London: Nicolas Brealey Publishing, 1993.

Malone, T. W., W. Crowston, J. Lee, B. Pentland, et al. "Tools for Inventing Organizations: Toward a Handbook for Organizational Processes." *Management Science*, 45:3(1999):425–443.

Morris, D. and J. Brandon. *Re-engineering Your Business*. New York: McGraw-Hill, 1993.

Rapid Application Development

Martin, J. *Rapid Application Development*. New York: MacMillan, 1991.

Petri Nets

Aalst, W. M. P. van der. "Putting Petri Nets to Work in Industry." *Computers in Industry*, 25:1(1994):45–54.

Desel, J. and J. Esparza. *Free Choice Petri Nets*, volume 40 of *Cambridge Tracts in Theoretical Computer Science*. Cambridge: Cambridge University Press, 1995.

Hee, K. M. van. *Information System Engineering: a Formal Approach*. Cambridge: Cambridge University Press, 1994.

Jensen, K. *Colored Petri Nets. Basic Concepts, Analysis Methods and Practical Use*. EATCS monographs on Theoretical Computer Science. Berlin: Springer-Verlag, 1996.

Murata, T. "Petri Nets: Properties, Analysis and Applications." *Proceedings of the IEEE*, 77:4 (April 1989):541–580.

Peterson, J. L. *Petri Net Theory and the Modeling of Systems*. Englewood Cliffs: Prentice-Hall, 1981.

Reisig, W. *Petri Nets: An Introduction*, volume 4 of *EATCS Monographs in Theoretical Computer Science*. Berlin: Springer-Verlag, 1985.

Reisig, W. and G. Rozenberg, Editors. *Lectures on Petri Nets I: Basic Models*, volume 1491 of *Lecture Notes in Computer Science*. Berlin: Springer-Verlag, 1998.

Reisig, W. and G. Rozenberg, Editors. *Lectures on Petri Nets II: Applications*, volume 1492 of *Lecture Notes in Computer Science*. Berlin: Springer-Verlag, 1998.

Workflow Modeling Using Petri Nets

Aalst, W. M. P. van der. "The Application of Petri Nets to Workflow Management." *The Journal of Circuits, Systems, and Computers*, 8:1(1998):21–66.

Adam, N. R., V. Atluri, and W. Huang. "Modeling and Analysis of Workflows using Petri Nets." *Journal of Intelligent Information Systems*, 10:2(1998):131–158.

Ellis, C. A. "Information Control Nets: A Mathematical Model of Office Information Flow." In *Proceedings of the Conference on Simulation, Measurement and Modeling of Computer Systems*, 225–240, Boulder, Colorado: ACM Press, 1979.

Ellis, C. A. and G. J. Nutt. "Modeling and Enactment of Workflow Systems." In *Application and Theory of Petri Nets 1993*, volume 691 of *Lecture Notes in Computer Science*, Edited by M. Ajmone Marsan. 1–16. Berlin: Springer-Verlag, 1993.

Workflow Management Systems and Tools

Aalst, W. M. P. van der, P. de Crom, R. Goverde, K. M. van Hee, W. Hofman, H. Reijers, and R. A. van der Toorn. "ExSpect 6.4: An Executable Specification Tool for Hierarchical Colored Petri Nets." In *Application and Theory of Petri Nets 2000, Lecture Notes in Computer Science*, Edited by M. Nielsen and D. Simpson. Berlin: Springer-Verlag, 2000.

FileNET. *Ensemble User Guide*. Costa Mesa, California: FileNET Corporation, 1998.

Hernandez, J. *The SAP R/3 Handbook*, 1997.

InConcert. *InConcert Process Designer's Guide*. Cambridge, Massachusetts: InConcert Inc., 1997.

IBM., *IBM MQseries Workflow: Concepts and Architecture*. Armonk: IBM Corporation, 1999.

Pallas Athena. *Protos User Manual*. Plasmolen, The Netherlands, Pallas Athena BV, Plasmolen, 1999.

Perreault, Y. and T. Vlasic. *Implementing Baan IV*. New York: Macmillan Computer Publishing, 1998.

Promatis. *Income Workflow User Manual*. Karlsbad, Germany: Promatis GmbH, 1998.

Software-Ley. *COSA User Manual*. Pullheim, Germany: Software-Ley GmbH, 1998.

Staffware. *Staffware 2000/GWD User Manual*. Berkshire, United Kingdom: Staffware plc, Berkshire, 1999.

Verbeek, H. M. W. and W. M. P. van der Aalst. "Woflan 2.0: A Petri-net-based Workflow Diagnosis Tool." In *Application and Theory of Petri Nets 2000, Lecture Notes in Computer Science*, Edited by M. Nielsen an D. Simpson. Berlin: Springer-Verlag, 2000.

Workflow Analysis

Aalst, W. M. P. van der. "Formalization and Verification of Event-driven Process Chains." *Information and Software Technology*, 41:10(1999):639–650.

————. "Woflan: A Petri-net-based Workflow Analyzer." *Systems Analysis—Modeling—Simulation*, 35:3(1999):345–357.

Aalst, W. M. P. van der, K. M. van Hee, and H. A. Reijers. "Analysis of Discrete-time Stochastic Petri Nets." *Statistica Neerlandica*, 2000 (forthcoming).

Aalst, W. M. P. van der and A. H. M. ter Hofstede. "Verification of Workflow Task Structures: A Petri-net-based Approach." *Information Systems*, 25:1(2000): 43–69.

Hofstede, A. H. M. ter, M. E. Orlowska, and J. Rajapakse. "Verification Problems in Conceptual Workflow Specifications." *Data and Knowledge Engineering*, 24:3(1998):239–256.

Sadiq, W. and M. E. Orlowska. "Applying Graph Reduction Techniques for Identifying Structural Conflicts in Process Models." In *Proceedings of the 11th International Conference on Advanced Information Systems Engineering (CAiSE '99)*, volume 1626 of *Lecture Notes in Computer Science*, 195–209. Berlin: Springer-Verlag, 1999.

Workflow Flexibility

Aalst, W. M. P. van der, and T. Basten. "Inheritance of Workflows: An Approach to Tackling Problems Related to Change." *Theoretical Computer Science*, 2000 (forthcoming).

Aalst, W. M. P. van der, T. Basten, H. M. W. Verbeek, P. A. C. Verkoulen, and M. Voorhoeve. "Adaptive Workflow: On the Interplay Between Flexibility and Support." In *Enterprise Information Systems*, Edited by J. Filipe. 61–68. Norwell: Kluwer Academic Publishers, 2000.

Ellis, C. A., K. Keddara, and G. Rozenberg. "Dynamic Change within Workflow Systems." In *Proceedings of the Conference on Organizational Computing Systems*, Edited by N. Comstock, C. Ellis, R. Kling, J. Mylopoulos, and S. Kaplan. 10–21, Milpitas, California, August 1995. New York: ACM SIGOIS, ACM Press, 1995.

Heinl, P., S. Horn, S. Jablonski, J. Neeb, K. Stein, and M. Teschke. "A Comprehensive Approach to Flexibility in Workflow Management Systems." In *Work Activities Coordination and Collaboration (WACC'99)*, 79–88, San Francisco, February 1999. New York: ACM Press, 1999.

Reichert, M. and P. Dadam. "ADEPTflex: Supporting Dynamic Changes of Workflow without Losing Control." *Journal of Intelligent Information Systems*, 10:2(1998):93–129.

Interorganizational Workflow

Aalst, W. M. P. van der. "Loosely Coupled Interorganizational Workflows: Modeling and Analyzing Workflows Crossing Organizational Boundaries." *Information and Management*, 37:2(March 2000):67–75.

———. "Process-oriented Architectures for Electronic Commerce and Interorganizational Workflow." *Information Systems*, 24:8(2000):639–671.

———. "Interorganizational Workflows: An Approach based on Message Sequence Charts and Petri Nets." *Systems Analysis—Modeling—Simulation*, 34:3(1999):335–367.

Operations Research

Baker, K. R. *Introduction to Sequencing and Scheduling.* New York: Wiley & Sons, 1974.

Buzacott, J. A. "Commonalities in Re-engineered Business Processes: Models and Issues." *Management Science*, 42:5(1996):768–782.

Kleinrock, L. *Queueing Systems, Vol. 1: Theory.* London: Wiley-Interscience, 1975.

Moder, J. J. and S. E. Elmaghraby. *Handbook of Operations Research: Foundations and Fundamentals.* New York: Van Nostrand Reinhold, 1978.

Pinedo, M. *Scheduling: Theory, Algorithms, and Systems.* Englewood Cliffs, Prentice-Hall, 1995.

Ross, S. M. *A Course in Simulation.* New York: Macmillan, 1990.

Unified Modeling Language (UML)

Booch, G., J. Rumbaugh, and I. Jacobson. *The Unified Modeling Language User Guide.* Reading, Massachusetts: Addison-Wesley, 1998.

Rumbaugh, J., I. Jacobson, and G. Booch. *The Unified Modeling Language Reference Manual.* Reading, Massachusetts: Addison-Wesley, 1999.

Marshall, C. *Enterprise Modeling With UML: Designing Successful Software Through Business Analysis.* Reading, Massachusetts: Addison-Wesley, 2000.

Index